Interrogating Caribbean Masculinities

Interrogating Caribbean Masculinities

Theoretical and Empirical Analyses

Edited by

Rhoda E. Reddock

University of the West Indies Press
Jamaica • Barbados • Trinidad and Tobago

The University of the West Indies Press
1A Aqueduct Flats   Mona
Kingston 7   Jamaica

©2004 by The University of the West Indies Press
All rights reserved. Published 2004

08 07 06 05 04   5 4 3 2 1

CATALOGUING IN PUBLICATION DATA

Interrogating Caribbean masculinities: theoretical and empirical
analyses / edited by Rhoda E. Reddock.
p. cm.
Papers presented at the symposium The Construction of Caribbean
Masculinity: Towards a Research Agenda held in St Augustine,
Trinidad, January 1996.
Includes bibliographical references.

ISBN: 976-640-138-1

1. Masculinity – Caribbean Area. 2. Sex (Psychology) – Caribbean
Area. 3. Men – Caribbean Area – Psychology. 4. Gender identity –
Caribbean Area. I. Reddock, Rhoda E.

BF692.5.I67 2004   155.3'32

Cover illustration: Dean Arlen, untitled (2003).
Book and cover design by Robert Harris.
Set in Sabon 10.5/15 x 24
Printed in Canada.

Contents

Part 3
Class, Ethnicity, Nation and Notions of Masculinity

Part 4
Popular Culture and Literary Images of Masculinity and Femininity

Foreword

RAFAEL L. RAMÍREZ

The papers published in this book were presented at the symposium "The Construction of Caribbean Masculinity: Towards a Research Agenda". The event was held at the University of the West Indies in St Augustine, Trinidad and Tobago, in January 1996. Dr Rhoda Reddock and her staff at the Centre for Gender and Development Studies organized the symposium. The conference was one of the first encounters between both male and female Caribbean scholars engaged in the study of the construction of masculinity in the region. For two days, both presenters and participants engaged in a vivid discussion about the nature of masculinity as a gender construct and its manifestations in the Caribbean region. With three exceptions – Michael Kaufman (Canada), Michael Kimmel (United States) and myself (Puerto Rico) – the participants were from the anglophone Caribbean.

The publication of these papers is a highlight in the development of masculinity studies in the Caribbean region. Most of the authors espouse a social constructivist approach. The constructivist approach maintains that the categories through which we perceive, evaluate and think are socially constructed. They do not exist independently of the subject. The categories are social constructions with cultural specificity. This point

---

*Sections of this text are drawn from previous publications and an unpublished manuscript.

of view emphasizes the active dimension of the subjects, who, employing the guidelines that their cultures lay down, construct their reality in
accordance with or in opposition to these guidelines. The artificiality of
cultural institutions, their historicism, diversity and relativity, is an old
theme in the human sciences. Contemporary social constructionism in
the analysis of sex, gender and sexual preference is characterized by the
systematic identification of social and cultural processes, which are articulated with our notions of sex and gender. Social constructionism
acknowledges that all societies establish gender differentiations. The masculine and the feminine domains are defined by specific attributes, tasks
and symbols. Subjects are recognized as male or female, and are evalu-
ated according to their compliance with gender expectations. What it
means to be a man, or a woman, is a cultural construction. Although
gender constructions are embedded on biological differences, they are
not biologically determined. They constitute a design sustained by a system of symbols, meanings, ascriptions and expectations.

Masculine ideologies are discursive constructions, which are dominant in societies structured on asymmetrical gender and power relations.
These relations are asymmetrical because tasks and attributes assigned
to each gender – prestige or power, for example – are not comparable,
or are not assigned in the same proportion. Asymmetrical relations are
established when the masculine domain is privileged, with the subsequent subordination and devaluation of the feminine domain. The origins, the manifestations and the reproduction of the androcentric
sex-gender system, designed by males and sustained by male dominance,
is a major concern of feminists and others in the human sciences.

In gender studies, masculinity is considered a multidimensional construct and not a normative referent, and special attention is paid to the
interaction of power and sexuality in the construction of masculine identities. Men perceive the power of masculinity in contradictory ways.
Collectively, men are considered to be powerful, but individually, there
are men who do not have much power – men subjugated to other men
and, on occasion, to women – and who evaluate themselves as individuals deprived of power. This situation responds to the fact that the power
of masculinity is constructed and unevenly manifested in homosocial

relationships (social relations among male actors, from which women are excluded). Masculine power is also interrelated with existing inequalities in a society. As Patricia Mohammed writes in her chapter, poor and destitute men have always been the victims of other men. To understand how men express and exert power, it is necessary to include the analysis of power in the context of structural relationships: the class system, political and economic inequalities, racism, colonialism, homophobia, and other systems of oppression and exclusion. In Caribbean societies homosocial relations are constructed in a hierarchical system. Therefore, there are diverse levels of differentiation and of relative equality between men, depending on their position in the hierarchy and on the various scenarios in which they relate to each other and weave their everyday living. The differential access of men to power also entails hypothesizing the existence of multiple masculinities, in which the margins of the representations of sexuality and gender identities are constantly being erased and redrawn. The differential access also leads us to question the notion of masculinity as a static, unitary and homogeneous gender construction based on the hegemonic masculinity model. Several papers in this book discuss the interrelations between hegemonic and non-hegemonic masculinities in the region.

Included in this collection is a chapter by E. Antonio de Moya about masculine power games in the Dominican Republic. Although de Moya was not present at the conference, his chapter is a welcome addition. I consider that the publication of this collection of papers will stimulate research and the production of more publications about masculine and sexual identities in the Caribbean region.

Preface

This publication was a long time in coming. It is the culmination of years of work in the emerging field of Caribbean masculinity studies. The majority of papers are revised and updated versions of papers presented at the 1996 symposium "The Construction of Caribbean Masculinity: Towards a Research Agenda", organized and hosted by the Centre for Gender and Development Studies at the St Augustine campus of the University of the West Indies. These were then supplemented with specially commissioned papers which, it was felt, were necessary to complete the collection. I would like to acknowledge the University of the West Indies Research and Publications Fund and the Netherlands Embassy Small Projects Programme for financial support to the symposium.

Since that time courses on men and masculinity in the Caribbean have been introduced on all three campuses of the University of the West Indies, and interest in the field is growing. The work in producing this collection was long and hard, but I hope that it is a welcome addition to our knowledge in this area. As with any project of this nature, this finished work owes much to many persons. I would like to especially acknowledge the work of Ms Raquel Sukhu, who, while a graduate assistant at the Centre for Gender and Development Studies, University of the West Indies, St Augustine, worked on editing the papers. Over the period of its development, Mr Amar Wahab and Ms Lara Roopnarine also worked on the project at various phases. Ms Glenda St Louis Ottley provided overall support at all stages of the project.

From January to June 2000, I was a visiting professor in African–New World studies at Florida International University. This space provided me with some time to consolidate work on this manuscript. I would also like to thank all the peer reviewers and contributors who responded to the many requests and who, like me, are happy to see this work finally in print.

I hope that you, the reader, will derive as much pleasure from reading this collection as I had in putting it together.

Interrogating Caribbean Masculinities

An Introduction

RHODA E. REDDOCK

The emergence of studies of masculinities in the Caribbean can be seen as one of the most recent developments in feminist and gender studies in that region. As with other parts of the world it is in many ways a response to the challenges posed by the second wave of feminism, which has had a significant impact on the region since the 1970s. Whereas this period began with a notion that something was wrong with femininity which had to be investigated, challenged and reconstructed, by the end of the twentieth century, concerns with masculinity had emerged with full force, giving rise to a men's movement with various tendencies. The men's movement has been characterized as "a collection of incompatible, separate movements" (Clatterbaugh 1997, vii), which of course would take different forms in differing social, political and economic contexts. Whereas some men have sought simply to fight back against the women's movement, others have seized the opportunity to reflect upon their experiences of masculinity and manhood, in the same way as women for the past four decades have done for femininity and womanhood.

Whereas masculinity studies in North America have been described as having their origins in the discourses on sexuality among homosexual men, in the anglophone Caribbean the origin has been quite different. Similarly, it has been argued that even in North America, black men's studies also had a different origin from its development among white males,[1] an origin located in concerns about the black family. Indeed, the specificities of family and gender relations in the Caribbean region, long the concern of social scientists, became the starting point for men's studies and the men's movement in this region.

By the end of the 1980s Barry Chevannes had started his men's group Fathers Incorporated, among predominantly working-class males in Kingston, Jamaica. To summarize roughly, the aims of this group as noted by Chevannes were: (1) to respond to the bad press which men, as fathers, were getting in the region through the labelling of Caribbean fathers as irresponsible, and (2) to instil in young men a sense of responsibility towards their children and the society in general.[2] While a number of early papers by Chevannes in the late 1980s began to deal with questions of manhood and masculinity, by far the most influential moment was the publication in 1986 of Errol Miller's *The Marginalization of the Black Male: Insights from the Development of the Teaching Profession*. This publication located concerns with masculinity at the heart of the postcolonial quest for upward social mobility, which for many Afro- and Indo-Caribbean people had been possible only through education. As noted by Patricia Mohammed (2000), however, although many never bothered to read the text, its title struck an empathetic chord with many men in Jamaica and indeed throughout the region, and the term "male marginalization" became a part of the popular vocabulary. This concept was attractive to men who had grown concerned over what they perceived as the unacceptable transformations in the discourse on gender relations, the challenge to male leadership and authority, and the new visibility of women and feminist politics in public life.

The marginalization thesis, as noted by Keisha Lindsay, received much of its empirical support, especially in Jamaica, from the data on education. As noted by her, and as has been well known for some time, the anglophone Caribbean is one of the few regions where secondary school enrolment of girls exceeds that of boys. Additionally, by the 1986–87 academic year, total female enrolment at the University of the West Indies slightly exceeded that of males. By the end of 1992, 70 per cent of all graduates from the University of the West Indies Mona campus were female (Lindsay 1997, 4). While a number of scholars have been able to challenge the marginalization thesis successfully (Lindsay 1997; Bailey 1997; de Alburquerque 1998; Chevannes 1999), it continues to have great impact, causing expressions of concern from the highest levels of government and from quasi-governmental institutions at national and regional levels.

The mid- and late 1980s was a period of consolidation for the new women's movement in the region. The formation of the Caribbean Association for Feminist Research and Action in 1985 marked the culmination of about fifteen years of incipient feminist organizing in the region. The late 1970s had seen the radicalization of a number of traditional women's groups of an earlier era, such as the Business and Professional Women's Clubs, and the emergence of smaller feminist-oriented groups among younger women in the region.

One of the earliest of these, the Jamaica Association for the Repeal of Abortion Laws, was formed in 1969, and by 1977 the Sistren Women's Theatre Collective had been formed among working-class Jamaican women. Throughout the 1980s we saw the emergence of groups in Belize, Trinidad and Tobago, St Vincent and the Grenadines, Guyana, and later Barbados. These groups, usually with small memberships, were involved in consciousness raising through popular education, income-generating projects, radio programming, media monitoring, and skill-training programmes in traditional and non-traditional areas, as well as in lobbying and advocacy on women's and broader socio-political issues (see Reddock 1998b).

In addition to the emergence of popular movements, developments also took place within governmental structures. Jamaica became one of the first countries to establish a Women's Desk, then a Women's Bureau in 1974, before the United Nations Declaration of International Women's Year in 1975. Throughout the decade 1976–85, women's "machinery" – desks, bureaux, departments and divisions – were established throughout the region. Through the advocacy work of the older and the more contemporary women's organizations, a number of regional mechanisms were put in place, including the Women's Desk of the Caribbean Community (CARICOM) Secretariat, the Women and Development Programme of the United Nations Economic Commission for Latin America and the Caribbean, and the Women and Development Unit within the Extra-Mural Department of the University of the West Indies.[3] In 1982, on the initiative of the Women and Development Unit, women and development studies groups were formed on each of the three campuses of the University of the West Indies, which led to the establishment of the Centre for Gender and Development Studies in 1993. While some of these agencies catered only to the anglophone Caribbean, others, like the Caribbean Association for Feminist Research and Action and the United Nations Economic Commission for Latin America and the Caribbean, dealt with the Caribbean as a whole, including Cuba; in any case, they all served to give women's issues increased visibility in national and regional fora.

During this period, and continuing to the present, violence against women emerged as the single issue capable of uniting women of all sectors, classes and ethnic groups. Over the last two decades the delegitimization of violence against women, once thought to be the natural prerogative of men and canonized in a number of famous calypsos, has been one of the greatest achievements of the movement. Unfortunately, as we shall see later, this did not translate into a reduction in the prevalence of violence. In many territories legislation against sexual offences and domestic violence was enacted. In Trinidad and Tobago, for example, by 2000 there were: two rape crisis centres; approximately eight shelters for battered women; a toll-free domestic violence hotline run by the government Domestic Violence Unit; and a community policing unit which had a focus on domestic violence and child abuse. In addition, legislation on sexual offences, including rape in marriage and domestic violence, was passed and had in some cases been revised.

In many ways the concern with masculinity was also fuelled by the intransigence of the problem of sexual violence and the apparent ineffectiveness of all solutions used to deal with it. After close to two decades of action against violence, most practitioners and observers of the scene came to the conclusion that maybe the answer lay in greater attention to the perpetrator than to the victim, who had been the previous focus. This has resulted in the emergence of a number of initiatives, at community and state levels, focused on men. For example, in recognition of the need to focus on men, the government Division of Women's Affairs in Trinidad and Tobago introduced a male support programme, and later changed its name to the Division of Gender Affairs to reflect its dual concern with women and men. The Rape Crisis Society instituted a male support programme, many community-based intervention programmes established counselling programmes for males, and the first serious men's group, Men Against Violence to Women, was formed by the mid-1990s.

As noted earlier, the 1986 publication of Errol Miller's book, as well as early essays by Barry Chevannes, heralded the emergence of a new literature on masculinity in the anglophone Caribbean region. To some extent, as we have seen with the formation of Fathers Incorporated, the new movement could not help but come to terms with an earlier literature on Caribbean masculinity which could be found in the family studies of the 1950s and 1960s. In that literature, the "disorganized" Afro-Caribbean family was characterized by what was seen as an unnatural "matrifocality", and an equally unacceptable level of "male irresponsibility and marginality". The Afro-Caribbean family, the product of its West African origins and its transformations during slavery, was never understood in its own right but always as a deviant form of a Western or European norm. These concerns were not transferred to the more overtly patriarchal Indo-Caribbean family, whose structure fitted more closely that of the hegemonic norm.

Although much of the present discourse has focused on male marginality in education, the debate on male marginality in the Afro-Caribbean context has a longer history. The now classic work of Peter J. Wilson (1969, 1973) established the dichotomy of the male quest for "reputation" and the female desire for "respectability" as a counter to the notion of male marginality reflected in the early family studies of the 1950s and 1960s. In those studies (Smith 1956; Clarke 1957; Smith

1973) the concern with what was perceived as an abnormal centrality of mothers and an "absence" of fathers in conjugal households was a common thread. Drawing on the *casa/calle* distinction of scholars of the Spanish-speaking Caribbean (such as Manners 1956; Mintz 1956; Scheele 1956), Wilson sought to explain that lower-class men, if marginal, were so only in relation to the household, and certainly not to the wider society. And even in relation to the household this was not entirely the case. In Providencia, the site of Wilson's fieldwork, 71 per cent of landholders were male and 95 per cent of Providencian men owned land. In addition most house-spots, which formed the basis of family units, were owned by men (Wilson 1973). Wilson's work has generated much discussion and critique (Besson 1993); nevertheless it continues to be an influential starting point for discussions on masculinity in both the anglophone and the hispanophone Caribbean (Sampath 1993, 1997).

In 1991 Errol Miller published his second book on this subject, *Men at Risk,* putting forward a more developed argument on the same theme as his earlier publication. Once again, although few may actually have read it, the title alone has served as a rallying cry for Caribbean men. Basically, Miller argues that ruling minority males purposely restrict the numbers of black males who are allowed upward mobility, with the result that black women inadvertently benefit and enjoy greater socioeconomic advancement than black men. Black women and a small number of black men co-opted into the ruling minority therefore form an alliance which creates divisions in the black community, with the result that the ruling minority is able to maintain its wealth, power and status. Miller acknowledges that "having dominated society for so long, men are basically morally bankrupt and spiritually tired" and that "the male mentality has taken humanity to the brink of catyclysmic disaster", and men may need "to languish at the margins for a while" (Miller 1991, 283). Nevertheless, the book warns men of the ruling minority that if they continue this trend, "women will not only continue to progress, the unintended consequence of being used as pawns in male conflicts, but will go on to assert themselves and seize power from men in some societies" (p. 282).

It is in this context, therefore, that the Centre for Gender and Development Studies on the St Augustine campus of the University of the West Indies organized and hosted the symposium entitled "The Construction of Caribbean Masculinity: Towards a Research Agenda". This symposium brought together scholars and researchers beginning to work in this area in the region, along with some international scholars in the field. At this symposium, the first academic initiative of its kind in the region, a number of papers were presented, some of which are included in this volume in an updated and revised form. Absent from this event were Barry Chevannes and Janet Brown, who at that time were completing one of the first systematic research studies on masculinity in the region. Between 1993 and 1996 they coordinated a UNICEF-funded project on gender socialization in the Caribbean, with special emphasis on male socialization. The study was carried out in five communities in Dominica, Guyana and Jamaica. The full research is now completed and a summary report written in popular form was published in 1998 (Brown and Chevannes 1998) and the full study in 2001 (Chevannes 2001).

In 1999 Chevannes challenged the marginalization thesis, offering a more nuanced analysis of the problematic. In his 1999 Grace, Kennedy lecture, *What We Sow and What We Reap: Problems in the Cultivation of Male Identity in Jamaica,* Chevannes concludes that males are not marginalized in the wider society or in education, but following Figueroa (this volume), he argues that the present patterns of gender socialization which privilege boys do have potentially problematic implications for male youth in a work environment which is increasingly being determined by educational competence (Chevannes 1999, 34).

While education, socialization and sexual violence have emerged as starting points for studies on masculinity in the anglophone Caribbean, the papers in this volume suggest that interests have now moved beyond this. This volume in many ways marks the emergence of scholarship on masculinity as a growing and significant area of new work in gender studies in the Caribbean. The establishment of the Caribbean Network for Studies on Masculinity based at the Centro de Investigación y Educación de VIH/SIDA of the University of Puerto Rico, Rio Piedras, in which the University of the West Indies Gender Studies Centres are represented and which brings together Caribbean and international scholars, is another manifestation of the significance of this new area of interdisciplinary and multidisciplinary work.

Some of the areas in which early work has begun are: hegemonic and subordinate masculinities (Ramírez 1999); literary theory and popular culture (Ramchand, this volume; Morgan, this volume; Rohlehr 1988 and this volume; Lewis 1998; Meeks 2000); masculinity, nationalism, ethnicity and identity (Sampath 1993; Mohammed 1995; Reddock 1998a; Lewis 2000); sexuality and sex work (de Moya and Garcia 1996; Phillips 1999; de Albuquerque 1999). In addition to work in academic circles, public policy organizations such as the International Planned Parenthood Federation and the Instituto de Sexualidad Humana of the Autonomous University of Santo Domingo have initiated research on male sexualities, attitudes and behaviours, also a concern of the Caribbean Epidemiology Centre, which has begun research on homo-sexuality and male sexual behaviours in the context of the HIV/AIDS pandemic.

Indeed, the HIV/AIDS pandemic has provided the space to examine one of the most controversial and pivotal subjects related to masculin-ity construction – homophobia. As noted by Michael Kimmel (1996), homophobia represents more than just a fear of homosexual men; it reflects male terror of being exposed as something other than heterosex-ual, as "not a real man". Homophobia therefore acts as a policing force, so to speak, monitoring and guiding boys and men's behaviour (Kimmel 1996). The anglophone Caribbean, and Jamaica in particular, has been characterized as homophobic and this issue has begun to emerge in dis-cussions of popular culture (Chin 1999); education and socialization (Parry 1996 and this volume); and is tentatively being explored by nov-elists and writers (Thomas 1994, cited in Chin 1999).

Another area of particular importance to the Caribbean region, bear-ing in mind the specificities of its history and contemporary reality, is that of the interrelations of masculinity, nationalism, ethnicity and iden-tity. In a recent work Linden Lewis identifies the masculinist orienta-tion which emerging black nationalism took during the early years of the twentieth century. This, he argues, "was normalized as a general process of struggle rather than a specific struggle, by one group of men to wrestle control from another, more powerful group of men". The assumption of leadership, therefore, "by men in the nationalist project appeared both to men and women as a natural evolution, given the relation of men to power, access to resources and privilege" (Lewis 2000, 262). In my own examination of this phenomenon in Trinidad and Tobago in the aftermath of the 1995 general election, where for the first time a predominantly Indo-Trinidadian government came to power, I argued that interethnic relations in these societies are often expressed as a contest among men, where control of political power and the state serves to legitimize claims of citizenship and becomes a symbol of "manhood".

These arguments are all in line with Patricia Mohammed's theorization, which posits the existence of three competing patriarchies in Trinidad society in 1917, the end of the indentureship period. She delineates these as the dominant white patriarchy, which controlled state power as it existed then, a "creole" patriarchy comprising Africans and a mixed group which was emerging, and finally an Indian patriarchy, seeking to construct itself out of some aspects of the cultural baggage brought from India and in the context of the systems functioning in Trinidad at that time (Mohammed 1994, 32). By the 1990s, however, one could argue that this contest for power had also become interwoven with competing victimhoods, victimhood in a postcolonial context being seen as moral grounds for recuperating postcolonial leadership and political, social and sexual power.

Writing on the rural, predominantly Hindu village of "Indian Wood" in Trinidad in the 1980s, Niels Sampath found that the construction of masculinity among young Indian males was based both on a rejection of the perceived negative images of their Indian identity and a celebration of its "positive" aspects. He portrays Indo-Caribbean masculinity as a difficult and sometimes confusing struggle against creolization, on the one hand seeking acceptance within its paradigm, but at the same time seeking to maintain Indian domestic patriarchal power. This is a struggle, following Wilson (1969), between the values of honour (Indian) and reputation (creole) (Sampath 1993). As noted in an earlier publication, this is a contradiction which is clearly played out in the struggle for citizenship and political power, a struggle which seeks recognition within the Afro-Creole political and cultural context but which at the same time rejects the legitimacy of the very context (Reddock 1998a, 8).

Interrogating Caribbean Masculinities

This volume is divided into four sections, each exploring a different aspect of this subject, many of them developing the themes raised above, some entering new areas. In section one, "Theorizing Caribbean Masculinities", some of the theoretical and conceptual issues related to the field are examined. Patricia Mohammed, in her chapter, establishes the complexity and dynamism of the construction of masculinity and stresses its interdependence with the construction of femininity. Further to this, she argues that the intersection of postmodernism and feminism provides a favourable environment for the deconstruction of patriarchy and for understanding Caribbean masculinity and femininity. This, one could add, is really the project in which feminists are involved. To this end, Mohammed argues that the deconstruction of masculinity, as of femininity, is an enterprise in which both men and women should be involved.

Keith Nurse, in his chapter, relates the discourse on masculinity to his area of intellectual concern: international relations. He sees this chapter as an attempt to redress the lack of critical treatment or exploration of masculinity in the field of international relations. This is so although the theme of gender in international relations and the work of feminist international relations scholars like Cynthia Enloe and Spike Peterson is relatively well developed.[4] Nurse places "masculinism" at the core of the global problematiques of sexism, racism, patriarchy and imperialism, and argues that, as the Caribbean was the first area of Western economic expansion overseas, Caribbean gender order has been influenced by occidentally defined masculinism. In his book *Masculinity and Power*, Arthur Brittan distinguishes "masculinism" from "masculinity". Masculinity he defines as those aspects of men's behaviour which fluctuate from time to time, a concept which exists only in relation to femininity. Masculinism, on the other hand, he defines as an ideology which justifies and naturalizes male domination and power, accepts heterosexuality and the existing sexual division of labour as normal, and is resistant to change and not subject to fluctuation over time (Brittan 1989, 4, 195). It is this masculinism, therefore, which Nurse argues is responsible for the unease within hegemonic masculinities at the changing gender order. These changes he sees as coming not only from the feminist challenge or the gay rights movement, but also from changes in the world capitalist system – changes in production and consumption which contribute to this reconfiguration of masculine identity.

The third chapter in this section, by E. Antonio de Moya, critically reflects on the international literature and theory on masculinity and relates it to the Caribbean context, in particular that of the Dominican Republic. In so doing he draws heavily on his own work on sexuality and sex work over the decade of the 1990s as well as the work of Rafael Ramírez (1993) in *Dime Capitán.*[5] De Moya develops a complex and intricate analysis based on the old theme of the *casa/calle* divide and the marked double standard which underlies it. Building on Ramírez's work, he also produces an interesting typology of masculinities, subordinate and hegemonic, which characterize Dominican and, he posits, other Afro-Caribbean contexts.

Section two, "Gender Socialization, Educational Performance and Peer Group Relations", explores this area, which is one of the best developed in the anglophone Caribbean at this time. As noted earlier, the debates on what has become known as the "Miller thesis", as well as concerns about education systems at all levels, has led to the emergence of a growing body of research on this subject (Figueroa 1996; Lindsay 1997; Jules and Kutnick 1997; Bailey 1997; Bailey and Brown 1999). The papers in this section provide a good representation of the range. The chapter by Aviston Downes explores this subject historically, seeking to examine "how the education system in Barbados . . . contributed to the creation of a version of masculinity intended to sustain the domination of white ruling class men". Focusing on the beginnings of boys' secondary education in British-colonized Barbados in the 1800s, he traces its development up to the early years of the twentieth century. In an examination of the complexities of race, class and gender in post-colonial Barbados, Downes shows the specific character of elite boys' education, aimed at promoting "homosociability" and male solidarity, which would eventually become a model for boys' education generally.

This historical examination provides a useful backdrop for Mark Figueroa's chapter. While he focuses on the now popular subject of so-called male underperformance, Figueroa advances an interesting argument, locating this problem as one of "male privilege" which is characteristic of Caribbean gender ideology. This is a controversial position in a climate emphasizing "male marginalization", however Figueroa presents a convincing argument of internal (related to the home) and external (related to public and social life) factors which contribute to male privileging, privileges which contradictorily work against boys at this present conjuncture.

The chapter by Odette Parry is a useful ethnographic study that allows us to look empirically at the situation in schools. Based on a symbolic interactionist study of teachers and pupils in Barbados, Jamaica, and St Vincent and the Grenadines, Parry argues that contemporary explanations of so-called male underachievement usually use what she calls the "woman as villain" thesis, where women and girls as mothers, teachers and pupils are held responsible for male academic performance. In her study Parry found that, on the contrary, notions of acceptable masculinity and male behaviour and homophobia contribute greatly to this situation. This section, along with the recent work of Brown and Chevannes, goes a long way towards answering some of the questions related to this very controversial topic.

The last chapter in this section breaks new ground in Caribbean scholarship generally and in Caribbean gender studies in particular. Wesley Crichlow presents, following Audre Lorde's (1982) notion of biomythography, an analysis of his personal experience as a homosexual growing up in the hegemonic heterosexist context of Trinidad and Tobago. Crichlow laments the absence of a dialogue on same-sex practices within black communities in general and Caribbean communities in particular. Like other persons of same-sex orientation in the Third World context, Crichlow challenges the pre-eminence of Northern terminologies. His conscious claiming of the pejorative Trinidadian term "buller man" to define himself can be seen as an effort to restore and reclaim indigenous terms and knowledge systems and a challenge to the hegemony of Euro-American terminology and conceptualization. This chapter can be seen as the beginning of an interrogation of same-sex relations in this region, in a conversation in which those involved in same-sex practices are centrally involved.

The third section, "Class, Ethnicity, Nation and Notions of Masculinity", explores those issues of ethnicity, class and identity which have always been central to writing on the Caribbean. In so doing, the papers add to the larger international literature which identifies the link between struggles for national and ethnic identity and citizenship, both at the personal and political levels, and the valorization of masculinity and manhood. The chapter by Hilary Beckles locates the early construction of black or Afro-Caribbean masculinity in the competitive and exploitative relationship between European and African males during the slave period. Noting that, for most of the slave period, males formed the majority of the Caribbean slave population, Beckles argues that the masculinity of enslaved blacks was constructed through its interaction with hegemonic structures of white masculinity, the principal site of interaction being the property relation. Here white male power was based on the monopolistic control, ownership and possession of all power and property, including black women and men.

This process, according to Beckles, occurred in a context where black men shared the same basic patriarchal values as white men and, when possible during slavery, sought to assert their masculine authority and power over women with deleterious effect. The inability to live this reality confirmed their subordinated masculinity, a subordinated masculinity which they would seek to assert at any given opportunity.

Linden Lewis's chapter explores the situation confronting Caribbean men as they enter the twenty-first century. Periods such as these, he notes, are usually times of reflection, and he suggests that this may be as good a time as any for men to pay some attention theoretically, ideologically and intellectually to the issue of their own gendered identities. At this conjuncture, he suggests Caribbean men appear to be facing two inter-related types of crises: one economic in orientation and the other social and gender related. These crises, he notes, cannot be seen as crises for men only, as when men are in crisis, so too are women and children. This is an interesting argument, as commentators have linked the current escalation of violence against women in the region and the heightening of the backlash against the women's movement to the economic restructuring more commonly referred to as structural adjustment policies (SAPS), at the behest of international financial institutions. Lewis calls for more research on the changing context and reality of masculinity in the region and its relationship to other factors such as labour. The development of masculinity studies as part of gender studies in the region, he suggests, is crucial.

The final chapter in this section, by Matthei and Smith, looks at a problem common to the region but in the specific context of the Garifuna people of Belize. The phenomenon of children left in the region by migrating parents, especially mothers, has emerged as an area of concern. One of the reasons leading to this concern has been the link made between this phenomenon and youth criminality, especially among male youth. Matthei and Smith begin by noting what they call the globalization of Belizean space. This so-called globalization, as in other parts of the region, may more correctly be seen as an "Americanization". They note the identification with US icons as demonstrated by t-shirts, baseball caps, and so on with sports logos of US basketball teams. The generalization of US cable television and the continuous interaction with that country through electronic and other communication systems highlight the extent of the influence on this predominantly rural Central American community.

This chapter traces the transnationalized processes through which patterns of US urban masculine ideology influence Garifuna youth who migrate to Los Angeles and those who are left at home with relatives. One of these is the "gangsta" ideology current in Los Angeles and transported to the Garifuna town of Stann Creek. Although focusing on Belize, the authors speak to a reality throughout the region, one that is beginning to receive greater attention.

The final section examines the fields of literature, visual arts and popular culture, media through which discourses on masculinity and femininity are not only represented but vigorously contested. The first chapter, by Paula Morgan, sets out to explore Caribbean women writers' "representations of their male counterparts" in their writings. She does so in order to answer a number of questions relating to women's and men's understanding of each other, through examining a number of female-authored texts. While noting that portrayals of men tend in the main to reflect common stereotypes, she notes that there are some exceptions to this rule. Additionally she finds that even when these portrayals are negative, they are sympathetically dealt with by the authors in a way which, quoting Marion O'Callaghan, acknowledges their having "fallen prey to social and historical factors that sanction male tyranny".

Kenneth Ramchand's chapter explores the figure of the badjohn in Earl Lovelace's text *The Dragon Can't Dance*. This icon of the black male warrior, on a mission to valorize his masculinity and become visible, is well represented in the literary writings of Trinidadian writer Earl Lovelace. Lovelace's novels and analyses of them have been central to discourses of urban masculinity within the anglophone Caribbean region. In a 1986 article, Kenneth Ramchand describes Lovelace's writing in these words:

> For in all his novels there are two overriding themes. There is first the theme of the liberation of the individual from imposed roles and attitudes, the salvaging of the real self from the role self, an exploration as in Walcott of New World possibility, "the possibility of the individual Caribbean man, African, European, Asian in ancestry, the gently enormous, gently opening morning of his possibility, his body touched with dew, his nerves as subtilised to sensation as the mimosa, his memory whether of grandeur or of pain gradually erasing itself as recurrent drizzles cleanse the ancestral or tribal markings from the coral skull, the possibility of a man and his language waking to wonder here". (Ramchand 1986, 5)

In his chapter here, Ramchand tackles Lovelace's treatment of masculinity in *The Dragon Can't Dance*, highlighting its significance as the

1960s version of the black urban warrior. For Lovelace, Ramchand notes, while not excusing the violence of the characters, the badjohn represents in the extreme the black man's need to be seen and acknowledged as a person. Interestingly, Ramchand notes a similar identification with the badjohn in the much earlier writings of Seepersad Naipaul, father of Vidia S. Naipaul, in his novel *Tales of Gurudeva*. In this novel, according to Ramchand, badjohns are referred to as "heroes of their race, champions of their culture and figures of defiance against the authorities in the new land", a group to which Gurudeva, like Fisheye in *Dragon*, yearns to belong.

This identification with the badjohn was reflected in the connection made with the heroes of US Westerns by men of subordinated masculinities of the Caribbean. As late as the 1980s Laurie Gunst, in writing about Jamaican badmen who later went on to form the posses in the United States, noted the influence of the bandits like Django on their imagination. She had this to say:

> the gunmen infused their cruelty with a certain cinematic style, a cool detachment from the agony they inflicted. Most of these paladins had come of age in the 1950s and 1960s, when Hollywood churned out countless westerns and Jamaicans began a long love affair with the legendary bandits of the silver screen . . . . I discovered the power of the myth as I came to know the gunmen and sufferers of Kingston. We shared an affinity with the Wild West, and this carried us across many a cultural bridge . . . there were the veteran outlaws who were brought to tears by "Ghost Riders in The Sky". There was the tense afternoon in a shantytown near Kingston where I had gone to meet a ranking named "Billy the Kid" who was very reluctant to talk to me until someone mentioned that I'd only recently come to Jamaica from Wyoming.
>
> "Whoy," Billy breathed in a reverent whisper. "I know 'bout that place! Nuff-nuff bad-mon come from out there! Hole-in-the-Wall, Butch Cassidy an' the Sundance Kid . . ." (Gunst 1986, xxii)

In the cases of both Gurudeva and Fisheye, their violence in the home and community is legendary, yet both authors are able to go beyond this to identify their yearnings to stand out and be noticed as part of their communities. Ramchand's reading of these two novels suggests commonalities in the subordinated masculinities of Afro- and Indo-Caribbean men which is not often acknowledged in the tension of interethnic rivalry, especially in Guyana and Trinidad and Tobago.

The third chapter in this section, by Gordon Rohlehr, deals with a very important avenue for giving voice to Afro-Trinidadian, and in particular Afro-Caribbean, working-class male concerns and aspirations. Using the Trinidad calypso as text, Rohlehr likens the calypsonian's space to the gayelle or stickfighting yard, where indeed many of the early calypsos were sung, and notes that the calypso is one of the strongest modes of the working-class performance of masculinity. He weaves a tale of the calypsonian as legendary stickman, phallic hero and boasting celebrant of his own prowess, metamorphosed as the Saga Boy or the Cocksman. Rohlehr argues that, because of its range of content – "everything under the sun" – and its variety of styles, the calypso becomes a useful basis for research, analysis and eventual theorizing about masculinity, a masculinity which it simultaneously masks and unmasks.

The final chapter in this section and also in this volume is by Christopher Cozier. It is a commentary and reflexive piece written in 1998, based on a series of installations presented by the artist/writer between 1991 and 1994. The first two of these, *The Shirt-Jac* and *The Whip*, are both interactive performance installations where the artist first interacts with the object then members of the audience are called upon to do the same. The author, the artist, reflects upon three installations, all representing aspects of masculine performance which are visually represented within this piece. Cozier is particularly interested in the issue of nationalism and the ways in which men sought to position and relocate themselves in the transition from colonialism to independence and what can be termed neocolonialism. In responding to the shirt-jac performance/installation, fellow artist Dean Arlen sees this as a case of

> an artist taking the role of actor. The shirt-jac – the seat, the prop, metamorphoses as a stage, the audience looks up to the artist. The work is set in real time . . . the artist brought the surface of the canvas into the 3-dimensional round and the audience was invited to participate in the discussion, adjusting the seat to their comfort zone. The work becomes more than itself – interactive, like he said talking to the shirt was like talking to your father

when he was reading the newspaper, using one discourse to define another agenda . . . [taking] his art and intellectual and national thoughts to the personal. (Arlen 2000, 1)

The last section of Cozier's chapter examines the 1994 Blue Soap exhibition, which reflects on the police, priest and politician – three masculine images representing neocolonial control.

From the above we get a picture, in the main, of Caribbean masculinities as conceptualized and experienced as subordinated and struggling, to varying degrees in the post- and neocolonial context, for the personhood, recognition, visibility, citizenship and power felt to be their birthright. So far the discourse has highlighted the conflict with other men, which often takes place through the bodies of women. The female, often depersonalized, may be the ground, the territory over or upon which fierce battles are fought, but increasingly as women challenge accepted notions of masculinity and enter spaces perceived as male preserves, the battle also becomes one directly against them.

This volume should be seen as an early contributor to what will eventually emerge as a vigorous and important area of scholarship and activism in this region – a process which, as with other endeavours in feminist politics and gender studies, has as its aim the transformation of human relations and the creation of a more just and humane society.

Notes

1. I owe this insight to Jafari Allen.
2. This was given at a verbal presentation organized by the Women and Development Studies Group at the University of the West Indies, Mona, *c.*1994.
3. The Extra-Mural Department of the University of the West Indies is now the School of Continuing Studies.
4. At the time of writing the author may not have been aware of *The "Man Question" in International Relations* (Zalewsky and Parpart 1998).
5. Also published in English as *Learning to Be a Man.*

References

Arlen, Dean. 2000. "The Shirt-Jac: Passages of Modern Sculpture". Typescript.

Bailey, Barbara. 1997. "Not an Open Book: Gender Achievement and Education in the Caribbean". Working Paper no. 1, edited by Patricia Mohammed, 22–44. Mona, Jamaica: Centre for Gender and Development Studies, University of the West Indies.

Bailey, Barbara, and Monica Brown. 1999. *Schooling and Masculinity: Boys' Perspective on the School Experience.* Kingston, Jamaica: Centre for Gender and Development Studies.

Besson, Jean. 1993. "Reputation and Respectability Reconsidered: A New Perspective on Afro-Caribbean Peasant Women". In *Women and Change in the Caribbean,* edited by Janet Momsen. Kingston, Jamaica: Ian Randle.

Brittan, Arthur. 1989. *Masculinity and Power.* Oxford: Basil Blackwell.

Brown, Janet, and Barry Chevannes. 1998. *"Why Man Stay So": Tie the Heifer, Loose the Bull.* Kingston, Jamaica: University of the West Indies.

Chevannes, Barry. 1999. *What We Sow and What We Reap: Problems in the Cultivation of Male Identity in Jamaica.* Grace, Kennedy Foundation Lecture. Kingston, Jamaica: Grace, Kennedy Foundation.

———. 2001. *Learning to Be a Man: Culture, Socialization and Gender Identity in Five Caribbean Communities.* Kingston, Jamaica: University of the West Indies Press.

Chin, Timothy S. 1999. "Jamaican Popular Culture, Caribbean Literature
    and the Representation of Gay and Lesbian Sexuality in the Discourses of
    Race and Nation". *Small Axe,* no. 5 (March).
Clarke, Edith. 1957. *My Mother Who Fathered Me: A Study of Three
    Selected Communities in Jamaica.* London: George Allen and Unwin.
Clatterbaugh, Kenneth. 1997. *Contemporary Perspectives on Masculinity.*
    Boulder: Westview Press.
de Alburquerque, Klaus. 1998. " 'Men Day Done': Are Women Really
    Ascendant in the Caribbean?" In *Caribbean Portraits: Essays on Gender
    Ideologies and Identities,* edited by Christine Barrow. Kingston, Jamaica:
    Ian Randle and Centre for Gender and Development Studies.
———. 1999. "In Search of the Big Bamboo: Among the Sex Tourists of the
    Caribbean". *Transition* 77.
de Moya, Antonio, and R. Garcia. 1996. "AIDS and the Enigma of
    Bisexuality in the Dominican Republic". In *Bisexualities and AIDS:
    International Perspectives,* edited by P. Aggleton. London: Taylor and
    Francis.
Enloe, Cynthia. 1989. *Bananas, Beaches and Bases: Making Feminist Sense of
    International Relations.* Berkeley: University of California Press.
Figueroa, Mark. 1996. "Gender Differentials in Educational Achievement in
    Jamaica and Other Caribbean Territories". Paper presented at the confer-
    ence Intervention Strategies to Address Male Underperformance in
    Primary and Secondary Education, Government of Trinidad and Tobago
    and the National Commission for UNESCO, Chaguaramas, Trinidad,
    November.
Gunst, Laurie. 1986. *Born Fi' Dead: A Journey through the Jamaican Posse
    Underworld.* New York: Henry Holt.
Jules, Vena, and Peter Kutnick. 1997. *Gender and School Achievement in the
    Caribbean.* London: Department of International Development.
Kimmel, Michael. 1996. "Masculinity as Homophobia: Fear, Shame and
    Silence in the Construction of Gender Identity". Paper presented to the
    symposium The Construction of Caribbean Masculinity: Towards a
    Research Agenda, Centre for Gender and Development Studies, St
    Augustine, Trinidad.
Lewis, Linden. 1998. "Masculinity and the Dance of the Dragon". *Feminist
    Review,* no. 59 (Summer).
———. 2000. "Nationalism and Caribbean Masculinity". In *Gender Ironies
    of Nationalism: Sexing the Nation,* edited by Tamar Mayer. London:
    Routledge.

Lindsay, Keisha. 1997. "Caribbean Male: An Endangered Species?" Working Paper no. 1, edited by Patricia Mohammed, 1–20. Mona, Jamaica: Centre for Gender and Development Studies, University of the West Indies.

Lorde, Audre. 1982. *Zami: A New Spelling of My Name.* Freedom, Calif.: Crossing Press.

Manners, R. 1956. "Tabara: Subcultures of a Tobacco and Mixed Crop Municipality". In *The People of Puerto Rico,* edited by J. Steward, et al. Urbana: University of Illinois Press.

Meeks, Brian. 2000. *Narratives of Resistance: Jamaica, Trinidad, the Caribbean.* Kingston, Jamaica: University of the West Indies Press.

Miller, Errol. 1986. *The Marginalization of the Black Male: Insights from the Development of the Teaching Profession.* Kingston, Jamaica: Institute of Social and Economic Research.

———. 1991. *Men at Risk.* Kingston, Jamaica: Jamaica Publishing House.

Mintz, Sidney. 1956. "Canamelar: The Subculture of a Rural Sugar Plantation Proletariat". In *The People of Puerto Rico,* edited by J. Steward, et al. Urbana: University of Illinois Press.

Mohammed, Patricia. 1994. "A Social History of Indians in Trinidad, 1917–1947: A Gender Perspective". PhD diss., Institute of Social Studies, The Hague.

———. 1995. "Writing Gender into History: The Negotiations of Gender Relations between Indian Men and Women". In *Engendering History: Caribbean Women in Historical Perspective,* edited by Verene Shepherd, Bridget Brereton and Barbara Bailey. Kingston, Jamaica: Ian Randle, 1995.

———. 2000. "Engendering Masculinity: Cross-Cultural Caribbean Research Initiatives". Paper presented to the Latin American Studies Association annual conference, March.

Parry, Odette. 1996. "In One Ear and Out the Other: Unmasking Masculinities in the Caribbean Classroom". *Sociological Research Online* 1, no. 2.

Peterson, V. Spike. 1992. *Gendered States: Feminist Revisions of International Relations Theory.* Boulder: Lynne Rienner.

Phillips, Joan. 1999. "Tourist-Oriented Prostitution in Barbados: The Case of the Beach Boy and the White Female Tourist". In *Sun, Sex and Gold: Tourism and Sex Work in the Caribbean,* edited by Kamala Kempadoo. Lanham, Md.: Rowman and Littlefield.

Ramchand, Kenneth. 1986. "An Approach to Earl Lovelace's Novel, through an Examination of Indian-African Relations in *The Dragon Can't Dance*". *Caribbean Quarterly* 32, nos. 1 and 2 (March–June).

Ramírez, Rafael. 1993. *Dime Capitán: Reflexiones sobre la Masculinidad.*
    Rio Piedras: Ediciones Huracán.
———. 1999. *What It Means to Be a Man: Reflections on Puerto Rican
    Masculinity.* New Brunswick, N.J.: Rutgers University Press.
Reddock, Rhoda. 1998a. "Masculinity, Ethnicity and Identity in the
    Contemporary Socio-Political Context of Trinidad and Tobago". Paper
    presented at Conference on the African Diaspora, University of California,
    Berkeley, April.
———. 1998b. "Women's Organizations and Movements in the
    Commonwealth Caribbean: The Response to the Global Economic Crisis
    in the 1980s". *Feminist Review,* no. 59 (Summer).
Rohlehr, Gordon. 1988. "Images of Men and Women in the 1930s Calypsos:
    The Sociology of Food Acquisition in the Context of Survivalism". In
    Gender in Caribbean Development, edited by Patricia Mohammed and
    Catherine Shepherd. St Augustine, Trinidad: Women and Development
    Studies Project, University of the West Indies.
Sampath, Niels. 1993. "An Evaluation of the 'Creolisation' of Trinidad East
    Indian Adolescent Masculinity". In *Trinidad Ethnicity,* edited by Kevin
    Yelvington. Knoxville: University of Tennessee Press.
———. 1997. "Crabs in a Bucket: Reforming Male Identities in Trinidad". In
    Men and Masculinity, edited by Caroline Sweetman. Oxford: Oxfam.
Scheele, Raymond. 1956. "The Prominent Families of Puerto Rico". In *The
    People of Puerto Rico,* edited by J. Steward, et al. Urbana: University of
    Illinois Press.
Smith, M.G. 1973. "A Survey of West Indian Family Studies". In *Work and
    Family Life: West Indian Perspectives,* edited by Lambros Comitas and
    David Lowenthal. Garden City, NY: Anchor Press.
Smith, R.T. 1956. *The Negro Family in British Guiana: Family Structure and
    Social Status in the Villages.* London: Routledge and Kegan Paul.
Thomas, H. Nigel. 1994. *Spirits in the Dark.* Oxford: Heinemann.
Wilson, Peter. 1969. "Reputation and Respectability: A Suggestion for
    Caribbean Ethnography". *Man* 4, no. 2.
———. 1973. *Crab Antics: The Anthropology of English-Speaking Negro
    Societies of the Caribbean.* New Haven: Yale University Press.
Zalewsky, Marysia, and Jane Parpart. 1998. *The "Man Question" in
    International Relations.* Boulder: Westview Press.

PART ONE

Theorizing Caribbean Masculinities

CHAPTER 1

Masculinities in Transition

Gender and the Global Problematique

KEITH NURSE

The attention that masculinity is now receiving is due in part to the erosion of the "myth that men are neither a problem nor have problems" (Rutherford 1988, 44). Myths, according to Roland Barthes (1989), play the role of depoliticization by marginalizing historical reality and replacing it with notions of the natural and the eternal. "The myth of masculinity is its attempt to pass itself off as natural and universal, free of problems" (Rutherford 1988, 23). As a consequence, gendered politics are made invisible. For instance, men rarely see themselves as a gender, and society generally treats masculine characteristics as the prototype of human behaviour, irrespective of time and space. Masculinism, therefore, operates as a hegemonic ideology and exerts a profound influence on the structure of modern society.

Gender is considered to be one of the main conflict formations in the modern world-system (Galtung 1991). The masculine/feminine schism is one of the fault lines in the modern human condition that facilitates epistemic violence and compromises social justice and harmonious global relations. Masculinism is the dominant philosophical value system in the gender framework. It is a totalizing philosophy in that it operates with a high level of consensus, as a well-constructed myth (Barthes 1989) and as an instrument of disciplinary power (Foucault 1980). In the nature of myths, it goes largely uncriticized and unquestioned. The pervasiveness and seeming permanence of masculinism is explained by the fact that gender, like other arenas of oppression, "is not only 'out there' structuring activities and institutions, and 'in our heads' structuring discourse and ideologies; it is also 'in here' – in our hearts and bodies – structuring our intimate desires, our sexuality, our self-esteem and our dreams" (Peterson 1997, 199).

The contention in this chapter is that masculinism is a core philosophy embedded in sexism, modernism, capitalism and imperialism. Consequently, it should be viewed as one of the core features of the *global problematique* (Addo 1985) and the *longue durée* of human history (Peterson 1997). This chapter is limited in terms of the cases cited and the examples used, because of the paucity of information on masculinism outside of the Euro/American sociocultural framework. This is as much a reflection of the intellectual division of labour as it is a function of the processes of globalization. Most of the information about the world is generated, published and distributed by the West. This presents some difficulties about generalization. Nonetheless, the approach adopted here is that a significant measure of the global gender dynamic is a result of the "export of the European/American gender order to the colonised world" through institutions like the church, the military, Western education, the modern state, transnational corporations and the worldwide media (Connell 1995, 199). In this regard, this chapter is of great relevance to the Caribbean, given that it was the first area of European overseas expansion, and that it has the unique distinction of being a virtual microcosm of a hybridized global culture (Addo 1980; James 1980; Mintz 1993).

Masculinity has emerged as a critical area of enquiry in the field of gender and cultural studies in the last decade. In the field of international relations or global politics, however, the subject is largely untouched. This is somewhat understandable given that the discipline is one of the most masculinist fields in the social sciences, with its traditional emphasis on statecraft, militarism and economic competitiveness. This chapter attempts to address this lacuna by analysing the contemporary transitions in masculinity as part of the long-term, large-scale transformations in the modern capitalist world-system. The aim here is to contextualize the current transitions in gender relations by exploring the relationship between the social construction of masculine identity and the perpetuation or transcendence of global problematiques such as sexism, racism and patriarchy.

Theorizing/Historicizing Masculinities

We start from the premise that masculinism is a gendered ideology that is socially constructed and therefore not static or immutable but shaped by the historical and cultural context (Kimmel and Messner 1995). A distinction is therefore made between masculinities and men, because the values of the former may not correspond to the personality or preferences of some biological men (for example, feminized masculinities) while this may be the case for some women (masculinized femininity). This view contrasts with conceptions of a biologically determined "male sex role" which suggests that male behaviour is informed by some essential, preprogrammed genetic code. There is much debate among scientists about whether gender differences are a result of differences in sex hormones like testosterone, which predisposes males towards aggression, competition and violence, and oestrogen, which predisposes females towards passivity, tenderness and exaggerated emotionality (Gorman 1992). In essence, the debate on gender differences is part of the long-standing "nature versus nurture" argument that is at the core of social science epistemology.

Male sex-role theory, by essentializing gender differences in the biological, the "natural", makes invisible the structural and systemic bases of power in gender relations. The claim of political neutrality rings hollow because the definition of what is natural or normal is informed by the characteristics and practices of dominant males. The characteristics of the "ideal" male in modern, globalized society are that he is white, heterosexual, married, middle-aged, university educated and upper middle class: what is termed *hegemonic masculinity* (Connell 1995). This is the hegemonic conception of Western masculinity by which all men – irrespective of age, class, race, sexual orientation or cultural background – are measured. Here the "white male" is constructed as an ideal for all "others" to emulate. The irony of the situation is that the hegemonic male ideal is a mythic construction that few can attain. Also, the white male is used as a *metaphor* for hegemonic masculinity but is not exclusive, because in different cultural contexts the ideal can take on a darker hue.

The behavioural norms within hegemonic masculinity are generally extrapolated as a universal. This approach has explanatory limitations in that it abstracts from a "false cultural universalism" which legitimizes and normalizes certain forms of masculinity (hegemonic ones) and marginalizes others (subordinate ones), for example, working-class men, gay men and non-Western men or ethnic minorities. Such theorizing is problematic because it is "ill equipped to understand the ways in which sex roles change, and the ways in which individuals modify those roles through the enactment of gender expectations" (Kimmel and Messner 1995, xix). An alternative approach to biological essentialism is one that is informed in the following way: it is not that our biology is irrelevant but that it serves as a lower boundary condition through which and upon which we must construct symbolic reality, both internal and social. The content of our lives – consciousness, the unconscious, experience, even "self" – is constructed from semantic and semiotic symbols we encounter in our interactive dialogue with the world (O'Hara 1995, 154–55).

Masculinist notions of gender relations are grounded in modern Western thought. The epistemological roots are to be found in the Newtonian-Cartesian world-view which dichotomizes and hierarchizes cultural values in binary opposites: objectivity versus subjectivity, reason versus emotion, mind versus body, culture versus nature, competition versus cooperation, public versus private. These differences are usually used to differentiate between male and female traits. In the dominant masculinist phallocentric discourse, the "feminine" is conceptualized and actualized as the "ontological Other" (Persram 1994, 280). In this framework the feminine is "perceived in terms of matter, *physics,* the passions, the emotions, the irrational, characteristics traditionally associated with nature. The implications that follow is that the feminine must be mastered and controlled, since it does not represent the desirable (though it is considered the desiring) aspect of human life" (p. 276).

Masculine values, on the other hand, are taken as the prototype for human behaviour. Masculinism, as the hegemonic ideational construct, achieves a *logocentric* posture and thus becomes "a pervasive, familiar, and powerful narrative by which we organise our understanding of social reality" (Johnson 1991, 153). Masculinism therefore operates as an instrument of disciplinary power (Foucault 1980) through its surveillance, hierarchization, categorization and normalization of gender and global relations.

Masculinity is inherently relational in that "different masculinities are constituted in relation to other masculinities and to femininities – through the structure of gender relations" (Connell 1992, 736). Masculinity is thus multidimensional, since gender relations are intertwined with class, race, ethnicity, age, sexuality and nationality. Hence, it is more appropriate to speak of multiple masculini*ties* rather than "one" masculinity. In addition, it is also recognized that there is a power differential within masculinities. Some masculinities are hegemonic and dominant while others are subordinated and marginalized. Historically, subordinate masculinities have been constructed and represented as *effeminate* and *infantile* to distinguish them from the hegemonic forms. They have also been *racialized* and *sexualized* as a means to justify their oppression (Connell 1995).

The subjectification of the "other" through "difference" (stigmatization, stereotyping, and so forth) has proved to be fundamental to the constitution of hegemonic masculinity. The interplay of "otherness" and "difference" is recognized as an important mechanism of governance, for example, in the colonialist discourse (Bhabha 1994). However, paradoxically, it involves an ambivalence and a circularity in that "it also makes 'difference' powerful, strangely attractive precisely because it is forbidden, taboo, threatening to cultural order" (Hall 1997, 237). Thus, "it implicates the 'subjects' of power as well as those who are 'subjected to it' " (p. 263). The poetics and politics of representation are such that "victims" can be co-opted by strategies of resistance just as the "victors" can display their anxieties and repressed fantasies through the projection of power. This appreciation of the workings of power and powerlessness provides a useful framework for analysing the relationship between hegemonic and subordinated masculinities.

The antagonism to homosexuality in hegemonic masculinity provides some insights into gender politics. Homosexuality is generally seen as the negation of masculinity and thus effeminate. Homosexual men are defined as the most unmasculine or emasculated of men. It is suggested that homophobic responses to gay men are one of the means by which hegemonic masculinity polices the boundaries of a traditional male sex role and reinforces a strict heterosexual practice (Connell 1992). In this way, homophobia is one of the building blocks in the construction of masculinity. It is argued that this tendency suggests that masculinity has been historically defined as the "flight from women", the repudiation of the feminine and the rejection of male-male intimacy. Men are therefore in constant fear of being viewed as wimps, sissies or homosexuals. Manhood is affirmed through homosocial enactment and male validation (Kimmel 1996). For instance, the *machismo* found in Latin America and the Caribbean is premised on securing and bolstering male "reputation" (Sampath 1997), hence the pattern of "a masculine ideal stressing domination of women, competition between men, aggressive display, predatory sexuality and a double standard" (Connell 1995, 31).

The case of Jamaican dancehall music is often cited in reference to homophobic tendencies in Caribbean culture. An example is the protest which Buju Banton's song "Boom Bye-Bye" generated in the international media. It has been argued that the international reading of the lyrics of the song was far too literal and did not appreciate the cultural context and the metaphorical role-play evident in Caribbean popular culture, for example, the tradition of stylized, ritual verbal violence that is common in reggae, calypso and other cultural forms (Cooper 1995).

To support her argument Cooper refers to the fact that "clearly out" male homosexuals work as higglers in Jamaican markets and ply their trade with relatively little provocation. Many have mastered the art of "tracing" – ritualized verbal abuse – as a form of protection from the heterophobia of Jamaican society" (p. 439). This is not to deny the strong homophobic tendencies found in Jamaican and Caribbean culture; rather it is to suggest that the analysis is not so straightforward. For example, it may be possible to see the homophobia exhibited in dancehall music as a function of class warfare, especially in relations between men from different social strata.

The racialization and sexualization of Jewish, Asian and black men is also an important feature in the Western discourse on masculinities. Jewish, Asian and black men are each situated in somewhat different sociopolitical locations, in spite of the fact that they are each subjected to the discriminating gaze of white men. In the United States and other Western societies, the white supremacist discourse on men's bodies provides a useful arena for study because its "extreme images both create racism and reflect core, mainstream values" (Harper 1994, 17). In the supremacist discourse Jewish men are subordinated through constructions that position them as effeminate, desexualized, degenerate and sinister. They are often portrayed or stereotyped as "the supposed leaders of the international economic cabal" (p. 13). Thus, they are seen as the race that is closest to European culture and civilization. Consequently, Jewish masculinities, when considered a threat, are constructed as a threat to white men from above.

Asian masculinities, like that of Jewish men, have been constructed as effeminate, desexualized and degenerate. They are also viewed as being susceptible to despotism and thus dangerous, as exemplified by the concept of the "yellow peril" and other orientalist representations (Said 1978). Unlike Jewish men, who are able to assimilate easily into "whiteness", Asian masculinities are viewed as culturally different when compared with Eurocentric characteristics (Fung 1995). Nineteenth-century racial and colonial classifications, by anthropologists like Gobineau (see table below), position Asians as subordinate to whites but superior to blacks in terms of intellect and moral manifestations. It is only in terms

Table 1.1   A Summary of the Characteristics of the Races According to
                Gobineau (1856)

	Black Races	Yellow Races	White Races
Intellect	Feeble	Mediocre	Vigorous
Animal propensities	Very strong	Moderate	Strong
Moral manifestations	Partially latent	Comparatively developed	Highly cultivated

Source: Young 1995, 104.

of animal propensities (read sexuality) that Asians are situated in the
lowest ranking (desexualized) with whites in the intermediate position.

In contrast to Jews and Asians, the white supremacist discourse sees
black men as a threat from below because of their strong animal propensities (read sexuality). Black masculinities, in the context of slavery, colonialism and white supremacy, have been constructed as primal, debased
and infantile and thus in need of control and supervision by white men
(Harper 1994, 13). For example, in the United States this is expressed
in three stereotypes: "there is Bigger Thomas (the mad and mean predatory craver of white women), Jack Johnson, the super performer – be it
in athletics, entertainment or sex – who excels others naturally (and
prefers women of a lighter hue), or Uncle Tom (the spineless, sexless –
or is it impotent? – sidekick of whites)" (West 1993, 83). These stereotypes lead Cornel West to the conclusion that "white fear of black sexuality is a basic ingredient of white racism" (pp. 124–25).

The infantilization of black men is exemplified in the construction of
black men's "in-bred dependency on the leadership of White Europeans"
(Shohat and Stam 1994, 140). The transnational Western media is replete
with images of subordinate black males, a format that is shared with
other ethnic groups. The concept of the "faithful sidekick", whether
Asian, Arab, black, or native, is very pervasive and seems to be almost
permanent. For instance, recollection of comic strips like *Mandrake* and
The Phantom, television programmes such as *The Lone Ranger* and *The*

Green Hornet, and films like *Tarzan* and *Lawrence of Arabia* illustrate how non-white men were situated in subordinate and impotent positions in the media during the 1960s and 1970s. Some twenty-plus years later one can still see the same constructions represented in present-day movies, especially action movies like *Die Hard, Lethal Weapon* and *Predator* that portray a white hero, what Andrew Ross (1995) calls the "Great White Dude". These movies illustrate the ways in which hegemonic and subordinate masculinities are represented in the Western imperial imaginary. These modes of representation have a sociopolitical impact because they colonize the mind and the imagination. Reflecting on this issue, bell hooks makes the point that

> Socialising, via images, by a pedagogy of white supremacy, young whites who see such "innocent" images of black males eagerly affirming white male superiority come to expect this behaviour in real life. Black males who do not conform to the roles suggested in these films are deemed dangerous, bad, out of control – and most importantly, white-hating. The message that black males receive is that, to succeed, one must be self-effacing and consumed by a politics of envy and longing for white male power. (1995b, 104)

White masculinity is able to reap the benefits of the construction of subordinate masculinities by representing itself as "phallic, erect, impenetrable, imbued with creative power", thereby ensuring that "white men are valorized and given agency while simultaneously their hegemony is confirmed, the [subordination] of the subaltern is affirmed and resistance is rendered inconceivable" (Harper 1994, 13). Such a mode of representation or cultural construction *enables* the oppressor and further *disables* the oppressed. It is increasingly being accepted that a "cultural construction could be historically determining" (Young 1995, 159). As a mechanism of social control, once internalized, it becomes self-fulfilling prophecy. For instance, according to Fanon, "the most powerful tool in the hands of the oppressor is the minds of the oppressed", and thus the colonized is "forever in combat with his own image" (1967, 194). This mode of disciplinary power, embodied in racism and sexism, is ultimately translated into an occupational and reward hierarchy: "Racism has served as an overall ideology justifying inequality. But it has been much more. It has served to socialise groups into their own role in the economy . . . . Racism, just like sexism, functioned as a self-suppressive ideology, fashioning expectations and limiting them" (Wallerstein 1983, 79).

The logic of supremacist discourse, as discussed above, does not only run along the hegemonic-subordinate continuum. It also exploits the schisms within subordinate masculinities. For example, under the old strategy of "divide and rule", the colonialists were able to construct a "culture of ethnicity" that kept the colonial subjects at each others' throats and kept the elite safe. The case of ethnic identity formation in Trinidad in the postemancipation period, where Indian indentured labourers were imported to replace ex-slave African labour (mostly male in both cases) is illustrative of how the *commodification of ethnicity* (Yelvington 1993, 11) relates to the division of labour in a colonial plantation economy.

> By claiming that blacks were poor workers and that East Indians were industrious and docile they [the colonialists] rationalized a programme that involved, among other things, the taxation of working-class blacks and other groups to subsidize the planters so they could import workers who would (at least indirectly) compete as labour. This lowered the price of labour, and, ultimately, divided the subjugated groups. The symbolization process was and is, in a large part, monopolized by those who have had access to the "symbolic capital" to perpetrate "symbolic violence" against less-endowed groups. (p. 10)

Masculinities and Patriarchy

The above observations suggest that masculinity is not just a simple reflex of patriarchal power because of the various cultural representations and institutionalized practices of men's gendered lives. The dominant feminist conception of patriarchy implies an unchanging universal domination of women by men (Walby 1990). Men are viewed as the *global ruling social class* and gender relations are presumed to be a virtual *sexual apartheid* (Jones 1996). This approach has its limitations because it operates with a categorical model of gender issues as women's issues and treats men as an undifferentiated class: the male-as-power-broker stereotype. Jones argues that this is problematic because "the result is a *de facto* equating of gender primarily with females/femininity. It is, in its way, a new logocentrism, whereby (elite) male actions and (hegemonic) masculinity are drawn into the narrative mainly as independent variables explaining 'gender' oppression" (pp. 420–21).

Similar reservations are expressed by bell hooks. She recounts:

> When I first began to study feminist theory, I was puzzled by feminist scholarship that would talk in universalizing generalizations about how patriarchy equates the female being with the body and the male with the mind, because I was so acutely conscious of the way in which black males have always been seen as more body than mind. (1995a, 205)

It is recognized, however, that most masculinities are complicit in patriarchy or tied together through the oppression of women, and that the marginalization of subordinate masculinities is an essential component in the reproduction of the myth of male power (Kimmel and Messner 1995). "Left" politics, for example, is replete with male imagery: the clenched fist, the haranguing oration, the rhetoric of fighting and struggling (Rutherford 1988, 42). Similarly, in commenting on the black antiracist, nationalist discourse, bell hooks argues that

> the discourse of black resistance has almost always equated freedom with manhood, the economic and material domination of black men with castration, emasculation. Accepting these sexual metaphors forged a bond between oppressed black men and their white male oppressors. They share the patriarchal belief that revolutionary struggle was really about the erect phallus. (quoted in ICA 1995, 38)

Phallocentrism (the power associated with the erect penis) can therefore be viewed as a defensive mechanism for men of all stripes. Most men are not as powerful as they are made out to be. The problem is that they are socialized to see male power and privilege as an entitlement, if not an endowment; this is the essential contradiction in the dominant construction of masculinity. Indeed, it suggests that men, especially those who experience their masculinity in contradictory terms, live in constant fear of being perceived as effeminate by other men and particularly by women. The fear of being unmasked may be viewed as the basis for homophobia, the backlash against feminism, male-on-male violence, and domestic violence against women.

The hegemonic white male ideal/myth serves a politico-cultural purpose. The white male is positioned at the apex of the pyramid of social hierarchy. All others are subordinate, including all women. Additionally, the white male experience is constructed as a universal one. The essence of this view is that the white male is conceptualized as the role model for all times, all places and all peoples. The white male is not just respected but revered and worshipped. For the subordinated "others", especially those who see themselves as inadequate, this ideal instils a desire to "catch up" or "follow the leader". Fear, guilt and the promise of pleasure combine together to act as the driving motors in sustaining and perpetuating the ideal, the hierarchy and the myth. In this way hegemonic masculinity, as an elevated and mythic cultural construct, operates like the "colonial desiring machine": a dialectic of attraction and repulsion where the subordinate "other" is always left wanting or unfulfilled (Young 1995, 175). In a similar vein, bell hooks argues that "patriarchy invites us all to learn how to 'do it for daddy,' and to find ultimate pleasure, satisfaction, and fulfilment in that act of performance and submission" (1995b, 98). Representations of hegemonic masculinity, subordinate masculinities and patriarchy work hand-in-hand to perpetuate the status quo. As hooks observes:

> Representations that socialise black males to see themselves as always lacking, as always subordinated to more powerful white males whose approval they need to survive, matter in white patriarchy. Since competition between males is sanctioned within male-dominated society, from the standpoint of white patriarchy, black masculinity must be kept "in check." Black males must be made subordinate in as many cultural arenas as possible. Representations that socialize black males to embrace subordination as "natural" tend to construct a world-view where white men are depicted as all powerful. To become powerful, then, to occupy that omnipotent location, black males (and white females) must spend their lives striving to emulate white men. This striving is the breeding ground among black males for a

politics of envy that reinforces the underlying sense that they lack worth unless they receive the affirmation of white males. (1995b, 99)

This analysis suggests that women's liberation from patriarchy is intimately intertwined with men's deconstruction and debunking of hegemonic notions of masculinity because "in white-supremacist capitalist patriarchy, black males and white females are uniquely positioned to compete with one another for the favours white 'daddies' in power can extend to them" (hooks 1995b, 99). It also suggests that an understanding of subordinate masculinities must begin with a critical examination of how institutionalized racism and sexism shape and constrain the possibilities, choices and personal lifestyles of men and women.

A case in point is the traditional male breadwinner role. In the feminist literature it is seen as the main source for patriarchy in the household and by extension the workplace and state policy. An alternative view would be to see the breadwinner role as a mechanism of patriarchal oppression of men which is then directed at women. Men's masculinity and perception of self-worth is most often defined in terms of their work and their ability to be providers for their family. Male breadwinners are portrayed as *real men*. Patriarchy encourages men to pride themselves on the "hard work and personal sacrifice they are making to be breadwinners for their families" (Pleck 1995, 11). It also trains men "to accept payment for work in feelings of masculinity rather than in feelings of satisfaction", consequently "men accept unemployment as their personal failing as males". The social construction of the male breadwinner role is therefore an important mechanism by which men are ensnared into their own oppression. And because it is mythologized – taken out of historical context and made natural and eternal – it becomes an invisible force, especially to men. This leads Pleck to the conclusion that the "false consciousness of privilege men get from sexism plays a critical role in reconciling men to their subordination in the larger political economy" (p. 12).

The collusion between patriarchy and masculinity operates in global politics as well. For example, hegemonic masculinity has been organized around perceptions of reason, rationality, self-control and the mastery

over others. In this regard, it is argued that "European/American masculinities were deeply implicated in the worldwide violence through
which European/American culture became dominant" (Connell 1995,
186). The masculinity problematique is implicated in the Western impe-
rialist project. In the history of European expansion, non-Western societies have been constructed and represented as either feminine or
child-like and therefore as having unmasculine traits. For example, during slavery in Trinidad the white men from the French planter class, in
celebrating Carnival – thereby playing out their fears and fantasies –
would pretend to be *negre jardin* (garden niggers or field slaves) based
on the "beliefs that the slaves were childish, sensuous, hedonistic, and
the planters were responsible, serious and civilised" (Johnson 1988, xiii).
"Colonised people are projected as body rather than mind, much as the
colonised world was seen as a raw material rather than as mental activity and manufacture" (Shohat and Stam 1994, 138). These observations
coincide with Connell's argument that "with masculinity defined as a
character structure marked by rationality, and Western civilisation
defined as the bearer of reason to a benighted world, a cultural link
between the legitimisation of patriarchy and the legitimisation of empire
was forged" (1995, 187).

It is also suggested that there is a link between masculinism and
nationalism (Bhabha 1995). The "nation" is often portrayed as the patriarchal father figure. Serving the nation is thus equivalent to serving the
hegemonic masculine. Nation building is about phallic identification and
thus naturalism. The "other", the foreigner, is feminized. Bhabha argues
that "this gendering of the nation's familial, domestic metaphor makes
its masculinism and its naturalism neurotic" (p. 60). In many respects
it is this sense of insecurity which makes the dividing line between nationalism and fascism so tenuous. Fascism is noted to be one of the responses to crisis tendencies in hegemonic masculinity. Fascism has acted as
a means to reassert or restore a dominant masculinity. For example, in
Germany at the turn of the twentieth century, fascist sexual politics
emerged "in the aftermath of the suffrage movement and German defeat
in the Great War" (Connell 1995, 84). In the United States it was
observed that the rise of the women's liberation movement in the 1960s

and the defeat in the Vietnam War stirred up "new cults of true masculinity which are informed by violent 'adventure' movies (e.g. the *Rambo* series), the expansion of the gun cult (e.g. the gun lobby of the National Rifle Association) and the rise of a paramilitary culture (e.g. right wing militia groups)" (Connell 1995, 84). The emergence of neofascism, in tandem with a resurgent sexism and racism throughout the West, is indicative of a violent reassertion of white male supremacy in societies that have been moving towards equality for women and subordinated groups.

The above analysis illustrates how far and deep the masculinist ideational construct runs. It shows that the legacy of masculinism is multidimensional and pervasive. It also illustrates that there are ebbs and flows, periods when there are crisis tendencies as opposed to times of relaxation. It appears that we are at such a historical conjuncture. This cyclical pattern is explained as part of the ideological tensions of historical capitalism. Wallerstein (1991) argues that there is a dynamic tension between the doctrine of "universalism", which promotes equality and democracy, and those of "racism" and "sexism", which fuel ethnicization, patriarchy and other anti-universalist principles. He argues that the latter doctrines operate as a "non-meritocratic basis to justify inequality", thereby fuelling capitalism's expansion as a system (p. 34). Masculinism is implicated in the racism-sexism doctrine because of its anti-universalistic value system. Based on the foregoing discussion, it appears that we are currently embroiled in that dynamic ideological tension, as women and subordinate men surge forward (under universalist doctrines) and confront the challenges of fundamentalist masculinism grounded in the doctrines of racism and sexism.

Transitions in Masculinities

The signs of a shift or transition in the gender order are everywhere it seems, especially in the West. The main observation is that men's traditional roles have been eroding and that women have begun to inhabit parts of the historic male domain. Safa (1995), for example, juxtaposes the "myth of the male breadwinner" with the rise in the partici-

pation of women in industrialization in the Caribbean. The conclusion
being touted by some analysts is that "men are at risk", to borrow
from the controversial title of Errol Miller's book (1991). The shift
appears to be most pronounced and most pervasive in the field of education. For example, in the United States educational statistics show that

> girls take more academic courses than boys; are more likely to finish high
> school than boys; and are more likely to go to college than their male class-
> mates. For 15 years, more women than men have been enrolling in college.
> Women are now a majority of all college students. Women receive a major-
> ity of undergraduate degrees and a majority of master's degrees. (Ravitch
> 1996, 168)

The situation described here is not just restricted to industrialized societies. In the case of the Caribbean this process is also very advanced. For
example, in Barbados, one of the territories with the highest levels of
educational achievement, girls have been outstripping boys at the secondary level for decades (*Trinidad Guardian* 1997). Tertiary education
has also begun to exhibit similar trends. This trend is often referred to
when the "male marginalization" thesis is being articulated. The problem with these arguments is that they tend either to construct men as
victims of the women's movement or to pathologize them as under-
achievers and deviants. This approach to dealing with the transitions in
masculinities is fraught with serious implications for gender relations,
as the following discussion illustrates.

An article in the *Economist*, entitled "Men: Tomorrow's Second Sex",
argues that men pose a growing social problem in the West because an
increasing number of them are uneducated, unemployed and unmarried.
The article goes on to say that

> they are failing at school, at work and in families. Their failure shows up in
> crime and unemployment figures. The problem seems to be related in some
> way to male behaviour and instincts. It is more than merely a matter of eco-
> nomic adjustment. And (considering the growth in "knowledge-based"
> employment) it is likely to get worse. (1996, 23)

In summary, the article highlights the following: boys are doing worse
than girls at every age in school, except university where girls are nar-

rowing the gap; women dominate the jobs that are growing, while men (especially those with the least education) are trapped in jobs that are declining; for some reason, men are not even trying to do "women's work"; there is a loose connection between work and marriage: joblessness reduces the attractiveness of men as marriage partners; men do not necessarily adopt "social behaviour" (obeying the law, looking after women and children) if left to themselves; rather, they seem to learn it through some combination of work and marriage (p. 23).

In Britain a recent study of men and women in the under-thirty-five age group argues that the society is in the throes of a "genderquake", as power tilts towards women in this demographic group. The study points out that "women have won many of the new jobs created over the past two decades – earning more money, increasing their share of the household income and strengthening their hold on the professions." In a noteworthy moment, the study also says that "young women show the characteristics previously considered typically male, such as a willingness to take risks, a desire for adventure in sport, foreign travel and a much greater interest in sexuality." It concludes that "we are in the middle of an historic change in relations between men and women: a shift in power and values that is unravelling many of the assumptions not only of 200 years of industrial society, but also of millennia of traditions and beliefs" (Bunting 1994).

These trends are considered problematic because school, work and family are perceived to be the three key socializing institutions without which men become *uncontrollable*. This conclusion is based on the age-old and unquestioned conception of the role of the male "breadwinner" as being essential to the full realization of male identity. It is also based on the assumption that male violence is endemic or part of some "state of nature".

> When men find it impossible to provide, they also seem to find it difficult to learn the nurturing bits. They may retreat into fundamentalist masculinity – the world of gangs which provide for their members a kind of rule-based behaviour that boys do not get elsewhere. For everyone else (and, in the long run, for boys too), the effects of failing to learn nurturing are universally bad. (*Economist* 1996, 26)

The problematique is not just gendered; it appears to be racialized as well. White male fear is now recognized as a phenomenon. A *Business Week* cover story reported that "white men are frustrated, resentful and, most of all afraid", as traditional economic sectors disappear and companies downsize and adopt diversity policies that white men feel discriminate against them in favour of women, blacks, Hispanics and Asians. One of the indicators for this, *Business Week* claims, is that white men are becoming a minority in the workforce: in the last decade the white male share of all professional and managerial positions in the United States dropped from 55 per cent to 47 per cent (Gates 1993). What is interesting about the *Business Week* story is that white male fear is coming just at the time when middle-class women and minority groups have made some economic advancement. Such white male fear is exhibited in the barrage of movies that depict women as sexual savages and "hot pussies" preying on unsuspecting men. Movies like *Disclosure, Fatal Attraction* and *Basic Instinct* are examples of what can be considered a reactionary backlash from Hollywood. This response belies the fact, however, that most women and minority men are still subordinate to most white men. In fact, one can argue that their situation is deteriorating. For women, the phenomenon referred to as the *feminization of poverty* is alive and well.

For minority men or subordinated masculinities the problem looms even larger in the changing world order. In the United States, for instance, studies on the impact of de-industrialization and economic restructuring show that employment opportunities for Afro-Americans, especially men, have declined significantly. Afro-American male joblessness is estimated to be two to three times higher than that for white men. The mismatch between the location of Afro-Americans (disproportionately concentrated in metropolitan areas) and the location of jobs is generally posited as one of the possible explanations. However, when this is taken into account it has been found that "the jobless rates for Black males in the *economically prosperous* metropolitan areas are nearly double the rates for their white counterparts in the *economically declining* metropolitan areas" (Johnson and Oliver 1992, 16).

In Britain, "Afro-Caribbean boys are three times as likely to be excluded from school as whites; they are also twice as likely as other boys to leave school unemployed, leaving about half of all Afro-Caribbean men under the age of 25 on the dole." Afro-Caribbean girls, on the other hand, "perform as well as white girls and better than white boys" (Younge 1996, 13). One can conclude, therefore, that male minority groups in the West appear to be at greater risk in the evolving gender order than their white counterparts. This should not be a surprising conclusion, given the historical experience of colonialism and white-male supremacy. What is critical to note, though, is that white men, particularly working-class men, are beginning to experience many of the same problems that others have lived with for centuries.

Nonetheless, the above discussion illustrates that there is a certain kind of unease that has emerged within hegemonic masculinity. An article in the *Economist* suggests that "what is really happening is merely a mutation in the Darwinian struggle for the survival of white-male supremacy. Threatened on the fringes of their power, white men are finding new ways to protect their interests – counter-attacking, counter-complaining, adopting the language and tactics used by minorities" (1994, 56).

Similar sentiments are expressed in the following quote from an article that comments on the implications of educational underachievement among white working-class boys in England:

> We have every reason to be extremely worried about failing boys. A generation of unemployable white men, seeing the jobs they thought were theirs being taken by women and the children of immigrants, are recruiting potential for white supremacists and neofascists. It was all well when you could point out to the public bore, ranting on about the foreigners taking our jobs, that those posts in the hospitals and on the buses were the low paid kind that he would not dream of applying for himself . . . . But when women and ethnic minorities are becoming the new technological proletariat in a computer-based economy, the wasted white youth of Britain is really going to imagine it has a beef. (Grant 1996, 19)

The phenomenon of white male fear appears to be at the base of white male supremacy as exemplified in the rise of neofascist and militia groups in the West. The New Right and anti–political correctness movements also seem to share some of the above-mentioned fears about the displacement of hegemonic masculinity. The main targets for these groups and movements have been black men, Jewish men, Asian men, gay men and feminists. The contest over hegemonic masculinity has been played out in the debates over issues like AIDS, affirmative action, abortion and family values. The main impetus in these debates, one can argue, is the resurgence of hegemonic masculinity through the control of the bodies of women and subordinate men. Recent scholarship suggests that the body and sexuality are central to white supremacist discourse (Harper 1994, 1). Other analysts assert that "race and gender oppression may both revolve around the same axis of disdain for the body; both portray the sexuality of subordinate groups as animalistic and therefore deviant" (Collins 1990, 171).

One of the interesting responses to the perceived threat to hegemonic male privilege and identity has been the resurgence of male bodybuilding. It has been observed in recent years that the visual media and consumer culture have been idealizing the hypermasculine body. This is viewed as problematic because "the male body as the embodiment of physical power has symbolic significance for the reproduction of the gender order" through the reassertion and reproduction of male privilege (Gillett and White 1992, 358). The argument is premised on the notion that there is some "affinity between psychocultural anxieties typically expressed by bodybuilders and their quest to reassert positive feelings of self through disciplining and sculpting hypermasculine bodies" (p. 359). This strategy for resurgent masculinity is seen as being contradictory, in that while it produces "physical capital which can then be converted into other forms of cultural and social capital", the tendency is for "the bodybuilder to be subordinated to and controlled by his objectified, sculpted body" (p. 359).

The objectification of men's bodies and the emergence of a new consumer ethic that incorporates men are relatively new phenomena. Men have long held the power of "the gaze" over women's bodies. Now, with the growth of men's style magazines and male modelling, men are being subjected to "the look" of both women and men. Their filmic and media images are increasingly being sexualized, eroticized and so feminized. It is also observed that masculinity has become a marketing tool with the growing commodification and aestheticism of consumer society (Edwards 1997). For example, the sale of male toiletries has been increasing in recent years. In addition, it is men who are doing the bulk of the purchasing, as opposed to ten years ago when women were the main purchasers of men's cosmetics. Men are also proving to be just as susceptible to "a loss of self esteem and dissatisfaction with their body image as women" when called upon to evaluate male attractiveness (Lury 1996, 150).

These transitions in masculinities are viewed as indicative of the decline of patriarchy. Barbara Ehrenreich (1995) argues that the traditional meaning of patriarchy (the rule of the father, including the rule of older men over younger men and of fathers over daughters, as well as husbands over wives) is being eroded by fundamental shifts in the sexual division of labour and gender ideology. For instance, she points out that in the West:

- men no longer depend on women for physical survival;
- masculinity, like femininity, is now being exploited by American consumer culture;
- men no longer need women to express their status;
- male wages have declined and so has the breadwinning role;
- young white males' wages and job opportunities have declined;
- women's gender identity is becoming masculinized.

Ehrenreich, however, cautions that "the end of patriarchy is not the same as women's liberation" (1995, 288). For her, patriarchy involves a process of mutual obligation which means protectiveness on the part of men, in terms of either comforting or infantilizing women (p. 288). She argues that those days are over. She identifies two parallel trends: male flight from female companionship and the masculinization of women. She forecasts an increase in male violence, especially that against women, and suggests that "'the battle of the sexes' may stop being a metaphor and become an armed struggle" (p. 290).

Other analysts have made the same conclusions but from slightly different angles. For example, Pleck makes the point that in contemporary times men have become more dependent upon women for emotional and sex-role validation because male-male friendships have been declining, while male-female relations have expanded with dating and marriage occurring more universally (1995, 7). As a result women have gained more expressive power and more masculinity-validating power over men. In this framework a woman's role is essentially that of the *masculinity-validating script*. This script is played out in the four following scenarios:

- women are used as *symbols of success* in men's competition with each other;
- women play a *mediating* role by smoothing over men's inability to relate to each other non-competitively;
- relationships with women provide men a *refuge* from the dangers and stresses of relating to other males;
- women reduce the stress of competition by serving as an *underclass*.

These scripts not only define what "true masculinity" is, or is not, they also inform what femininity is all about as well. Deviation from these roles is seen as a threat to the natural order of patriarchy. Consequently, the challenges that have arisen through "women's liberation [mean] that the stakes of patriarchal failure for men are higher than they have been before, and that it is even more important for men not to lose" (Pleck 1995, 10).

Seeking Explanations

How do we explain the current shifts or transitions in the gender order? A reading of the literature suggests that the answer is complex and multifaceted. However, there appear to be four critical areas: transformations in the capitalist mode of production and consumption; the rise of feminism; the gay rights movement; and resistance to racialized masculinities.

Masculine identity is very bound up with work. The concept of the male breadwinner seems to be one of those values that have become universal. Having a job and earning a good income are essential mechanisms for men to gain power and prestige as well as attract women. The role of the breadwinner is an important source of authority for men within the context of patriarchy. A decline in this role, for example through unemployment, has been manifested to result in the loss of self-esteem and problems like domestic violence and reduced sexual potency (Miles 1992, 98). Kimmel (1996) makes the point that male access to women is determined and measured by the length of a man's "CV" rather than the length of his penis. Sampath argues similarly that "just as women are socially valued as 'sex objects', so men are valued as 'success objects' in a context of *reputation*" (1997, 51). Sampath also suggests that these two values complement each other and therefore lead to the reproduction and perpetuation of patriarchy. This perspective is validated, in part, by a recent survey in the United States which identifies that "for women, cash flow out-ranks a man's physical attractions, education or occupation, while men place only physical beauty above a woman's bank statement" (Rhodes 1997). The survey also points to a new development: the value that men now place on a woman's economic status. This trend suggests that relationships and sexuality are being impacted by transformations in the economic sphere, such as the emergence of the two-income family and the decline of male wages.

Recent transformations in the world of work and the global capitalist accumulation process have exacted a huge toll on traditional conceptions of masculinity. The microelectronics revolution has automated (through labour-saving technologies) several aspects of the work practice, such that there has been the de-skilling of working-class jobs, particularly in manufacturing. Along with the process of de-skilling, these jobs have been made flexible – responsive to the demands of the new technologies and shifts in the market place. Most of these new jobs have seen rapid growth in women's participation in occupations which were formerly dominated by men. Women predominate in these new low-wage, low-skill jobs (for example, in enterprise or export processing zones) because they are more likely to accept routinized and dead-end jobs. This has resulted in what is referred to as female-led industri-alization (Joekes 1982) and the "global feminization" of manufacturing (Standing 1989).

The dematerialization of production, with the introduction of syn-thetic products, has resulted in the recession of jobs in the resource-based industries where male brawn and affinity to outdoor and physically risky work were valued and rewarded. The rise of the service economy has also dealt a critical blow to male employment. Service jobs tend to reward so-called feminine traits such as empathy and cooperation. It is estimated in the United States, for instance, that the five fastest grow-ing sectors (residential care, computer and data processing, health serv-ices, child care, and business services) are dominated by women. In contrast, men dominate in the five fastest declining sectors (footwear, ammunition making, shipbuilding, leather working and photographic supplies) (*Economist* 1996, 24). In addition, many of the new service jobs that have been created in the last two decades are low paying as well as part time. High-paying jobs are very knowledge intensive and require at least a university degree, an area where men seem to be under-achieving.

These shifts in global production structures have had a dramatic impact on the economic situation in the Caribbean region. There have been increasing levels of structural and technological unemployment in male-oriented jobs. This has occurred in a context of export marginal-ization in traditional sectors and massive reductions in public-sector employment under the banner of structural adjustment programmes. Economic panaceas like export-oriented industrialization have exacer-bated the tendencies inherent in these externally propelled economies, rather than expanding or deepening the industrial and export base (Nurse 1995). This suggests that the prospects for new and expanding job opportunities for working-class men in developing areas like the Caribbean are limited at best.

What appears to be emerging is a three-tiered society/economy with an entrepreneurial and technological elite at the top; in the middle stra-tum, a reserve army of service and industrial workers, some of whose incomes place them among the working poor; and a mass of underemployed, unemployed (and in many cases unemployable) people who are defined as the permanent underclass. Men have traditionally dominated in the top category, and all indicators suggest that they will continue to do so for some time. The real problem for men is in the middle and lower strata. Many are slipping out of the middle stratum to join the lower ranks. In this sense one can argue that what we are seeing is the *masculinization of poverty*. Unlike the equivalent phenomenon among women, which is much larger in scope, it is evident that men will resort to more antisocial behaviour. This makes their poverty a great threat to society.

Masculine identity is also being reconfigured from another direction within the capitalist accumulation process. Men's image has become objectified in the consumer market, very much like its female counterpart (Edwards 1997). Rutherford argues that "the marketplace has produced a plurality of masculine identities; different models of fatherhood, sexualised images of men and new sensibilities" (1988, 36). The *New Man* is portrayed as being more fashion conscious, and so his consumption style has emerged as an important signifier of his status in replacement of, or alongside, his job in a post-Fordist context. It is "a masculinity that has partly detached itself from its formative links to traditional class identities" (Rutherford 1988, 39). Nixon argues that "the formation of a new subject-position for men in relation to the practices of fashion, style and individual consumption" has disrupted traditional male sexual identity because male models tend to be feminized – to be the object of another man's gaze (1997, 315). He suggests that these "images draw on forms of looking which were historically the prerogative of gay men – without pathologising that look" (p. 314).

A parallel, yet seemingly contradictory, phenomenon is the hardening of men's bodies. The image of the successful man today is one who has a hard, lean body. An overweight body is seen as a sign of failure. This is exemplified by the range of new body-sculpting magazines and exercise machines that are being promoted. Men are being encouraged to have "rock hard abs" and a totally toned physique (a hard body). This social trend mirrors the experience of women, who have been subject to the critical gaze of the media and have long been judging their self-worth in terms of their appearance. Eating disorders like anorexia and bulimia, which emerged as problematic for young women, appear to be rising markedly for young men as well, as illustrated by the case of Argentina (Faiola 1997).

The marketing of masculinity is explained as an aesthetic innovation in response to the recession in the West since the late 1960s. Haug (1986) explains that the clothing industry had gone through a downturn and had decided to target the male population for market expansion. The clothing industry, however, was faced with the challenge of changing Western men's austere dress paradigm to one that was a bit more adventurous. The aim was the "outdating of what existed, its denunciation, devaluation, and replacement". The strategy employed was based on using slogans to "mobilize the *anxiety* potential and so undermine the then current standards of appearance of the sober, orderly and well-groomed bourgeois" (Haug 1986, 43). The aesthetic innovations were likened to youthfulness, in comparison to the standard grey outfit which was equated with cowardice, obesity, tiredness and boredom.

The third critical area in the transition of masculinities is the impact of the feminist or women's movement. Arising from the feminist movement has been a reordering of the global gender framework. Virtually no corner of the globe has been untouched by the movement. The universal rights of women do not go unquestioned anymore. From the struggles for universal suffrage to the current battles over sexual harassment, the gender context has been impacted. It is this movement that put gender relations on the academic and public agenda. The feminist movement emerged from the watershed period of the late 1960s with a revolutionary zeal. Since then the more radical movement has been involved in the "unthinking" and deconstruction of gender oppression. Patriarchy has been the main target; it is seen as the primary source for all the asymmetrical relations between men and women (Walby 1990). Equal access to education, equal pay for equal work, women's control of their reproductive rights and ending violence against women have been at the top of the agenda. All of these challenge traditional male power and privilege. The discourse has moved from just a focus on direct violence (for example, rape and domestic violence) to an examination of the sources of structural violence (for example, legal codes and discrimination in the workplace) and cultural violence (epistemologies of patriarchy and masculinism) that perpetuate female subordination (True 1996). In essence, the feminist movement contends that "women and the feminine constitute historically underprivileged, under-represented, and under-recognized social groups and 'standpoints'; and this should change in the direction of greater equality" (Jones 1996, 406).

The pursuit of equality between the sexes has not been unproblematic. The feminist or women's movement has been subjected to a conservative backlash from hegemonic masculinity. Most of the debate about issues like family values, male marginalization, single-headed households, the rate of divorce, and female sexual assertiveness are essentially aimed at disciplining women into their traditional roles. In tandem with these debates has been a masculinization of femininity in the media. Women are now free to be as violent, aggressive and exploitative as men. No longer are they portrayed as helpless damsels in distress; increasingly, they are constructed as "tough women, killer women, bitchy women" (Ehrenreich 1995, 290). Recent movies and television programmes like *Thelma and Louise, Serial Mom, Bad Girls, Alien, La Femme Nikita* and *Xena: Warrior Princess* position white women as violent and almost as dangerous as their male counterparts. Interestingly, black women had an earlier stint in these roles. The "blaxploitation" movies of the mid-1970s had actresses like Pam Grier and Tamara Dobson "kicking butt" in movies like *Cleopatra Jones, Cuffy, Foxy Brown* and *Friday Foster.* One analyst makes the point, however, that these female action heroes pleased rather than threatened men because of their sexy imagery (Bogle 1989). A similar conclusion could be drawn about the new genre of female action movies.

The gay rights movement has also had an important impact on the way we see masculinities. As discussed, homophobia is one of the principal ways in which hegemonic masculinity is defined. The gay man is constructed as the "other". The prominence that gay issues have gained in recent years indicates that some fundamental changes have taken place. Debates over gays in the military in the United States, gay marriages and gay people in the priesthood have challenged some of the main institutions of masculinism. Hegemonic heterosexuality has also come up for scrutiny; as a result it can no longer monopolize the sexual terrain (Connell 1995, 202). Homosexuality has emerged to be a valid alternative for many. The victimization of homosexuals has been rendered problematic from a political standpoint, even though there are still many instances where it is used to gain political mileage. Nonetheless, what this signals is that the binarisms of the hegemonic gender order are being fragmented.

One of the main sources for hegemonic masculinity has been the construction of "otherness". Racialized masculinities inhabit this domain. The anticolonial and anti-imperialist movements were confronted with the self-suppressive and limiting stereotypes and stigmas of otherness. The struggle has been long and hard with some successes along the way, for example, the civil rights movement and Third World nationalism. Feminist critics have noted, however, that the modes of resistance to imperial subjectification and governance have been accompanied by a *"machismo"* that facilitated the subordination of women. It has also been argued that the form of nationalism and development policy that emerged was largely imitative and therefore integrated with the dominant masculinist paradigm. The result has been a scenario where the social context has become more culturally pluralist without the core values of masculinism being undermined.

The relative decline of the West and the rise of the Pacific Rim countries is one example of how the relationship between hegemonic masculinity and a racialized masculinity has been reconfigured. In many respects Asian masculinities have been co-opted and made "honorary Whites", a term used by the apartheid South African government to facilitate Japanese investors. Asians have been elevated in this scheme, as exemplified by the recent publication of the "bell curve" which positions Asians above whites in terms of "IQ". Blacks still pull up the rear.

Subordinate masculinities are still faced with an uphill battle, in spite of the fact that hegemonic masculinity has been challenged in so many quarters. For example, black masculinity has impacted on hegemonic masculinity, particularly in the fields of sport and entertainment. The quintessential example is that of Michael Jordan, who is one of the most identifiable people on the planet. His advertising appeal has been virtually unparalleled: "Jordan eats Wheaties, drives Chevrolets, wears Hanes, drinks Coca Cola, consumes McDonalds's, guzzles Gatorade, and, of course, wears Nikes" (Dyson 1994, 123). For Dyson, although Jordan operates within a depoliticized cultural context, his achievements are remarkable for a "six-foot-six man of obvious African descent" in contemporary American culture (p. 126). However, what remains problematic is that the fields of sport and entertainment are considered to emphasize body more than mind, and therefore recast black masculinity within the traditional racialized, sexualized, infantilized and feminized framework. In the new context the hypermasculine black male body is increasingly commodified and fetishized (Wallace 1995). It is also the case that the US popular culture and media have constructed two stereotypes of black men: "the successful ones who do nothing but promote themselves, and the underclass ones who spend all their time robbing, stealing, doing drugs, and killing" (Wallace 1995, 302). The heavily publicized cases of O.J. Simpson, Clarence Thomas and Mike Tyson are examples where the "double image" of black masculinities is unified and used to maximum political advantage to reinforce old stereotypes and update established modes of political governance.

Conclusion

The question that emerges from the foregoing discussion is: To what extent are the transitions in masculinities transformational in terms of redressing the global problematique? It is very much in vogue these days to argue that everything has changed, hence the popularity of the prefix "post", which is now attached to almost anything. The "mythology of change", as Addo calls it (1986), has much currency in the academy as well as the popular media, but it lacks a critical appreciation of the ways in which capitalism has been able to adapt to, if not co-opt, various modes of resistance.

This chapter has approached the issue of *transitions in masculinities* with a more discerning eye. It has examined the discontinuities as well as the continuities in the construction of the various masculinities at the world level, the changing forms and the enduring tensions implicit in patriarchy, and the relationship between the two and the reproduction of capitalist development on a world scale. From this perspective, this chapter fully endorses Andrew Ross's position on the "changingness" in patriarchy and masculinity. He argues:

> Patriarchy is constantly reforming masculinity, minute by minute, day by day. Indeed, the reason why patriarchy remains so powerful is due less to its entrenched traditions than to its versatile capacity to shape-change and morph the contours of masculinity to fit with shifts in the social climate; in this it shares with capitalism a modernising hunger to seize the present and dictate the future. (1995, 172)

This chapter employed a method of gender analysis that was fully conscious of the ways in which power flows through a network of disciplinary codes (for example, white supremacy, racial stereotyping, homophobia) and governing institutions and how they ultimately determine social relations and create subject positions. As illustrated here, modern masculinism is cotemporal with global capitalism and operates as a mechanism to perpetuate epistemic violence through its articulation with sexism, racism, imperialism, Eurocentrism and even fascism. As such, it involved an analysis of how social formations (for example, the household, interest groups, the state) and identity constructions (gender, race, class, ethnicity and sexuality) interact in the practice of the multiple masculinities and femininities, locally and globally.

The crisis tendencies in masculinism share with other crises in the modern world-system (for example, environmentalism, racism, poverty, inequality and so forth) the problem of invisibility on the part of beneficiaries and aspirants. Consequently, the problems associated with masculinism remain largely invisible to men as a collective. As such it has generated very little internal debate. The critique and deconstruction of hegemonic masculinity has essentially come from gay men, working-class male popular culture, and women, and thus has been easy to sideline as peripheral. A backlash from elite men has emerged as a consequence.

The mainstream debate on the transitions in masculinities has come from elite men who have bemoaned the relative decline of male privilege and status. From this quarter the perspective has been informed either by a fear of feminism and the women's movement, or by a critique of subordinate masculinities, for example, by pathologizing male deviation from expected norms in education, sexuality and work. Efforts to reclaim hegemonic masculinity are exemplified in the current discourse about issues like male educational underachievement, family values, single-headed households and homosexuality. These are examples of how resurgent masculinity is reinscribing the strict codes of hegemonic masculinity.

The defensive posture of hegemonic masculinity is understandable because masculinism is one of the pillars upon which modern capitalism rests. The ideology of masculinism is able to exploit male insecurities and vulnerabilities about sexuality and work, for instance, to advance the interests of capitalist development. By the same token it is also used as a basis to perpetuate sexism and racism, thereby reinforcing traditional occupational and reward hierarchies. From a revolutionary standpoint, the traditional myth of male privilege, power and status blinds men to their own gender oppression, and therefore limits the possibilities for an emancipatory transition from within the boundaries of masculinism. This illustrates that the prospects for a preferred future in gender relations are dependent on the continued unmasking and deconstructing of the core components of hegemonic masculinism.

References

Addo, Herb. 1980. *Approaching the Peculiarity of the Caribbean Plight within the Paradox of the Representative State in the Contemporary World-System*. Tokyo: United Nations University.

———. 1986. *Imperialism: The Permanent Stage of Capitalism*. Tokyo: United Nations University.

Addo, Herb, et al. 1985. *Development as Social Transformation: Reflections on the Global Problematique*. London: Hodder and Stoughton.

Barthes, Roland. 1989. *Mythologies*. New York: Noonday Press.

Bhabha, Homi. 1994. *The Location of Culture*. London: Routledge.

———. 1995. "Are You a Man or a Mouse?" In *Constructing Masculinity*, edited by M. Berger, B. Wallis and S. Watson. New York: Routledge.

Bogle, Donald 1989. *Toms, Coons, Mulattoes, Mammies, and Bucks: An Inter-pretative History of Blacks in American Films*. New York: Viking Press.

Bunting, M. 1994. " 'Genderquake' Tilts Power Towards Women Under 35". *Guardian Weekly*, 9 October.

Collins, Patricia Hill. 1990. *Black Feminist Thought: Knowledge, Consciousness, and the Politics of Empowerment*. Boston: Unwin Hyman.

Connell, R.W. 1992. "A Very Straight Gay: Masculinity, Homosexual Experience and the Dynamics of Gender". *American Sociological Review* 57, no. 6.

———. 1995. *Masculinities*. Cambridge: Polity Press.

Cooper, Caroline. 1995. " 'Lyrical Gun': Metaphor and Role Play in Jamaican Dancehall Culture". *Massachusetts Review* 35, nos. 3 & 4.

Dyson, Michael. 1994. "Be Like Mike? Michael Jordan and the Pedagogy of Desire". In *Between Borders: Pedagogy and the Politics of Cultural Studies*, edited by H. Giroux and P. McLaren. New York: Routledge.

Economist. 1994. "White Male Fear", 29 January.

———. 1996. "Men: Tomorrow's Second Sex", 28 September.

Edwards, Tim. 1997. *Men in the Mirror: Men's Fashion, Masculinity and Consumer Society*. London: Cassell.

Ehrenreich, Barbara. 1995. "The Decline of Patriarchy". In *Constructing Masculinity*, edited by M. Berger, B. Wallis and S. Watson. New York: Routledge.

Faiola, A. 1997. "Argentine Teens Desperate to be Thin". *Guardian Weekly*, 20 July.

Fanon, Frantz. 1967. *Black Skin, White Masks.* New York: Grove Press.

Foucault, Michel. 1980. *History of Sexuality. Volume I: An Introduction.* New York: Vintage.

Fung, Richard. 1995. "Burdens of Representation, Burdens of Responsibility". In *Constructing Masculinity,* edited by M. Berger, B. Wallis and S. Watson. New York: Routledge.

Galtung, Johan. 1991. "The Emerging Conflict Formations". In *Restructuring for World Peace: On the Threshold of the Twenty-First Century,* edited by K. Tehranian and M. Tehranian. Cresskill, N.J.: Hampton Press.

Gates, D. 1993. "White Male Paranoia: Are They the Newest Victims or Just Bad Sports?" *Newsweek,* 29 March.

Gillett, James, and Philip White. 1992. "Male Bodybuilding and the Reassertion of Hegemonic Masculinity: A Critical Feminist Perspective". *Play and Culture 5.*

Gorman, C. 1992. "Sizing up the Sexes". *Time,* 20 January.

Grant, L. 1996. "Lessons to Be Learnt". *Guardian Weekly,* 24 March.

Hall, Stuart. 1997. "The Spectacle of the 'Other' ". In *Representation: Cultural Representations and Signifying Practices,* edited by S. Hall. London: Sage.

Harper, Suzanne. 1994. "Subordinating Masculinities/Racializing Masculinities: Writing White Supremacist Discourse on Men's Bodies". *Masculinities 2,* no. 4.

Haug, Wolfgang. 1986. *Critique of Commodity Aesthetics: Appearance, Sexuality and Advertising in Capitalist Society.* Minneapolis: University of Minnesota Press.

hooks, bell. 1995a. *Art on My Mind: Visual Politics.* New York: The New Press.

———. 1995b. "Doing It for Daddy". In *Constructing Masculinity,* edited by M. Berger, B. Wallis and S. Watson. New York: Routledge.

Institute of Contemporary Arts (ICA). 1995. *Mirage: Enigmas of Race, Difference and Desire.* London: Institute of Contemporary Arts.

James, C.L.R. 1980. *The Black Jacobins.* London: Allison and Busby.

Joekes, Susan 1982. *Female-Led Industrialisation: Women's Jobs in Third World Export Manufacturing: The Case of the Moroccan Clothing Industry.* Sussex: Institute of Development Studies.

Johnson, D. 1991. "Constructing the Periphery in Modern Global Politics". In *The New International Political Economy,* edited by C. Murphy and R. Tooze. Boulder: Lynne Rienner.

Johnson, J.H., and M. Oliver. 1992. "Economic Restructuring and the Socio-Economic Well-Being of African Americans". *UCLA CAAS Report* 14, nos. 1 and 2.

Johnson, K. 1988. Introduction to *Trinidad Carnival.* Port of Spain, Trinidad: Paria Publishing.

Jones, A. 1996. "Does Gender Make the World Go Round? Feminist Critiques of International Relations". *Review of International Studies* 22.

Kimmel, Michael. 1996. "Masculinity as Homophobia: Fear, Shame and Silence in the Construction of Gender Identity". Paper presented to the symposium The Construction of Caribbean Masculinity: Towards a Research Agenda, Centre for Gender and Development Studies, St Augustine, Trinidad.

Kimmel, Michael, and M. Messner. 1995. *Men's Lives.* New York: Allyn and Bacon.

Lury, Celia. 1996. *Consumer Culture.* New Brunswick, N.J.: Rutgers University Press.

Miles, I. 1992. "Consequences of the Changing Sexual Division of Labour". *ANNALS, AAPS,* no. 522.

Miller, Errol. 1991. *Men at Risk.* Kingston, Jamaica: Jamaica Publishing House.

Mintz, Sidney. 1993. *Goodbye Columbus: Second Thoughts on the Caribbean Region at Mid-Millennium.* Coventry: University of Warwick, Centre for Caribbean Studies.

Nixon, Sean. 1997. "Exhibiting Masculinity". In *Representation: Cultural Representations and Signifying Practices,* edited by S. Hall. London: Sage.

Nurse, Keith. 1995. "The Developmental Efficacy of the Export-Oriented Clothing Industry: The Case of Jamaica". *Social and Economic Studies* 44, nos. 2 & 3.

O'Hara, Maureen. 1995. "Constructing Emancipatory Realities". In *The Truth about the Truth: De-confusing and Re-constructing the Postmodern World,* edited by W.T. Anderson. New York: Putnam.

Persram, Nalini. 1994. "Politicizing the Feminine, Globalizing the Feminist". *Alternatives* 19.

Peterson, V. Spike. 1997. "Whose Crisis? Early and Post-Modern Masculinism". In *Innovation and Transformation in International Studies,* edited by S. Gill and J. Mittelman. Cambridge: Cambridge University Press.

Pleck, Joseph. 1995. "Men's Power with Women, Other Men, and Society: A Men's Movement Analysis". In *Men's Lives,* edited by M. Kimmel and M. Messner. New York: Allyn and Bacon.

Ravitch, Diane. 1996. "The Gender Bias Myth". *Forbes,* 20 May.

Rhodes, T. 1997. "Sure Way to the Heart Is through the Wallet". *The Times,* 20 August.

Ross, Andrew. 1995. "The Great White Dude". In *Constructing Masculinity,* edited by M. Berger, B. Wallis and S. Watson. New York: Routledge.

Rutherford, Jonathan. 1988. "Who's That Man?" In *Male Order: Unwrapping Masculinity,* edited by R. Chapman and J. Rutherford. London: Lawrence and Wishet.

Said, Edward. 1979. *Orientalism.* New York: Vintage.

Safa, Helen. 1995. *The Myth of the Male Breadwinner: Women and Industrialization in the Caribbean.* Boulder: Westview.

Sampath, Niels. 1997. "Crabs in a Bucket: Reforming Male Identities in Trinidad". In *Men and Masculinity,* edited by Caroline Sweetman. Oxford: Oxfam.

Shohat, Ella, and Robert Stam. 1994. *Unthinking Eurocentrism: Multiculturalism and the Media.* London: Routledge.

Standing, Guy. 1989. "Global Feminization through Flexible Labour". *World Development* 17, no. 7.

Trinidad Guardian. 1997. "Battle of the Sexes", 3 May.

True, Jacqui. 1996. "Feminism". In *Theories of International Relations,* edited by S. Burchill, et al. London: Macmillan.

Walby, Sylvia. 1990. *Theorizing Patriarchy.* London: Blackwell.

Wallace, Michele. 1995. "Masculinity in Black Popular Culture: Could It Be that Political Correctness Is the Problem?" In *Constructing Masculinity,* edited by M. Berger, B. Wallis and S. Watson. New York: Routledge.

Wallerstein, Immanuel. 1983. *Historical Capitalism.* London: Verso.

———. 1991. "The Ideological Tensions of Capitalism: Universalism versus Racism and Sexism". In *Race, Nation, Class: Ambiguous Identities,* edited by E. Balibar and I. Wallerstein. London: Verso.

West, Cornel. 1993. *Race Matters.* Boston: Beacon Press.

Yelvington, Kelvin. 1993. "Introduction: Trinidad Ethnicity". In *Trinidad Ethnicity,* edited by K. Yelvington. London: Macmillan.

Young, Robert J. 1995. *Colonial Desire: Hybridity in Theory, Culture and Race.* London: Routledge.

Younge, G. 1996. "School Ban on Blacks Caused Brixton Riot". *Guardian Weekly,* 23 June.

CHAPTER 2

Unmasking Masculinity and Deconstructing Patriarchy
Problems and Possibilities within Feminist Epistemology

PATRICIA MOHAMMED

The experience of being a man, of being Indian or African, of being Muslim or Anglican, of being a Trinidadian or a Jamaican, a priest or a fisherman, is never an isolated one. At each point the individual man is a product of a number of constructed identities. For instance, an Indian man attending a traditional Muslim wedding night in village Trinidad may find himself cut off from the women and interacting with a primarily male grouping. Here he is expected to behave like his male peers, share their jokes, be a man in a male culture. He may or may not be comfortable in this situation, and may change drastically when confronted with another situation, say a masquerade band in Trinidad Carnival in which mixing with the other sex is not only indiscriminate, but altogether desirable. Here both the multicultural setting and the flirtation with women bring out another aspect of his masculinity, one which may be quite different from his interaction with other men from his ethnic group and class. Identities are never constructed in isolation from our experiences, but our experiences are themselves mediated through the material body. A male Ghanaian colleague who shared student life with me in The Hague and came from a prestigious background in Ghana was appalled that when he entered a tram in Holland, invariably people would immediately clutch their bags and purses closer to them. Black women did not have the same experience. In sheltered cities of Europe, as a black male he immediately represented an ethnic group and a sex who are feared for this or that reason. Our material bodies – whether outwardly biologically male or female – our race or ethnic group, the colour of our skin and the class we typify within a particular culture constantly inform and mediate our social experiences and influence how we express our masculinity and femininity, as well as the expectations by others of our masculinity and femininity. The black working-class dancehall queen in downtown Kingston is not expected to exhibit the same "femininity" as the uptown "browning"[1] of St Andrew.

"The material world that surrounds us is one in which we use our living bodies to give substance to the social distinctions and differences which underpin social relations, symbolic systems, forms of labour and quotidian intimacies", writes Henrietta Moore (1994, 71). The manner in which we use and experience our bodies to interact with the social is, nonetheless, more similar than different for any grouping of individuals within a culture, and in some cases across cultures. One such grouping is gender identification. Gender identity is not a static achievement for each individual or group, in that age and experience themselves change us within our span of life, as does the way in which cultures collectively or individually shift symbolic interpretations or expectations of ethnic groups, sexes and even classes over time. Experience acts ontologically for all of us, but it does so consciously, through a technique of construction. Our identities, whether racial, ethnic, gender, class, national or political, are constantly undergoing construction. Wars or struggles for independence in a society; poverty caused by famines and drought; political rivalries between ethnic groups; nationalistic programmes aimed at building a state; consciousness-raising movements such as Black Power or the women's movement all influence the ongoing construction of the multiple parts which make up the identity of an individual. But the material base from which this construction takes place is our bodies. The body is both a repository of our conscious and unconscious and, simultaneously, the physical medium through which we experience the world and engage actively with it.

One of the major epistemological tasks in feminist scholarship is to reunite the individual experience of the body with the ongoing and continuous process of constructing identities. A preliminary way in which feminist epistemology has entered this discourse is to consider how the biological script of the male and female body gets inscribed with different messages from birth and therefore influences the way in which knowledge about life is constructed by each sex. Men and women experience their environment differently, and this experience itself provides the knowledge which they formulate about reality, about their life chances, about their sexuality, about themselves. This difference has not been fully incorporated into received knowledge thus far, and this has limited the extent to which feminist scholarship and gender theory have managed to influence other disciplines in the academy. An anecdote by leading feminist historian Joan Scott introduces one dimension of the issue. In the foreword to *Connecting Spheres,* edited by Marilyn Boxer and Jean Quaertert (1987), Scott writes:

> In the fall of 1984, I arrived in Paris on my way to a conference at UNESCO on the history of women. At the airport an officious customs officer asked the usual questions about the nature of my business in France, and then queried me on the topic of the conference I was attending. When I replied "the history of women", he responded mockingly, "Do women have a history, Professor? And what might it be?" I was taken aback not only by the hostility, but by the difficulty of answering such questions. Of course women had a history, but one so rich and unmined that no single phrase or storyline could capture it.

I have used this anecdote deliberately, as it echoes the experience of most who write and speak on feminism with commitment, whether in

Europe or in the Caribbean. Women's absence from historical writing, from the early development of Western philosophy, has not just created an omission of their group and sex, but limited their contribution to the ideas which have come to shape knowledge as we receive it on a daily basis. For example, we have the idea that women are "imperfect males", as Aristotle in early patriarchal conviction branded the female sex. Many of the ideas which have shaped femininity as emotional and irrational emerged primarily as a result of women's absence from the process of knowledge creation in the earlier centuries. There was also a marked lack of knowledge of the biology of women, and especially of the contribution that the female sex made to the biological reproduction of human society. Until the nineteenth century, theories of "embryology attributed to the father's seed the major contribution to the characteristics of the offspring" (Cline Horowitz 1987, 86). The discovery of the existence of the female ovum in 1827 then led to further scientific research on the contribution of the ovum to reproduction and thus the complementary rather than secondary role of the female in reproduction. In other words, women not only did not "make" history, they were also assigned a secondary role in the continuous recreation of society itself.

Feminist epistemology, or feminist theory of knowledge, engages directly in these debates about who determines what is truth and what is important, about who creates knowledge and for whom. It proposes that women's experience of life – largely relegated to the domestic sphere, in the care of children and the sick and elderly – produces new ideas about existence which add to the font of knowledge creation. At the same time it does not attempt to *replace* received knowledge by new knowledge gleaned from a feminist standpoint of experience. What it attempts to do is to *challenge* received knowledge and *amplify* it. The construction of knowledge in the Western world until the middle of the twentieth century was heavily androcentric and Eurocentric. Feminist epistemology has begun to establish new parameters of thought, to contest what is accepted and valued as admissible levels of knowledge, and to confront the gatekeepers and conveyors of knowledge. And it began by returning to the lived experience of women, by investigating the way in which the roles, sexual division of labour and expectations of women were shaped largely through their biology.

From the middle of the twentieth century onwards, feminism began a concerted and accelerated search for "femininity" in opposition to a received "masculinity". Man and manhood were taken as given, the known factor against which a femininity was inscribed as the second-ary term, the "Other", as coined by Simone de Beauvoir in *The Second Sex* (first published in 1949). The project of feminism in the twentieth century after women had won the right to vote and recognition of their civil rights, and had begun the movement for sexual liberation, was to discover the basis on which the subordination of one sex was justified, to understand the origins of patriarchal thought and the persistence of a male dominant ideology. Western philosophical thought had construc-ted masculinity and femininity as two oppositional sets of characteris-tics, simultaneously positioning masculinity and men as superior, and femininity and women as inferior. Interestingly, a similar opposition is also evident in Eastern philosophy, although this is couched in more mediated terms. For instance, women and men are viewed as comple-mentary beings in Hindu philosophy: women are the earth while men are the seed. In essence, the earth lies fallow and barren without the seed, and eventually it is the seed that is valued over the earth which gives it life. This schema of female-to-male in both Western and Eastern thought is embedded in language through dichotomies which symbolize man/woman as culture/nature, rational/emotional, assertive/passive, strong/weak, or public/private. These strategic oppositions continuou-sly privilege men in the superior position of the hierarchy and place women in the inferior position, as the second sex.

Dichotomous thinking remains useful for linguistic purposes and appears valid enough in terms of legitimizing human actions (as, for example, good and evil) or for purposes of description (as, for example, white and black) and, for that matter, was inherited from "scientific" discourses (action/reaction). It has also been used for other, unsavoury purposes. The first term generally takes its place in the hierarchy over the position of the second, such that good is better than evil and white is superior to black. Dichotomous thought therefore entrenches the superiority of the former term over the latter; for example, racially, white-ness was deemed superior to blackness. The hegemony of these ideolog-ical discourses can be traced as far back as the ideas of Plato and Aristotle who, formulating reason over emotion, and culture over nature, justified the domination of women by men, enslaving women in domes-tic activities and excluding them from public life in the name of reason and objectivity.

The problem with this dichotomy when it is related to human expe-rience is that it misrepresents the relationship between mind and body, between reason and emotion, and between culture and nature. It sit-uates human nature as itself dichotomous. If mind, reason and cul-ture are deemed superior, then logically the survival of human civilizations could be traced back to a superior male – the hunter, who conquered nature by producing tools and weaponry and began to control not only women's reproductive labour but also the labour and resources of other tribes to ensure the survival of the fittest. The role of woman therefore becomes non-essential in the progression of human life on earth. Biological reproduction of the species is deemed a secondary activity, domestication of animals and grain cultivation and gathering, developed by women to provide the staple for the tribe, are perceived as inferior contributions compared to the protein sup-plied largely by the men from the hunt and chase. The latter activity was viewed as requiring superior skills of coordination and social coop-eration, thus enhancing brain capacity of the species (Slocum 1995; Fagan 2002). A contemporary analogy which comes to mind is the value attached to housework as compared to that attached labour which is considered skilled – for instance, driving a truck. Housework and childcare are not only considered non-work, but non-productive work, demanding little skill and no training, and somehow natural to women's lesser capabilities. They are in most societies allocated the lowest wages.

Feminist epistemology has attempted to challenge this dominant clas-sificatory scheme and in doing so has lent support to the contestation of other dichotomies which have affected the development of society – dichotomies which have led to racial stereotyping based on colour and ethnicity, dichotomies which have produced disadvantaged castes and classes. In this sense, feminist epistemology intersects with postmodernism. Postmodernism calls for a commitment to the deconstruction of universalities and stereotypes. Postmodern thought is rejected by many because of its apparent self-serving nature, its preoccupation with literature, linguistics, psychoanalysis and philosophy. It has become rather fashionable to reject postmodernism as a new fad produced by armchair intellectuals of more "developed" societies who have no relationship to the real world. Clearly we need to be selective about new paradigms of thought, especially when their explanatory powers are obfuscated through language itself. Nonetheless, it seems to me that the methodology of deconstruction and narrative creation which postmodernism proposes, as well as the thought regarding the processes of identity creation – political, national and racial or ethnic, and gender-based – speak directly to the Caribbean social experience, a precocious experiment in the settling of different groups of migrant people.

Why is postmodern feminist epistemology useful for understanding Caribbean masculinity and femininity? For many reasons, but two are contained in the ideas thus far expressed. First, what is taken for granted as natural – as for instance a natural sexual division of labour and natural sexual differences between men and women – can be seen as constructed over time and thus can be deconstructed. We therefore need to re-examine in our histories and in our ongoing experience how the natural is persistently being transformed, or can have different meanings simultaneously in a particular culture. For instance, *Lady Nugent's Journal of Her Residence in Jamaica from 1801 to 1805* ([1966] 2002) depicts a clear distinction between the femininity of the white woman and the "unfeminine" physical strength of the black woman. Childbearing was somehow more "natural and easy" for the black woman, who also had a strenuous workload in the fields. It was expected that the white women would be frail, while the opposite was simultaneously being proposed for black women. Parallel if not similar readings of masculinity are also evident in Thistlewood's diary (Hall 1999), where black masculinity is constantly being denigrated in favour of white masculinity.

Second, postmodern thought allows the researcher to employ the method of deconstruction, which strives not to replace one stereotype by another nor to redefine other universalistic paradigms (as for instance the archetypal Caribbean man, or the Caribbean woman, undifferentiated by class or ethnic group). It allows diversity to explain different historical and social experiences. Thus, for example, it allows for differentiation by country and ethnic grouping of the African peoples themselves who comprise the Caribbean. Postmodernism also presents another dilemma: How do we translate so many diversities into notions of universality such that differences do not become reified and fetishized, "producing barriers between individuals and groups, leading to a replication of special interest group politics" (Best and Kellner 1991, 205)?

The question which this chapter sets out to answer is how do we continue to investigate masculinity and femininity in general, provided as we are with a new set of gendered lenses? Having established the study of femininity as the paradigm for feminism, how and where do we fit the study of masculinity without falling into the trap of dichotomous and oppositional thinking? How do we begin to study masculinity not in isolation from femininity but as its counterpart, closely interconnected with and reciprocally shaped by femininity? More precisely, how do we examine Caribbean masculinity in relation to Caribbean femininity, in particular so that we do not persistently replicate the stereotyped notions we have inherited from our predecessors who wrote the anthropological script of the region as follows: the white male as powerful and dominant; the black male as promiscuous and irresponsible; the Indian male as violent and quick tempered and excessively patriarchal in his relations with his household; the white woman as frail, weak, either rich or the object of class ridicule; the coloured woman as sexual object; the black woman as strong and independent, running a matrifocal household and distrustful of men; the Indian woman as a passive and subservient creature, and so on?

Gendered lenses provide us with a set of ideas and tools which allow investigation from many angles. The burgeoning interest in masculinity is not coincidental; for many men it is a reaction to feminism. This is a natural and expected outcome. The relationship between the sexes is a constantly negotiated one, whether this negotiation takes place through the lyrics of popular culture (as for instance in dancehall or calypso), in individual households, in state institutions or in the academy. At this historical moment the negotiations are more consciously motivated than, say, two decades ago. Teresa de Lauretis (1987) observed that the construction of gender identities (and the same can be said for the construction of other political identities) at this point in world history has become a self-conscious one. We are far more aware of ourselves, our ethnic identities, our political power in the world, the limits and strengths of our class position, and the reasons for differentiating one from the other – even if not respectful enough of these differences – than we were in the first half of the twentieth century, when racial apartheid was still openly practiced and supported in the southern United States and in South Africa.

Differences expressed by the practices of diverse ethnic groups, the knowledge that there are imbalances in the amount of power and privilege between some peoples of the North and the South, that there are different world-views between the East and the West, have become more apparent. Rapid technological change, mass communication, travel and increased literacy have made us far more sophisticated in knowledge than previous generations could have imagined. This heightened consciousness also ensures that symbolic interpretations are not left unchallenged. For example in Jamaica, Buju Banton's famous dancehall lyrics "but most of all mi love me browning" did not go unchallenged by women, who resented the insinuation that blackness was not also beautiful and desirable. His subsequent song, "Mi No Stop Cry fi All Black Women", made amends. Later, Beenie Man's song entitled "De Wickedess Slam", while reinforcing sexual stereotypes about uptown and downtown girls, also validated the sexuality and desirability of the downtown (primarily black) woman.

With regard to gender identity, there have been tremendous strides in some countries in the increased access which women have to education, jobs, self-actualization and sexual liberation. How we continue to present and represent sexual difference cannot be detached from concepts and ideas about sexual equality which have been fought for over the last few decades, in a global thrust of women's activism. The idea of equal education for girls is now so taken for granted that we forget that it was only in the latter part of the twentieth century that education and equal access to employment became available to women in some societies. We also overlook the fact that in others, some girls still do not have access to equal education, and that practices such as female infanticide still indicate a preference for the male sex.

The ambiguity, paradox and ambivalence of gender must, however, be retained (De Lauretis 1987). Identity has become an overused word, and a negative one when its politics leads to the repression of heterogeneity. Identity has positive connotations insofar as it acknowledges that individuality is formed through one's historical and cultural background and through one's gender, class and ethnic status. The conception of the female identity and femininity as equal to masculinity should not be an attempt to homogenize both sexes into an identical whole, or to suggest that difference between the sexes must be denied. To discard the notion of such difference is both dangerous and impossible. It assumes that one can disregard the complexity and manifold variety, and thus the richness, of human social experience, including that of human ontological experience. The male is not the same as the female; masculinity is not the same as femininity, although they may be more similar than different. The most fundamental difference between the two may very well be the biological difference: thus far in most species, only the female mammal can actually physically reproduce. This fact raises the issue of what (biological) ontology means for the construction of manhood and womanhood, for concepts and practices of masculinity and femininity, and therefore for the contribution of feminist epistemology to mainstream knowledge.

At the same time we need to be cautious about – in fact, we must challenge – returning to a pure essentialism of the body as male and female. Essentialism has proven to be both useful and destructive; it can be fundamental to the creation and retention of hegemonic ideologies which place power in the hands of those who actively maintain these ideologies (for instance, essentialist ideas of race, caste/class or gender). This primary difference between masculinity and femininity prompts alists to hold fast to an argument that there are different roles for men and women in society, that the male is naturally the breadwinner and protector and, by extension, the female is the dependent sex. Essentialism also views male sexuality as aggressive and dominant, with female sexuality as passive, to be controlled by the male. Notions such as these, along with the idea of the female as an imperfect male, actively sustain a particular social order. For instance, whiteness is deemed superior to blackness due to nineteenth-century scientific claims that the larger brain size of Caucasians represented a higher level of evolution. Class structure was maintained on the basis of royal bloodlines, and for that matter caste is formulated as a product of birth, and not derived from the occupational and hierarchical division of Hindu society which accompanies it. With regard to the male and female, men are perceived as physically stronger and intellectually more agile than women, and so on.

Constructivism arose as a reaction to the essentialist school of thought in the latter half of the twentieth century, and was clearly stimulated by shifting notions of class (Marxist analysis), race and sexuality. Michel Foucault's treatment of sexuality in his *History of Sexuality, Volume 1* (1980) is a prime example of constructivism at work. Foucault demonstrates that sexuality must be conceived of not only as a natural given with drives and instincts over which we have no control, but as also constructed over time by historical and cultural factors. As a result of constructivist thinking, to exemplify the point, it is more difficult to argue that rape of a woman by a man is a crime stimulated by the instinctual and uncontrollable hormonal impulses of a male aroused by a tempting female. Instead it could be viewed as the result of the relations of power and dominance embedded in the gender system, between masculinity and femininity, deriving from the sexual metaphor of man as aggressor and woman as either temptress or conditioned to be afraid of the generic male. Constructivist thinking also influenced Simone de Beauvoir to create her famous dictum that "woman is made, not born". Thus was also derived the conceptualization of gender which moved it away from the concept of sex as biology. Gender was social and cultural, therefore changeable; sex was biological, therefore fixed.

Gender theorists latched on to the ideas of constructivism, as it allowed the possibility of change. If woman's position was not secondary to man but socially constructed, then there was scope for change. Institutions were viewed as having responsibility for the reinforcement of patriarchal ideologies and the continuous construction of gender differences. A good example is found in religion. In Christianity it is said that the woman, Eve, was made from the rib of Adam and she was the temptress in the Garden of Eden. She is depicted and thereafter cast as inferior and sexually untrustworthy, and therefore women must be controlled by men. Religion itself relies on essentialist interpretations. If we regard femininity and what is deemed feminine as being constructed over time, then the same applies to masculinity, which could also be transformed.

The earlier feminist struggles for gender equality, however, could not have anticipated how difficult it would be to change, in a relatively short historical time span, ideas built over centuries. They also did not fully appreciate the notions which do still exist, in my view, about essential differences between maleness and femaleness. If men and women are the same, then maternity leave must be made available to both. If what is masculine and feminine is only constructed, then the future vision for feminism is either androgynous societies or the production of Amazonian women. The dilemma in feminist theory at this point is how do we reject some of the more debilitating aspects of essentialism while still taking account of it? How do we retain the components of constructivism which are relevant – in other words, how do we deconstruct femininity and masculinity without falling prey to the idea that the characteristics of our maleness and femaleness can be explained fully by the social and cultural? As one theorist has asked, "What are the boundaries between the social and the individual, both in a psychological and in a sexual sense?" (Wieringa 2002, 18). How do we employ the theoretical frames of essentialism and constructivism without creating other binary oppositions in thought? One way of viewing the issue is to frame essentialism and constructivism not in opposition but, as Wieringa has suggested, by seeing that "indeed many essentialist arguments are contained in constructivist writing" (2002, 18). What is needed therefore is the element of difference which is still contained in the complementarity of both axioms.

In a seminal essay entitled "The Traffic in Women" (1975), anthropologist Gayle Rubin suggested the term "sex/gender system" to get away from the dichotomy then being developed in feminist theory, of sex as biological and gender as socially constructed and culturally specific. She attempted to demonstrate not only the difference between the two terms but their relation to each other. In other words, this is an attempt to engage more harmoniously the essentialist and constructivist arguments which separated biological sex from social gender. The construction of gender identity becomes a rapprochement with biological sex, between essentialism and constructivism, and consequently a rapprochement between masculinity and femininity rather than a perceived (natural) opposition.

The rest of this chapter attempts nothing more ambitious than a set of notes and guidelines in the study of masculinity, posited within the ideas raised in the first part of the chapter. To summarize, these were: the application of a gender lens, the politics of identity creation, the concept of equality within sexual difference, the determination of masculinity and femininity as both essential and constructed in history, culture and society, and the employment of the method of postmodern deconstruction. I move on first to a metaphorical unmasking of masculinity, and next to a deconstruction of some of the notions associated with patriarchy.

Unmasking Masculinity

There are many ways in which masculinity is viewed by men themselves in their writings on the subject. I examine briefly some of these approaches and the ideas being expressed. Geoff Dench, in a book entitled *The Frog, the Prince and the Problem of Men* (1995), argues that women have more to lose by attempting to reshape common wisdom about what constitutes masculinity, thereby disrupting the natural harmony between the sexes. For Dench, masculinity is defined by the role of protector and breadwinner, giving men a primary role in society. If that is taken away from them he fears they will become like the frog, ugly and irresponsible, without the kiss of the princess to humanize them and turn them into princes. In other words, men are culture, only because natural woman creates cultured man. Dench's argument relies on an essentialist frame of reference. He fears that generations of men and women and human civilization thus far have worked out a natural division of responsibility which, if reordered, could prove to be destructive to continued social relations between the sexes. Women, he thinks, have more to lose by attempting to be more "like men". Part of the misunderstanding with which Dench enters this discourse and polemic with feminism is his assumption that feminism is about women trying to ape a dominant man's culture. If women have rejected the paradigm of male power and the opposition of mind and body, reason and emotion, then it is hardly likely that they are attempting to replace it by another, equally limiting, female dominant paradigm.

Michael Kaufman, in *Beyond Patriarchy: Essays by Men on Pleasure, Power and Change* (1987), puts forward a perspective which engages more readily with contemporary feminist readings of masculinity and patriarchy: "Much of the literature by men on male-female relations tends to be at one extreme or another: many look at how men are scarred and deformed by our roles but do not examine men's privileges and power over women". At the same time he places himself candidly in the shoes of men and observes that "what makes feminism a threat for so many men, or at least a source of confusion and struggle, is not only that we have privileges to lose, but that it appears – or at least feels – as if our very manhood is at stake" (p. xiv).

Like Kaufman, Linden Lewis, in an essay entitled "Constructing the Masculine in the Context of the Caribbean", also situates himself in both male and female perspectives, recognizing the power and privilege which masculinity confers on Caribbean men and the resistance they have to losing ground. He acknowledges that analyses of gender in the Caribbean (and elsewhere), which have focused on women, lack a serious examination of masculinity. The result is that masculinity has been conceived primarily in negative terms, in which "Caribbean men are homogenized, and identified as a part of a reactionary backlash against feminist intervention in the region" (1994). Lewis notes, and I agree, that this kind of interrogation has failed to promote understanding between men and women and, like Kaufman, he consistently presses for analyses which enhance a relational understanding rather than a widening of the gap with further misunderstandings.

At the risk of being pedantic at this point, perhaps somewhat late in the essay, but deliberately so, I want to argue that this inquiry into masculinity in relation to femininity requires a precision with terminology. When we speak of masculinity in intellectual discourse, are we speaking the same language as the politician, the journalist, the calypsonian or my father and yours? What do we mean by the words male, man, manhood and masculinity? Can they be interchangeably used? It might be useful to revisit the etymology of the word itself and its parent in feminist discourse: gender. Donna Haraway notes that the equivalent words in different languages are *gender* in English, *Geshlecht* in German, *genre* in French, and *genero* in Spanish.

> The root of the English, French and Spanish words is the Latin verb, *generare,* to beget, and the Latin stem *gener-* race or kind. . . . The substantives *"Geshlecht"*, *"gender"*, *"genre"* and *"genero"* refer to the notions of sort, kind, and class. . . . The modern English and German words, *"gender"* and *"Geshlecht"* adhere closely to concepts of sex, sexuality, sexual difference, generation, engendering, and so on, while the French and Spanish seem not to carry those meanings as readily. (Haraway 1991)

The words associated with gender in all Western languages are entangled with concepts of kinship, race, language and nationality, all of which in the present-day discourse speak to the politics of identity. The puzzlement with the word and concept of gender will no doubt continue. When we begin to examine and deconstruct masculinity itself, the term must not be unproblematically taken within the still puzzling terminology of gender, particularly as regards its cultural differentiation. Masculinity, like femininity, must be constantly interrogated by class, race and culture, as well as assigned historical variation.

Given the need to establish both essentialist elements as well as socially constructed ones, a useful differentiation in terminology can be that "male" is a biological referent, while the terms man, manhood and masculinity are more socially ascribed and, in fact, constructed in terms of what it is not: male is not female; masculinity is not femininity. In fact the most common definition of masculinity seems to be its distance from what is denoted as feminine in most cultures. This may be more true of contemporary Western culture than of others, causing us to historicize the concept of masculinity just as femininity itself has undergone historical scrutiny. For instance, in parts of New Guinea studied by Margaret Mead in 1935, "men are (like Victorian women) at once prudish and flirtatious, fearful of sex yet preoccupied with love magic and cosmetics that will lead the maidens – who take the initiative in courtship, to be interested in them" ([1935] 1949). In other areas Mead found instances of sexual asymmetry in which the roles of men and women were seen as cooperative and complementary, suggesting that economic factors were not the main reasons for the emergence of this asymmetry. For instance, among the Tchambuli the women were traders, controlling family economics; the men were artists and ritual specialists. Although it appeared to Mead that women had little respect for masculine skills and secrets, they still found it necessary to ritually pretend inferiority in morality and knowledge in comparison to men (Zimbalist Rosaldo 1974, 18–19).

In contemporary Caribbean society discussions on the marginality of men and the independence and "overachievement" of women suggest other asymmetries of recent vintage which have not been put under the microscope of the anthropologist but which raise the same questions. Studies of the lived relationships between contemporary men and women may assist in clarifying the correlation which exists between essentialism and constructivism in understanding gender. To unmask masculinity is not to reduce what is deemed masculine or manhood to the known and therefore without mystique, nor is it to deprive masculinity of its difference from femininity. To unmask masculinity is to remove some of the stereotypes associated with the term, and to subject men themselves to an interrogation of what it means to be a man, how their masculinity is defined and to question who determines where the boundaries of masculinity lie.

In the once virtually unchallenged division of society into masculine and feminine, nature and culture and other binary oppositions, within the process of writing the history of Western man into culture, masculinity was assumed to be fixed. The word patriarch itself, associated with manhood, was invested with power, assurance, knowledge and confidence. What emerged in history was the notion that man was the known quantity, with woman the unknown, to be defined in relation to man, as terms such as "the fairer sex", "the better half" and so on patronizingly imply. The feminist project has been to reinscribe the woman as existent and to recover her in history. This project has become a more self-conscious one in the twentieth century. Femininity and female gender identity needed to be uncovered through conscious interpretation and representation, by examining conceptions of womanhood and femininity in different cultures. The point which is speculative but worthy of inquiry is that in the ongoing construction of both identities (or the dialectic of both), in retrospect, the feminine seems much less problematic and more fixed, perhaps even more timelessly inscribed in some way than the masculine.

Feminine gender identity was always implanted more firmly through the ontology of the female body – the monthly menstrual cycle which ordered female time more precisely, the act of giving birth and the dependence of the newborn on mother's milk, the knowledge which women had to have of their bodies if sexual activity was not to produce unwanted children. The nature of women's being was premised on knowing their bodies and learning how to ensure that the children they gave birth to survived. This required and continues to demand relative stability and seriousness of purpose; whether we speak of women in the past or of women today, similar ideas apply.

For the male, masculine gender identity has generally derived from the promise of what a man can do, not what he is. Manhood and masculinity were/are linked to power, status, control, and the execution of his role as provider and breadwinner. If the male could not fulfil this promise, then he was not a man. If femininity was largely about bearing children, then woman's status, class and power were linked to that of her mate or male kin. The shift in occupational roles and the knowledge we now admit to, that women have also been providers and bread-winners, have challenged notions of masculinity, while allowing women to expand concepts of femininity.

Femininity now incorporates the role of provider, education and careers, intelligence, physical strength and agility in sport, and so on. Has masculinity really been able to absorb with equanimity some of the "traits" generally deemed feminine, such as nurturance and monogamy? This perhaps is at the root of male fear that they are losing ground and privilege, that manhood is under siege. The idea of losing ground puts an increasing psychological pressure on men to retain notions of mas-culinity which perhaps were possible under different economic circum-stances but are increasingly a luxury in the political economy of the contemporary world order. Men feel threatened when they cannot fulfil their "God-given and natural role". What consequences this has for delinquency among young men, and how this provides an explana-tion as to why women appear to emerge as the stronger rather than the weaker sex when there is an increase in unemployment and poverty, are issues which must be debated in relation to masculinity.

The legendary thesis of man the hunter and woman the gatherer took firm root, and transformed itself into an explanation as well as an argument for the timeless persistence of a normative and natural sex-ual division of labour within society. Explanations provided by feminist interpretations of this thesis give useful food for thought among men and women who unquestionably support these notions. While the sex-ual division of labour has changed over time due to the demands of the existing modes of economic production of goods and services, it is uncer-tain why the task of the hunter has emerged as more important than that of the gatherer and nurturer. Is this a projection of contemporary human values and hierarchical ordering onto the past? In both previous and current modes of production, the burden of breadwinner must always have been a difficult one for the man to bear. One must also question why this essentialist idea was so readily appropriated by capitalism to pay a family wage to the man, with the assumption that the provider is always male. Even a cursory understanding of the history of Caribbean societies refutes the notion that women have been solely dependent on a male breadwinner. Both sexes have contributed continuously throughout the development of human society to the support of the family. Research on the family in history has recorded that among many systems of production, for example the peasant family, there was no real division in a practical sense. Either through collectivities or in extended families which included household helpers, both men and women performed tasks which accumulated surplus for household survival.[2] This debunking of different roles of both male and female in society is neatly summed up by anthropologist Eleanor Burke Leacock: "the notion of a somehow separate 'woman's role' hides the reality of the family as an economic unit, an institution as crucial for the continued exploitation of working men, as it is for the oppression of women" (1979, 13).

The privileges accorded to men were and are still based on class, status and their access to economic and social power. By extension, impoverished men have equally been the victims of other men. In the thirteenth and fourteenth centuries in parts of western Europe the rights of the lord over his tenant included the *droit de seigneur* or *prima nocte* – the right of the lord to have sexual relations with the serf's newly wedded wife. The dishonouring of a man and his masculinity through the female body has been and remains literally a blow below the belt for masculinity. This, incidentally, persists as a feature of war today; the dishonour of the losing group is made more complete if its women are raped and impregnated. In general, this act is carried out by other men. In this sense, masculinity is a public more than a private arrangement, between men and men, rather than primarily a relation between men and women.

Masculinity as a social construct is fashioned differently at different ages. Anthropological insights offer a wealth of illustrations of the cultural variations in what can be considered masculinity in more "primitive" cultures, as seen for instance in the works of Maurice Godelier (1981), Margaret Mead (1949) and Eleanor Burke Leacock (1979). The notions held in Western society are not universal ones. History also reveals tremendous differences in the trappings of masculinity, in dress style, length of hair, the use of cosmetics and adornment and so on. In twentieth-century society the re-emergence of long hair and ponytails among men signifies either a challenge to bourgeois society or a willingness to bend gender lines of demarcation. My own reading of the Rastafarian hairstyle for men is that it reaffirmed biblical notions of manhood, control and power while also being mimetic of the symbolic Lion, the personification of strength. Hair therefore signified for African men in Jamaica the reclamation of gender identity, of blackness, of origins, of defiance against a history of colonization which weakened the patriarchal base and of regaining control over the women of the tribe. The "dreadlocks" appeal to men not only of the Rastafarian faith, and appropriation by other cultures outside of Jamaica suggest that this message is a universal one for many black men throughout the Western world.

The willingness to challenge notions of masculinity in a culture seems to also change with the chronological age of the individual man, in negotiation with individual women. While symbolic notions of masculinity may be retained outside of the intimacy of the household, within the closed environment many changes are negotiated, such that household chores become more shared. For example, men may openly profess to like cooking. But, interestingly, this seems to come with the age, experience and confidence in maleness which a man possesses, so that his "feminine" activities will not be misinterpreted by his peers.

Several questions suggest themselves in relation to the study of masculinity in the Caribbean. What is Caribbean masculinity, if such a thing exists? What are Caribbean men if they are not irresponsible and emasculated as a result of their history of colonization? How do we move away from the stereotypes which have been associated with manhood in the Caribbean and which themselves create the psychological barriers, in my view, to change in gender relations? Are women in the Caribbean really antagonistic to men, or is it towards the ideas of masculinity which inform group male behaviour? Do Caribbean men fully understand the additional burdens which women bear by being labelled independent and strong? These are the questions to which the ongoing deconstruction of masculinity must respond. The unmasking of masculinity also requires a parallel deconstructing of patriarchy. In my view the ideologies and practice of male dominance, while privileging some men, also keep masculinity imprisoned behind invisible bars.

Deconstructing Patriarchy

The archetypal patriarch is the dominant father or powerful man who rules over the household or community – including women, younger men, sons, daughters and slaves. Patriarchy itself can be defined as a prescribed power relationship in which the patriarch or father rules over the others for the benefit of the household or clan. Built into the notion of power and control by the father or leader of a clan is the idea of a "benevolent patriarchy" at work. Anthropological findings have revealed that the rule of father over sons, or older men over younger men, was, in many cases, not premised on benevolence but designed to ensure that power and privilege remained the hands of the older men. A parallel in female-female relationships can be seen between mother-in-law and daughter-in-law in the Indian household. The mother-in-law has herself experienced the debased position in the household into which she married, but reinforces this same hierarchy when her son brings another female into the household. By reproducing the same mechanism of authority and control, the older woman is able to channel and keep her status and privileges in her household. A question we might then ask of masculinity: What power and resources do men gain by controlling other men and younger men? One explanation derives from the essentialist paradigm, in that younger males have the virility to supersede the sexual authority of the older male and must therefore be restricted. In addition, like the mother-in-law and daughter-in-law association, such control ensures that the labour power of the younger or less privileged male is controlled by the older.

Feminism has revealed many faces of patriarchy as societies progressed into twentieth century. Both ideologies and practices of patriarchy served to control female labour, female reproduction and female sexuality, while also inscribing a pecking order or control and power among men themselves. A contemporary deconstruction of patriarchy requires a revisiting of the term patriarchy, moving away from the glibness or the taking-for-granted with which we have come to use the term in feminist discourse.[3] The recognition of patriarchy as both ideology and practice led feminism into a search for origins, a search which, though proving inconclusive, has still been necessary and worthwhile.[4] The findings suggest that if patriarchy has been constructed through history, then it can also be deconstructed.

Several important notions in the concept of patriarchy have surfaced through feminist scholarship. First, the universality of its ideology and practices. Again anthropology has revealed more similarities and differences between cultures in this respect, despite the fascinating and remarkable exceptions which have been uncovered. Second has been the tenacity of patriarchy once it takes root. In an attempt to illustrate the concept of patriarchy to a colleague, an insightful postgraduate student of mine5 once used a very graphic and penetrating metaphor which can be appropriately borrowed here. Patriarchy is not fixed or the same during all historical periods; rather, like an amoeba, it changes form and takes different shapes in different historical moments. This very transformation and division, and the capacity to do so, in fact account for its persistence over time.

In the Caribbean a popular notion is that patriarchy was introduced by the white colonial ideology, as if it had not existed in the communities which inhabited previously these islands or within the cultures from which the major migrant groups were derived. This point of view is a very limiting one. It puts the blame for the subordination of women and the emasculation of men squarely in the hands of another greater patriarchy and not on the gender relations negotiated between men and women as these societies continue to undergo additional transformation. Lewis (1994) argues that through a developed and sophisticated European system of patriarchy, colonial rule in the Caribbean inscribed notions of masculine superiority into the culture and political economy of the region, laying another foundation for the institutionalization of gender inequality in the region. Although they were excluded from control over resources and from equal access to power with their European counterparts, African men, and later Indian, Chinese, and Portuguese men came to internalize and support these very same patriarchal standards. Lewis suggests that the social relations of men and women in Caribbean society before European colonization have still, however, to undergo serious scholarly investigation. In deconstructing patriarchy the social relations between the migrant men and women who came or were transported, and the gender systems which emerged within these groups, need closer scrutiny. The issue is not that relations of patriarchy did not exist before forced or voluntary forms of migration took place, but rather that the forms of patriarchy which existed were different and, like the metaphoric amoeba, took on a different countenance in the new settings.

I can draw on two key examples of deconstructing gender relations within an ethnic group, areas in which I have carried out research, to make this point clearer. Indian men and women were largely brought as individuals, even though some migrated in families. The shortage of women in the earlier periods of indentureship in the nineteenth century allowed a flagrant challenging of the rules of kinship which bound both sexes to family, monogamy and sexual mores. The notable outburst of violence against Indian women, especially during indentureship, was the Indian males' response to women's challenge of the dominant patriarchal notions according in India which had placed Indian women in subservience to the male. The Indian female was in shorter supply in the Caribbean and she had greater opportunity to select a male partner or to desert him if he did not fulfil her sexual or material needs. The result was a major disruption in Indian family patterns and in the gender system. Indian patriarchy suffered a major blow. The suicide rate among Indian men was also very high, and was worrisome to the colonial officials, who blamed this on the immorality of women when they could offer no other explanations. Indian women emerged during indentureship as threatening the internal patriarchal order of the group. They had gained a degree of independence and freedom which they could not have possessed under the patriarchal ideologies and practices which were still dominant in India at the time. This trend was partially reversed in the later and postindentureship period when a reorganized kinship system, family and household structure, institutions such as religion and the panchayat[6] began to enforce norms which had been established for centuries in Indian society, but which were also undergoing changes there.

In a previous article entitled "Fragments of the Colonial Legacy: The Representation of Masculinity in Caribbean Thought", I asked and attempted to answer the following questions: Why is it that the brutal system of slavery resulted in an emasculated male and a strong independent female who single-handedly was deemed to be responsible for the well-being of the family? What is it about slavery and colonialism which brought on a legacy of antagonistic relations between men and women of African descent in Caribbean society? In a selection from the Thistlewood diaries 1750–86 (compiled by Douglas Hall [1999]), I was struck by the plurality and diversity in intimate relations within the slave population itself. As with Indian migrants, the African slave population also suffered serious disruptions in their internal arrangements as a result of an uprooting and displacement of norms and traditions. The slave population at this time exhibited a marked degree of inconstancy – both men and women changing partners, baby mothers and baby fathers with consummate ease, even though it appeared possible to develop long-term and binding relationships in the plantation if they wished. This area requires systematic investigation to substantiate the point I wish to develop. Nonetheless, my reading of the diary extract suggests that while one of the reasons for so-called male irresponsibility can be attributed to the licentiousness of the colonial masters themselves, there was a startling parallel between the disruption of gender relations among Africans under slavery and that of Indians in the early stages of indentureship. The breakdown of kinship rules and tradition allowed more flexibility for both men and women during slavery, and insofar as this could be exploited within slave society, African men and women were themselves not indifferent to the possibilities.

A parallel between these two experiences, of shifts in patriarchal dominance and a reshaping of an internal gender system, was also echoed by an Australian colleague who had knowledge of gender relations among some Aboriginal tribes of Australia. She pointed out that colonization had disempowered both Aboriginal men and women in this postcolonial state. Women nevertheless emerged as independent, strong and responsible, while the Aboriginal men were largely seen as irresponsible, weak and quick to drown their sorrows in the bottle. Again the connections between the essentialism of biology and the constructed nature of social gender needs to be questioned here across cultures. Why is it that women emerge as independent and resourceful in the face of adversity?

While this reading of gender relations within ethnic groups presents one facet of deconstruction, we also need to examine how patriarchy is being reformulated continuously by the interactions and power relations between the different groups. If we look at Jamaican society after emancipation, a new patriarchal order between men and men is being formed. In Jamaica we have the emergence of a white, creole society, coloured society and black marginal male grouping. In Trinidad after indentureship a similar hierarchy was created, with the dominant white male, the French creole grouping, the middle-class coloured group, the emancipated African descendants and the Indian male at the bottom of the ladder. Within each group there are gender relations to be negotiated between men and women, but the dominant patriarchal group provides the rules for the creation of a new order and this provides the fresh base for the negotiations between men and men for power, status and privilege. Patriarchal manifestations of power take on dimensions specific to the historical moment. Since patriarchy and public power appear to go hand-in-hand, the process is simultaneously about holding on to and controlling power in the society at any time. The group which maintains the strongest patriarchal control also holds the power.

In deconstructing patriarchy we must therefore see masculinity as being negotiated between men and men for the visible gains which power allows: money, status, privilege, control over one's life and livelihood, access to one's own and other men's women, and so on. If the echelons of state or high commerce present arenas in which men trade for power with other men, then at a different level the production of popular culture provides another powerful space through which symbols of masculinity are being traded. A good example is found in the classic Trinidadian calypso "Jean and Dinah", sung by the Mighty Sparrow after the end of the Second World War. Soldiers on the US military base in Trinidad packed up and went home, taking with them the US dollars which had given them greater access to prostitutes and other women in urban Trinidad. A new patriarchal order in Trinidad began to take shape after they left:

Jean and Dinah, Rosita and Clementina
Round the corner posing,
bet yuh life is something they selling
And if you catch them broken
Yuh could get it all for nothing
Don't make a row
The Yankees gone and Sparrow take over now
              (Might Sparrow 1956)

In Jamaica, Errol Miller's *Marginalization of the Black Male* (1986) resonates with the masculinist discourse of slavery, a continuous emasculation in which men are again the victims of the dominant colonial order – black men must not be educated to challenge their former colonial masters. While recognizing that patriarchy is about the power relations between men and men as well as between men and women, Miller still works within the ideological paradigm of male dominance, implying that this ideology is a natural one, an inherent gender order for society. The burden of emasculation is placed subtly on the backs of women, who benefit from the power plays between men and men. While Miller accurately observes that Jamaican women have taken advantage of educational opportunities and have achieved greater mobility than men, he does not question the notion of manhood itself and the way in which this may be at variance with the requirements of the changing education system and the changing occupational and wage structure of developing capitalism. Insofar as capital will persistently draw more on female labour, then patriarchal notions of manhood will also have to undergo a significant shift. The answer does not lie in resorting to opposition and antagonism against women.[7]

The corollary to this deconstruction of patriarchy is as follows: how does the power relationship between men and men impact the relations between men and women? If the benefits of patriarchy are in the control of female sexuality, the control of female labour power, and the continued establishment of superiority over the female sex, then the mechanisms of negotiation between men and women will follow from these premises. At the same time, one must continuously examine the way in which the blueprint for patriarchy, that of benevolence and protection, has had universal and seemingly timeless appeal. The interrogation of patriarchy therefore must become not a dissection of masculinity to expose its raw desire for power and strength, but an investigation of the factors which have led to and continue to demand such qualities as benevolence and protection from masculinity. As Jeffrey Weeks (1986) has pointed out insightfully, we appear as a species to remain committed to sexual difference. Answering the questions why and for what purpose may require us to enter other disciplines to examine the origins and persistence of patriarchy and therefore the ideas of masculinity which endure. The analysis of patriarchy should not be restricted to the designs for power and privilege between men and men, or that between men and women. As the few examples of history I have drawn on have illustrated, patriarchy is equally about the establishment and retention of power between races or ethnic groups, classes and sexes. This continued understanding of patriarchy alongside a more profound interrogation of masculinity has now been become one of the key points for focus on the feminist agenda.

Conclusion

Some of the present male discourse on patriarchy and masculinity appears to do little more than reinscribe the old order rather than creating a more equitable one. It is therefore necessary and strategic for women and men to enter into dialogue on these questions, as it may be impossible for patriarchy to examine its own weaknesses. If masculinity and femininity are ultimately about the definition and retention of an opposition in human society which we must respect and nourish, then the feminist project may depend on the creation of new essentialist ideas of human nature, undifferentiated by sex, but celebratory of difference.

Notes

1. Browning is a term developed in the late twentieth century to refer to persons, especially women, of "light brown" complexion.
2. See, for example, evidence in Goody 1983.
3. Foremost among the scholars who have carried out research in this area is Gerda Lerner (1989).
4. It must be noted that Kate Millett's earlier work, published in 1970, retained both notions of patriarchy as the rule of older men over younger men, but Millet looked more systematically at the way in which patriarchy defined the ideology and practices of male dominance as they were manifested in the twentieth century. In subsequent developments of feminist perspectives, patriarchy attained the stature of a key conceptual advance in feminist theory. Radical feminists viewed the ideology of male dominance as key in the subordination of women, while socialist feminists looked at the intersection between patriarchy and capitalism in ensuring male dominance in society.
5. This observation was made by Michelle Rowley, a young Trinidadian student who was one of the first candidates for the MSc in Gender and Development Studies offered by the Centre for Gender and Development Studies at the University of the West Indies, Mona, Jamaica.
6. The panchayat referred to the council of five male elders who were chosen in the villages from among the men held in esteem. Their duties were wide ranging, but essentially they were the gatekeepers of norms and the voices of authority in the village.
7. The work of Keisha Lindsay, another former postgraduate student, is important here. Lindsay's critique, now published in the Working Paper no. 1 of the Centre for Gender and Development Studies Mona Unit (1997), expands the critique of Miller.

References

Best, Steven, and Douglas Kellner. 1991. *Critical Interrogations*. Houndmills: Macmillan.

Burke Leacock, Eleanor. 1979. "Engels and the History of Women's Oppression". In *Myths of Male Dominance: Collected Articles on Women Cros-Culturally*. New York: Monthly Review Press.

Cline Horowitz, Maryanne. 1987. "The 'Science' of Embryology before the Discovery of the Ovum". In *Connecting Spheres*, edited by Marilyn Boxer and Jean Quaertert. New York: Oxford University Press.

De Beauvoir, Simone. [1949] 1972. *The Second Sex*. Reprint, Harmondsworth: Penguin.

De Lauretis, Teresa. 1987. *Technologies of Gender: Essays on Theory, Film and Fiction*. Bloomingdale: Indiana University Press.

Dench, Geoff. 1995. *The Frog, the Prince and the Problem of Men*. London: Neanderthal Press.

Fagan, Brian M. 2002. *World Prehistory: A Brief Introduction*. Englewood, NJ: Prentice Hall.

Foucault, Michel. 1980. *History of Sexuality. Volume I: An Introduction*. New York: Vintage.

Godelier, Maurice. 1981. "The Origins of Male Domination". *New Left Review*, no. 127 (May–June).

Goody, Jack. 1983. *The Development of the Family and Marriage in Europe*. Cambridge: Cambridge University Press.

Hall, Douglas. 1999. *In Miserable Slavery: Thomas Thistlewood in Jamaica, 1750–86*. Kingston, Jamaica: University of the West Indies Press.

Haraway, Donna. 1991. "Gender for a Marxist Dictionary". In *Simians, Cyborgs and Women: The Reinvention of Nature*. London: Free Association Books.

Kaufman, Michael, ed. 1987. *Beyond Patriarchy: Essays by Men on Pleasure, Power and Change*. Toronto: Oxford University Press.

Lerner, Gerda. 1989. *The Creation of Patriarchy*. Oxford: Oxford University Press.

Lewis, Linden. 1994. "Constructing the Masculine in the Context of the Caribbean". Paper presented at the Nineteenth Annual Caribbean Association Conference, Merida.

Lindsay, Keisha. 1997. "Caribbean Male: An Endangered Species?" Working Paper no. 1, edited by Patricia Mohammed, 1–20. Mona, Jamaica: Centre for Gender and Development Studies, University of the West Indies.

Mead, Margaret. [1935] 1949. *Sex and Temperament in Three Primitive Societies*. New York: William Morrow.

———. 1949. *Male and Female*. New York: William Morrow.

Mighty Sparrow. 1956. "Jean and Dinah". Kay CRS008.

Miller, Errol. 1986. *Marginalization of the Black Male*. Kingston, Jamaica: Institute of Social and Economic Research.

Mohammed, Patricia. 1995. "Fragments of the Colonial Legacy: The Representation of Masculinity in Caribbean Thought". Paper presented at the Annual Conference of the Society for Caribbean Studies, London, July.

Moore, Henrietta. 1994. *A Passion for Difference: Essays in Anthropology and Gender.* Cambridge: Polity Press.

Nugent, Maria. [1966] 2002. *Lady Nugent's Journal of Her Residence in Jamaica from 1801 to 1805.* Edited by Philip Wright. Reprint, Kingston, Jamaica: University of the West Indies Press.

Rubin, Gayle. 1975. "The Traffic in Women: Notes on the Political Economy of Sex". In *Toward an Anthropology of Women,* edited by Rayna Reiter. New York: Monthly Review Press.

Scott, Joan. 1987. Foreword to *Connecting Spheres,* edited by Marilyn Boxer and Jean Quaertert. New York: Oxford University Press.

Slocum, Sally. 1995. "Woman the Gatherer: Male Bias in Anthropology". In *Issues in Feminism: An Introduction to Women's Studies,* edited by Sheila Ruth. Mountain View, Calif.: Mayfield.

Weeks, Jeffrey. 1986. *Sexuality.* London: Tavistock Publications.

Wieringa, Saskia. 2002. "Essentialism versus Constructivism: Time for a Rapprochement?" In *Gendered Realities: Essays in Caribbean Feminist Thought,* edited by Patricia Mohammed. Kingston, Jamaica: University of the West Indies Press.

Zimbalist Rosaldo, Michelle. 1974. "Woman, Culture and Society: A Theoretical Overview". In *Woman, Culture and Society,* edited by Michelle Zimbalist Rosaldo and Louise Lamphere. Stanford, Calif.: Stanford University Press.

CHAPTER 3

Power Games and Totalitarian Masculinity in the Dominican Republic

E. ANTONIO DE MOYA

El dictador Trujillo pasea ante sus aduladores taconeando fuerte, con estudiada afectación de dominio, y nadie osa sentarse antes que él dé orden para ello.

[Dictator Trujillo walks in front of his flatterers beating noisily with his heels, with a studied pretence of dominion, and nobody dares to sit down before he orders them to do so.]

   – J. Almoina, *Una Satrapía en el Caribe*

¿Quién se *ve* más hombre de nosotros dos?

[Who *looks* manlier of the two of us?]

   – One Dominican male talking to another

Around the beginning of the 1990s, a patriarchal satirical Central American folk song, "*El Venao*" (literally "the deer", but metaphorically "the cuckold"), recorded by a local "Christian" singer, became a top *merengue* hit on pop music radio stations all over the Dominican Republic. It soon became popular in Puerto Rico, Venezuela, Mexico and among the Hispanic population in US cities (Caroit 1996). The song told the tragicomic story of a man whose wife was unfaithful to him. As a result, the man was viciously harassed, ridiculed, and scorned as a scapegoat by other men in his neighbourhood. In Dominican lower-class communities the song helped to draw attention to a high prevalence of sexual infidelity in the times of AIDS. It also became a collective innuendo directed at unsuspecting male victims of adultery, as well as the stage of an ongoing drama akin to the Theatre of Cruelty.

The untoward song was anonymously whistled to those men by the telephone, or loudly and reiteratively played on the jukeboxes of street-corner *colmados* (grocery stores) every time they passed nearby. To the despair of the victims, mocking customers joyfully danced and sang to the chorus "*El Venao, El Venao*" while drinking beer and rum. When the fashion of this biting jest faded away in the country several years later, no less than a dozen women had been killed (at least one man beheaded his wife with a machete). Dozens of women had been badly battered and injured by jealous husbands, and some men had committed homicide or suicide as a consequence of the "killing" *merengue*.

As a likely sequel to this, a small town in the northwestern part of the country has celebrated a peculiar, emasculating Carnival for the last four or five years. In it, the so-called Community Cuckold of the Year receives as an "award" the "Crown of Horns" in a *Fiesta de Cuernos* (cuckoldry festival). Any unwitting married man could be the year's chosen antihero, the winner of this catastrophic, discrediting and disqualifying surprise. Even worse, as a disclaimer, he would be pressed to prove to others that the accusation is false; if true, he must guarantee that the infidelity was not culturally "justified" by his presumable lack of masculinity. He must show that he is "still" a man by taking "due" revenge on his wife and her lover. Otherwise he will have to submissively accept the defiling stigma of a cuckold, a synonym for abjection, of being an outcast or a contemptible individual.

Although it is not totally clear how this selection is made in the community, it is known that there are consultations with many individuals in different neighbourhoods for potential candidates. Informal interviews are also conducted with key informants such as likely eyewitnesses, motorbike taxi drivers who have transported the couples to hotels and motels, go-betweens, and male perpetrators, the latter glorified as everyday-life heroes. Later on, in the Carnival parade throughout the few streets in town, a dancing crowd of community members carrying the cuckold's crown proceeds towards the house of the unfortunate husband. His reaction, of course, should be one of shock, denial and anger, but the crowd will prompt and encourage him to action. As a result, the "celebration" has invariably ended in violent fights, and one or more deaths have occurred every year in the community for this reason. In 2000 the police banned the celebration of this violent festival, but this might not be the end of the story.

These two apparently trivial social events reflect the unfortunate public salience of conjugal infidelity, among other phenomena, for the construction of masculinity, power relations and social control in Dominican society and in cultural affinity areas. As such, the central theme of this chapter is masculinity as a totalitarian and contradictory political discourse. Christian Krohn-Hansen (1996) has convincingly shown that this discourse is produced, reproduced and modified by ordinary people in everyday life in the Dominican Republic. As such, notions of masculinity play a central part in the production of political legitimacy in this country. Verbal categories mainly based on sexual orientation, and labels used by Dominican men for classifying and evaluating each other as men (for example, *venao*), structure masculinity as a dominant discourse. According to Krohn-Hansen, this "problematic of legitimation", of establishing differences between themselves as men, helps to produce what is politically conceivable as well as a particular set of power relations.

Masculinity as a Part of the "Problematic of Legitimation"

Several attempts have been made internationally to define and study masculinity as an important part of the "problematic of legitimation" (Habermas 1976) for men in the last few years. Robert Brannon's 1976 definition of virility, for instance, summarizes it in four main components: (1) absolute rejection of the feminine; (2) power, success, wealth and social position; (3) emotional control in crises; and (4) being daring and aggressive (see Kimmel 1997). According to semiotic definitions, masculinity exists only in contrast to femininity. Following poststructuralism and Jacques Lacan's ideas, Connell says that masculinity is nonfemininity, the locus of symbolic authority; the phallus is the "signifying property" and femininity is symbolically defined by its absence (1997, 32).

Kimmel (1997) has reviewed some other definitions of masculinity. He quotes Kenneth Wayne (1912), who wrote that a man's measure of himself is usually another man. Similarly, in 1991 David Leverenz proposed that virility ideologies have evolved mainly in relation to peer regards and masculine authority. Later on, David Mamet (1993) added that what men need is approval from men. Finally, Kimmel stated that as adolescents we learn that our peers are a sort of "gender police", constantly threatening with unmasking us as effeminate, as not men enough. He concluded that, *ceteris paribus,* masculinity is "homosocial" approval: "We test each other, perform heroic acts, take tremendous risks, only because we want other men to attest to our virility" (1997, 55).

Popular discourses about gender still present women as naturally sexually passive and receptive, and men as naturally indiscriminate and sexually voracious (O'Connell Davidson and Sánchez Taylor 1999). In the Dominican Republic the ideal partner for most males seems to be, in their words, a commodity: "*dama en la calle, cuero en la cama y chopa en la casa*" (a lady in the streets, a nymphet in bed and a servant at home). Women are expected to seduce men by preparing exquisite meals for them, since it is believed that *por la boca muere el pez* (roughly: men and fish alike, they are caught by their "hunger"). Perhaps beyond gender differences, as we will see, it does not matter that much whether the partner is female or male, provided that the domination-subordination dynamic is present.

Gender Work, Homophobia and Compulsory Heterosexuality

Kaufman (1997) coined the concept of gender work to refer to the process of internalization of gender relations, which is seen as an element in the construction of our personalities. Consciously or unconsciously, he reasoned, we help to preserve patriarchal systems.

From ancient times in the Dominican Republic, women have been seen as playing a pivotal role in the cultural transmission of gender anxiety and homophobia to younger generations. Parents strongly fear that their children could eventually "become" homosexual and, because of this, the mother tends to behave as the guardian of child sexuality, probably in order to avoid casting aspersions on the father's masculinity (de Moya and García 1996). This is closely linked to the instillation of homophobia.

Kimmel (1993) defines homophobia as the effort to suppress homoerotic desire, to purify a man's relations with men, women and children, and to insure that nobody could ever confound him with a homosexual. In his words, it is "the fear that other men . . . reveal to ourselves and to the world that we do not meet standards, that we are not true men". For Kaufman (1997) homophobia simultaneously transmits and alleviates fear – a fear that is inconsistent with the dominant masculinity.

Mostly in the upper-middle and middle classes in the Dominican Republic, who are mainly concerned with social power, there is a relatively basic, clear-cut, stereotyped and paranoid (totalitarian) etiquette for gendering both the verbal and non-verbal behaviour of young boys away from "femininity". Adrienne Rich (1993) has called the product of this gender work "compulsory heterosexuality". This spiral of no-no rules, this *panopticum,* is meant to avert any possible "femininity" in boys' body language. It works as a straightjacket that automatically warns them, as a thermostat, against any innocent gesture, movement, word or action that is not the best choice for prospective true males. Paradoxically, these rearing practices might increase *and* decrease the threshold of resistance to taboo homosexual – phallicist – temptation. In this way Dominican males are socialized in a strongly restrictive and prohibitive environment, which surely cripples their spontaneity, authenticity and joy, and produces much hypocrisy and neurosis.

Some examples of this, primarily gathered by the author from participant observation of mother-child and children's interaction, and from informal conversations and semistructured interviews with men and women over three years, are worth mentioning, for they guide what I propose is a totalitarian image of dominant masculinity. This etiquette is generalized knowledge in at least the last three generations, and has been validated as "normal" or "God-given" rearing practices of boys by dozens of mothers. The examples are:

- A boy should not adopt the prone position raising his buttocks in bed ("expose him"), as if asking to be mounted by a male ("asking for children").
- He definitely cannot play with dolls or show an interest in "women's things" or feminine activities.
- He must stand up, walk and sit down in a straight fashion.
- He should not rest hands on his waist, let hands hang loosely, intertwine the fingers of both hands, look at his own nails with the hand open (palm facing down), cross his arms, or cross his legs at the ankle level (rather than above the knee).
- He should not gesticulate much or show "feminine gestures", such as soft hand movements.
- He cannot maintain eye contact with a male for more than a fraction of a second, hail him more than two or three times in the same day, or stare at him with *ojos deseosos* (a longing look).
- He cannot wear his mother or sisters' clothes, shoes, make-up or jewels.
- He cannot learn how to dance classical ballet or to play piano or violin.
- He should put on shirts from behind, without raising his arms.

- He is not welcome to enter the household's kitchen (hegemonic female territory) nor taught how to prepare any meal, no matter how simple it is.
- He should not sweep or mop the floor at home if there are available women.
- He should not touch his own face or let anybody else touch it.
- He has to fight if he is insulted or slapped on his face.
- He cannot publicly show fear of anything.
- He should not sob nor cry, even when hurt.
- He must speak forcefully and loudly.
- He should not be too sophisticated or courteous in speech; he should use "masculine" four-letter words.
- He must not use the words of women or "faggots" (such as "divine" or "fabulous").
- He should flee from affectionate men.
- He must learn to spit as far as possible, to whistle loudly with his fingers, and to play rough in sports.
- And by age twelve or thirteen, at puberty, he should show a vivid and visible erotic interest in all females that come close to him (mostly girls his age and their mothers) when he is with his peers.

The Concept of Hegemony

Masculinity studies in the last few years have pointed to a vast array of cultural representations of power relations among men, closely linked to a fusion of "social class and ethnicity-race culture" (a notion akin to Micheline Labelle's 1987 "ethnoclass"), sexual orientation and age. According to Kaufman (1997), instead of thinking about a single masculinity, "hegemonic" and "subordinate" forms should be recognized and studied, thus positing masculinity as a hierarchical construct. For him, patriarchy not only exists as a men's power system over women, but as a system of power hierarchies between different groups of men and also between different masculinities (pp. 66–67). He advances the idea that each subgroup within the hierarchy, on the basis of race, class and sexual orientation, among others, defines being a man according to the social and economic possibilities of the group. Patricia Mohammed (1996), for example, intelligently points out that poor and destitute men are, and have always been, victims of other men.

In 1987 Connell (quoted in Kimmel 1997) borrowed from Antonio Gramsci (1971) the concept of "hegemony" to be applied to gender relations. Gramsci understood this as a cultural dynamic by which a group demands and sustains a position of leadership in social life. Connell (1997, 34–40) defined hegemonic masculinity as the "*image* of masculinity of those men who control power" (my emphasis). He understood this concept as "the configuration of gender practice which embodies the currently accepted answer to the problem of the legitimacy of patriarchy, which guarantees (or is taken to guarantee) the dominant position of men and the subordination of women". Connell establishes the distinction between so-called hegemonic, accomplice (ally) and subordinate masculinities. He also emphasizes that the successful resort to authority, more than direct violence, is the mark of hegemony, although violence often underlies or sustains authority. For Connell, gender is a way of ordering social practice. He claims that "by adopting a dynamic view of social practice organization, we may reach an understanding of masculinity and femininity as *gender projects*. Hegemonic masculinity is not a kind of fixed character, but a model of gender relations, an ever-contestable position, historically mobile" (Connell 1995, 76–77).

Kimmel (1997) also states that virility is not static or timeless, for it is a set of always changing meanings, constructed through men's relations with themselves, with other men and with the world. In this sense, it could be hypothesized that every individual might have multiple, situational and fluid masculine "identities" ("multiple selves", unstable and vaguely integrated identities, in Laclau's 1993 terms), which are discriminately displayed or attributed according to perceived characteristics of the actors and the requirements of the environment, as an endless power game. According to Mosse (1996), today's hegemonic masculinity is a stereotype transformed into the norm by the rising European bourgeoisie at the end of the eighteenth century. Connell (1997) applies the concept "legitimation crisis", also borrowing it from Habermas

(1976), to refer to attempts to restore a dominant masculinity. In Cruz-Malavé's terms, although masculinity keeps being hegemonic, the discourses that have traditionally validated it are in crisis (personal communication).

Kaufman adds, "much of what we associate with masculinity is based on a man's capacity to exercise power and control" (1997, 63). In Gilmore's words, "the image of masculinity confers respect to its carrier and security to his family, lineage or people, since these groups, by sharing a collective identity, reflect the reputation of the man and this reputation protects them" (1997, 83).

Davis (1977) and Gilmore (1997) state that in given contexts and cultures virility can be interpreted as a kind of moral obligation to provide for the family. This view, of course, is a specific historical and cultural outcome, far from being universal, as I intend to show in the next section. Gilmore studied Mediterranean masculinity, particularly in the south of Spain, where he identified four "types" of masculinities that do not meet the standards of dominant males. These are the adult bachelor, the married man without children, the father who spends "too much" time at home during the day and with women, and the "obvious" homosexual man.

Similarly, Norma Fuller writes that masculinity produces several "marginal versions" in Peru, corresponding to the different ways in which the male "does not attain or refuses to attain" what she calls "adult" masculinity. These versions are the *Don Juan* (womanizer), the irresponsible, the idealist, the sacred man and the delinquent, "among others". For her, "these are the phantom-frontiers against which every male constitutes the script of his gender identity" (1997, 147).

Masculinities and the *Casa/Calle* Divide

Two opposite *and* complementary cultures constructed around the stereotypes of the household and the street as sacred and profane spaces, respectively, constitute the guiding principles of most political and social life in the Dominican Republic. In these two cultures, notions of social class intersect with ethnicity and race. The ruling class attempts to champion the sacred (respectable) component while the oppressed classes are expected to vindicate its profane (reputation) counterpart. Of course, both classes reserve the right to conveniently endorse the values and norms of the opposite and complementary culture when opportune, in a kind of yin-yang interaction. According to Fuller (1997) the household, the inner aspect of life, is feminine. It is the reign of the wife and the mother. The street is masculine, and men belong to it. The dual nature of masculinity allows men to circulate through both worlds, at the same time keeping the monopoly of the street.

The household space is seen as the one that defines those actions and institutions that are socially sanctioned by the dominant ideology. This space encompasses social institutions such as marriage, the nuclear family, dominant religions (Catholic and Christian), formal economy, private and official educational institutions, heterosexual sexual practices, and traditional gender roles and mores (Cáceres et al. 1998).

In popular ideology, on the other hand, the street space is a direct contradiction to this. Streets are ruled by the "other", "the Man" (Cruz-Malavé 1996). This space sets the limits on those institutions, practices and situations that are not officially sanctioned, such as the informal economy, the sex industry, extramarital relations and *tigueraje* (tiger-like behaviour; shrewd and slick opportunistic predators). Family, fidelity, seriousness, and respect for institutions and dominant values are not prominent in the street space. On the contrary, these are consistently subverted, and the man "gets vacations" from the ties that join him to the sobriety of the household, through participation in street activities (Cáceres et al. 1998).

Notions of honesty, fidelity and trust, established within the household space, are ethical values vested with much social meaning and seen as necessary for establishing conjugal relations. The collective appreciation of these values coexists, in a contradictory way, with equally rooted cultural ethics of the inherent unfaithfulness of men. At the same time that trust and fidelity are valued, it is acknowledged that men are "naturally" unfaithful (Cáceres et al. 1998).

The Christian ideology of monogamous marriage as a sacrament emphasizes values such as premarital chastity, the nuclear family, fidelity, motherhood, and care of children and elders, among others. This conjugal arrangement is understood in the country with a marked double standard. Highly differentiated and unequal gender roles are frequently emphasized. Women place their loyalties at the service of their husbands, children and households, while men can place loyalties both at home and in the street, trying to strike a viable balance between the two sets of moral ideals.

The wife, when financially dependent on her husband, may understand marriage as a kind of lottery, where she could have the *mala suerte* (ill fate) that he may not comply with her social-class role expectations, in the sense that he may abide more by the rules of the street. In the more traditional and rural culture the man can be a *mujeriego* (womanizer), *gallero* or *jugador* (gambler), and *borrachón* (heavy drinker). The traditional wife has to resign herself to this, raise *her* children (with "true" household values and norms) and be conformist with "God's will", until the husband *siente cabeza* (appeases himself), which usually occurs around his andropause ("male menopause"), if ever. These meanings are hard to extricate from Christian values, and reflect the strong influence of Judaeo-Christian archetypes such as the original sin, the weakness of flesh, and the woman as a seducer (Cáceres et al. 1998).

Upon looking at Dominican masculinity as part of the "problematic of legitimation" for men, and at labels used throughout the *casa/calle* divide, consensus on three general themes seems to be evident. These themes are the following: (1) Men are the "exact opposite" of women, whatever any or both of them could be. (2) Procreation is a necessary but insufficient condition for legitimizing masculinity. And (3) homosocial relations among men are experienced as competitive gendered relations in terms of domination-subordination, at least at the "definitory stage" of new dyadic relationships, where they establish, probably on an unconscious basis, who is "the male" (leader, initiator) and who is "the female" (follower) among them. As suggested before, each man's positioning in the dyad will be dependent on the power he displays in the interaction.

Masculinity, Virility and Manhood: Tigers and Lions in the Gender Jungle

Although gender work seems to be relatively generalized for the social-ization of boys, a major distinction between the cultural perspectives of the household and those of the street seems to exist. Masculinity, viril-ity and manhood have usually been regarded as synonyms, but the two cultures, according to the differential power associated with social class, seem to invest those concepts with distinct meanings, apparently based on ancient archetypes of social life patterned on the mythical "laws of the jungle".

The street culture, consistent with the claim of the profane, empha-sizes the notion of "maleness" or "virility", understood here as chasing behaviour and showing male potency. This culture, contrary to the obser-vations of Davis (1977) and Kimmel (1997) in the Mediterranean, is rel-atively unconcerned with family duties, probably as a defence against political and economic powerlessness. The *tíguere* (Bengal tiger or American jaguar), shrewd and fast, is the icon of this culture, waiting for its opportunity to act.

The origins of this mostly transgressive culture in the Dominican Republic are probably related to a history of slavery, oppression and political instability, but few studies have been conducted in this regard. Krohn-Hansen (1996), for example, states that the Dominican *tíguere* is the product of a protracted national history of political turbulence and repression. The label *tigre* was also used in Cuba before 1959, and is presently used as *títere* in Puerto Rico. Collado (1992) dates the height of the "cult of the *tíguere*" in the Dominican Republic to "*Generalísimo*" Trujillo's rule. A closer historical look, nonetheless, suggests that terms used in previous centuries, such as Carib, *criollo* (creole), *cimarrón* (maroon), *alzado* (bushman), pirate, *bandolero* and *gavillero* (bandit), and *machetero* ("macheteer") may convey similar transgressive mean-ings.

On the other hand, the household culture, consistent with the claim of the sacred, emphasizes the notion of *hombría* (manliness or man-hood), understood here as courage, determination and power, closely related to provision of resources for the family ("responsible father-hood", for instance). The *león* (African lion), as the king of the jungle, *comehombre* (ready to eat men) and prepotent, is its symbol. This has historically been the general authoritarian attitude of the Dominican ruling class. Interestingly enough, the two main professional baseball teams in Santo Domingo are the *Tigres del Licey* (Licey's Tigers) and the *Leones del Escogido* (Chosen Lions).

Masculinity Categories, Subcategories and Labels

Manifestations of virility and manhood combine in multiple ways to produce an attribution of the "kind of man" any male is. This is probably also true for the virilized female, a theme that I will address below.

In terms of research methods, around one-third of the labels for masculinities collected come from my personal fieldwork during the last three years. In this regard, I have made many participant-observation sessions of informal homosocial and heterosocial gatherings in public places. I have also initiated many informal conversations on this topic, for example, in public transportation facilities (buses, *carros públicos*), and interviewed many individuals of both sexes, Dominican and foreign, in different social class, sexual orientation, ethnicity/race and age groups. Another third of the data was retrieved from a lifetime of memories and experiences, and validated through informal group discussions with men and women. The last third, mostly material from the first seven decades of the twentieth century, was abridged from a broad study of the Dominican vocabulary (Rodríguez Demorizi 1983).

From this triangulation of sources, four main inductive categories of masculinity, primarily based on the perception of sexual orientation, arose and are discussed in this section. Some of the categories proposed by Connell (1997), Gilmore (1997) and Fuller (1997), based on Mediterranean and Latin American experiences, were found in this research in the Dominican Republic.

These categories are "hegemonic" masculinities, "subordinate" masculinities, "marginal" masculinities and "residual" masculinities. They can be depicted as concentric circles centred on the notion of power and control, superimposed on the yin-yang dialectic of the household and street cultures. Hegemonic masculinities are those shown by both virile and manly, exclusively heterosexual men, who are regularly called "true" or "real" men in everyday conversation.

Next, the category of subordinate masculinities emerges. For purposes of simplicity, I have divided subordinate men into heterosexual and bisexual, as two subcategories. This does not mean that I believe that they could really be separated as groups of special character, except in the mind of the dominant male. This issue, however, needs further research in terms of the attribution of potency and/or power to each of the many labels used within each category.

Subordinate heterosexual men are regarded as "still-men", but not "true" or "real" men. Subordinate bisexual men are regarded as "not real men" or "charlatans". At the next layer there is a marginal category that comprises "non-virile" and "non-manly", "effeminate" men, homosexual by choice, stereotypically perceived and treated by hegemonic males as females or "social women". I finally propose a residual category, which includes "mannish" females (not necessarily lesbians), virilized by attitudes, hormones or medication, stereotypically regarded and treated by hegemonic males as males or "social men".

I have identified an exuberant array of more than two hundred labels, and tried to classify them according to the four categories used to refer to dynamic social representations of masculinities in the *casa/calle* divide, which are defined in power relations within a constantly changing and conflictive field. In this section I attempt to make an initial description of this classification. This typology should allow us to venture into future analyses of the likely relations between pairs of labels within and between subcategories and categories within concrete contexts and situations (such as the case of *el venao*), thus retaining their density, plurality and conflictiveness. In each category and subcategory I present, first, labels indistinctly used in both cultures, if any, and second, labels used exclusively in each one. This approach, of course, will need further examination in concrete, ongoing social relationships between men.

Hegemonic Heterosexual Masculinities ("True, Real Men")

Hegemonic heterosexual masculinities characterize dominant men. In the street and household cultures no common labels seem to be used for hegemonic masculinities. This is consistent with our claim that different emphasis (virility versus manhood) is put in each perspective. In the household culture the expressions *hombre serio* (truly straight, "serious man"), *hombre de palabra* (man of words), *hombre de pelo en pecho* (daring man) and *padre de familia* (*pater familias*, Roman patriarch) are used. Any dominant male in the ruling class can be referred to by any of these labels, which convey respect and deference. A man in this rank is usually addressed as *señor don* (roughly equivalent to "His Honour" or "Sir"). He is frequently appointed to political positions that need an image of administrative honesty and determination, and is then referred to as *hombre público* ("public man") or *político* (politician), the most powerful of men.

Three decades ago the words *tutumpote* (*totum potens*, omnipotent man) or *burgués* (bourgeois) were frequently used in a despondent way to designate very rich and powerful men. The word *cacique* (Indian chief) is customarily used for local community leaders or otherwise powerful and rich men in Dominican towns. Nowadays the terms *ejecutivo* (executive) and *empresario* (entrepreneur) are used as synonyms for powerful men.

All men in this household-culture category are embodiments of the Father figure in the ideology of the patrifocal Christian Sacred Family. They are exclusively heterosexual and nominally monogamous, fathering children of both sexes who are kept and educated at least until eighteen years of age or until marriage. Sporadic or recurrent unfaithfulness to one's wife, or having a mistress and children, may be a common power display, as part of a certain transgressiveness allowed to the hegemonic male (the "street vocation", the "weakness of the flesh"). Men's loyalty is directed towards their children, mostly to boys, who are supposed to "inherit" their father's masculinity (Cáceres et al. 1998).

In the street culture there are several labels that represent hegemonic males. These are the *macho proba'o* (tested male), the *tíguere-gallo* (rooster-tiger), the *barraco* or *verraco* (male swine), the *pato macho* (male duck, head of the flock), the *machazo* or *macharrán* (supermacho), the *braga'o* (firm, lecherous) and, more recently, the *güebú* (large penis), *machomén* and *machómetro* (male's measure). These seven are supposed to be exclusively heterosexual, and often have multiple serial and/or simultaneous female partners. They usually father children to several women and regularly fail to provide for children's well-being and education. Among descendants of Haitian migrants, the words *papá bocó* (*bokor*, *shaman*) and *lugarú* (*loup-garoux*) are also used, the last with the same meaning as *comegente* (being ready to eat people). These men impersonate the "Absent Father" figure in the ideology of the matrifocal serial monogamous family, headed by a woman who bears children by different fathers (Cáceres et al. 1998).

Other labels for relatively successful men in the street culture also entail virility and potency. Here I found the words *toro* (bull), *bilíguer* (big leaguer, extraordinary man) and *bichán* (big champ, champion) which have become old-fashioned. Present labels are *líder* (leader), *jefe* (chief), *duro* (hard), *comando* (commando), *mayimbe* (charismatic leader, usually a *merengue* or *bachata* musician or artist followed by many feminine fans), *caballo* (horse, stud), *bacano* (star, sex symbol), *pachá* (*bon vivant,* sheik) and, more recently, *matatán* (lady killer).

Subordinate Heterosexual Masculinities

Many heterosexual males can be classified as subordinate to hegemonic males; that is, they occupy a second position in the hierarchy. I have divided this category into four subcategories of labels for less powerful heterosexual men, according to terms used by ordinary people. These are *hombres incompletos* (incomplete men), *hombres en apariencia* (virtual men), *hombres sospechosos* (dudes), and *sobrevivientes* (survivors) and *fracasados* (losers).

Hombres Incompletos *(Incomplete Men)*

In both the household and the street cultures some men are not regarded as "complete" or hegemonic, because some deficit is attributed, mostly to their virility. This is very close to the observations of Gilmore (1997) on Mediterranean masculinity.

The first label found in this subcategory is the *hombre soltero* or *jamón* (pejoratively called "ham" or singleton), a bachelor or single adult man, over twenty-eight years of age, who has shown through the years that he is "incapable of forming and maintaining a family and a household" (Rodriquez Demorizi 1983). The second label is the *hombre casado sin hijos* (married man without children), seen as a family disgrace, a "product" of some ancestor's phallic deficit or mother's infertility. The third is the *hombre que sólo da hijas* (*chancletas*) (man that procreates only daughters, called "sandals"), seen as a signal of male weakness, phallic deficit or female dominance.

Hombres en Apariencia *(Virtual Men)*

Some other men are neither "true, real men" nor "incomplete" men. They are "virtual" men, only "appearing" or "looking" like men. On closer inspection they "behave as women", that is, are probably cowardly, shy and not aggressive. This is Gilmore's (1997) man who prefers to stay at home, called *casero* (homely), or to be with women, called *faldero* (surrounded by women's skirts) or *embatola'o* (wearing a woman's frock) in the Dominican Republic. This subcategory includes passive men, weak men, "unimportant" men, short men and cuckolds. Several defiling labels for these men are used, mostly in the household culture, mainly as they show lack of power, courage and determination.

Passive men. The terms found in this group are *pariguayo* (jerk, clumsy, slow); *manilo* (large, clumsy rooster); *mamita* (undetermined); *mamao* (good-for-nothing); *bolsa* (scrotum); *bolsón* (big good-for-nothing); *tipito* (little guy); *m'hijo* and *mi'jijo* (my child); and *ñemón* (dumb, "big glans"). Also *pendejo, pendengo, penderengue* (coward, literally "anal hair"); *pendejón* (big chicken); *gallina* (hen); *gallo pelón* (dull rooster); *ñoño* (spoiled brat); *guanajo* (simpleton); *beato* (pious man); and *santo* (saint, faithful man) are used for these men.

Men of weak character. These men are called *hombrecito* (little man); *medio hombre* (half-man); *pelele, mequetrefe, ñeñeñé, flin-flin* (whipster); *menea'o, de'telenga'o, flojo, blandito, bobalicón, acoña'o, tembleque* (flabby, wimp); *suave* (soft); *poquito* (few); *toto* (pussy-man); *totico* (little pussy-man); *pupú* (shit-man); *mojón* and *buena mierda* (big shit).

"Unimportant" men. Other terms are also used, mostly in the household culture, for men regarded as unimportant. These are the *insignificante* (insignificant), *pelagato* (cat-skinner) or *don nadie* (mister nobody); *infeliz* (unlucky); *carajo* and *carajo a la vela* (ordinary man); *bocón* (braggart); *buchi-pluma, allantoso* (pretender); *figurero* (show off); *fantoche* (puppet); *payaso* (clown); *boque-burro* (absurd); *loco viejo* (unpredictable); and *pobre diablo* (poor devil).

Small men. These are also regarded as lacking, and words such as *enano* (dwarf), *tapón* (shorty) and *pineo* (pygmy) are applied to them.

Cuckolds. Mostly in the street culture, labels used for less powerful heterosexual men mostly refer to victims of female infidelity, presumably as a result of lack of sexual potency. These labels are *cuernú* (cuckold) and *venao* (deer).

Hombres Sospechosos *(Dudes)*

Some men are regarded as "under suspicion" of not being real men. The main reasons for this are: (1) being delicate, handsome or physically attractive as a woman; (2) being dependent on mother or wife; and (3) being a gigolo (living off women). In other words, men should not be either too handsome or financially dependent, as these are regarded as feminine traits.

Delicate and attractive men. In the household culture, the delicate types are *príncipe* (prince, magnificent); *caballero* (*cavalier,* gentleman); *dama* (lady, delicate, soft-spoken, kind man); *señorito de su casa* (homeboy, virginal boy); *pichirilo* (*petit-maitre*); *cura* (priest) and *sacristán* (sexton). The attractive ones are *gallo* (rooster), *pollo* (chick); *pepillito, lindo, lindón, lindoro, buenmozo, priti* (good looking, handsome, pretty boy); *belleza* (beauty); *muñeco* (doll); *carita de niño, carita lavada* (baby face); *osito* and *peluche* (teddy bear). All of these terms refer to lack of power. In the street culture we find the *chopero* (man who sexually likes female servants); *cuero macho* (male whore); *hembro* (male sexy as a female); *nalgú* (big buttocks); *bololo* or *gustavito* (man unusually attractive to women); and *paganini* (generous client of female sex workers). As expected, these labels relate to sex and potency.

Dependent men. In the household culture these men are "not real" or "not yet real". These are the *arrima'o* (loafer); *manganzón, tajalán* and *zángano* (big boy, slugger); *gevito* (lad, *ephebe*); *tineyer* (teenager); *muchacho, muchachito,* and *muchachón* (boy, big boy); *carajito* (child, childish, young adolescent, literally "small penis"); *monaguillo* (acolyte); and *pajuilito* (little peacock). More demeaning labels are *piojo* (louse); *mime* (small flying insect); *porquería* (pork shit); *culo-caga'o* (dirty asshole boy); and *pedazo de gente* (piece of a person). In rural areas the term *niño de oro* (golden boy) is similarly used. In the street culture we find the *vaca-muerta* (dead head), a man who, in a group, at the moment of paying for meals or other services, is always broke.

Gigolos. A label used in both cultures for heterosexual gigolos, but with different meanings, is *chulo* (pimp). In the household culture he is a man kept by a woman (power dimension), and is also called *rubirosa* (dandy), *prostituto* (prostitute) or stripper (if he is a dancer). In the street culture he is the lover (potency dimension) of one or more female sex workers, off of whom he usually lives. He is called *chulo, papi, papichulo, papi-de-nylon* (an outdated label) or *control*.

Sobrevivientes *(Survivors)* and Fracasados *(Losers)*

Men who are at the bottom of subordinate heterosexual categories of masculinity are seen as either *sobrevivientes* or *fracasados,* and are generally treated as outcasts, pariahs or non-persons. They generally have difficulty in finding and retaining female partners, mostly because of their social and economic powerlessness. Labels used for survivors in the household culture are *tíguere-tíguere* (tiger-tiger, reduplicated for emphasis; shrewd man); *tíguere bimbín* (phallic tiger); *verdugo* (scourge); *bárbaro, barbarazo* (barbarian); *perro* (dog); *tranca, trinquete* (stick, pawl); *liebre* (hare); *lince* (a keen-sighted man); *crápula* (scum); *plebe* (plebeian); and *lumpen.*

Labels used for losers or socially and economically debased men are *pata por suelo* (barefoot); *salta p'atrá* (regressive, less than ordinary); *pate-puerco, jocico'e'puerco, boque-burro, tarúpido* (stupid, retarded, ignorant, nonsensical); *hijo de Machepa* (son of nobody); and *limpia-saco, lambe-ojo, lambe-culo, tumba-polvo* or *lambón* (gross flatterer, inferior man). Also used for them are *seboruco, ñame con corbata, sarataco* (dumb man); *tarugo* (servile); *desbarata'o, pitifui* or *pitifuiche, fundillo vacío* (empty pockets); and *viralata* (stray dog). *Lambe-plato* and *muerto de hambre* (starving man); *purgón, plaga, ladilla, sanguijuela* (persistent beggar, plague, lice, leech); *vomitivo* (emetic); *tiesto* (potsherd); and *sorullo* ("ugly thing") are added to this group. *Chopo* (servant, maid, cook or gardener) is usually applied to ordinary and unsophisticated men dedicated to "feminine" tasks in domestic service.

Labels used for survivors in the street culture are *culebro* (male snake); *labioso* or *muelú* (eloquent, convincing); *bregador* or *jodedor* (fucker); *joseador* (hustler); *busca-vida* (go for, opportunist); *turpén* (daring); *brigán, levente* (rule-less); and *truchimán* (trickster, probably from the Arabic *turyuman* – see Rodríguez Demorizi 1983, 258–59). *Mangrino* and *palomo* (cock pigeon, street kid) are applied to a destitute child, adolescent or adult man working on the streets, runaway or homeless (de Moya 1989). *Buzo* ("diver", garbage collector) is a man who picks and separates garbage products (metal, glass, plastic, paper and food) from household refuse, and who lives in a dumping ground. *Mal nacío, mal parío* (ill bred) is someone who is alive "only by miracle".

Subordinate Bisexual Masculinities

Many men's apparent attraction to sexual partners of both sexes, and their presumed interest in sexually "subordinating" or being "subordinated" by other men via oral and/or anal penetration, appears to be socially understood as a test of their degree of masculinity. The merging of phallicism and homophobia has resulted in a peculiar construction of masculinity. This conception appears to be centred on how a male uses his anus rather than on how he uses his genitals, as only the male who is anally receptive *by choice* "loses" his masculine attributes (de Moya and García 1996).

In the household culture bisexual behaviour is not an easily conceivable notion, to the extent that such ambiguity is generally expelled on the basis of denial. In the Dominican Republic the hegemonic heterosexual male usually defines having sexual relations with both women and men as the attempt of a "really" homosexual man to deceive society about his sexual orientation. The labels found for this presentation of masculinity are *bisexual* or *ambidiestro* (ambidextrous); *redondo* (all-around); and *medio pájaro* (half-bird or half-queer). These men are identified as homosexual by choice, but most remain relatively clandestine (*tapados* or "closeted") if they want to enjoy part of the patriarchal dividend. To do so, they usually marry a woman and have children, but also engage in insertive and/or receptive sex for pleasure with gay males, and frequently pay subordinate bisexual or marginal homosexual men from the street culture for sex.

Interaction seems to be more complex in the street culture. Many men, mostly between seventeen and twenty-four years old, have sex relations with women and with men identified as homosexual (Ramah, Pareja and Hasbún 1995). For doing so, these bisexual men usually receive payment or a token as a destigmatizing device from men, that is, they always have sex *with* money, not necessarily *for* money, and as a rule they do not (publicly) adopt the anally receptive role. When involved in bisexual behaviour beyond age twenty-four, men are frequently referred to as "charlatans" (not serious), shameless men, not-good-as-men. They are generally seen as more despicable than subordinate heterosexual males, but less so than marginal homosexual men. De Moya and García (1999) explain that these bisexual men consider themselves as "normal", definitely heterosexual, and separate from the more "stigmatized" and "deviant" men who adopt the receptive, "feminine" sex role.

In the street culture we find several versions of bisexual masculinities, closely associated with sex work, shrewdness and *tigueraje*. First is the *hombre normal* (normal man) or *macho* (male, he-man). He has female partners with whom he practices vaginal sex for pleasure ("normal" sex), and may practice insertive oral and anal sex to paying male clients. He does not self-identify as either gay or a sex worker, since he is usually the insertive ("male") partner in sex and he "needs the money"; this is sufficient cultural justification. Second is the *heliogábalo* or *tíguere-rapa-tíguere* (tiger who penetrates tigers). He is a predominantly heterosexual male with multiple feminine partners who seduces heterosexual and bisexual subordinate men (mostly dudes and inexperienced sex workers) into receptive anal sex. He is not necessarily a sex worker, but an emasculating male.

Third is the *bugarrón or bugato* (bugger, sodomite, butch, hustler), *bugarroncito* (teenage bugger, beginner), or *bugarronazo* (professional hustler, veteran), variously named according to his age and expertise in sex work. He has sex with both women and men, but self-identifies as heterosexual. He usually has a steady feminine partner and girlfriends. He practises insertive anal sex both with men, for/with money, and with women, for pleasure.

The fourth is the *sanky-panky* (hanky-panky, beach boy, gigolo), with several variants: *sanky-sanky* (true beach-boy, professional gigolo), *sanky* (sporadic gigolo), *sanky chipi-chipi* (very poor, marginal gigolo) and *poli-panky* (policeman gigolo). Initially these beach boys perform as guides and escorts for foreign tourists. They soon become their friends, dancing and drinking partners, lovers, and frequently end up as their kept men or pimps, living off them. They can have sex with both women and men for/with money, and self-identify as gigolos and sex workers only among their peers. Having sex with men is not necessarily the rule for them, as this entails doing so clandestinely to avoid stigmatization. A few of them have become international gigolos, performing as models or strippers in discotheques of the United States and European countries.

Marginal Homosexual Masculinities

The emphatic social stigma attached to the homosexual identity in predominantly patriarchal societies imposes public silence upon sexual

relations between men. The stigma against male homosexuality partially results in the perception of this role as feminine, weak and lacking
power. These characteristics are understood as antagonistic to those possessed by the hegemonic, patriarchal male, self-described as "normal"
and respectable (Cáceres et al. 1998). Nonetheless, in the popular imagination angry homosexual men can be as brave, daring, dangerous and
jealous as angry women are supposed to be. In this regard, Cruz-Malavé
(1996) asks whether the homosexual man would be able to subvert the
structure that both repudiates him and absorbs him, a structure analo-
gous to our conception of an ambivalent homophobic-phallicist culture.

According to Fuller (1997) homosexuality is an ever-present phantom, which forms an intrinsic part of the constitution of the identity of
the gender role. This issue is more urgent during adolescence, when the
threat of being feminized acts as an attraction/repulsion pole. Similarly,
Connell asserts that homosexuality is the "cellar of all that is symbolically expelled from hegemonic masculinity" (1997, 40). As a result, from
the dominant point of view, homosexuality is easily assimilated to femininity. Cruz-Malavé puts it in a more radical tone when referring to
prisons:

> Dead man, spectre, the homosexual is a hole, and through that hole slips in
> all that otherness that the community seeks to repel, "treason", the porous,
> the permeable . . . . Sodomy is what subdues the subject, both what subjects
> and subjectifies him, fixing him into place within the network of distinctions
> of the prison system, assigning him a name and a space. (1996, 134–41)

In both the household and the street cultures, the words *pájaro* (bird),
maricón or *cundango* (faggot) and *mamagüebo* (cocksucker) are regularly used to designate in a pejorative way men who are homosexual by
choice. *Virao* and *volteao* (invert) are used infrequently nowadays. Some
of the most demeaning labels such as *manfloro, maca-grano, mama-
bolsa, maricón de orilla* (plebeian faggot) and *pingüino* (penguin) have
disappeared from people's talk in the last three decades. Other labels are
almost exclusively used in the household culture, namely *mujercita* (little woman); *afeminado* (effeminate); *afectado, amanerado* or *partido*

(womanish); gay; and *mariconazo* (big faggot). These men are usually *declarados* (out of the closet) and are assumed to adopt the receptive role in anal sex, although this is far from being a rule, especially in the times of AIDS.

In the street culture, mostly as a secret identifying code among male sex workers, the label *nueve* ("nine", perhaps in relation to "69" or reciprocal oral sex) is used to refer to foreign homosexual men, who are not necessarily effeminate. Three other labels are used in the local gay "environments" to designate homosexual men by choice. These are *loca* (crazy woman), *maricona* (queen or fairy, the "feminine" of the faggot) and *lonfa* (an old gay man).

Four other labels are reserved for gay preadolescent and adolescent males. *Loquita, pajarito, mariquita* and *mariconcito* (young bird, little faggot) are used in both the household and the street cultures. *Pajarita* and *pajarolita* (young "female" queen or fairy) are terms used only in the street culture. Depending on the tone of voice with which these words are uttered, they may signal contempt or complicity. Popular ideology asserts that many presumably gay boys (aged eight to twelve years old) "awake" to homosexuality when they are raped during childhood by adolescents or men who practise abuse and violence in their interest in virginity and juvenile sexuality. These *maniguas* (literally, "jungle's law" in ancient Taíno-Arawac language), individual or gang rapes, are supposedly caused by the provocative "feminine" behaviour (manners, gestures, speech, action) of those boys, who are blamed for being violated (Cáceres et al. 1998).

Also in the street culture there are the labels *bugarrona* and *bugaloca* (faggot who likes to penetrate male partners) and *marigarrón* (gay man who practises both sexual roles). These terms designate men who exhibit effeminate gestures and manners (are *declarados,* or "out of the closet"), but may seduce and have insertive anal sex with more masculine men. This tends to occur in vulnerable situations, such as the end of dancing parties when many men are drunk (and horny). The word *bugatriz* ("buggeress") is reserved for very masculine-looking men (for example, bodybuilders, gym boys) who are anally receptive in sex, and *tabarrón* is reserved for the bugger who may adopt both sexual roles.

Cruz-Malavé (1996) proposes that the "queen" and the "faggot" are not so much the antithesis of their "macho" characters and poetic personae as that "proximate other" in whose likeness the latter see reflected the catastrophic condition of their own manhood.

The *maipiolo* (procurer, bawd, intermediary, go-between) is usually the homosexual street equivalent of the heterosexual household *chopo*. Most often he is a middle-aged gay man, who receives the assignment of being the confidant of female sex workers in brothels, and the procurer between them and male clients.

In general, feminine behaviour in young males is repressed, silenced and expelled in the household culture as a broken taboo and a family stigma. In the street culture it is tolerated to the extent that it parallels (and sometimes excels) women's make-up, talk, gestures, poise and behaviour, provided that this behaviour does not compete with "true" females' appeal for their real or imaginary male partners, lovers and husbands. Paradoxically, feminine behaviour in boys with androgynous characteristics may be tolerated and even reinforced in this culture. This can occur under special borderline circumstances, such as being the only boy in a family of five or more sisters, or being the last boy in a long family (more than five to seven children) and, perhaps, being exceptionally endowed in his genitalia, that is, having a "sacred phallus".

It seems that mothers and/or grandmothers tend to rear these boys as social girls, probably to ensure their allegiance in old age. Girls will grow up and are expected to get married and be more loyal to husband and children than to mother and/or grandmother. Often grandmothers reserve these boys for companionship and exemplary socialization, that is, to be raised as *señoritos de su casa* (homeboys, virginal boys, previously discussed as dudes) (de Moya and García 1996). They will probably never get married nor have children, and if they do so, their main loyalty will be to the mother figure. This seems to be the exact continuation of what has been called the *berdache* or two-spirited person tradition.

This mostly Amerindian more is very much alive today in the Dominican Republic, and probably elsewhere in the continent and islands. *Travesti* (transvestite) or *draga* (drag queen) is a label used in both the household and the street cultures to designate these modern *berdaches* in urban areas. In the last twenty years, transvestites have become an important part of show business, sex work and nightlife in large Dominican cities. In the household culture the word *vestida* (cross-dresser) is frequently used for men raised as women, who presumably look, think and behave as such, often deceiving "real" men. Frequently many of them compete with each other to decide who most resembles a female. As a paradox, male group dominance and power is usually conceded to the one who shows as the most aggressively feminine.

In the street culture five other labels – *pájara mala* (evil female-bird), *maldita* (damned woman), *perra* (bitch), *puerca* (pig) and *venenosa* (venomous) – are also used either as a "recognition" or as an insult (depending also on tone of voice), mostly as an internal designation within transvestites' environments. Interestingly enough, about half of transvestites tend to adopt the insertive role in homosexual anal sex (de Moya and García 1996), via the partner's seduction or choice, or with publicly masculine steady partners (*maridos* or husbands), who are usually *bugarroncitos* (teenage buggers). Relationships between adult transvestites and adolescent male sex workers seem to be an important part of the street-culture construction of masculinity.

A special case of the *berdache* tradition is the *masissí calembé* (big-dick sissy), a homosexual Haitian, Dominican-Haitian or Dominican man in the agricultural sugar-cane colonies (*bateyes*), raised and treated as a social and most "expensive" woman in his/her community. It is not yet clear why and how a specific boy is picked to be socialized in this way, but he is frequently seen as the son and heir of a "mystery", *luá* (*loa*) or supernatural spirit. In other words, he is born with a "light", according to syncretic popular religiousness.

I have speculated that these newborns are probably the healthiest, largest and brightest in the community, as they will have to perform all the duties of several women, and that they also could have a large penis size, which is the meaning of *calembo* (tobacco loaf). This seems to be supported by the fact that she/he may also adopt the insertive role in heterosexual vaginal sex and homosexual anal sex, via the partner's seduction or choice. There is some evidence that these persons have parapsychological powers, undergo intensive trance experiences and are dedicated to shamanistic religious services such as divination, healing and counselling from puberty on.

A final label that is found mostly in the street culture within this broad marginal homosexual category is the *cambiada* (transgendered). They are men who say that they feel as "women trapped in masculine bodies", and endure cosmetic intervention or surgery for modifying the shape of breasts, eyes, nose and so on, without penis extirpation. Most of Dominican transgenders only go as far as putting on make-up, waxing or depilating, receiving hormone treatment, and implanting silicone and similar substances in their bodies to resemble females. Only a few transgendered migrants to the United States or Europe have become transsexuals, undergoing genital surgery, probably because of high economic costs, and primarily because of the social value of being a "phallic woman" in a phallicist-homophobic society.

Residual Masculinities

The final category, "residual masculinities", might look surprising and perhaps far-fetched for many readers, as it entails the stereotype of so-called viragos, virilized women or Amazons. They often develop masculine attitudes and secondary sexual characteristics, such as being deep mouthed, and having muscular strength, beard, mustache, and abundant hair on the chest and arms. Most Dominican women in this situation react with embarrassment, often waxing or depilating and decolouring facial and arm hair, although a few cultivate these traits, since some of these signs seem to be culturally invested with sensuality. It seems legitimate to us to include this category within masculinities, to the extent that men often tend to react to these women and label them as if they were competitive social men.

In both the household and the street cultures we encounter very demeaning labels attached to these women. In the household culture terms used are *hombruna* (mannish), *marimacho* (tomboy, butch), *machómetra* (macho's measure), *amachada* (mannish woman), *tortillera* and *cachapera* (dyke), and *lesbiana* (lesbian). In the street culture the labels are *machorra* (sterile), *maricona* (female faggot) and *bugarrona* (female bugger, lesbian-oriented female sex worker). In a sense, most of these labels are an extrapolation derived from their apparent similarity with men who have sex with men. No attention has been paid to studying and understanding the multiplicity of their true characteristics.

Women who have sex with women but do not exhibit masculine traits remain invisible and ignored. According to Young-Bruehl (2000), the "female homosexual, conceived as masculine and a competitor to the male, was and is more threatening to the patriarchal order than the woman she might compete for, so she had to be confronted as a stereotype before any more nuanced view of female homosexuality could emerge". We have found no label in the household culture for the "feminine" partner in the relationship (*femme* in English), except *la mujer* ("the" woman) and *carajita* (young girl), attesting to the invisibility of the role. The only street culture label that we have found is *bolola,* a very attractive young female.

The Dynamics of Hegemony

It remains in our research agenda to start untangling the likely relationships of men who receive specific labels with other men who "carry" the same or different labels, regarded as more, equally, or less virile and/or manly than them. For further research, Table 3.1 presents some tentative and rough ideas of what could probably happen when occupants of similar or different categories start relating to each other, and the likely course of the relationship. Relationships between men classified within each single category could be regarded as relatively symmetrical in terms of power. On the other hand, relationships between men belonging to different categories could be considered as relatively asymmetrical. Cultural and historical norms and expectations should pattern their interactions. In general terms, each dyadic relationship between men should be defined by their respective social positioning.

Symmetrical interactions should probably be initially ambivalent, and later on should turn to either cooperation, competition or no interaction (being friends, enemies or just acquaintances) in order to establish,

Table 3.1   Hypothetical Response Set of Masculine Categories in Dyadic
Relations

Categories	Heterosexual hegemonic	Heterosexual subordinate	Bisexual subordinate	Homosexual marginal	Residual
Heterosexual hegemonic	Ambivalence	Leadership/ deference	Despise/ submission	Repulsion/ Admiration, contempt	Curiosity, rage/ challenge
Heterosexual subordinate		Ambivalence	Admiration/ compassion, disdain	Repulsion, compassion/ rage	Rage/ compas- sion
Bisexual subordinate			Ambivalence	Exploitation/ attraction	Distance/ empathy
Homosexual marginal				Ambivalence	Perplexity/ distance
Residual					Ambival- ence

sustain or terminate a relationship that was not previously defined. Asymmetrical interactions may produce a host of reactions, depending also on the "historical etiquette" of these relationships.

I would expect that when most hegemonic men interact with heterosexual men perceived as subordinate, the first would adopt the role of leaders, whereas the second would display the role of deferent followers. When hegemonic men meet men labelled as bisexual (having sexual relations with both women and men), they would probably show disdain, while these bisexual men would probably show submission. When encountering men perceived as homosexual (orally and/or anally receptive in sex), the hegemonic would probably exhibit repulsion, while these homosexuals would show admiration or contempt, depending on the degree of rejection or acceptance of their sexual identity. With women labelled as virilized, hegemonic men would probably display curiosity and then rage, while these women would probably challenge their masculinity.

Subordinate heterosexual men would probably feel admiration for men labelled as bisexuals (as daring and courageous), who in turn may respond with compassion and disdain for these heterosexual men. For men perceived as homosexual, subordinate heterosexual men may show a mixture of repulsion and compassion, whereas homosexuals may exhibit rage towards them. For women labelled as virilized, subordinate heterosexual men would display rage, while these women would respond with compassion for them.

An illustrative case of the interaction of one of these women with hegemonic and subordinate males and females was found as part of our observations:

> Brunilda (not her real name) was an assertive Spanish globetrotter nurse in her mid-forties, visiting Santo Domingo for the first time. She was heterosexual but was physically virilized, apparently by prescription drugs. As a Mediterranean, she usually dressed in a white, semitransparent gown (*galabbeia*), and loved the streets. She displayed a long and visible goatee, shaved her head, and constantly demanded respect for her human rights. She was often also "noisy", and loved to recite flippant (anticlerical, antivirginal and proanal) poems learned as a child in Catholic nuns' schools in Spain. She also urinated in the street as men frequently do in the Dominican Republic. Most men (usually hegemonic and subordinate heterosexuals) showed much curiosity and were quickly attracted to her. Nonetheless, she soon violently clashed in conversation with individuals from both groups, in a competition geared to demonstrate who was more of a man between the two; often the conversations threatened to become fights. Women usually feared her and fled from her because of her cavalier manners, pressing courtesy and deceitful seductiveness, perceiving her as a likely lesbian.

Many bisexuals seem to relate to men labelled as homosexual mostly in an exploitative manner, while most homosexuals respond to them with erotic attraction and an ingratiating demeanour. As an example, gay men frequently pay men self-defined as heterosexual for having sex, thus accepting the "gendered" definition of the relationship, but sometimes they expect to reverse the situation. With females labelled as virilized, bisexual men tend to maintain a distance, not to look suspicious to hegemonic men, while these women show some empathy and identification with them. Finally, when men labelled as homosexual meet virilized women, they reveal perplexity and sometimes fascination, while these women tend to keep a distance from them, not wanting to be confused as their allies.

Conclusion

Throughout this chapter I have tried to show how masculine identity is an important part of the "problematic of legitimation" for political and social life in the Dominican Republic, opening or closing opportunities for men's personal endeavours. Masculinity is thus a totalitarian notion that produces intricate strategies (power games) for men to oppress other men and to prevent oppression by them. In a sense, every dyadic relationship between men seems to be "gendered" or rank-ordered by actors' characteristics and behaviour. The outcome, of course, is a multiplicity of (situational) masculine identities displayed by each man.

Masculine identities can be said to be fragile since they do not depend only on a man's behaviour, but also on the ways other men and women relate to him or to "his" women. I illustrated this basic point with two examples of collective behaviour, in which the reputation of men had been questioned and easily destroyed by the accusation of being the victims of adultery, which for men is equal to becoming a woman, a contemptible situation. Symbolically threatening to emasculate each other (probably as a defence mechanism against anxiety) is a recursive, pervasive and deadly power game in this country. The 1930–61 dictatorship of Rafael L. Trujillo was shown as a theatre-state in which hegemonic masculinity (and its inversion) was the star.

From early childhood, males are led to become self-conscious about those verbal and non-verbal behaviours which could lead others to suspect that they are not "true" or "real" men. This self-consciousness, which may become quasi-paranoid by adolescence for non-conforming males, is the product of an ongoing process of stringent, totalitarian "gender work", oriented towards the construction of a hegemonic male. In this process both men and women, young and old, relatives and strangers, probably under the lead of the mother, conspire to instil homophobia in the maturing boy (and may, paradoxically, increase the threshold of taboo homosexual – phallic – temptation). This irrational fear of becoming a woman, as I have said, of "degenerating", helps to compulsorily construct – and simultaneously deconstruct – exclusive heterosexuality.

I have termed as "hegemonic" these presumptive absolutely straight men, following Gramsci (1971) and Connell (1997). They are the ones who must produce and reproduce as a ritual the patriarchal power game of masculinities, primarily on the basis of sexual orientation. As a symbol, hegemonic men embody the measure against which all men will compare themselves. They have to define, patrol and preserve the borders of patriarchal "normalcy". That is why men in the Dominican Republic, probably from ancient times, have to be the "exact opposite" of women. They have to comply with the rules of sound, proven and "balanced-gender" fatherhood (that is, having children of both sexes), and should show that they are not less masculine than any other man in their own social position.

I have also tried to show that a necessary distinction for understanding Dominican and probably other Afro-Caribbean masculinities has to do with what I called social class and ethnicity/race culture (ethnoclass). This complex interplay broadly defines two intertwining, opposite *and* complementary cultures. The household culture is constructed around the concepts of the feminine, the sacred and the respectable. The street culture is built on the basis of reputation as well as the masculine and the profane. Then I argued that the household culture leans on the notion of *hombría* (manliness or manhood, for example, "responsible fatherhood") as a way to reproduce power through the family. Destitution and homelessness constitute emasculation for this culture. The street culture, on the other hand, is centred on the notion of *virilidad* (maleness or virility, that is, sexual potency). Female infidelity and male impotence, then, represent emasculation for this culture.

I proceeded to describe a hierarchy of categories, subcategories and labels used by ordinary people in the Dominican Republic for comparing men. The fact that most of the labels have been successfully translated from Spanish into English is a suggestion that this kind of taxonomy is probably not restricted to a few geographical or historical social realities. They do exist and are probably relevant elsewhere, although the premises for ranking men may be quite variable. In this sense, these categories are basically intended as an invitation for linguistic and ethnographic cross-cultural research, mostly in the Caribbean.

The four main categories of masculinities that I have proposed for analysis, primarily based on sexual orientation, are the hegemonic heterosexual, the subordinate heterosexual, the subordinate bisexual, the marginal homosexual and the residual virilized female. Subordinate heterosexual men, going by the proliferation of labels, seem to constitute the majority of males. They have been subclassified as: (1) incomplete men, (2) virtual men, (3) dudes, and (4) survivors and losers.

Finally I introduced the idea of analysing relations within and between dyads of labels, subcategories and categories in future research. This should be a promising step for understanding what Habermas (1976) has termed "legitimation crisis tendencies" in postmodernity, and prospectively looking at transformations of masculinities as ongoing processes. Such an ambitious project would probably shed much light on the dynamics of legitimating and simultaneously transgressing hegemonic masculinity. Although masculinity seems to keep being hegemonic, the discourses that have traditionally validated it are in crisis.

After this long journey of discovery, we feel that, some way or another, the masculinity-femininity polarity seems to be paradoxically reluctant to dissolve. This might be true to the extent that, consciously or unconsciously, we seem to help to keep the ghost of the patriarch alive in our minds, even when we question and attempt to deconstruct it.

References

Almoina, J. 1999. *Una Satrapía en el Caribe. Historia Puntual de la Mala Vida del Déspota Rafael Leónidas Trujillo.* Santo Domingo: Editora Cole.

Cáceres, F., et al. 1998. *Análisis de la Situación y la Respuesta al VIH-SIDA en la República Dominicana.* Santo Domingo: CONASIDA, ONUSIDA, AcciónSIDA, UNESCO and Profamilia.

Caroit, J.M. 1996. " '*El Venao*' ou le *merengue* qui tue". *Le Monde,* 20 May.

Collado, L. 1992. *El Tíguere Dominicano.* Santo Domingo: Editora Panamericana.

Connell, R.W. 1995. *Masculinities.* Berkeley: University of California Press.

———. 1997. "La organización social de la masculinidad". In *Masculinidad/es. Poder y Crisis,* edited by T. Valdés and J. Olavarría.

Santiago, Chile: Ediciones de las Mujeres no. 24, Isis Internacional/ FLACSO.

Cruz-Malavé, A. 1996. " 'What a Tangled Web!' Masculinity, Abjection, and the Foundations of Puerto Rican Literature in the United States". *Differences: A Journal of Feminist Cultural Studies* 8, no. 1.

Davis, J. 1977. *People of the Mediterranean*. London: Routledge and Kegan Paul.

de Moya, E.A. 1989. "La Alfombra de Guazábara o el Reino de los Desterrados". *Primer Congreso Dominicano sobre Menores en Circunstancias Especialmente Difíciles*. Paper presented at the conference Congreso Dominicano, Santo Domingo, 9–11 October.

de Moya, E.A., and R. García. 1996. "AIDS and the Enigma of Bisexuality in the Dominican Republic". In *Bisexualities and AIDS: International Perspectives,* edited by P. Aggleton. London: Taylor and Francis.

———. 1999. "Three Decades of Male Sex Work in Santo Domingo". In *Men Who Sell Sex: International Perspectives on Male Prostitution and HIV/AIDS,* edited by P. Aggleton. London: Taylor and Francis.

Fuller, N. 1997. "Fronteras y retos: varones de clase media del Perú". In *Masculinidad/es. Poder y Crisis,* edited by T. Valdés and J. Olavarría. Santiago, Chile: Ediciones de las Mujeres no. 24, Isis Internacional/ FLACSO.

Gilmore, D.D. 1997. "Cuenca mediterránea: la excelencia en la actuación". In *Masculinidad/es. Poder y Crisis,* edited by T. Valdés and J. Olavarría. Santiago, Chile: Ediciones de las Mujeres no. 24, Isis Internacional/ FLACSO.

Gramsci, A. [1929–35] 1971. *Selections from Prison Notes*. New York: International.

Habermas, J. 1976. *Legitimation Crisis*. London: Heinemann.

Kaufman, M. 1997. "Las experiencias contradictorias del poder entre los hombres". In *Masculinidad/es. Poder y Crisis,* edited by T. Valdés and J. Olavarría. Santiago, Chile: Ediciones de las Mujeres no. 24, Isis Internacional/FLACSO.

Kimmel, M.S. 1993. "Masculinity as Homophobia". In *Cracking the Armour: Power, Pain and the Lives of Men,* edited by M. Kaufman. Toronto: Viking Canada.

———. 1997. "Homofobia, temor, vergüenza y silencio en la identidad masculina". In *Masculinidad/es. Poder y Crisis,* edited by T. Valdés and J. Olavarría. Santiago, Chile: Ediciones de las Mujeres no. 24, Isis Internacional/FLACSO.

Krohn-Hansen, C. 1996. "Masculinity and the Political among Dominicans: The Dominican Tigre". In *Machos, Mistresses, and Madonnas: Contesting the Power of Latin American Gender Imagery*, edited by M. Malkaus and K.A. Stolen. London: Verso Books.

Labelle, M. 1987. *Ideologie de couleur et classes sociales en Haïti*. Montreal: Presses de l'Université de Montréal.

Laclau, E. 1993. "Power and Representation". In *Politics, Theory and Contemporary Culture*, edited by M. Poster. New York: Columbia University Press.

Leverenz, D. 1991. "The Last Real Man in America: From Natty Bumppo to Batman". *American Literary Review 3*.

Mamet, D. 1993. "What Men Need Is Men's Approval". *New York Times*, 3 January.

Mohammed, P. 1996. "Unmasking Masculinity and Deconstructing Patriarchy: Problems and Possibilities within Feminist Epistemology". Paper presented at the symposium The Construction of Masculinity: Towards a Research Agenda, Centre for Gender and Development Studies, University of the West Indies, St Augustine, Trinidad.

Mosse, G.L. 1996. *The Image of Man: The Creation of Modern Masculinity*. New York: Oxford University Press.

O'Connell Davidson, J., and J. Sánchez Taylor. 1999. "Fantasy Islands: Exploring the Demand for Sex Tourism". In *Sun, Sex, and Gold: Tourism and Sex Work in the Caribbean*, edited by K. Kempadoo. Lanham, Md.: Rowman and Littlefield.

Ramah, M., R. Pareja, and J. Hasbún. 1995. "Dominican Republic: Lifestyles and Sexual Practices Results of KABP Research Conducted among Homosexual and Bisexual Men". In *Inventario de Recursos de Investigación en SIDA. América Latina y el Caribe (1991–1994)*, Washington: OPS/OMS [PAHO/WHO].

Rich, A. 1993. "Compulsory Heterosexuality and Lesbian Existence". In *The Lesbian and Gay Studies Reader*, edited by H. Abelove, M.A. Barale, and D. Halperin. New York: Routledge.

Rodríguez Demorizi, E. 1983. *Del Vocabulario Dominicano*. Santo Domingo: Editora Taller.

Wayne, K. 1912. *Building the Young Man*. Chicago: A.C. McClurg.

Young-Bruehl, E. 2000. "Beyond the Female Homosexual". *Studies in Gender and Sexuality* 1, no. 1.

PART TWO

Gender Socialization, Educational Performance and Peer Group Relations

CHAPTER 4

Boys of the Empire

Elite Education and the Construction of Hegemonic Masculinity in Barbados, 1875–1920

AVISTON D. DOWNES

Attempts at "engendering" history in the anglophone Caribbean over the past two decades have concentrated almost exclusively on retrieving Caribbean women from historical "invisibility" (Brereton 1988, 123–41; Brereton 1992; Beckles 1995b, 125–40). However, there is a growing body of historiographical literature which suggests that men and masculinity remain obscured, in spite of the predominant androcentric authorship within the discipline of history. Gisela Bock, for example, has argued that "questions about gender have mainly focused on the female sex, on the 'woman question'. Men appear to exist beyond gender relations to the same degree that they dominate them" (1989, 17). Similarly, John Tosh has observed for Britain that "in the historical record it is as though masculinity is everywhere but nowhere" (1994, 180). Beckles, in his assessment of the historiography of Caribbean slave societies, posits that historians of this period have traditionally utilized a corpus of archival sources which "says considerably more about enslaved women than it does about enslaved men. The slave male, in fact, is the one who was rendered largely invisible" (1996, 5).

Concepts of "visibility" and "invisibility", then, are theoretically and methodologically limited and cannot advance the intellectual discourse on gender in Caribbean history beyond the retrieval stage. Moreover, Caribbean "women's history" has focused on the commodification of the black woman's "biology", and to complement this with "men's history" will not necessarily extricate the discussion from the predominant paradigm of "sex". If the "engendering" of Caribbean history is really to be completed, the study of masculinity must be given its due attention. However, this agenda should be pursued in the context of a "gender history" which opens vistas on how Caribbean "women" and "men" were both socially and discursively constructed.[1]

A methodological advance from the reclamation stage also necessitates a theoretical shift from the "additive" paradigm. It is evident from the Caribbean context that race and class – at least – are integral to any understanding of gender constructs. But neither the class-reductionist nor the "add gender and stir" approach is adequate. Reddock has suggested that "the major emphasis may not be in locating a person within a hierarchy of oppressions but in conceiving the extent to which each of these mechanisms of oppression/exploitation impinges on the other and determines the way in which the other is experienced" (1993, 52).

Brewer also rejects the "additive" approach and advocates analyses which recognize the "simultaneity" of these forces (1993, 27–28). Similarly, Lorber and Farrell argue that race, class and gender operate in a synergistic fashion as vehicles of oppression (1991, 9).

Hegemonic Masculinity

Kimmel has noted that "masculinity and femininity are relational constructs, the definition of either depends upon the definition of the other" (1989, 12). The "othering" process which gives birth to gender identities can only be usefully studied in concrete historical contexts, with all the complexities inherent in social relations. Hegemonic masculinity is a discursively constructed masculinity which gains and maintains its pre-eminence through its ideological linkages with socially dominant men. Whereas the masculinity of superordinate men secures legitimacy and normative status, oppressed men have their masculinity either devalued or negated. As Messner and Sabo point out, "hegemonic masculinity is constructed in relation to various subordinated masculinities as well as in relation to femininities" (1990, 12). Indeed, for any representation of masculinity to become hegemonic, the co-optation or complicity of "lesser masculinities" is necessary. The consequence is empowerment of most men over women, but a control predicated also on the control of men (Donaldson 1993, 655; Carrigan, Connell and Lee 1985, 551–604).

Gender is not an integral part of Gramsci's conceptualization of hege-mony. Nevertheless, his identification of the education system, church and other vehicles as critical purveyors of ruling-class hegemony is rel-evant to an understanding of hegemonic masculinity. This chapter will examine how the education system of Barbados with its imperial dic-tates, and its functional linkages with Euro-Christianity, contributed to the creation of a version of masculinity intended to sustain the domi-nance of white ruling-class men.

The appropriate values of colonial hegemonic masculinity were those represented by the English gentleman, since historically creoles were viewed as inferior to their metropolitan cousins. The features of hege-monic masculinity, then, were precisely those which were privileged with-in England in the Victorian and Edwardian periods: sociopolitical leadership; economic dominance; heterosexuality; headship of nuclear family; chivalric defence of property, empire and family. Moreover, there was a renewed emphasis on physical prowess, expressed in sports and war, which served to reinforce the "naturalness" of male power. This expression of masculinity was also aggressive, racist and expansionist, but Euro-Christianity played a pivotal role in lending moral authority to this version of masculinity.

Colonial Education Ideology

While there is already a rich body of English historiography which has addressed the development of imperial masculinities in the English public school system (Mangan 1981, 1985, 1988a, 1988b; MacKenzie 1984; Mangan and Walvin 1987), there are few studies written from the experiences of the colonial British West Indian periphery. Historical research on education in the Caribbean has been preoccupied with government policy, access and formal curricula, to the exclusion of cocurricular activities and the culture of schooling. However, this chapter contends that it was through activities organized outside the formal classroom that educators were very successful in inculcating desired gender identities and imperial loyalty.

Historians of West Indian colonial education agree that colonial educational systems were underpinned by an agenda of social stability, rather than one for social change. The implementation from 1878 of the recommendations of the Bishop Mitchinson Commission Report (1875) in Barbados established the basis of the "modern" education system in Barbados. Deteriorating socioeconomic conditions in the island created fertile ground for social unrest, which the 1876 Confederation riots fulfilled. The reason for improving the education system was, in part, to create a small, educated, non-white middle class to serve as a social buffer between the agro-commercial bourgeoisie and the masses. It was envisaged that "a few well selected examples", elevated from their working-class origin, "would secure general conformity to the law from the rest", and that the local elite, like England's hereditary aristocracy, would be strengthened by the co-optation of this new middle class (MCA 1874–75, pt. 2, app. X, 4–5).

The ever-declining fortunes of the sugar industry in the latter half of the nineteenth century prompted changes in the ownership and control of that enterprise elsewhere in the British Caribbean, but in Barbados the planter class consolidated itself through an accommodation with the merchant class. The numerically declining white elite recommitted itself to ensuring the hegemonic entrenchment of anglocentric culture which reinforced the superiority of whiteness. During the heyday of the sugar industry, planters sent their boys to the best English schools and universities to validate their Englishness. As one beneficiary noted, "My father brought up his eight children and sent me to Oxford on an estate of only one hundred acres" (PP 1898 [C–8650–29], LIX, 17). Late-nineteenth-century economic woes resulted in the white elite's support for transforming some local schools, formerly established for the "lesser whites", into elite institutions fashioned after the English public-school pattern.

Foremost among these schools was Harrison College, which was founded as the Harrison Free School in Bridgetown in 1733, as a "Public and Free School for the poor and indigent boys of the Parish", but reorganized under an act of the legislature in 1870 as a "good grammar school" for the education of "the better classes". Harrison College became one of the two first-grade boys' schools in the island, catering to boys up to age eighteen and offering a curriculum firmly grounded in the classics. The task of transforming Harrison College was assigned in 1872 to Horace Deighton, a master of arts graduate (1854) of Queen's College, Cambridge.[2]

Deighton had already succeeded in making Queen's Royal College (formerly the Queen's Collegiate School) in Trinidad the premier elite school in that colony, during his tenure as head (1859–72). For the next thirty-four years, under Deighton, Harrison College consolidated its position at the apex of the island's school system, and also became one of the more reputable schools in the entire British colonial empire.

The other first-grade school was Lodge, which first opened in 1745 as the Codrington Grammar School and from its inception offered classics, mathematics, philosophy and religious studies. The Barbados legislature recognized it as a first-class grammar school in 1869 and as a first-grade school, as recommended by the Mitchinson Commission. The school catered primarily to the sons of the planters and their functionaries in the windward part of the island. The vicissitudes of the sugar industry, however, impacted on the consistent development of that institution. After a few closures and frequent change of headmasters, the fortunes of the school were reversed with the 1899 appointment, and subsequent thirty-two-year tenure, of O. Decourcy "Bill" Emtage. He had been a "Deighton boy" at Harrison College who won the Barbados

Scholarship to Oxford in 1886, subsequently graduating with a first-class bachelor of arts in mathematics and a master of arts in physics. Under his leadership Lodge was permanently transformed into an institution modelled after the English public school, and it earned the reputation of the premier elite boarding school in the West Indies (Foster 1891, 426; LSR 33, 1943, 7; Hoyos 1945, 48; Hoyos 1953, 125–29).

Whereas Harrison College and Lodge catered for the boys of the upper and upper-middle strata of planters and merchants, Combermere School, reorganized in 1879 to replace the old Central Boys' School in Bridgetown, emerged as the premier second-grade school in Barbados. Alleyne School in St Andrew, Coleridge School in St Peter and Parry School in St Lucy were three other government-supported second-grade boys' schools, but their contribution to the creation and expansion of a middle class paled in significance when compared to Combermere. Under the dynamic leadership of Bishop George Richardson Burton from 1897 to 1925, Combermere offered Spanish, French, shorthand, typing, book-keeping and commercial arithmetic, thus orienting the curriculum to prepare Combermerians for the expanding Bridgetown-based commercial sector (Sandiford and Newton 1995, 26–33). The school therefore became the mecca and nursery for the rising urban and peri-urban poor white and non-white middle class. By 1899 it had 127 pupils; from the 1900s its enrolment began to surpass that of Harrison College, and did so consistently after 1910.

But, while secondary education for boys resulted in the growth of a male middle class, secondary school opportunities remained restricted for girls (Cole 1982, 1–31; Drayton 1984; Mayers 1995, 258–75). The all-male Mitchinson Commission was unsure of the intellectual capacity of girls to pursue a curriculum similar to that for boys. Nonetheless, the commission was concerned that the "unsound", "flimsy" and "narrow" female education that was provided would prove inimical to the intellectual development of boys. Early child development depended on good maternal teaching, without which "it is idle to expect the boys in our first and second-grade schools to go there receptive of culture till this defect is remedied" (MCA 1874–75, app. X, 11). Middle and upper-class women were therefore perceived by dominant men as destined to be refined and respectable wives to enhance the status of their husbands and to nurture their sons for future leadership.

This ideology of male hegemony was entrenched by the persistence of limited access to secondary education for female students. Up to 1893 the first-grade school, Queen's College, was the only government-supported high school for girls, compared to six schools for boys: two first-grade and four second-grade. Queen's College's enrolment rarely exceeded a hundred and was limited to the daughters of the (mainly urban) agro-commercial bourgeoisie. The founding in 1894 of Alexandra School in the rural parish of St Peter only slightly increased the secondary school places for girls, but was insignificant in extending the class base of that education. Its enrolment averaged thirty-seven students; between 1894 and 1914 the daughters of eleven artisans and six shopkeepers were educated there, compared to 183 from planter and estate managerial backgrounds (Downes 1994, 170).

The roll of Victoria School for Girls, founded in St Andrew in 1898, never exceeded eleven, owing to the smaller and less viable planter base in that part of the island. Consequently, that school closed after its enrolment plummeted to six in 1903. Nevertheless, the gender bias in the education system is well illustrated by the fact that whereas Victoria was closed, Alleyne School in the same parish, with a similar enrolment profile, was spared. Clearly, then, the strengthening of the mainly white upper stratum of Barbadian society by a growing corpus of non-white middle-class functionaries was predicated on the intellectual empowerment of males. Not more than 1.5 per cent of the total school population up to 1911 received secondary education. But whereas 2.5 per cent of the male school population enjoyed secondary education, a meagre 0.6 per cent of the female school population so benefited.

Gender, Sport and Empire

But formal education was only a small part of the preparation of the middle and upper classes for their gendered destinies. The reorganization of the elite boys' schools in Barbados coincided with the emergence of "muscular Christianity" in the English public school. This philosophy encouraged the marriage of education, morality and physical strenuousness, expressed particularly in sport and typified by Thomas Hughes's *Tom Brown's Schooldays* (1857) (Winn 1960, 64–73; Newsome 1961; Mangan 1981). Although Sandiford and Stoddart (1987) have examined the evolution of this ethic in elite-school cricket in Barbados, in the context of colonial class and racial configurations, their analysis virtually ignores gender.

But it was the profound devotion to athleticism which was central to the cultic pursuit of manliness from the 1870s (Newsome 1961, 199). A major factor behind the relocation of Harrison College in 1871 from Spry Street, Bridgetown to its present location was to have access to a playing field, because

> such an adjunct is considered in the mother country to be absolutely necessary to the success of a good school for the following reasons – that it is in the playground that the manly bearing of the boys is encouraged and the master is enabled to see much of the habits and character of the boys; and that it would give a healthy tone to their training, in addition to their "intellectual culture". (Jemmott 1983, 12)

When Deighton arrived at Harrison College two years later, he vigorously pursued a programme which involved a commitment to sport, and wherever possible he encouraged the appointment of fellow muscular Christians to his staff. Lodge's financial difficulties had threatened the consistent development of the cult of athletic manliness, although the school had been a pioneer in cricket in Barbados. The school's eleven was in a premier position among the island's cricket clubs when the school closed in 1879. After it reopened in 1881 it struggled for over a decade to recapture its former cricketing glory, partly because the school did not insist on the recruitment of committed sportsmen, as Deighton of Harrison College did. "Whenever a new master arrived from England", R.H. Smith, a former cricket captain, recalls, "we used to collect in the porch in front of the school to see whether we could discover a cricket bag among his luggage, but we were disappointed each time" (1968, 100). Athleticism at Lodge was reinvigorated by the appointment of Bill Emtage as headmaster in 1899.

Combermere's second-grade status did not hinder the development of muscular Christianity in that school. The foundation of Christian manliness was established at Combermere by Reverend T. Lyall Speed, between 1879 and 1896, and consolidated under G.B.R. Burton, during his twenty-eight years of leadership there. As a former "Deighton boy" at Harrison College, Burton needed no further convincing of the importance of sport to character formation and masculine identity. Support for the almost obsessive devotion to manly sports in the elite schools of Barbados by the 1880s is illustrated by a letter from one correspondent, who argued that

> all enlightened parents . . . will know that the knowledge of foreign languages and Mathematics (however excellent that knowledge is in itself) is to be counted as nothing when compared with the moral training which we seek to instil in our little ones by means of the public schools, and that the play ground, and not the school desk, as [sic] the forge whereon the characters of our boys are principally moulded for their good. (*Herald,* 30 November 1885)

Cricket, especially, was represented as the quintessential manly sport. The Combermerian E. Dalyrmple Laborde stated while he was a master at the Lodge School:

> It [cricket] trains the boy to be a sportsman, thus giving him one of the essential qualities of a gentleman. Many a boy would mope around contracting selfish ideas in solitude, if he were not dragged into the society of his fellows by the influence of cricket. Through the same influence all selfish tendencies are eradicated before the youth leaves school. In other words cricket teaches a boy how to mix with his fellows, and, as a man, how to mix with men. (1910–11, 111)

Evidently, to be a "man" necessitated male homosociability; to be a loner or a "house boy" was to be "unmanly". According to Whitson (1990), sporting activity "has served as an important site in the construction of male solidarity, an institution that encourages men to identify with other men and provides for the regular rehearsal of such identification" (p. 21).

Moreover, cricket was said to be ideal training for future leaders. It inculcated "discipline, unity and responsibility – *esprit de corps*". To captain a cricket team provided an ideal opportunity to learn the leadership skills of responsible authority, stamina, courage and vigilance. As the sphere for the exercise and inculcation of these leadership values, the playing field itself was a metaphor for the colonial state. The playing fields of Harrison College, Lodge and Combermere were the nurseries for the training of the future leaders of Barbados. Good elite-school cricket was a measure of the viability of future leadership in the country. One commentator sensed that Barbadian civilization was under threat when, in the 1911–12 cricket season, the elite schools did not perform as expected. Aghast, he observed:

> The failure of Harrison College, the Lodge or the Combermere, to supply worthy recruits to the ranks of the adult clubs, is a much more serious happening than the failure to win a game would at first suggest. The form displayed at these schools from season to season is to us what the meeting of Oxford and Cambridge is to English cricket or Harvard and Yale to American baseball. (*Barbados Cricketers' Annual* 1911–12, 86)

The exclusion of women from active participation in both school and club cricket was an indication of their perceived intellectual inferiority and incapacity for public leadership. Although it was acceptable for women to play croquet, tennis or any other sport which emphasized their poise and grace, cricket was too physically manly, "intelligent and serious". The point was not lost on Penelope Lawrence, cofounder of Rodean School in Brighton, England. She stoutly argued that senior girls should also be exposed to "scientific" games like cricket because "a boy or girl who plays cricket enters a world larger than his or her own narrow sphere, and is induced to care for impersonal ends beyond the immediate circle of the home or school." After all, cricket was not confined to a small group; it was a national sport, "a strong social bond between the mother country and the colonies, between class and class, and race and race" (PP 1898 [C–8943], XXIV, II, 155).

In 1910 Helen Laborde headed a cricket team of girls from Queen's College, coached by Mike Mayers, but this seemed to be a one-off novelty game and no real challenge to elite masculinity (Queen's College 1982, 2). Women may have been kept beyond the boundary, but their presence in marquees, carriages or ladies' pavilions on the periphery was necessary to validate the masculinity of those chivalrous knights in white flannel jostling with willow and ball. As Percy Goodman asked rhetorically, "What is cricket without the ladies?" (*Barbados Cricketers' Annual* 1903–4, 54).

Cricket was also a celebration of heterosexuality and patriarchal nuclear-family values. There was complicity between white middle and upper-class men and their female partners in supporting this construct of hegemonic masculinity. White women, as Beckles observes, were "required to surround the game with an aura of respectability that represented a barricade designed to exclude men of other races" (1995a, 223–24). The annual reports of marriages and engagements of cricketers in the *Barbados Cricketers' Annual* are a good indication of how cricket provided a milieu for the marital consolidation of the plantocratic and mercantile bourgeoisie (Downes 1994, 249–50).

The fact that the playing field became the quintessential metonym and metaphor for war further entrenched most team sports as "defeminized" spheres. It did not matter that the Duke of Wellington never said that the "Battle of Waterloo was won on the playing fields of Eton" (Haley 1978, 161); headmasters of boys' schools rehearsed it at many speech days anyway. Aggression and war did not negate the construct of the English Christian gentleman. Indeed, from the period of the Crimean War, muscular Christianity and militant masculinity were beginning to converge. Charles Kingsley, one of the founding fathers of muscular Christianity, in his *Brave Words for Brave Soldiers,* exhorted: "the Lord Jesus Christ is not only the Prince of Peace; He is the Prince of War too" (cited in Winn 1960, 67). Many hymns of the period, such as "Onward Christian Soldiers", created an image of a "manly Christ" leading the saints to war (Tamke 1978, 150–55). Evangelism and imperialism could coexist without contradiction, and the masculine icon of the brave public school boy-soldier was born. Henry Newbolt powerfully captured this image in his "Vitaï Lampada", penned in 1898 on the eve of the South African War:

> There's a breathless hush in the Close tonight
> Ten to make and the match to win –

A bumping pitch and a blinding light,
An hour to play and the last man in.
And it's not for the sake of a ribboned coat,
Or the selfish hope of a season's fame,
But his Captain's hand on his shoulder smote –
"Play up! Play up! And play the game!"
The sand of the desert is sodden red, –
Red with the wreck of the square that broke; –
The Gatling's jammed and the Colonel dead,
And the regiment blind with dust and smoke.
The river of death has brimmed his banks,
And England's far and Honour a name,
But the voice of a schoolboy rallies the ranks:
"Play up! Play up! and play the game!"

This spartan-schoolboy-sportsman-soldier construct of masculinity, so common in late Victorian public schools (Mangan 1988a; Best 1975), is well illustrated by the Barbadian Robert Richard Challenor (*c.*1870–1902). His experience during the South African War in 1902 was a case of real life mirroring Newboltian poetry. Robert and his brother, Edward Lacy Challenor (1873–1935), fought with British regiments during the South African War. Both were "Deighton boys"; both were keen cricketers who played for Wanderers and subsequently for their regiments. Robert became a captain in the Lancashire Fusiliers and was sent to South Africa in December 1901. On the afternoon of 31 March 1902, Robert led a column of his soldiers which was hopelessly outgunned by 1,200 Boers. Nonetheless, he was reported to be "conspicuous in this crisis of the fight, giving hope and encouragement to those who were in reach of his voice". He shouted, "Play the game!" to one section of the battalion and continued (in "Vitaï Lampada" style) to encourage the ranks even after he was shot through the head. He was shot again, and that was the end of his innings and captaincy (Smyth 1904, 441). The sanitized, heroic account of Challenor's "gamesmanship" was a classic case of exemplary British imperial masculinity. As Mangan notes, "the national hero was now a warrior and a patriotic death in battle was the finest masculine virtue" (1995, 15).

By the end of the first decade of the twentieth century, a new militancy was also evident in Barbados Cup cricket, which puzzled some sections of the society still wedded to a fading idealistic version of Christian manliness. This militancy coincided with the crisis in local club cricket following Spartan's admission of a coloured working-class young man to its Cup Competition team in 1899. The admission of Fitz "Lilly" Hinds to the competition represented a breach in the hegemonic class and gender configurations of local cricket, which then slumped into "crisis" for four successive seasons. Many of the prominent gentlemen withdrew from the competition; fewer members of the "fairer sex" attended the matches, and others turned their attention to other sports like polo (Downes 1994, 241). The annual rivalry between Pickwick and Wanderers took a new twist in 1909, after a member of Pickwick was criticized for bowling over the head of a Wanderers batsman. In stout defence of this action, G.O'D. Walton argued that cricket

> is essentially a manly game played by men; there is nothing of the soft, or feminine about it, you must keep within the prescribed rules . . . . But within those rules you are entitled to use all your wits, every stratagem, coupled with your skill, to accomplish your object[.] Find out what is effective under the conditions present, and do it. Cricket of all games approaches nearer to the dread game of war, and herein lies the secret of its great hold on men. As in war, so in cricket, there is no mercy or quarter till you have won. (*Weekly Recorder*, 16 October 1909, 5)

The editor of the *Weekly Recorder* felt that this new approach would "lead to moral degeneracy in the youth", but he was clearly out of step with the times. Cricket, above all sports, retained its masculine codes by resisting technological changes. Whereas various new forms of vulcanized rubber revolutionized ball games in the late nineteenth century, the only change to the leather and cork cricket ball was the addition of a seam and a new finish (Sandiford 1984, 278). To face a "hard ball" speeding from the arm of a fast bowler was a sure test of masculinity:

> Who could, for instance, picture to his imagination the phlegmatic Dutchman, with his capacious round stern, chasing or sending the ball whizzing through the air like a cannon shot, and getting a run with the speed of a roebuck

. . . . The effeminate inhabitants of cloudless Italy, Spain and Portugal would sooner face a solid square of British infantry than an approaching ball from the sinewy arm of a first-class bowler. Instead of the bat, their backs would be turned for the purpose of stopping it. (Mandle 1973, 525)

While by 1860 the Americans had gone crazy about the faster-paced and innovative game of baseball (Kirsch 1989, 100–102), Britain and her cricket-loving colonies remained steadfast to king cricket because it best encapsulated the social Darwinism of British imperialism. Moreover, because of its serious didactic value it could not be rushed. Cricket was

an intricate and leisurely warfare, and the fact that every moment of it is equally fraught with possibilities and openings for glorious uncertainties makes it peculiarly the delight of intelligent observers, none of whom find dullness in the stubborn, defending his wicket successfully against eleven opponents. First-class cricket calls for such very special gifts of temperament and skill that only the fittest survive, and all their actions are worthy study. (cited in Warner 1920, 104)

The connection between games and imperial defence and manhood intensified in the years leading to, and throughout, the First World War. In an editorial of the *Combermere School Magazine* (*CSM*), Charles Wilkinson Springer wrote,

Boys, Mother England is calling you.
Join in our wonderful game!
Show what you are, sterling grit all through,
Bred of the stuff that has made England's fame.
(*CSM* 1, no. 4 [Third Term 1913–14]: 1–2)

W.R. Allen, a thirteen-year-old pupil of Form III, Combermere, lauded the importance of physical culture against the rising threat of the Germans:

The praises of Physical Culture I sing:
Physical culture is a very fine thing.
It preserves the life and strength of a nation.
And in every city there should be a station
For teaching young fellows to swim, box and drill,
And then you would find they would never be ill.

They'd never be sickly, pale-faced, or thin,
And the German invaders would never get in
To the Land where the Union Jack ever shall
wave – Barbados! the land of the free and the brave.
    (*CSM* 1, no. 2 [October 1913]: 2)

Another Combermerian, Hilton A. Vaughan of Form IV, in his poem
"Press On!", issued the rallying cry:

Press on for home and honour
For all to us most dear
Press on, the game is worthy
And Britons know no fear
    (*CSM* 2, no. 3 [Third Term 1914–15]: 7).

Burton of Combermere, in a speech given at the end of the 1918–19
school year, said,

but ladies and gentlemen, I think that a great war memorial for the
Combermere school would be a good play field. (Cheers) . . . I still hope that
we shall have in time a big play field to train the boys to go to the help of
the Empire if it should require them again and make it our war memorial.
(Cheers). (*CSM* 6, no. 3 [Third Term 1918–19]: 14)

It is very clear, then, that the boys of the elite Barbadian schools, like
their English counterparts, had embraced the representation of masculinity embodied in "the sacrificial subaltern" seduced by the "heroic myths
of empire" (Mangan 1995, 18–19).

Imperial Imagination and Masculinity

These myths were fuelled further by the popular literature, especially the
much-maligned "penny dreadfuls". In 1886 the editorial of the *Taxpayer*
lamented:

The press also deluges us with literature that panders to the low tastes of
certain classes of people. We have "penny dreadfuls" in which highwaymen,
burglars, and grisettes figure as the heroes and heroines. There is the foolish
"boy literature," in which a bad boy who runs away from home joins a

ship, and has bloody encounters with pirates and savages, winding up a
startling career with discovering hidden treasure on a desert isle. (12 June
1886, 3)

The penny-dreadful genre, although maligned for subverting
respectable Victorian middle-class values, needed only slight revision to
bring it in line with the imperialistic and chauvinistic realities of the late
nineteenth century. The Religious Tract Society in England had been a
critic of penny dreadfuls, but its *Boys Own Paper,* launched in 1879,
retained the tales of aggression. What changed was that this aggression
was externalized from the highways and school hallways of England to
the "native" lands of Africans and Asians, and exercised by heroic
sports-loving missionaries, colonial officials and soldiers (Dunae 1980,
105–21; Marsden 1990, 333–53; MacKenzie 1984, 201). Moreover,
juvenile fiction became more gender specific from the late nineteenth
century: the male heroic adventure story for boys, stories set in domestic settings for girls. J.A. Hobson observed that the "spirit of adventure"
associated with imperial expansionism was "fed by a flood of the
literature of travel and of imaginative writing . . . imparting an ever-
growing fascination to the wilder portions of the earth" (1988, 213).

There was a steady flow of these juvenile periodicals, annuals and other
penny books into the British West Indies. Alfred Barrow, the stationer at
No. 9 High Street, Bridgetown, was always well stocked. Although as a
schoolboy C.L.R. James revelled in English canonical literature on the
school curriculum, it was the cheap boys' literature like the *Boys Own
Paper, The Captain* and *Young England* that captured his imagination.
He contends: "these we understood, these we lived by; the principles they
taught we absorbed through the pores and practised instinctively. The
books we read in class meant little to most of us" (1963, 35). According
to James, popular juvenile literature complemented the games ethic in the
school, and underscored the values of unquestioned obedience to authority, fair play, *esprit de corps* and puritan stoicism.

The experience of James in Trinidad had its resonance in the boyhood
of Frank Collymore, a coloured Barbadian, also from a lower-middle-
class background. As a sheltered boy, Frank found refuge in the world
of adventure provided by *The Children's Friend* and penny dreadfuls

like *Dick Turpin, Robin Hood, Deadwood Dick* and *Buffalo Bill,* which his father bought him weekly (Collymore 1969, 34; 1975, 85–86). Collymore's early vista on the wider world was through this literature, which exposed him to the life of "savage tribes" in remote lands. It is difficult to assess the impact of such literature. There is little surviving evidence to suggest that, as West Indian boys, James and Collymore seriously pondered the racist connotations of adventure stories in which white men always outsmarted and dominated non-white men. The textual heroic representations in boys' adventure stories may have permitted young middle and upper-class boys of Barbados to vicariously invest in the "imagined masculinity" of British imperialism (Dawson 1994). By the late 1890s there was an acceleration in attempts to transform fiction and metaphor into reality.

Popular Militarism and Hegemonic Masculinity

By the turn of the century headmasters of the boys' elite schools turned to popular militarism as the latest vehicle for transforming boys into men. According to Springhall and Summers, English voluntary youth movements during the 1900s were saturated with the theme of defensive militarism (Springhall 1971, 125–58; Summers 1976, 104–23).

Wilkinson concludes that adult leaders harnessed youthful energies to fulfil goals of "imperial defence, national defence, international cooperation, national efficiency, and so on" (Wilkinson 1969, 22). These themes resonated as well throughout the school-based organizations in Barbados. Boys were taught that the test of a real man was his willingness to defend country and, of course, hearth and home. Colonial defence was a matter for serious consideration by the governing class of Barbados at the turn of the century. The Colonial Office accepted the recommendation of an 1879 Royal Commission to rationalize its scattered military and naval resources in the region by consolidating them at the coaling stations of Jamaica and St Lucia (CO 854/26, Derby to Officer Administering the Government, 19 June 1885, confidential circular; Goodenough 1893, 490–91).

After intermittent debates beginning in 1885, the Barbados legislature eventually approved a bill in 1901 to re-establish a local volunteer
force (MCA 1891–92, doc. 107; DLC, 3 Dec. 1895; MCA 1900–1901,
doc. 30; DHA, 22 Oct. 1901, 138–46; DLC, 29 Oct. 1901, 45–47;
1901–21 Volunteer Act), a decision influenced, no doubt, by persistent
cane fires and organized potato raids throughout the 1890s (DHA, 22
Oct. 1901, 143).

From 1899 Burton instituted a physical drill programme for
Combermere boys, conducted by a drill master from the Volunteer
Force every Monday and Wednesday evening at three o'clock (*CSM* 1,
no. 1 [June 1913]: 6). At Lodge School physical drill was placed on the
curriculum in 1902 (LSR 2, 1912, 4). The introduction of physical
drill had been somewhat of an *avant-garde* action taken by Queen's
College and Alexandra. Middle and upper-class women in Barbados
had come a long way since 1886, when a newspaper correspondent had
deplored the "false modesty and gross ignorance" in the island where
"it is considered immodest and indelicate for women to ride, walk, row,
swim, run, or in fact do anything that their sisters in large countries
are permitted to do, without fear of 'Mrs Grundy' "(*Taxpayer*, 6
February 1886). In England, schools for upper and middle-class women
were pioneering physical education programmes (McCrone 1987,
97–129; Fletcher 1987, 145–57; Hargreaves 1994, 56–87) and the
English headmistresses of Queen's College and Alexandra brought similar ideas to Barbados.

In 1890 Katherine Gray of Queen's College informed the board of
governors of the school that she intended to secure a drill sergeant to
run an optional programme in drill for the girls (Queen's College
Governors' Minute Book, 5 May 1890). Alexandra, from its establishment in 1894, had been committed to physical drill, and M. Sophie
Arnold had no difficulty in securing wooden dumb-bells from the board
of governors (Log Book of the Alexandra School, 1894–1918, third term
report 1894 and first term report 1895). A student of Queen's College
in the early 1900s remembers the English, male drill sergeant ordering
the girls: "Hands to the seams of your trousers!" (*Queen's College
Historical Diary*, 28).

The fact that females were already engaged in physical drill in Barbados neutralized such an activity as a site for constructing masculinity. Not surprisingly, therefore, the headmasters of the elite boys' schools soon sought a more military type of drill. In 1902 Burton, dissatisfied with the limitations of physical drill, asked his board of governors for forty dollars to purchase wooden rifles, but this was denied (BDA: SCH 2/1/2, Combermere School Board of Governors' Minutes, 5 May 1902, 1). Lodge's physical drill programme, launched in 1902, was replaced the following year by company drill for senior boys (LSR 2, 1912, 4).

By 1904 the governing bodies of the three elite schools had approved a cadet corps scheme drawn up by R. Radcliffe Hall, science master at Lodge and officer of the Barbados Volunteers (BPL: BS 72, Harrison College Governors' Minutes, 11 January 1904, 33; ibid., 2 May 1904, 43; Minutes of Lodge School Governing Body, 26 February 1904; LSR 1, 1911, 28; LSR 2, 1912, 4; LSR 7, 1917, 17; LSR 33, 1943, 7; Hoyos 1945, 89; Sandiford and Newton 1995, 39). A full cadet scheme was in operation at Harrison College from 1905 (BPL: BS 72, Harrison College Governors' Minutes, 4 September 1905, 80).

The local organizers of cadets disclaimed chauvinist militarism and argued that the cadet corps was the latest character-building scheme for boys which, along with games and modern studies, would bring balance to the idealism of the classical curriculum. The "right view" of the corps was that it was "not meant as a nursery for a volunteer, militia or regular force" but that its "true use" was "to instil into the boys the most eminent of virtues – Discipline" (LSR 1, 1911, 32). As the principal organizer, R. Radcliffe Hall, wrote two decades later, the cadet corps provided systematic physical training and "opportunities to each boy to get practice in disciplining himself and in controlling others" (LSR 7, 1917, 18).

For all of the disclaimers of militarism, organizers of the cadets, with Governor Hodgson's assistance, soon replaced their dummy rifles with real ones out of the surplus provided by the War Office (LSR 1, 1911, 28). Lodge established a rifle club in 1906 which benefited from the financial support which the Colonial and War Offices extended to the sport of shooting in the colonies. The Barbados Rifle Association

received £77 in ammunition in 1907–08, plus an additional grant of
£108 to send a West Indian team to compete at Bisley (PP 1908 [319],
LXX, 5). The attorney general reminded the House during the debate
on the Volunteers Bill in 1901 that the performance of the Boers during
the South African War demonstrated the value of training volunteers in
their early manhood to use rifles (DHA, 22 October 1901, 139). The
amended Volunteer Act of 1907 confirmed the cadet companies of the
three elite boys' schools as attachments of the Volunteer Force (1907–42,
"An Act to Amend the Volunteer Act 1901 [1901–21]", sec. 2).

By the height of the Great War, headmasters were less apologetic
about militarism, and envisaged that the cadet corps would remain a
centrepiece of education reform after the war. "I feel certain in my
mind", said Burton, "that if the Cadet Corps and elementary military
drill had been compulsory in the schools of the British Empire, we should
not have had this disastrous War in which we are now engaged",
(Cheers) "because our young men would have been able to compete with
other nations; they would have been trained and known how to shoot
straight" (*CSM* 3, no. 2 [1915–16]: 6).

At Lodge the popularity of cadets was especially high and there was
a membership equivalent to 86.8 per cent of enrolment in 1909, compared to 46.5 per cent in 1903 at Rugby, the prestigious English public
school (PP 1904 [Cd. 2062], XXX, Militia and Volunteers [Royal

Table 4.1   Barbados Cadet Corps, 1909–1914

Years	Harrison College		Lodge		Combermere		Totals	
	Roll	Cadets	Roll	Cadets	Roll	Cadets	Roll	Cadets
1909	182	67	53	46	173	52	408	165
1910	172	61	52	44	171	51	395	156
1911	158	56	55	53	176	58	389	167
1914	151	77	71	68	181	58	403	203

Sources: Blue Books and Barbados Volunteers annual reports

Commission], paras. 11564, 11565). By 1914, 95.8 per cent of Lodge boys were cadets, which suggests that by then membership in the corps might have been compulsory for the senior boys. At Harrison College cadet corps membership rose from 36.8 per cent of enrolment in 1909 to 51 per cent of enrolment by 1914. Overall, 50 per cent of the total enrolment of the three elite secondary schools were in the cadet corps by 1914, up from 40.4 per cent in 1909.

Up to 1914, membership in Combermere's cadet corps did not exceed 32 per cent of enrolment, but this figure does not provide an accurate measurement of the fervour of imperial masculinity in that school. In the first place, as the fastest-growing secondary school in the island, Combermere would have had more boys under the age of twelve, ineligible for recruitment as cadets. Second, because the school drew its pupils from the lower middle class, many of them could not afford the extra 13s 6d (10s for the uniform and 3s 6d for the felt hat).[3] Indeed, Major Clarke observed that the company at Combermere consisted mainly of younger boys, whose parents were unwilling or unable to replace the suits when the boys outgrew them. A third reason for Combermere's smaller company lay in the fact that from 1912 the school was actually buzzing with the activity of two uniformed voluntary groups: the Boy Scouts and the Cadet Corps.

The Boy Scout movement was founded in 1908 by Robert Baden-Powell, a hero of the South African War. Two years later Reverend FitzPatrick, a former Harrison College master, wrote Baden-Powell offering to launch the movement in Barbados (SAA: TC "Barbados", FitzPatrick to Baden-Powell, 1 December 1910) and was sanguine that the Barbadian public schools would extend the movement to both blacks and whites (SAA: TC "Barbados", Baden-Powell to FitzPatrick, 6 December 1910). Following FitzPatrick's initial audiences with the governor and with Dr Dalton of Harrison College, meetings of headmasters and officials were held from April 1911 to March 1912, before the final agreement at a meeting of 9 March 1912 to establish the Barbados Boys Scouts Association (BBSA) (SAA: TC "Barbados", FitzPatrick to Baden-Powell, 22 March 1911; BBSA Minute Book no. 1 [1911–17], 21 April 1911, 28 April 1911, 1 July 1911, 9 March 1912).

Dalton said that the cadet corps and games were already consuming the time of masters and students at Harrison College but Burton, with his usual enthusiasm for things imperial, was convinced scouting could successfully coexist with the cadet company (BBSA minutes, 28 April 1911). Indeed, Burton had already decided to launch the first scout troop in the island. Baden-Powell himself had already granted his blessing to the initiative, on 15 January 1912, during the Barbados leg of his eight-month international tour (SAA: BSA 00097, R. Baden-Powell, "Reports etc. on Boy Scouts", 2). Combermere's two scout masters, C.W. Springer and V.A. Southwell, along with two assistants and fifty-six boys, comprised the first troop registered when the BBSA was formally launched (*CSM* 1 [June 1913]: 7; BBSA minutes, 9 March 1912).

There has been sustained interest over two decades in the Boy Scouts, and general agreement that scouting was promoted as a vehicle for shaping the masculinity of boys (Springhall 1971, 125–58; Hantover 1978, 184–95; Rosenthal 1980, 603–17; Warren 1986a, 232–56; Rosenthal 1986; Macleod 1983; MacDonald 1993). However, there has been a debate, as old as the movement itself, concerning the relationship between scouting and militarism. Springhall, in a seminal article, located scouting within the British imperialistic militarism of the early 1900s and argued that the movement was co-opted by Edwardian elites to further their imperial political agenda (Springhall 1971; also 1987, 934–42). While this view has been stoutly supported by Summers (1987, 943–50). Allen Warren and, more recently, Martin Dedman have discounted the militaristic imperial argument and reaffirmed the citizenship-training one (Warren 1986a, 232–56; 1986b, 376–98; Dedman 1993, 201–23).

The debate is perhaps academic. Citizenship training and military preparedness were not mutually exclusive aims. Scouting taught sexual sublimation, spontaneous heroism and selfless patriotism, expressed ultimately in "duty unto death". Fourteen-year-old Cyril A.D. Chase of Combermere, a first-class badge holder, patrol leader and King Scout, knew that lesson well. Explaining why he joined the Scouts, he wrote:

> I deduced, firstly, that an employer would prefer to employ a Boy Scout to an ordinary boy, and secondly, that the more boys there are with a scout's

training, the more liable is England to hold her place of supremacy in future generations. My next move was to read tales on scouting, and, when I saw how many scouts had saved life, some of them laying down their own while doing so, I was inspired with that enthusiasm which any descendant of Britain's heroes feels on hearing of deeds of bravery done by another be he friend or foe. (*CSM* 1, no. 2 [October 1913]: 4)

The response of this young Combermerian underscores the critique of jingoistic and militaristic constructions of masculinity and nationalism made by anti-imperialists and sections of the labour movement in Britain. Even before the Boy Scout movement was formally launched, J.A. Hobson, in his *Imperialism: A Study* (first published in 1902), offered a penetrating critique of imperialists who co-opted the British education system to conflate imperial militarism with patriotism:

Most serious of all is the persistent attempt to seize the school system for Imperialism masquerading as patriotism. To capture the childhood of the country, to mechanize its free play into the routine of military drill, to cultivate the savage survivals of combativeness, to poison its early understanding of history by false ideals and pseudo-heroes . . . to feed the always overweening pride of race at an age when self-confidence most commonly prevails, and by necessary implication to disparage other nations, so starting children in the world with false measures of value and unwillingness to learn from foreign sources – to fasten this base of insularity of mind and morals upon little children of a nation and to call it patriotism is as foul an abuse of education as it is possible to conceive. (1988, 217)

Baden-Powell insisted that scouting sought to inculcate healthy masculinity in boys without jingoistic militarism. He argued that

its object is far above that of merely obtaining a few hundred recruits for the Territorials. Its object is to train the individual boy, if possible, throughout the whole of the rising generation and to inculcate into him an idea of manliness, unselfishness, self-discipline and patriotism – in a word to promote good citizenship in the future nation. (SAA: BSA 01036, R. Baden-Powell to MacIlwain)

No evidence has yet come to light to suggest any opposition in Barbados to the militarist construction of masculinity . However, when

Brigadier-General Dalyrymple Hay inspected the Combermere troop in June 1914, he apologized for not having the opportunity to change his military uniform, and told the young Combermerians, "You are Boy Scouts, not scouts in the military sense" (*CSM* 2, no. 1 [1914–15]: 7). When Baden-Powell received a copy of the *Combermere School Magazine* and read the speech, he was so impressed that he wrote to congratulate Burton on the way scouting was progressing at Combermere (SAA: Baden-Powell to Burton, 20 November 1914; *CSM* 2, no. 2 [1914–15]: 14–15).

With the outbreak of the First World War, defensiveness diminished and a circular of 4 August 1914, from Scout headquarters, instructed commissioners to make the scouts available for any service towards the war effort (SAA: BSA 00930; *CSM* 2, no. 2 [1914–15]: 2). The many hours spent in ambulance drill, despatch running, mock battles and signalling would now be tested. In spite of the limited practical utility of some of these, E.D. Redman, a former officer of the Combermere Cadet Corps, acknowledged that "the soldierly spirit which the corps created in me has, I am sure, been the cause of my desire to join the colours, and to fight against the wretched Hun for a cause; and I am now proud of being a member of His Majesty's Army" (*CSM* 5, no. 3 [1917–18]: 3).[4]

J.C. Hope, a former patrol leader, first-class badge holder and the island's first King's Scout, wrote extolling the virtues of the vehicles of cultural imperialism to which Combermere exposed him: "It was there I learnt the rudiments of drill, there I became a scout, and there I started correspondence as a member of the League of the Empire. I mention these because of the advantages I have derived from them" (*CSM* 3, no. 3 [1915–16]: 5). However, behind the rhetoric of love for king and country was a genuine search, especially by non-white West Indians, for social justice, racial pride and an unequivocal validation of their masculinity.

Whereas education reform facilitated the creation of a non-white (predominantly male) middle class, relegation to the lowest ranks of business functions in the commercial or plantation enterprises and confinement to the lower rounds of the civil service was still their lot.[5] A persistent patriarchal-racist ideology represented black men as "boys"

– permanently infantilized and thus not yet ready for leadership, certainly not where whites were available.

Glenford Howe has indicated that there was a discourse (albeit a contested one) in which many black West Indian men believed that fighting in the "white man's war" was an opportunity for genuine social justice and colonial reform (1994, 30–33). Black middle-class men, especially, viewed the war as an opportunity to prove their equality to white men – to demonstrate that the educated black man could "play the game", could demonstrate initiative, sacrificial service and indispensability to British imperial fortitude. Douglas A. Haynes, a black Combermerian in the British West Indies Regiment, wrote to the *Combermere School Magazine* to clarify this issue for the pupils at his alma mater. He alluded to the discrimination against black Barbadians in civil service appointments, in the local taxation system and in the rule of law. However, from his perspective, participation in the Great War was a positive step towards dismantling "the 'Ante bellum' state of affairs" in which the black man "sat patiently waiting for bones". The war was the crucible within which the black man would demonstrate his masculinity unequivocally. According to Haynes, "Having proved himself a man, now, by doing and daring as a man, he can claim in the name of manhood" (*CSM* 6, no. 2 [Second Term 1918–19]: 8).

Haynes was wrong, because the ideological discourse on masculinity remained imprisoned within the metalanguage of "race". Not only was John Bull not yet ready to recognize or validate the masculinity of black men generally, but class and status divisions among non-white West Indians proved an obstacle to any pan-Afro-Caribbean masculinity. Take for instance the case of J.C. Hope (former Combermere King's Scout) and fellow petitioners who wrote to J. Challenor Lynch, the chairman of the local recruiting committee, and complained: "We were made to understand that we would have been [recruited] on an entirely different footing to the regular West India Regiment, and that we would have been enjoined every privilege just as any other British soldier, we find now that this is not the case. We have been deceived" (CO 28/294, encl. no. 2, Hope et al. to Lynch, 2 August 1918, in despatch no. 173, 14 Oct. 1918).

This petition clearly demonstrates that these black middle-class "old boys" of the elite school identified with their white British counterparts rather than with working-class blacks serving in the West India Regiment. Class and the command of elite English culture, not racial solidarity, were the bases of their definition of normative masculinity. Lynch confirmed that they were indeed "men of intelligence and good character" from middle-class backgrounds (CO 28/294, encl. no. 1, Lynch to Fell, 9 October 1918, in despatch no. 173, 14 October 1918). However, to their imperial masters such distinctions mattered little; they were simply "natives" and were denied commissions and equal pay because of their colour (CO 28/294, encl. no. 2, Hope et al. to Lynch, 2 August 1918, in despatch no. 173, 14 October 1918).[6]

Conclusion

Fundamentally, the construction of hegemonic masculinity in Barbados was formulated by the co-optation of the "lesser" masculinity of a black middle class by the socially dominant white males. This process was facilitated primarily through the school system. The myth of the education system of Barbados was that the Mitchinson reforms had created a meritocratic instrument for social justice, mobility and cultural "refinement". Like their white, public school–educated counterparts in England, these black "boys of the empire" associated socioeconomic and political dominance – whether in the local or wider imperial contexts – with masculinity itself. Consequently, a share in the fruits of hegemonic masculinity necessitated political enfranchisement, and social and economic justice. Nevertheless, the aggressive masculinity exercised by old boys of the elite schools of Barbados in protecting imperial and colonial interests did nothing to redress the social, political and economic inequities which faced blacks in the empire.

Clearly, gender emasculation, class exploitation and racism acted simultaneously as forces of oppression for non-white West Indian men. For black men the pursuit of masculinity defined in British imperial terms would prove illusory without redressing these oppressive forces. The revolt of black soldiers at Taranto, Italy in December 1918, as well as protests by demobilized black soldiers elsewhere, demonstrated an awakening against British colonial oppression. By 1920 many West Indian black men, influenced by the ideology of black nationalism, had begun to intensify their quest for human dignity rooted in racial integrity, social justice and economic enfranchisement. They were (and perhaps still are) far from fully disavowing constructs of masculinity predicated on aggression and the subjection of women but, ideologically, they had started to grow up.

Notes

1. For a good critique of the paradigmatic limitations of the historiography of slavery, see Beckles 1995b.
2. Venn 1944. For Deighton's early professional career, see CO 321/44, 26 November 1881, Deighton to Colonel Harley, encl. confidential in Harley to Earl of Kimberley, 28 November 1881.
3. Prices cited in MCA 1909–10, doc. 88, F.J. Clarke's Inspection Report, appendix A.
4. See also the following letters indicating the influence of the cadets and Boy Scouts: Letter from H.H. Williams, *CSM* 4, no. 3 (1916–17); Letter from C. Ivor Proverbs, *CSM* 5, no. 2 (1917–18): 5–6.
5. For a number of such cases in Barbados, see Straker 1896.
6. See also the recommendation of the Swaby Commission for financial aid for the corps, especially at Combermere: MCA 1908–1909, doc. 252, Education Commission Report 1907–09, 23. The general problem of clothing drew attention again in 1915–16; see MCA 1915–16, doc. 251, Barbados Volunteers Annual Report 1915–16, 11.

Abbreviations

BDA   Barbados Department of Archives
BPL   Barbados Public Library
CO   Colonial Office papers
CSM   *Combermere School Magazine*

DHA   Debates of the House of Assembly
DLC   Debates of the Legislative Council
LSR   Lodge School Record
MCA   Minutes of Legislative Council and Assembly (Barbados)
PP   British Parliamentary Papers
SAA   Scout Association Archives, London

References

Barbados Cricketers' Annual. Various years.

Beckles, Hilary. 1995a. "A Purely Natural Extension: Women's Cricket in West Indies Cricket Culture". In *Liberation Cricket: West Indies Cricket Culture,* edited by Hilary Beckles and Brian Stoddart. Kingston, Jamaica: Ian Randle.

———. 1995b. "Sex and Gender in the Historiography of Caribbean Slavery". In *Engendering History: Caribbean Women in Historical Perspective,* edited by Verene Shepherd, Bridget Brereton, and Barbara Bailey. Kingston, Jamaica: Ian Randle.

———. 1996. "Black Masculinity in Caribbean Slavery". Women and Development Unit Occasional Paper 2. St Augustine, Trinidad: Centre for Gender and Development Studies, University of the West Indies.

Best, Geoffrey. 1975. "Militarism and the Victorian Public School". In *The Victorian Public School,* edited by Brian Simon and Ian Bradley. Dublin: Gill and Macmillan.

Bock, Gisela. 1989. "Women's History and Gender History: Aspects of an International Debate". *Gender and History* 1, no. 1 (Spring).

Brereton, Bridget. 1988. "General Problems and Issues in Studying the History of Women". In *Gender in Caribbean Development,* edited by Patricia Mohammed and Catherine Shepherd. St Augustine, Trinidad: Women in Development Studies Project, University of the West Indies.

———. 1992. "Searching for the Invisible Woman". *Slavery and Abolition* 13, no. 2.

Brewer, Rose M. 1993. "Theorizing Race, Class and Gender: The New Scholarship of Black Feminist Intellectuals". In *Theorizing Black Feminisms: The Visionary Pragmatism of Black Women,* edited by Stanlie M. James and Abena P.A. Busia. London: Routledge.

Carrigan, Tim, Robert Connell, and John Lee. 1985. "Toward a New Sociology of Masculinity". *Theory and Society* 14, no. 5.

Cole, Joyce. 1982. "Official Ideology and the Education of Women in the English-Speaking Caribbean, 1835–1945". In *Women and Education,* edited by J. Massiah. Bridgetown, Barbados: Institute of Social and Economic Research.

Collymore, Frank. 1969. "At the Turn of the Century, 1898–1902". *Bim* 13, no. 49 (July–December).

———. 1975. "Non Immemor (Part Two)". *Bim* 15, no. 58 (June).

Combermere School Magazine. Various years.

Dawson, Graham. 1994. *Soldier Heroes: British Adventure, Empire and the Imagining of Masculinities.* London: Routledge.

Dedman, Martin. 1993. "Baden-Powell, Militarism, and the 'Invisible Contributors' to the Boy Scout Scheme, 1904–1920". *Twentieth Century British History* 4, no. 3.

Donaldson, Mike. 1993. "What is Hegemonic Masculinity?" *Theory and Society* 22, no. 5.

Downes, Aviston. 1994. "Barbados, 1880–1914: A Socio-Cultural History". DPhil thesis, University of York.

Drayton, Kathleen. 1984. "The Development of Higher Education for Women in the Commonwealth Caribbean with Special Reference to Barbados". Paper prepared for the Sixth Berkshire Conference on the History of Women, June 1–3.

Dunae, Patrick. 1980. "Boys' Literature and the Idea of Empire". *Victorian Studies* 24, no. 1 (Autumn).

Fletcher, Sheila. 1987. "The Making and Breaking of a Female Tradition: Women's Physical Education in England, 1880–1980". In *From "Fair Sex" to Feminism: Sport and the Socialization of Women in the Industrial and Post-Industrial Eras,* edited by J.A. Mangan and Roberta J. Park. London: Frank Cass.

Foster, Joseph, comp. 1891. *Alumni Oxonienses: The Members of the University of Oxford, 1715–1886.* Oxford: James Parker.

Goodenough, W.H., and J.C. Dalton. 1893. *The Army Book for the British Empire.* London: HMSO.

Haley, Bruce. 1978. *The Healthy Body and Victorian Culture.* Cambridge, Mass.: Harvard University Press.

Hantover, Jeffrey P. 1978. "The Boy Scouts and the Validation of Masculinity". *Journal of Social Issues* 34, no. 1.

Hargreaves, Jennifer. 1994. *Sporting Females: Critical Issues in the History and Sociology of Women's Sports.* London: Routledge.

Hobson, J.A. [1902] 1988. *Imperialism: A Study.* Reprint, London: Unwin Hyman.

Howe, Glenford. 1994. "West Indian Blacks and the Struggle for Participation in the First World War". *Journal of Caribbean History* 28, no. 1.

Hoyos, F.A. 1945. *Two Hundred Years: A History of the Lodge School.* Bridgetown, Barbados: Advocate.

———. 1953. *Our Common Heritage.* Bridgetown, Barbados: Advocate

James, C.L.R. 1963. *Beyond a Boundary.* London: Stanley Paul.

Jemmott, Ralph A. 1983. "A Brief History of Harrison College, 1733–1983". *Harrisonian: 250th Anniversary Commemorative Issue.* Bridgetown, Barbados: Harrison College.

Kimmel, Michael S. 1989. "Rethinking 'Masculinity', New Directions in Research". In *Changing Men: New Directions in Research on Men and Masculinity*, edited by Michael S. Kimmel. London: Sage.

Kirsch, George B. 1989. *The Creation of American Team Sports: Baseball and Cricket, 1838–1872.* Urbana: University of Illinois Press.

Laborde, E. Dalyrmple. 1910-11. "Public School Cricket". *Barbados Cricketers Annual.*

Lorber, Judith, and Susan A. Farrell, eds. 1991. *The Social Construction of Gender.* London: Sage.

MacDonald, Robert H. 1993. *Sons of the Empire: The Frontier and the Boy Scout Movement, 1890–1918.* Toronto: University of Toronto Press.

MacKenzie, John M. 1984. *Propaganda and Empire: The Manipulation of British Public Opinion, 1880–1960.* Manchester: Manchester University Press.

Macleod, David I. 1983. *Building Character in the American Boy: The Boy Scouts, YMCA, and Their Forerunners, 1870–1920.* Madison: University of Wisconsin Press.

Mandle, W.F. 1973. "Games People Played: Cricket and Football in England and Victoria in the Late Nineteenth Century". *Historical Studies* 15, no. 60 (April).

Mangan, J.A. 1981. *Athleticism in the Victorian and Edwardian Public School: The Emergence and Consolidation of an Educational Ideology.* Cambridge: Cambridge University Press.

———. 1985. *The Games Ethic and Imperialism: Aspects of the Diffusion of an Ideal.* Manchester: Viking.

———. 1988a. "Images of Empire in the Late Victorian Public School". *Journal of Educational Administration and History* 12, no. 1 (January).

———. 1995. "Duty unto Death: English Masculinity and Militarism in the Age of the New Imperialism". *International Journal of the History of Sport* 12, no. 2 (August).

————, ed. 1988b. *"Benefits Bestowed"?: Education and British Imperialism.* Manchester: Manchester University Press.

Mangan, J.A., and James Walvin, eds. 1987. *Manliness and Morality: Middle-Class Masculinity in Britain and America, 1800–1940.* Manchester: Manchester University Press.

Marsden, W.E. 1990. "Rooting Racism into the Educational Experience of Childhood and Youth in the Nineteenth- and Twentieth-Centuries". *History of Education* 19, no. 4.

Mayers, Janice. 1995. "Access to Secondary Education for Girls in Barbados, 1907–43: A Preliminary Analysis". In *Engendering History,* edited by Verene Shepherd, Bridget Brereton, and Barbara Bailey. New York: St Martin's.

McCrone, Kathleen E. 1987. "Play Up! Play Up! And Play the Game! Sport at the Late Victorian Girls' Public Schools". In *From "Fair Sex" to Feminism: Sport and the Socialization of Women in the Industrial and Post-Industrial Eras,* edited by J.A. Mangan and Roberta J. Park. London: Frank Cass.

Messner, Michael, and Donald Sabo, eds. 1990. *Sport, Men, and the Gender Order: Critical Feminist Perspectives.* Champaign, Ill.: Human Kinetics.

Newbolt, (Sir) Henry. 1918. *Collected Poems, 1897–1907.* London: Thomas Nelson.

Newsome, David. 1961. *Godliness and Good Learning: Four Studies on a Victorian Ideal.* London: John Murray.

Queen's College. *Queen's College 1883–1983.* 1982. Bridgetown, Barbados: Queen's College.

Reddock, Rhoda. 1993. "Primacy of Gender in Race and Class". In *Race, Class and Gender in the Future of the Caribbean,* edited by J. Edward Greene. Kingston, Jamaica: Institute of Social and Economic Research.

Rosenthal, Michael. 1980. "Knights and Retainers: The Earliest Version of Baden-Powell's Boy Scouts Scheme". *Journal of Contemporary History* 15.

————. 1986. *The Character Factory: Baden-Powell and the Origins of the Boy Scout Movement.* New York: Pantheon.

Sandiford, Keith A.P. 1984. "Victorian Cricket Technique and Industrial Technology". *British Journal of Sport History* 1, no. 3 (December).

Sandiford, Keith A.P., and Brian Stoddart. 1987. "The Elite Schools and Cricket in Barbados: A Study in Colonial Continuity". *International Journal of the History of Sport* 4 (December).

Sandiford, Keith A.P., and Earle H. Newton. 1995. *Combermere School and the Barbadian Society.* Kingston, Jamaica: The Press, University of the West Indies.

Smith, R.H. 1968. "Reminiscences of Lodge Cricket in 1891". *Lodge School Record* 57.

Smyth, Major B. 1904. *A History of the Lancashire Fusiliers.* Vol. 2, *1822–1903.* Dublin: Sackville Press.

Springhall, John. 1971. "Boy Scouts: Class and Militarism in Relation to British Youth Movements, 1908–1930". *International Review of Social History* 16.

———. 1987. "Baden-Powell and the Scout Movement before 1920: Citizen Training or Soldier of the Future?". *English Historical Review* 102, no. 405 (October).

Straker, D. Augustus. 1896. *A Trip to the Windward Islands; Or Then and Now.* Detroit: James H. Stone.

Summers, Anne. 1976. "Militarism in Britain before the Great War". *History Workshop* 2 (Autumn).

———. 1987. "Scouts, Guides and VADs: A Note in Reply to Allen Warren". *English Historical Review* 102, no. 405 (October).

Tamke, Susan S. 1978. *Make a Joyful Noise unto the Lord: Hymns as a Reflection of Victorian Social Attitudes.* Athens, Ohio: Ohio University Press.

Tosh, John. 1994. "What Should Historians Do with Masculinity? Reflections on Nineteenth-Century Britain". *History Workshop Journal* 38 (Autumn).

Venn, J.A., comp. 1944. *Alumni Cantabrigienses.* Vol. 2, no. 2. Cambridge: Cambridge University Press.

Warner, P.F. 1920. *Cricket Reminiscences.* London: Longman.

Warren, Allen. 1986a. "Citizens of the Empire: Baden-Powell, Scouts and Guides and an Imperial Ideal, 1900–40". In *Imperialism and Popular Culture,* edited by John M. Mackenzie. Manchester: Manchester University Press.

———. 1986b. "Sir Robert Baden-Powell, the Scout Movement and Citizen Training in Great Britain, 1900–1920". *English Historical Review* 101, no. 399 (April).

Whitson, David. 1990. "Sport in the Social Construction of Masculinity". In *Sport, Men, and the Gender Order: Critical Feminist Perspectives,* edited by M. Messner and D. Sabo. Champaign, Ill.: Human Kinetics.

Wilkinson, Paul. 1969. "English Youth Movements, 1908–1930". *Journal of Contemporary History* 4, no. 2.

Winn, William E. 1960. "Tom Brown's Schooldays and the Development of 'Muscular Christianity' ". *Church History* 29.

CHAPTER 5

Male Privileging and Male "Academic Underperformance" in Jamaica

MARK FIGUEROA

Academic underperformance can be seen as one aspect of maleness in Jamaica. This chapter seeks to ascertain the extent to which this "underperformance" can be understood in relation to the historical privileging of males.[1] The decline of male, relative to female, academic performance in the Caribbean and a number of other areas globally has captured the attention of professionals as well as lay persons. This decline has sometimes been portrayed within a conceptual framework of male marginalization/victimization. What I provide here is an alternative way of viewing the phenomenon. Instead of seeing the current "underperformance" as a result of male marginalization or victimization, I demonstrate how it might be conceptualized as an ironic consequence of historical male privileging. I consider Jamaica a good case for study, as the relative decline in overall male academic performance has been particularly striking. In addition, a wide range of research has been done on this issue relevant to the Jamaican case. At a conceptual level I am seeking to broaden the space within which existing and future research results can be used, to illuminate the way in which the dialectic of gender privileging manifests itself in the Caribbean.[2] At a more practical level I am seeking to provide an alternative framework for the development of policy in this controversial area.

I take as a given that the male gender has been privileged historically in Jamaican society. The male gender has had access to a broader social space; it has had greater control over a wider range of resources and has been more able to enjoy the resources that it has controlled; it has maintained a more prestigious position in society as a whole, and has exercised greater power in practice, regardless of the respective power potentialities of the genders in history. In taking this position I wish to make it clear that my reference to male privileging is always to the heritage of the "old" privileging of the male gender, unless I specify otherwise. My argument is not dependent on an assessment of the current state of gender privileging, whether taken globally or with respect to specific social spheres. What I explore is how the historical structure of male privileging can be linked to the contemporary result of male "academic underperformance".[3]

In doing this research I was struck by the wide range of material on which I was able to draw that tended to contradict the popular notions of male marginalization/victimization. As such, I claim no originality for many of the ideas I put forward.[4] Indeed, I present this work with the hope that it will stimulate others who have been working in this field (or who I might be so bold as to say should be working in this field) to come forward and publish their conclusions. My concern is that there are ideas that circulate with respect to male "academic underperformance" which have the possibility of becoming conventional wisdom in some circles but which cannot stand up to even a modicum of scrutiny. It is time for those who know better to speak up. Gender issues in the Caribbean are extremely complex, and often exhibit a texture that is somewhat different from those identified by gender scholars in other regions. The issue of male "academic underperformance" in the Caribbean deserves more sophisticated attention than it has received to date.

There are significant policy issues at stake, depending on what we identify as the underlying cause of male "academic underperformance" (Figueroa 2000, 72–73). In what follows, a link is made between male "academic underperformance" in Jamaica and gender socialization practices that are rooted in male gender privileging. These are reinforced by other tendencies in society that also have roots in the historical privileging of the male gender. These latter trends include the tendency for female-dominated professions to be relatively low status and low paying, for men to get higher pay for the same work, and for women to need more qualifications than men to hold the same jobs. If the underlying causes of the problem of male "academic underperformance" are to be found in male gender privileging, then a solution must be sought in the transformation of gender relations. To go the alternative route of creating new special accommodations for males within the education system would in fact be seeking to add a new dimension to male privileging, and could ultimately exacerbate rather than solve the problem.

In what follows I start with an examination of some of the statistical evidence available and demonstrate that, although females are often outperforming males in terms of overall numbers, a more detailed analysis of the statistics reveals the footprint of the old male privileging. Second, I seek to show how the increasing tendency of males to lose ground in academic fields where they had previously dominated can be seen as part of a process of cumulative causation in which cultural patterns rooted in the historical privileging of the male gender play an important role. Based on male privileging, certain patterns of gender socialization of boys have developed that tend to leave them deficient with respect to skills that are increasingly required for survival within the educational system. I consider the expectations that boys face, as well as the tasks that they are given at home, and show how these do not prepare them well for schooling, especially as it has developed in Jamaica. Third, I carry my analysis over into the educational system. Here I interrogate the gendered processes that are taking place inside the schoolroom and seek to show how these may be contributing to "male underperformance". Fourth, I turn my attention to the impact of motivational and other factors beyond the school gate. In particular I look at the prospects that males and females face in their efforts to realize a career that provides a high income, social prestige and self-fulfilment, as well as the images they face in the media. I examine these issues in the context of the social transformations that have taken place in Jamaica over the last few decades. I conclude by indicating how transformation of gender relations and the reform of the educational system might benefit all concerned and provide some suggestions for further research.

In presenting these arguments I am aware that there are two big issues that need to be addressed, both related to comparison. Much of what is said about male privileging in contemporary Jamaica was true for Jamaica in the past, when academic performance was quite different. In addition, there are societies where it could be argued that male gender privileging is more striking, yet academic results are also quite different. As such, it is necessary to assess the arguments provided here within a dynamic context. It has not always been possible to pay adequate attention to this dynamic element in this chapter; this is a significant limitation, but I do try to identify how the changes that have taken place over the last few decades, along with the particular forms of male privileging that exist in Jamaican society, might be linked with the outcome of male "academic underperformance". (For a more detailed treatment of some of the dynamic aspects see Figueroa 2000.) Comparisons are also made between Jamaica and some other societies where male privileging exists, with very different academic outcomes.

The Statistical Evidence

Jamaica's recent educational statistics demonstrate that, at all levels, females now outperform males in a wide range of areas, including some disciplines formerly dominated by males.[5] If we were to take an uncritical look at the global picture we might even conclude that women have finally overcome their age-old disadvantages, at least in this one area of achievement, and that they are now demonstrating academic dominance in the educational field. In my view this conclusion would be premature. A closer look at the data reveals the stamp of historical male privileging.

There are a number of data sets that can be examined from a gender perspective. A number of these have in fact been analysed.[6] At the primary level there are the (recently replaced) Common Entrance Examination scores. At the secondary level there are the Caribbean Examinations Council (CXC) O level and A level results, and at the tertiary level the statistics for most institutions are also available for study. Given the constraints of space I have only looked in detail at the data for the University of the West Indies (UWI), which provides a very good case for viewing the extent to which gender balances have changed in different disciplines.

In recent years approximately 70 per cent of those graduating from the Mona (Jamaica) campus of UWI have been women. This situation, and the context from which it has emerged, has brought about a number of expressions of concern from male opinion leaders and even from female gender specialists. See, for example, comments by UWI Chancellor Shridath Ramphal (1993, 1994, 1995), Errol Miller (1986, 1991), Donnovan Simon (1992), Raymond Forrest (1995), Carl Wint (1993a, 1993b), and Elsa Leo-Rhynie (1992). Miller's approach has been to discuss changes in education in terms of the marginalization/victimization of the black male, while Wint has called for "a study to determine the status of young men" in Jamaica as a necessary first step "before we can begin to plot a strategy to improve the status of men" (1993b). This view is closely related to a perspective present throughout the English-speaking Caribbean, that suggests that the way out of this problem is to give male students and even male staff special breaks within the educational system.[7]

An uncritical look at the global picture at UWI could lead us to conclude that in fact men are being marginalized, but a richer analysis tells a different story. Before looking more closely at the data, I am unable to restrain myself from making a polemical point. It is interesting that the emergence of women as a significant majority within the graduating class at UWI has been the occasion for a number of persons to speak of impending social doom: "No society can function effectively if this huge imbalance persists" (Forrest 1995, 7). Strangely, not one of the doom-seers seems to have wondered how Caribbean society functioned when the balance was going the other way, nor have they apparently stopped to wonder how large parts of Asia and Africa, where the balance goes the other way, function.

Indeed, those who are foretelling impending doom seem unaware of even more glaring gender imbalances *against* women that exist at the top of the academic pyramid at UWI. Moreover, female students have for decades dominated certain fields at UWI, while males have dominated others. This apparently was not a problem until women seemed poised to dominate the previously male-dominated, hence prestigious, fields as well. It seems that certain persons can only become gender sensitive when women are successful in a field traditionally dominated by men. The absence of women from a high-prestige, male-dominated field like engineering, or the absence of males from a low-paying, female-dominated field such as nursing, evokes little gender-based comment from some of these most concerned individuals. It would appear that male chauvinism is alive and well in certain quarters, and that the struggle for real gender equality has a long way to go.

In 1994–95 (provisional data) women represented just over 60 per cent of students registered in UWI as a whole.[8] This was the first year that female registration rose above 60 per cent at UWI. Male registration was over 60 per cent for all the years from 1948–49 until 1971–72. Female registration only went above 50 per cent for the first time in 1982–83. In the case of Jamaican students the picture at UWI is slightly different. Taking all three campuses together, women have been the majority among Jamaican students since 1974–75. (In that year they represented 51 per cent of all first-degree, certificate and diploma registrations.) We need to ask, How was this majority achieved? In this analysis, unless otherwise stated, I am referring to the registration of Jamaican students on all three campuses, not students at the Mona campus and not just Jamaican students at the Mona campus.[9]

To achieve just over 50 per cent of first-degree registrations as a whole in 1974–75, women had to reach nearly 80 per cent of first-degree registrations in the "low-prestige" areas of arts and education while being just about 40 per cent, or somewhat less, in the "high-prestige" areas of law, medicine and natural sciences. In the case of engineering and agriculture, women were less than 4 per cent and 20 per cent respectively. Only in social sciences were women 50 per cent, and this was accomplished by being over 86 per cent of the social-work class. Registrations for certificates and diplomas followed a similar pattern. (Unfortunately I do not have the data for higher-degree registrations disaggregated on a sex basis.)

By 1983–84 female students had made gains in most if not all faculties, to achieve an overall majority of 54 per cent in terms of first degrees, certificates and diploma registrations. The most significant changes with respect to first degrees came in the faculties of law, agriculture and engineering, where female registrations were 54 per cent, 33 per cent and 10 per cent respectively. The picture with respect to certificates and diplomas was more complex, with women losing ground slightly in some of the more traditional areas such as education and social work.

Between 1983–84 and 1993–94 we see a majority of females registered in the more arts-based areas, extended from arts and education to include law and social sciences. A rough parity was achieved in the faculties of medicine and natural sciences, while female registration in agriculture and engineering lagged behind. The certificates and diplomas tended to follow the pattern of the more arts-based degrees. This is not surprising, given that the vast majority of certificate and diploma programmes are outside of the natural science–based faculties. These courses are shorter than the first degree and therefore produce a disproportionate number in the graduating class. This is one reason that the graduating class has a larger proportion of women than total registrations would suggest.

What the figures for certificates and higher degrees suggest is that women require more education than men to get ahead professionally.[10] Given that their first jobs have often been in areas such as the clerical and secretarial field, they need to study again to move on in the male-dominated world of work. This could explain their dominance of the certificate programmes; their male counterparts do not need further qualifications to get ahead (CGDS 1995).

Even with a first degree women fall into the same problem; they find it necessary to return to get a diploma or masters degree to get ahead.

An alternative explanation, that women do higher degrees to climb to the top of the academic ladder, seems implausible. If this were so, they would have long dominated the staff at UWI. As we see below, this has not happened at all. The gender breakdown for registrations for higher degrees was only published beginning in 1987–88. In that year women constituted 63 per cent of registrations, as against 57 per cent for first degrees, diplomas and certificates. Over the next five years there was some variation but no clear trend with respect to the difference in registrations at the undergraduate and higher degree levels. This data can be compared with the gender breakdown of the staffing at UWI Mona, where Jamaicans constitute just less than 70 per cent of the academic and administrative staff (1993–94).

Education is the only faculty in which women constitute the majority of the academic staff at this time. This is a professional faculty, where the feminization of the particular profession is so long and well established that it would be hard for women not to be in the majority.[11] Nursing education, library studies, librarianship and administration are the fields in which we find gender parity or a majority of women staff members at UWI Mona. But even in disciplines that have long been feminized the dominance of males sometimes persists, especially at the top. The gender disaggregation of data was not available to me for the 1950s, so that I cannot say what the first year was in which women constituted the majority of registrations in the arts. Studies in these disciplines were introduced in the 1950s, and it seems likely that if women were not the majority right away they would have become so shortly thereafter. Among Jamaican students women have constituted approximately 80 per cent of registrations since 1973–74 (the first year for which I have data). Yet in 1992–93 they still only represented 42 per cent of the Mona academic staff (all nationalities), and at the professorial level they represented only 17 per cent.

The data presented above suggest a similar pattern to the one identified by Peter Whiteley (1995a) in his analysis of registration and passes for science subjects. What his work indicates is that behind the veil of equality evident in the relative parity of registrations in the natural sciences is a significant gender bias. Whereas women dominate in biology and achieve more or less equality in chemistry, men clearly dominate in physics. Whiteley's ironic comment on the extent to which these realities are understood is worth quoting at length:

> That there is far to go [with respect to sensitizing educators] may be inferred from the comment of the Dean of the Faculty of Natural Sciences . . . that there was "no problem" . . . because, *overall,* the registrations were approximately equally male and female. His views are reportedly shared by most of the faculty in the Department of Physics (all male); it is also noteworthy that in, 1993/94, [*sic*] 67 [84 per cent] of the 80 faculty members in the Faculty . . . were male. (1995a, 10)

Now that women are beginning to challenge men in the prestigious disciplines it is seen by some as a national crisis. The fact that women have long dominated education and the arts was never such a problem. Calls are going out for male role models for boys in the school system. But years of female "underperformance" at the highest academic level, even within fields they dominated, never led to the same urgent calls for serious analysis of the problem or for special measures to provide women with role models at the highest academic level. This stands in sharp contrast with Britain, for example, where gender inequalities in employment at the tertiary level had become a significant issue by the end of the 1990s.[12]

What the statistics show is that gender biases against women in Jamaica are still intact, despite the gains women have made at the level of overall admissions. In fact, the most startling gender imbalance at UWI is not at the level of student admissions or graduates at Mona, or with respect to the registration of Jamaican students. It continues to be at the level of professorial appointments on all three campuses. In 1993–94, for the whole university, 7 per cent of the appointments at this level were female. If we want greater gender balance at UWI we might wish to start where these imbalances are greatest. This would involve appointing more women at the top and persuading more males to go into fields like nursing, where women constitute the overwhelming majority. We might also consider appointing more women in agriculture and engineering, as well as persuading more women to register in these fields. In 1992–93, of the 102 members of staff in these two fields, nine were women, and female registrations represented 17 per cent of first-degree students. Meanwhile women represented 94 per cent of nursing registrations and 75 per cent of the staff.

The situation at UWI appears to be paralleled by the situation at the University of Technology in Jamaica (formally the College of Arts, Science and Technology, CAST). Data quoted by Boyd Carey (1993) indicate that "men were the majority in Architecture, 66 per cent; Building, 88 per cent; Engineering, 96 per cent, while women were in the ascendancy in Commerce, 66 per cent; Hospitality and Food Science, 89 per cent; Science and Health, 69 per cent; [and] Technical Education, 68 per cent".

The data for tertiary institutions in Jamaica do not show a simple takeover by women. What they show is that education remains extremely gendered, even if its gendered nature is now being manifested in a significantly different manner. My suggestion that male "academic underperformance" is rooted in male privileging is not an indication that I consider the problem to be a trivial or unimportant one to be brushed aside in favour of more pressing gender issues. There is no doubt that it is a serious problem; indeed, the extent of the problem should draw our attention to a need to come to terms with it at its roots, and not address it merely in terms of its most obvious symptoms. In addition, it is of special interest as it provides a very good opportunity to bring gender issues into the mainstream and demonstrate how gender bias can have negative consequences on men as well as women. Yet, to formulate the problem as one of male "academic underperformance" is misleading, just as it is misleading to see the issue as a female takeover, as the data clearly show that women are "underperforming" as well. What we have is differential gender performance, and we need to understand why it is so marked in the Jamaican case.

At first sight it may appear that it is male performance that is declining or female performance that is improving. Yet there are a number of other ways in which we might conceptualize the situation. It is possible that interest in and the status of academic pursuits are generally in decline (that is, beyond the direct instrumental values most narrowly seen with respect to the earning power they impart to the successful scholar). In this context the relative decline in male performance may be due in part to a more rapid decline in male interest in and respect for academic pursuits. So that while the interest in and respect for academic pursuits amongst women may also have declined somewhat below the level of a few decades ago, interest among men may be far below its former level. This is often discussed in terms of falling standards within the educational system, but whereas the issue of standards is a difficult one to measure, there is no doubt that there is an increasing focus on certification rather than education amongst students within the Jamaican educational system.

To understand what is taking place we need to adopt a dynamic analytic perspective on gender in the Jamaican educational system. More attention needs to be paid to the dynamic process of transformation in the performance of each gender, in terms of understanding what has accounted for changes within the group as opposed to comparisons between them. In starting to unravel the connection between educational outcomes and gender, I believe that it is necessary to start at the earliest stage of gendering: that is, with gender socialization.

Gender Socialization

The recently conducted UWI Gender Socialization Project summarized a major tendency in child-rearing practices in the Caribbean under the slogan "tie the heifer and loose the bull" (Brown 1995, 7; see also Brown and Chevannes 1995). This slogan points to the large gap in the gender socialization of Jamaican children. It embodies a vision of boys and girls that leads to the kind of upbringing that may well be the starting point for male "academic underperformance". That boys are naturally bad and girls are naturally good is a widely shared operational principle, even among fairly sophisticated persons who may well be quite gender conscious otherwise.

From the start boys and girls are treated differently in this self-fulfilling conception. In the home boys are expected to misbehave while girls are expected to conform to a rigid code. If a boy misbehaves it is essentially expected, but if a girl does so it is a serious matter. Expectations are very important in how children behave, and Jamaican children are raised under the noxious banners that "boys will be boys" while "girls can't do what the boys do and still be ladies". This underlying vision of gender socialization is not a mere accidental preference of many parents. It is connected to the historical privileging of males, which has provided them with a wider social space. Males exercise the freedom of the public space while females are considered more ideally suited to the private, domestic space where they are called on to minister to the needs of the males. The fact that so many Jamaican women work outside the home does not undermine this conception, as evidenced by the fact that women's work outside the home is not equally matched by men's work within the home.

To make matters worse, as boys grow older they are often exempted from many of the basic self-care and household tasks that girls are obliged to do. Where boys are involved in chores these are often related to the traditional privileging of males, embodied in the right to roam the streets at will. Whereas a girl is confined to her home, in the main, boys are allowed to run up and down as they please. Outdoor tasks such as going to the shop and running other errands, which are more frequently allocated to boys, open the door to a much wider social space than those such as cooking, washing clothes and cleaning the floor, which are more likely to be allocated to girls. This division is based on the historical privileging of males in terms of the space that the genders have occupied in patriarchal societies.

The different requirements of female versus male grooming has been given as one example of how differential socialization impacts on skills learnt that are later useful in school (Sobo 1993, 156). The most tedious task a boy might face is a trip to the barber once every few weeks. Here he is required to sit still for a few minutes while his hair is removed. Meanwhile his sisters, depending on the length and texture of their hair, and the household regime, may have to endure an even more taxing process every day.

Male privileging requires that girls take this extra care for two reasons, and there is evidence from the Gender Socialization Project that girls are taken care of for nearly twice as long as boys. First, girls are expected to be far better presented in public. Second, the taboos about women's bodies and their natural reproductive functions mean that there is a much greater effort made to instil in girls practices of personal care. For example, an effort is usually made to introduce girls to the basic elements of washing clothes at an early age. This is because the taboos require that a woman must wash her own underwear. At the same time there is no taboo against a woman washing a man's garments. Indeed, it is not unusual for a girl to be required to wash her brothers' underwear (see Sobo 1993).

Researchers have suggested that this gendered approach gives boys less exposure to tasks that would build self-discipline, time management and a sense of process (Davies and Evans 1997; Parry 1995b). The historical privileging of males leads to an upbringing that can leave boys without certain basic skills. These are precisely the skills that are needed for educational attainment, especially in a Jamaican-type school system. To get an indication of this we just have to consider a listing of some of the tasks that are essential for success within a largely rote learning–based system. These include: the ability to sit still and listen carefully to what one is not particularly interested in, the desire to please others, the habit of doing what one has to do rather than what one wants to do, the habit of following what others say rather than pursuing one's own aims, and the ability to perform uninteresting and repetitive tasks. In general these are not the skills instilled in Jamaican boys.

The question may well be asked, how can I link opposite practices and attitudes to historical male privileging? In some societies male privileging is manifested by the failure to educate women at all; that is, women are often not even exposed to basic literacy. In such societies male children are openly preferred. Such societies are very different from Jamaica. Women often never leave the home by themselves; their role is entirely domestic (including working within family enterprises), and they often have little or no choice in determining their fate in mating or marriage, and hence their future domestic role. Once they have left home they have little possibility of returning to help their parents in the future. In such societies sons are preferred as the ones who stay home and assist in the development of the family's fortunes. In Jamaican society, male privilege has manifested itself in male freedom to roam and often never to return, while their female relatives take care of the home base and any ageing or infirm family members. The more this is so, the more attractive girls become, especially where male employment is becoming less sure.

In the Jamaican case it is also necessary to ask what has changed which may explain how male privileging now produces a relatively improved female academic performance, where previously it produced the opposite. One factor has to do with changes in lifestyles. The shift from rural living has reduced the outdoor tasks that boys used to do, such as tying out the goats. The reduction in the number of yards that boys would in the past have had to sweep also means that there is much less of the typically "male" work left to be done. Meanwhile there has been less reduction in the comparable typically "female" work. Another dynamic change relates to the relative increase in the harshness of life in Jamaica which, it can be argued, has left boys less cared for. There is consistent evidence that it is within the communities of inner-city Kingston that the greatest gap exists in the rearing of boys and girls along the lines that I have been discussing. The point has been reached now where families are effectively saying that they prefer girls to boys. This is a far cry from the traditional upper-class values of well-to-do St Andrew dwellers (Leo-Rhynie 1997, 19).

A Gendered Schooling

Boys' gender socialization gives them less opportunity to gain the basic skills they need for schooling. They then enter a school system in which the teachers (and students) share the same gendered values that they faced in their preschool socialization. From the very beginning of the formal educational system, boys face a gender mismatch which is likely to have far-reaching consequences. It is well known that teacher expectations impact heavily on educational outcomes. We can, therefore, start with the issue of expectations concerning male behaviour. With respect to discipline it is clear that teachers have different expectations concerning boys and girls. Research indicates that teachers adopt different approaches to boys and girls in Jamaican schools (Evans 1987, 1988).

Two approaches to the discipline of boys have been observed; both of these are likely to lead to "male underperformance". For those teachers who seek to discipline the boys there is evidence that they adopt far more brutal methods than they would apply to girls. Such teachers are far more likely to punish boys, and in doing so are far more likely to apply the strap. Combined with this tendency is a sometimes separate and equally pernicious one: teachers, so much under pressure from large classes and lack of facilities, often do not even try to instil discipline in boys, taking it for granted that they will be bad. In fact both of these tendencies are rooted in the concept of the male that was presented above.

Thus boys may not receive the more subtle training in self-discipline that girls get in school, but when they play true to form and get far out of line there is an attempt to literally beat them back into shape. Boys therefore lose on two sides. First, they do not get the training in self-discipline necessary for academic success. Second, school becomes an uncomfortable place where they have to suffer the tedium of sitting still for most of the day when much of their previous training was in running up and down. When they behave in ways consistent with their earlier training they are often abused. Both of these disadvantages faced by boys can be traced back to the historic privileging of the male gender, insofar as the school draws on the skills children learn in the private (female) sphere rather than the public (male) sphere. In addition, the assumptions about maleness cause boys to be treated in educationally dysfunctional ways in school. (The same is true for femaleness/girls, but that requires a somewhat different discussion.) The problem is intensified in that Jamaican elementary schools depend more on teaching styles geared to children who have the qualities that girls have been socialized into (sometimes with limited success) than on the qualities that boys have been socialized into (usually with far more success).

As the boys progress in school they cannot keep pace with their sisters. Girls are expected home right after school (lest they learn to do what the boys do and get pregnant at a young age). They are also more likely to stay in the house until released in the morning again for school. They therefore have little alternative but to do their homework or take up the habit of reading books. Generally speaking, boys have stayed later at school to play and have "taken their time" to come home, have put down their bag and rushed out into the road or playing field. Sometimes with less sleep, often having done less homework and generally with less book exposure, the boys return to school the next day to continue to fall behind. It should be noted here that with the growing availability of television, girls might well be reading less and less at home. Even then, watching television is a sit-still and relatively passive activity, thus better training for school than being in the street. Television has probably contributed to the decline in academic pursuits discussed above; nevertheless, the evidence so far is that the boys' interest has declined more than the girls'.

Male privileging also comes to haunt boys in other ways. The feminization of the teaching profession has been part of a process that has seen a dramatic fall in levels of pay and, with them, in the status of the profession. As males leave the profession, education increasingly appears to boys as a "woman thing", acquiring in their minds an increasingly lower status. The absence of role models and the sit-still-and-listen methods of teaching, along with the chauvinist attitudes of the boys, put them at great disadvantage. There is evidence that boys actually actively assert their maleness by resisting school (Parry 1995b; Evans 1988, 91, 116). This is particularly true with respect to certain subjects that are seen as "feminine". Male-child subculture therefore exerts considerable peer pressure on boys to be disruptive in school and to underrate certain subjects.

One of the peculiarities of the Jamaican situation that is worthy of note is the language situation. In days gone by the acquisition of the "best" possible English was the goal of generations of colonial scholars. Increasingly there is resistance to the use of English as an imposition. It is not only considered more appropriate to express oneself in the Jamaican vernacular, but the need to be multilingual is not strongly felt. This has affected boys more than girls, who in 1995 got more than 70 per cent of the passes in English language in the CXC examinations.

(This compares with just over 50 per cent in maths). English has in fact been identified as one of the important targets of the male-child subculture. The assertion of manliness, with its macho value of toughness, includes the rejection of English as a more refined, softer, "feminine" form of communication. This places boys at a disadvantage where English remains the prime language of instruction, especially at the higher levels of the school and in the printed instructional materials. This may further be reinforced by male teachers who adopt similar attitudes to the boys. These male teachers are more concentrated in the more "male" subjects such as physics, and have been identified as being resistant to correcting English errors (Parry 1995a, 5; 1995b).

The declining quality of school administration is another dynamic gender-linked factor that helps to explain the more rapid fall in overall performance in certain boys' schools. The exodus from the teaching profession often took with it the most capable male teachers and administrators. This meant that the most capable teachers and school administrators who remained were often women. Gender bias prevented these women from becoming the heads of boys' schools. This left some of Jamaica's leading boys' schools with less than ideal heads. It should be noted that this bias also operates throughout the entire coeducational system, where there is a bias towards appointing male heads as well.

It could be argued that Jamaica's practices of gender socialization and the pedagogical methods used over many years would have resulted in superior performances by girls had they been given equal opportunities for education in the past. There is no doubt that the relative better performance of boys as against girls in the past was in part due to the greater restrictions placed on female education. This is most obvious in disciplines such as physics, which were not even taught in some of the leading girls' high schools until long after they were standard in boys' schools. Over time these restrictions have been relaxed. With a more level playing field, the advantages that their early gender socialization give girls have emerged in terms of their improved relative academic performance.

The broadening of opportunities for women in education has promoted, as much as it has been promoted by, the entry of women into careers that were previously dominated by men. In effect what I have been arguing is that the more level the playing field outside of the home, that is, within the educational system and the job market, the more likely girls are to outperform boys. This is because the girls' home training puts them at such an advantage. This has been intensified by the feminization of education, the devaluation of education by society and the consequent reduction in resources going to education, with the effect of demotivating boys and an increased tendency towards the use of rote-learning methods that do not mesh with boys' early gender training. To these factors, that are internal to the educational system, we need to add those external to the system.

Factors Beyond the School Gate

There are a range of wider social changes that have taken place which can be seen as operating to undermine male academic performance. Despite some movement towards a more level playing field at school and work, there are still a number of factors within the world of work that would tend to provide males with less incentive towards upgrading their qualifications. Research done by the UWI Centre for Gender and Development Studies (CGDS 1995) for the Jamaica Employers' Federation confirmed that women have to be more qualified to get the same jobs as men. In addition, even the most qualified women find it difficult to rise above the middle-management group that women dominate in some businesses. The motivation is there for women to become more qualified, but men find other ways of advancing their careers. In fact the Centre for Gender and Development Studies pilot study suggests that women are not even doing as well at this level as is popularly believed. Within the organizations studied there are at least two men to every woman from the supervisory level upwards, with six men to one woman at the executive management level, and eleven men to one woman at the level of the board of directors.

The drawing of more and more women into the workforce outside the home has had an effect on society that is yet to be calculated. This is not to suggest that they should be "sent back home", as some would

have it. The problem is that the unwaged services women used to provide to society have not always been replaced. Elsewhere I have discussed
this in terms of women's contribution to the formation of social capital
(Figueroa 1995). There are fewer hands available to care for children
and to do voluntary work in community and caring organizations (formal and informal). Men have not taken up the slack, and even if they
did make a comparable contribution to childcare it is doubtful that the
gap would be filled in other areas. This is just one aspect of the stress
that society is facing. All manner of social interactions, institutions, traditional attitudes and values are facing rapid change. In this context the
transformation of gender socialization and gender relations is lagging.

Thus, instead of responding to the social transformation that has
taken place by insisting that all children pull their weight within the
house, girls are (relative to boys) given more responsibility, afforded
more watchful attention, prepared for school and in effect often preferred, although the persistence of the ideology of male privileging makes
it difficult for some parents to recognize and admit this. As noted above,
in traditional rural life there may well have been a more even balance
of chores between the genders, hence the preference for boys may have
been more solidly based.

Boys are increasingly left to fend for themselves, in keeping with the
notions of historical male privileging, associated with male strength
and male control of public spaces. In addition, given historical patterns
of gender socialization, boys are likely to be even more aggressive and
disruptive in a period when social norms are under pressure. Social instability has promoted all the tendencies that make boys perform badly in
school, while probably having a similar but lesser effect on girls. A relatively greater effort is being made to save the girls, in keeping with the
historical male-privileging notions of the need to "protect" women. The
main concern for girls remains the probability that they may become
pregnant in their teenage years or before they have a suitable level
of potential independence or have acquired a mate acceptable to their
family. The effort to avoid early pregnancy itself leads to more attention to girls. The concern for boys' involvement in violence is also strong
but many parents, given their gender perspectives and socialization

practices, end up simply hoping for the best. In addition, given the gender roles in the home, girls become an increasingly important asset for families with single parents or where all the adults work, especially if the males are not pulling their weight with respect to domestic chores.

The tendency towards male "academic underperformance" appears to cut across classes but it seems to be particularly marked in the inner-city areas, where the issues of instability and harshness of life are most evident. There is a need for further research with particular attention to the issue of social-class differences in relation to gender over time. But the research done for the Gender Socialization Project indicates that girls in these communities follow the stereotypes suggested above to a great extent. In addition it is clear that when a choice has to be made, it is the girls rather than the boys who are sent to school. All the attitudes that support this behaviour are rooted in the historical privileging of males, in particular the more protective attitude towards girls, the belief that boys need to learn to fend for themselves, and the view that girls need to have an education so that they will not be taken advantage of by men.[13]

While there are fewer positive role models for boys within the educational system, there are many role models for them on the streets of inner-city communities. While it is the exceptional teacher who even has a modest car to drive, the boys can witness within their communities men but a few years older than they are with all the trappings of modern living: jewellery, cars, household appliances, the latest in fashions and all the lifestyle attributes that go with these. Few of these successful young men have any education to speak of. They may have an incomplete high school education or no high school education worth mentioning, but this has not hindered them from acquiring great wealth and streetwise status. These are the youth who dominate the streets where the boys roam. The values of their working parents, assuming their parents are working people, have little chance of being picked up as the boys are not even home long enough to do so. There can be little doubt that the growth of opportunities in the underground economy has tended to tarnish the myth of the meritocracy, and with it the motivation to acquire an education.

Beyond the social transformations discussed we need also to examine the increasing role of the media. Many of the negative aspects of gender socialization are being strengthened by media images. The media images of a good life would tend to suggest that it is those involved in the illegal drug trade rather than artisan and working-class parents, neighbours, and hard-working teachers who are living the good life. Along with the image of a good life, the media also presents many gender stereotypes that would reinforce the type of macho socialization that boys receive, while failing to present images of women that are in keeping with their achievements in Jamaica. Women remain the underprivileged sex in Jamaica but despite this, they have made enormous advances. They have also made contributions in practically all spheres of life, including many where men make only a minor contribution, if any at all. This is not the portrayal given in the media. This contributes to the chauvinist socialization of boys, which I have argued above undermines their effective participation in schooling. What the media does promote is a cult of the "beautiful" young woman. Much of the advertising and a large part of the programming are focused on this cult. All manner of merchandise is sold and many a film story is told in relation to this "beautiful" young woman. The ultimate case is the beauty contest and, to a lesser extent, the fashion show. Jamaica is beauty contest and fashion show capital, boasting three Miss Worlds since Independence in 1962.

We might wonder whether there are any positive ways males have responded to the situation in which females are often outperforming them and gaining access to social spaces that were formally more firmly under male control. Above I have noted the response of certain members of the male establishment. It is probably true to say that many Jamaican males share these sentiments. Indeed, anecdotal evidence suggests that it is not uncommon for young male students to express what amounts to a feeling of victimization. This often comes with some indication that the system favours females. Ironically it is sometimes argued that female teachers favour girls because they are girls, and in the same breath that male teachers favour girls because they are girls.

At a different level there is one response that I find particularly inter-esting. If the boys are in fact making any new move to learn from the girls, it is not in a way that is likely to advance them educationally. Faced with their own limited possibilities in the last twenty years, boys have sought to take on one aspect of female privilege. This is the privilege of being pretty. Thus, if the boys have taken anything from the girls it has been an enormous preoccupation with their appearance. This is not to say that Caribbean males have not always been acutely concerned with their appearance; we just have to think of the proverbial "Colon" man (returning from working on the Panama Canal with his fancy stuff). Still, what has happened in Jamaica over the last decade is something quali-tatively different for a society where just a generation or so ago the wear-ing of cologne by a man was seen as a sign of effeminacy. Jewellery, including ear and other body piercing, elaborate hairstyles including chemical processing and dyeing, the latest styles in clothes and shoes as well as the use of perfumes, all unthinkable within Jamaican society a generation ago, are now the typical attributes of young males.

Conclusion

It is possible to link male "academic underperformance" to male privi-leging and the manner in which this has been played out in relation to education in a period of social change and crisis in social relations, insti-tutions, values and norms. A long-term solution to the problem that rec-ognizes this connection is likely to be more effective than one that is based on a notion of some kind of conspiracy to marginalize males of any shade or colour. The problem can be attacked at three levels: the home and community, the school, and the workplace. The equal shar-ing of all domestic tasks at home is ultimately likely to have a salutary effect on boys' schoolwork. As long as boys continue to be marginal-ized in cooking, cleaning and washing, they are likely to be increas-ingly marginalized in the classroom.

The problem in the classroom has elements that go far beyond the gender issue. The fact is that the pedagogical methods used in Jamaican schools often lead one to despair. The teacher-centred, sit-and-listen, rote-learning, knowledge-based, memory-driven, overtaught, extra-lessoned, physically violent, verbally abusive system we have is just not suited to the development of the type of citizens who can help to transform their country. But this is not an article on pedagogy. What this chapter does raise is the extent to which the system can accommodate the needs of different types of students who have different types of talents, needs and learning abilities. The case for a change in teaching methods does not even begin to rest on the gender issue. Thus I make the point solely for the purposes of this work: so long as the system depends on repetitive rote teaching, boys coming out of contemporary Jamaican culture will fail to utilize their abilities fully and will continue to underperform.

Further, it should be noted that as long as subjects continue to be defined as "male" or "female", boys will be at a disadvantage in choosing a career in keeping with their aptitudes. Meanwhile girls will be less constrained, as a female doing a "man's job" is always more acceptable than the obverse. Increasingly, as women "take over" so-called male academic subjects, the options for boys will be more and more limited. Ultimately there will be little that boys can safely do without threatening their masculinity.

The blame for the disgraceful state of affairs in education rests with the entire society. What many teachers do with the available resources is nothing short of miraculous. It is a bad system, and good teachers ought not to defend it out of loyalty or because of the blood, sweat and tears they and their colleagues have put into it. We have allowed the devaluation of education. One large contributor to this has been the increasing focus on narrowly defined economic and financial calculations. Certain trends in economics must take special blame for this, insofar as they have taught society to value what the market values. The fact is that the market, as even the economists know, cannot be expected to give more than some vague approximation of the value of certain things, and one of them is education.[14]

Education, like childcare, contributes far more to society than has been recognized. Both are essential to the development of what is now being called social capital. When we devalue education we devalue social capital, and we do so at our peril. Education needs more resources of every type, but resources are not everything. Teachers, parents and students need to be more conscious of gender issues and the way in which gendering operates consciously and unconsciously within the system.

At the workplace there needs to be a levelling of the playing field. As long as women have to be more qualified than men for the same job, women will and men will not have the motivation for study. It is not the erection of, but the removal of, barriers to the advancement of women that will ultimately stimulate male academic achievement. In the short run a major example of this would be the opening-up of top posts in boys' schools to the best person for the job. It is this type of gender-conscious but not gender-biased thinking that is required to tackle the problem at hand.

In tackling the problem, there are many aspects of the issue that call out for careful investigation. Before considering some of these, it is well to note that there is a great deal of ongoing research on gender and education and male "academic underperformance". As such, while there is definitely a need for more research there is also the need for the presentation of a synthesis of existing work. This chapter can be seen as a small contribution to such an effort.

Despite much ongoing data analysis there are many trends that remain to be unravelled. Trends that appear based on a few data points sometimes fail to hold up when new figures become available. In addition, conclusions based on global figures sometimes are contradicted by a process of disaggregation. There is much opportunity as well for comparative analysis, regionally and internationally. Within this context, the question can be posed: How great is the problem in Jamaica and the rest of the Caribbean in relation to what is taking place elsewhere?

Some data already exist on how boys and girls spend their time, but there is need for more careful analysis if we are to base our conclusions about gender socialization on a firm foundation. Differences in attitudes towards gender and gender socialization between different social strata call for study. Along with this there is need to see how gender issues relate to social class, race and shade, as well as rural-urban differences within the home, the classroom and the world of work. In this regard

attitudes need to be considered, in particular the extent of the sophisti-
cation of gender awareness, and the extent to which the framework of
male marginalization/victimization has captured the consciousness of
students, teachers and the wider community.

Research relevant to what takes place within the classroom is also
important. Foremost among these questions are the education processes and the pedagogical approaches needed to respond to different
learning styles, abilities and intelligences. To what extent have exceptions already been granted to boys, and what have been the consequences? The entire discourse within the classroom needs to be
interrogated to ascertain its true gender content and effect. To what
extent do boys and girls have different developmental paths, what is
behind these, and how should the curriculum be ordered, if necessary,
to take this into account?

Within the world of work, what are the specific mechanisms that
allow men to get ahead despite their "academic underperformance"?
How are the skill requirements developing and how well does the contemporary process of gendering prepare boys and girls for their adult
careers? In particular, given the ways boys and girls grow up today, will
they be ready for a transformed global labour market?

Methodologically the research on gender difference needs to be more
dynamic, looking at the factors that determine how the performance of
each sex is transformed over time. In this regard it is important to go
beyond a comparison of performance to an understanding of the differential processes affecting males and females. It is also important to understand the dynamic interaction between them and see how one may affect
or be affected by changes in the gender profile of the other. Beyond this
it is important to understand that the sexes react to factors outside of
gender. We need to examine the factors affecting each sex, because
changes in society may affect each disproportionately. We can see this
in relation to the issues discussed in this chapter. Ultimately it is the differential impact of social processes on boys and girls, some very long
term and some of more recent vintage, that has brought us to the point
of male "academic underperformance".

Notes

1. I am using male "academic underperformance" to mean a failure to achieve the same level of entry, passes and distinctions as females do within programmes of study at the various levels of the educational system. I use the term because it is current, but I always put it in quotation marks because I consider that the issue is wrongly posed as just one of male "academic underperformance". The reality is one of uneven gender performance, with areas of both male and female "underperfomance".

2. For a fuller discussion of how I use the idea of gender privileging and the dialectic of gender privileging, see Figueroa 1998.

3. My argument is not that maleness has been an advantage at every moment (of time and space) in Jamaica's history. It is also not based on an insistence that current gender socialization practices generally privilege boys over girls. Those who agree with my assessment of contemporary gender privileging may find greater support for my arguments, but differences of opinion on the extent to which gender relations have been transformed are not central to my discussion. In particular, differences of opinion as to whether male or female children are now being privileged in their upbringing do not affect the core of my argument. Whether the privileging of the male child is in fact still the norm, or whether it is the norm within some social groups and not others, is not central to my basic argument.

4. Even where I have come to an idea myself someone else has usually put forward the idea previously in academic or popular work. I have sought to mention and to acknowledge others, but a search of the relevant literature would provide many more references. In writing this chapter I had the research assistance of Diana Thorburn, who also contributed ideas of her own.

5. For evidence that Jamaican females outperform males in a range of disciplines at all levels of the system see Bailey 1997; Buttrick 1995; Leo-Rhynie, Bailey and Whiteley 1995; and Whiteley 1995a, 1995b. There are certain fields that remain exceptions to the general rule of superior female performance. Some of these retain a very strong male bias. This tendency is discussed below.

6. See, for example, Buttrick 1995; Carey 1993; Hamilton 1985; and Whiteley 1994, 1995a, 1995b.

7. See, for example, "Report on the Conference on Intervention Strategies to Address Male Underperformance in Primary and Secondary

Education" by the Ministry of Education and the National Commission for UNESCO, Port of Spain, Trinidad, 1997.

8. All statistics on UWI are taken from *Official Statistics of the University of the West Indies* of various years. Note that since this research was done there has been a reorganization of some of the teaching units at UWI, including a merger of some departments and faculties.

9. There seem to be significant differences with respect to gender balances between different Caribbean territories. Space does not allow me to attempt to unravel these. For some indication of differences between different territories at the secondary level, see Figueroa 1997. It should also be noted that the data are being analysed with one major gap unplugged: the gender distribution of Jamaican students studying abroad. Buttrick (1994) estimates that there are probably just about as many Jamaican students studying abroad at various kinds of tertiary institutions as there are Jamaican students at UWI, but he gives no indication of gender balance.

10. This is consistent with the work of Sudhanshu Handa (1995). Based on human capital assumptions, his econometric analysis of the "Survey of Living Conditions in Jamaica" shows that women have a much higher rate of return to investment in education. That is, relative to women, men get less out of improving their educational status.

11. Throughout the chapter the term "feminization" is used essentially in a quantitative sense, implying that there are more women than men where formerly the opposite was true. I do not use the term with any deeper meaning, such as a flip from male to female values or the like.

12. See, for example, discussions in the press in June 1999 on the "Report on Independent Review of Higher Education Pay and Conditions" (the Bett Report). The difference between the two cases is not a matter of a lack of research on UWI. See, for example, Carty 1988.

13. The most dramatic evidence that I have seen for this is a report that of the 180 students in the 1994 graduating class for Tivoli Comprehensive, more than 130 were girls (*Daily Gleaner*, 5 July 1994). Whereas Trench Town Comprehensive also tends to follow the national trend, the neighbouring Charlie Smith Comprehensive is quite the opposite, with male registrations outpacing female registrations 318 to 185. This dramatic deviation from national trends is yet to be explained, but two possibilities have been suggested. First, that parents have removed promising girls from this very violence-prone area. Second, that girls have gone to other, more prestigious schools that fall within the same catchment area.

(Conversation with Paulette Chevannes, principal of Charlie Smith
Comprehensive, 1 January 1996).

14. There are economists who have studied and stressed the importance of
    investing in education. Despite this, I would argue that the entire thrust
    of the mainstream paradigms has been to downgrade non-market values.

References

Bailey, Barbara. 1997. "Not an Open Book: Gender Achievement and
    Education in the Caribbean". Working Paper no. 1, edited by Patricia
    Mohammed, 22–44. Mona, Jamaica: Centre for Gender and Development
    Studies, University of the West Indies.
Brown, Janet. 1995. "The Caribbean Gender Socialization Project". Paper
    presented at symposium on the University of the West Indies Gender
    Socialization Research Project, Mona, Jamaica, 12 October.
Brown, Janet, and Barry Chevannes. 1995. *Report to UNICEF on the
    Gender Socialization Project of the University of the West Indies.*
    Kingston, Jamaica: University of the West Indies.
Buttrick, John. 1994. "Jamaicans Who Study Abroad". *Social and Economic
    Studies* 43, no. 3.
———. 1995. "About the Common Entrance Examination". *Social and
    Economic Studies* 44, nos. 2 and 3.
Carey, Boyd. 1993. Address to Kingston College Founders' Day Luncheon.
    Reported in the *Daily Gleaner,* 10 May.
Carty, Linda. 1988. "Political Economy of Gender Inequality at the
    University of the West Indies". PhD diss., University of Toronto.
Centre for Gender and Development Studies (CGDS). 1995. *Report of
    Jamaica Employers' Federation Symposium on Maximizing Women's
    Potential in the Jamaican Work Place.* Kingston, Jamaica: Centre for
    Gender and Development Studies, University of the West Indies.
Chevannes, Barry. 1995. "Male Socialization in the Caribbean: Community
    Profiles". Paper presented at symposium on the University of the West
    Indies Gender Socialization Research Project, Mona, Jamaica, 12 October.
Davies, Rose, and Hyacinth Evans. 1997. "Overview Issues in Childhood
    Socialization in the Caribbean". In *Caribbean Families: Diversity among
    Ethnic Groups,* edited by Jaipaul Roopnarine and Janet Brown. London:
    Ablex.

Evans, Hyacinth. 1987. *Strengthening of Secondary Education (Phase II – General Curriculum)*. Final report, Government of Jamaica/United Nations Development Programme. Kingston, Jamaica: Faculty of Education, University of the West Indies.

———. 1988. *Strengthening of Secondary Education (General Curriculum) – A Study of Five Parishes*. Final report, Government of Jamaica/United Nations Development Programme. Kingston, Jamaica: Faculty of Education, University of the West Indies.

Figueroa, Mark. 1995. "Does the Market Undermine Its Social (Resource) Base?" Paper presented to Department of Economics Seminar Series, University of the West Indies, Mona, Jamaica, February.

———. 1997. "Gender Differentials in Educational Achievement in Jamaica and Other Caribbean Territories". Paper presented at Conference on Intervention Strategies to Address Male Underperformance in Primary and Secondary Education, Port of Spain, Trinidad, 26–28 November.

———. 1998. "Gender Privileging and Socio-Economic Outcomes: The Case of Health and Education in Jamaica". In *Gender and the Family in the Caribbean,* edited by Wilma Bailey. Kingston, Jamaica: Institute of Social and Economic Research.

———. 2000. "Making Sense of the Male Experience: The Case of Academic Underachievement in the English-Speaking Caribbean". *IDS Bulletin* 31, no. 2.

Forrest, Raymond. 1995. "Why Are Fewer Men Entering Tertiary Institutions?" *Financial Gleaner,* 5 May.

Hamilton, Marlene. 1985. "The Performance Levels in Science and Other Subjects for Jamaican Adolescents Attending Single-Sex and Co-educational High Schools". *Science Education* 64, no. 4.

Handa, Sudhanshu. 1995. *Employment, Income and Labour Supply.* Policy Development Unit Working Paper no. 1. Kingston, Jamaica: Planning Institute of Jamaica.

Leo-Rhynie, Elsa. 1992. "Women and Development Studies: Moving from the Periphery". Inaugural Professorial Lecture. University of the West Indies, Mona, Jamaica, December.

———. 1997. "Class, Race and Gender Issues in Child Rearing in the Caribbean". In *Caribbean Families: Diversity among Ethnic Groups,* edited by Jaipaul Roopnarine and Janet Brown. London: Ablex.

Leo-Rhynie, Elsa, Barbara Bailey, and Peter Whiteley. 1995. *The Status of Science and Technological Education in the Anglophone Caribbean with Special Reference to Gender.* Report of survey conducted in ten anglophone Caribbean countries by the Centre for Gender and Development Studies. Kingston, Jamaica: University of the West Indies.

Miller, Errol. 1986. *The Marginalization of the Black Male: Insights from the Development of the Teaching Profession.* Kingston, Jamaica: Institute of Social and Economic Research.

———. 1991. *Men at Risk.* Kingston, Jamaica: Jamaica Publishing House.

Parry, Odette. 1995a. "What's Sex Got to Do with It?" *Guardian,* 5 September, education supplement.

———. 1995b. "Inside Out: The Production and Reproduction of Gender Difference in the High School Classroom". Unpublished.

Ramphal, Shridath. Various years. "Chancellor's Graduation Address". University of the West Indies, Mona, Jamaica.

Simon, Donnovan. 1992. "Male 'Non-Performance' Causing Concern". *Daily Gleaner,* 3 December.

Sobo, Elisa. 1993. *One Blood.* Albany: State University of New York Press.

Trinidad and Tobago. Ministry of Education and National Commission for UNESCO. 1997. "Report on the Conference on Intervention Strategies to Address Male Underperformance in Primary and Secondary Education". Port of Spain, Trinidad.

University of the West Indies (UWI). Various years. *Official Statistics.* St Augustine, Trinidad: Office of Planning and Development.

Whiteley, Peter. 1994. "Equal Opportunity? – Gender and Participation in Science Education in Jamaica". Paper presented at Third Biennial Cross-Campus Conference of the Faculty of Education, University of the West Indies, Cave Hill, Barbados.

———. 1995a. "Science Education in the Caribbean: A Gender Perspective". Paper presented at the International Conference of the National Science Teachers' Association, Ocho Rios, Jamaica, July.

———. 1995b. "Gender Difference in Physics Education: Evidence from the Caribbean". Paper presented at AAPT Summer Meeting, Gonzaga University, Spokane, Washington.

Wint, Carl. 1993a. "The Question of Motivating Men". *Daily Gleaner,* 19 January.

———. 1993b. "Men's Worth Need to Be Recognised". *Daily Gleaner,* 26 January.

CHAPTER 6

Masculinities, Myths and Educational Underachievement

Jamaica, Barbados, St Vincent and the Grenadines

ODETTE PARRY

The vulnerability of males, and black males in particular, is currently at the centre of a discourse prevalent within popular culture and enjoying a growing appeal among social scientists. The focus of this account, namely masculinities, reflects both Caribbean regional and international concern that males in society are becoming increasingly vulnerable, marginalized and at risk. This chapter sets out to challenge some dominant myths about Caribbean male educational underachievement.

In the Caribbean, and in Jamaica in particular, it has become popular not only to talk about "male marginalization" in the context of education (Miller 1986, 1989, 1991), but also to see educational successes of females and educational failure of males as two sides of the same equation. That is, males fail because females do well. Hence in some Caribbean territories educational policy attempts to redress the balance by discriminating against females in order to compensate for the poor performance of males. I have argued elsewhere (Parry 1995) that this is seen as acceptable because females are perceived as villains and males as victims of the education system.

Here I explore some aspects of the "female as villain" thesis by focusing upon females as both pupils and teachers in the secondary education systems of Jamaica, Barbados, and St Vincent and the Grenadines. This chapter sets out to illustrate some of the ways in which females are perceived as problematic and how, as teachers and pupils, they are held responsible for the poor educational performances of males. In highlighting the crucial role of male gender identity which is central to the "female villain" thesis, as it relates to both teachers and pupils, this chapter offers an alternative perspective on male educational underachievement.

This account is based on data collected between September 1994 and December 1995 for a research project at the Institute of Social and Economic Research, University of the West Indies, Jamaica which focuses upon gender and education in the English-speaking Caribbean. The methodological approach was informed by naturalism, and the main data collection methods were classroom observation of fourth-form pupils (fourteen-year-olds) and ethnographic-style interviews with head teachers, guidance counsellors and fourth-form teachers in selected subjects. The interviews, which were unstructured, were carried out at the schools, during and after the school day. Fourth-form classes in English A (language), biology and physics provided the main focus of classroom observation.

This analysis is based upon data from the unstructured interviews carried out in eight Jamaican high schools, four high schools in Barbados and three in St Vincent. Data were also collected from two schools in the Grenadines. The participating institutions included rural and urban schools, single-sex and coeducational schools. Of the eight Jamaican schools which took part in the research, two were all-male schools, two were all-female schools and four were coeducational. In Barbados all four were coeducational schools; three had previously been all-male schools and one had previously been an all-female school. In St Vincent one all-male school, one all-female school and one coeducational school participated in the research; both schools in the Grenadines were coeducational.

In total 110 interviews were carried out. These comprised 17 heads, 13 guidance counsellors and 82 teachers. Of the 82 teachers, 34 taught English, 21 biology and 20 physics. The remainder taught other arts, science and vocational subjects. Five of the 34 English teachers were male; 6 of the 21 biology teachers were male, and 15 of the 20 physics teachers were male. In Jamaica 10 of our total of 42 teachers were male. In Barbados 11 of the 21 teachers were male and in St Vincent and the Grenadines 10 of our 22 teachers were male. Of the 18 head teachers, 10 were male and one of the 13 guidance counsellors who participated in the research was male.

All teachers interviewed were observed teaching fourth-form pupils prior to the interview taking place. Field notes recorded during observation were analysed and used to inform areas which were explored with the teachers during interviews. Areas probed in the interviews included background information on teachers (length and type of experience), aspects of classroom behaviour, motivation and performance and pupil-teacher relationships.

Men are under-represented in the teaching profession in the Caribbean, and this is particularly apparent in Jamaica (Miller 1989; Leo-Rhynie 1989; Scheifelbein and Peruzzi 1991). Our "sample" attempted to reflect the gender ratio of teachers (less than one male to four females in some cases) in the schools which we visited. Of the three subjects which we looked at, the only subject in which male teachers were more visible than females was physics.

In addition to observation and interviews, questionnaires were completed by pupils from one fourth form at each of the fifteen schools which made up the main "sample". In total, 668 questionnaire schedules were completed. The schedules provided some demographic data about students and focused upon their educational choices, future occupational plans and what they saw as major influencing factors in their lives. Although at the time of writing, analysis on this data is ongoing, questionnaire responses have been used to illustrate the issue of homophobia raised in this account.

Background to the Research

In the industrialized world, whilst the domains of academic achievement continue to differ by gender, the popular stereotype of the female under-achiever is now largely unfounded (Stockard and Wood 1984; Klein 1985). It appears rather that women are motivated to achieve equally with men or to surpass them in educational attainment (Klein 1985; Stockard 1985; Stockard and Wood 1984; Mickelson 1992; Saltzman 1994), and this is despite unequal opportunities which they face in the occupational structure upon leaving school (Mickelson 1992).

Jamaican females are largely outperforming their male counterparts. Girls do better than boys at both primary and secondary levels of school-ing (World Bank 1993). Gender differences in performance are most noticeable at the first level of testing, the common entrance examination (CEE), where females achieve a higher proportion of high school places even where assessment policies have attempted to redress the gender imbalance by discriminating in favour of males.

The 1995 CEE passes in Jamaica showed an overall increase of 3 per cent over the previous year's figures. The gender differential, however, remained the same, with 44 per cent of the awards going to males and 56 per cent going to females, despite the fact that females have to score more points on the exam than males to get the coveted award. In the previous year, results for St Vincent and the Grenadines showed that of the 313 pupils who passed, 65 per cent were female and 35 per cent were male.

World Bank figures show that the majority of Caribbean Examination Council (CXC) passes (General Certificate of Secondary Education [GCSE] O level equivalent) are claimed by females, although results indi-cate that subject choices follow a traditional pattern, with females high-ly visible in arts and males in science (Whiteley 1994). In 1993, 54.3 per cent of the entries for all subjects were from females and 45.7 per cent from males. Of the total Grade I results, 35.4 per cent went to males and 64.6 per cent went to females. When we compare English to physics results we see 81.4 per cent of the Grade I English results were taken by females and 60.7 per cent of the Grade I physics results went to males.

Figures available for Barbados and St Vincent show similar trends in that, overall, females are outperforming males. In Barbados 59.6 per cent of passes in English A went to females and also 63.9 per cent of passes in biology. In physics, however, males did marginally better than females, taking 55.5 per cent of the passes. In St Vincent 58.1 per cent of English A passes went to females and also 58.7 per cent of passes in biology. In physics, however, gender differences in performance were negligible, with males claiming 50.7 per cent of the passes. Overall in Barbados, for all subjects females secured 60.4 per cent of the passes and in St Vincent 61.1 per cent.

Theoretical Background

Theoretically this study is informed by interactionist sociology, where the social world is seen as emerging through interaction and interpretation. Although the research is located at the level of the school, it understands classroom interaction as both informing and informed by the wider contexts in which it is imbedded (Mac an Ghaill 1994). Whilst based on the premise that schools do not merely reflect the dominant gender ideology of the wider society but actively produce gender divisions, this chapter does not position teachers as being wholly responsible for these divisions (Stanworth 1983). What goes on in the classroom must therefore be understood in the context of wider societal issues as they relate to power and social control (Bernstein 1975).

The focus here is upon issues arising from the data which relate to ways in which females, as both pupils and teachers, are held responsible for male underachievement. The first addresses the perception of heads, teachers and guidance counsellors that females are sexually reprehensible. The second issue focuses upon the perception that female teachers are over-represented in the schools. Both these observations are linked, in respondents' accounts, to the wider issue of male educational underachievement, and have been used to justify the position that females, as either teachers or pupils, are at least partially responsible for this underachievement.

Female Pupils and Sexuality

When discussing aspects of male underachievement, teachers talked about the way in which males rejected education as a viable route through which to realize their objectives. That is, males bypass the education system in order to obtain material wealth. In this respect teachers felt males "want to get rich quick", that they reject education as an ineffective route to realizing this goal and that in this respect many males felt "schooling is fooling". Both male and female respondents felt that at the root of the objective to gain material wealth lay a desire to attract females, and that this was linked to an inability of male pupils to attract females of their own age. In acknowledging this a female teacher from Barbados explained: "It is my observation that if a girl gets pregnant it probably won't be by a boy in school. It's usually by someone outside and they are usually older."

Respondents from all three territories talked about the sexual relationships which females at school formed with older men. Some respondents, like the head teacher from an urban all-male school in Jamaica, described the motivation for selecting older men as mercenary: "Girls want men to buy them presents and expensive meals . . . some girls go out with really old men." A female English teacher at an urban coeducational school in Jamaica described how female pupils reject males of their own age for this reason: "The girls don't want the boys because they don't have the money."

Not all the respondents described the females' motivations as mercenary. The guidance counsellor at a rural coeducational school in Jamaica explained females' sexual rejection of their peers in terms of sexual maturation: "The girls do mature faster than the boys and say the boys in school are too immature for them even though they are the same age. They go with older men who aren't in school." Also some of the respondents, like the guidance counsellor at an urban all-female school, felt that it was difficult to judge the behaviour of females by the standards of the school, which might run contrary to the expectations of the communities in which the girls live:

You see if they aren't getting any attention at home they may feel no one loves them. So when someone, a man, shows an interest in them and tells them they are pretty it is hard to resist. They are under a lot of pressure. It is difficult because although we present a different picture of life in the school, the culture at home is so different and they live it every day.

Other respondents acknowledged how female pupils may be under pressure to assist with the family budget. In this respect, as illustrated in an account provided by the head of a Jamaican urban all-female school, respondents were ambivalent about the behaviour of female pupils:

We do get girls who are sponsored by older men. Maybe they will provide for the girl and all her family. It could be a butcher who will provide the family with fresh meat. She will be having a relationship with him. Sometimes I see girls on the bus flirting with the drivers and the conductor. I think they are either having a relationship with the driver or they are about to. They stand behind the drivers and vie for attention. Sometimes competing with each other.

Whether the motivation for involvement with older men was described as biological, mercenary or cultural, respondents clearly condemned females for the sexual relationships which they formed with men outside of the school. Sexual responsibility was laid squarely at the feet of female pupils. For example, the guidance counsellor cited below locates the responsibility for sexual diseases with females:

Because the sexual responsibility is not there in the family with the father this can lead to problems and we do have problems with sexually transmitted diseases. The girls don't know any better. Even though they are warned it's not until it happens to them that it gets through.

The guidance counsellor at an urban coeducational school acknowledged how issues of responsibility and blame were reinforced by school policies and practices, in that a pregnant female would be required to leave the school whereas the baby's father could remain at school with no interruption to his education:

Some of the pupils are sexually active and I try to make sure they are using contraceptives. There is no doubt the girls are at a disadvantage. If a girl at school gets pregnant from a boy at school she really has nothing on that boy. The boy has no problem. The girl will have to leave the school, for maybe a year, or maybe she won't come back. But the boy he doesn't have to leave. He can stay at school.

In taking responsibility for sexual relationships, females are subjected to a double standard which, as the guidance counsellor at the rural coeducational school explained, means taking the blame: "Girls can't do what boys do. They think they are probably right, that we will be judgemental. In this respect a girl will feel condemnation."

Females are condemned by teachers for their sexual relationships with older men. Implicit in this condemnation is the notion that in sexually rejecting their male peers, females contribute to the educational failure of males. Sexual rejection was felt to affect males performance in two ways. The first was that in order to attract females, teachers felt, males are pressured into bypassing the education system. The argument in its crudest form goes like this: Males understand that females of their own age seek out older men for sexual relationships. They see this as a function of the gifts and money which older men can provide and interpret the motives of the females as mercenary. In the words of one respondent: "The boys know this so they want to get money fast", and another: "The boys are under pressure so they see a route to get a nice girl."

Because it is commonly held that males reject education and schooling in order to attract women, female pupils are felt to be responsible for the underachievement of their male peers. While this position reflects a link made by educationalists between sexuality and male underachievement, it ignores the fact that fourth-form males, who were the focus of this research, had access to first, second and third-form females. Indeed some respondents, when talking about the relative maturity of males and females, described how older males in the school dated younger pupils. Also, the admission by guidance counsellors that "baby fathers" are allowed to remain at school whilst pregnant females are expelled suggests that the extent of sexual rejection of male students may be less than respondents described.

The second way in which sexual rejection was felt to affect the males' performance relates to the development of sex/gender identity. It was clear in respondents' accounts how the sex/gender identity of females is forged through the heterosexual relationships which they form with older males, relationships for which they are condemned. For males, the development of sex/gender identity is clearly felt to be more problematic. According to teachers, males are sexually rejected by their female peers, which means that the development of male sex/gender identity cannot be forged in the same way as the females, that is, through identification with heterosexual relationships. Conversely, the sex/gender identity for males emerged, in teachers' accounts, through the rejection of non-heterosexual relationships. The difference between male and female sex/gender identification is captured by an English teacher at an urban all-female school: "Girls seem to be more interested in sex at this age whereas I think the boys are more afraid of homosexuality. Jamaican men have to be macho. Homosexuals are run out of the community because of this fear that they have of sexuality."

This position is clearly problematic, in that while male pupils may be denied sexual access to females of their own age, they do have access to younger female pupils. Yet in the respondents' accounts issues of homosexuality in relation to gender identity development of males were a recurrent theme. For example, the (male) head teacher at an urban all-male school reinforced the fear expressed by the respondent above:

> Homosexuality is seen as a sin here [in Jamaica] . . . . And you know it's terrible but a lot of men could fall into their clutches because of poverty . . . I don't come out and tell the boys straight but I talk to them in small groups and say things like "If you don't keep yourself clean and tidy then no girl is going to want you".

While this account does not propose the existence of any relationship between homosexuality and school underachievement, the data do suggest a link between homophobic attitudes such as those expressed above and male educational performance. This phenomenon materializes in the extremely anti-academic male sex/gender identity which develops as a result of homophobic attitudes. Respondents described the ways in which being masculine or "macho" affects both behaviour and academic performance; being masculine or macho was not felt to be compatible with either diligent study or good grades. A female biology teacher from an urban all-female school explained how it is only when examinations approach that males really begin to apply themselves to their school work to any serious extent: "A boy may enter high school and for the first two years just get by. Then in the last two his attitude seems to change and he begins to put more effort into his school work. They may feel it's the macho way to act."

Masculine or macho identity appears to characterize both attitudes to school work and classroom behaviour. The guidance counsellor at an urban all-male school describes below how inappropriate gender behaviour could affect peer attitudes to the perpetrator. She felt gender inappropriate behaviour on the part of males undermines pupil status and authority:

> Boys have a real macho image to live up to. If a boy acts in an effeminate way he will be targeted and teased by the other students. Especially if he has a position of authority like a prefect he will have a really hard time and no-one will listen to him. The attitude will be "I don't want him talking to me lest of course I become identified with him".

This respondent expressed a clear attitude towards what she felt was inappropriate male behaviour and illustrated her position accordingly: "There is one particular problem with a boy in the first form. He is so effeminate he even gets me annoyed. He gets a really hard time. One boy in the class took a piece of wood and gave him a little spanking." While giving this account the respondent picked up a substantial piece of wood (part of a school desk) and told us that it was the particular instrument which was used to administer the "little spanking".

Although it seems that macho behaviour is encouraged at school, it clearly runs contrary to the academic ethos of education. For example, many of our respondents described English, which is a core curriculum subject, as "too effeminate", "not macho enough", "nerdish" and "too girlish" for males. The head of a rural coeducational school in Jamaica explained how this was a cultural problem: "Boys don't read because of our culture orientation. Reading is not macho or masculine enough for them. It's maybe too girlish." We found similar views to these among our respondents in Barbados, as expressed by a female head teacher: "Of course where ever you go you hear about 'nerds' who just work and work but here a nerd is a boy who shows academic inclinations. It takes on a special meaning, as sissy and effeminate does."

These views are reiterated by a female teacher in Barbados: "Boys prefer to be seen not to work. It's not popular to be male and studious. It's not macho. So some work on the sly. When they do work and apply themselves they will perform very well." Although many of our respondents felt that pupils had equal opportunities to pursue subjects of their choice, at the same time they felt certain skills were inappropriate for males. The female guidance counsellor at a rural coeducational school argued,

> Boys need to be masculine here. They must do certain subjects like technical drawing, physics and maths. They think these are the subjects which they are best at because that is the information we feed them. If a boy wants to do food nutrition, and not many do, it's not as if we encourage it. If a boy wanted to do textiles it would not be a done thing. It would cause some excitement, yes it would cause a stir.

Similar views are expressed by an English teacher in St Vincent: "It's like reading is the worst thing you can do. It's sissy and nerdish. They are very short sighted and don't see that failure to read affects their other subjects."

Homophobic attitudes were also apparent from the student questionnaire responses. On the questionnaires, pupils were asked whether they would prefer to be taught in a single-sex or a coeducational classroom. Overall, 14 per cent said single-sex and 86 per cent said coed. There was little difference in responses from males and females on this question (50 per cent of those who said coed were females and 49 per cent were males).

Students were then asked to explain the reasons for their response to this question. In Jamaica 17 per cent of males said they preferred coeducation because they did not want to be seen as homosexual. The question was open ended and provoked answers such as "I'm not gay", and "I don't love a man" . None of the female pupils gave homosexuality as a reason for preferring coeducation. The Jamaican responses to this question were more marked than in either of the other two territories. In Barbados 5.6 per cent and in St Vincent 2.6 per cent of males cited denial of homosexuality as their reason for preferring coeducation over single-sex schools. These responses may reflect a more tolerant attitude towards homosexuality in territories other than Jamaica. However, while it is clear that other Caribbean territories are also characterized by the high levels of male underachievement apparent in Jamaica, it is in Jamaica that the gender differences in educational outcome are most marked.

Female Teachers

Head teachers, teachers and guidance counsellors recognized how masculine or macho attitudes and behaviour contributed to educational failure. At the same time, however, they expressed deep concern, which echoes international concern (Elliott 1995), that the development of male sex/gender identity is threatened by a lack of suitable role models in school. In this respect both male and female respondents talked about an "over-presence of female teachers" in schools. The invisibility of male teachers, it was argued, fails to redress the absence of a father figure in the home. This was held by the male head of an urban all-male school to be particularly salient for the males from single-parent, female-headed households: "I think it's good for the boys to have exposure to male teachers and I'm happy about their presence in the school. Many of the boys lack a male father figure at home."

Jamaican families are characterized by a large percentage of single-parent, female-headed units. Respondents were concerned about the adverse effects of absentee fathers on the attitudes and behaviour of adolescent males, and some clearly felt Jamaican women to be responsible: "You know in Jamaica it is the women who are wrecking the men. In this society most households don't have men . . . ." Respondents felt that "schools have too many women teachers", and that "boys are sick of seeing women". This concern was stressed by head teachers, including the female head of an urban all-male school:

Of the sixty-six teachers I have nine are men. I try to attract men but I don't discriminate in recruitment. In some ways the male members of staff are easier to handle than the females. They take instructions from the principal easier, despite the fact that it's a female principal. They aren't as touchy as the women are.

Discussion

This chapter has examined two examples of ways in which females, as pupils and teachers, are linked, in teachers' accounts, to the educational underachievement of Jamaican males. To reiterate, these are through the sexual rejection of male pupils by their female peers, and through the "over-presence" of female teachers in school. These views reflect popular explanations for male educational failure and are reinforced by educational policy which discriminates against females at the first level of educational testing. However, what these explanations fail to make explicit, in both cases, is the crucial role which male sex/gender identity plays in educational failure.

This account suggests that an important contributory factor to male educational underachievement in Caribbean classrooms is the "hard", "macho", "masculine" attitudes and behaviour which run contrary to the academic ethos of school. Macho attitudes and behaviour were claimed by heads, teachers and guidance counsellors to affect attitudes to school, behaviour in class and subject choice.

While condemning these attitudes and behaviours, heads teachers and counsellors admit to encouraging them amongst male pupils. The homophobic fears expressed by staff and the resulting censure of attitudes and behaviours which were felt to be "effeminate", "girlish", "sissy like" and "nerdish" reinforce a masculine gender identity which rejects many aspects of schooling as all of the above. Furthermore, the importance of masculine gender identity is clearly expressed in teachers' fears about the lack of male role models for boys. Together, single-parent, female-headed households and a predominance of female teachers were felt to compound problems which boys experienced in development of male sex/gender identity.

There are several reasons for challenging this thinking. The first is that research has shown that it is often an erroneous supposition that single-parent, female-headed family units do not have access to role models from which children can learn (Epstein 1993; Stack 1974). Furthermore, research suggests that there is no firm basis for assuming that men who grow up in fatherless families are more likely in adulthood to suffer from a lack of masculine identity because they lacked male role models as children (Herzog and Sudia 1971). More recent research focuses on the way in which fathers, rather than contributing to traditional masculine identity, may usefully help to break it down via supportive, caring roles (Mac an Ghaill 1994). The analysis presented here fully supports this position, given that masculine gender identity, as it exists in its present construction, appears wholly detrimental to the educational interests of Jamaican males.

Furthermore, any link made between fatherless families and poor educational performance of males should consider home and school research in this area. Just as men and women have radically different experiences of family life (Bernard 1982), so there are two types of parent-school relationships: his and hers (Lareau 1992). In terms of schooling and relationships with the school, "parents" invariably means "mothers".

The contention that it might be more appropriate to break down traditional masculine identity patterns in preference to reinforcing them relates to my second point, and is highlighted by a head teacher in St Vincent in relation to appropriate role models: "The main problem is that our men are too irresponsible and are not appropriate role models for our children."

Concerning teachers, and more specifically the under-representation of male teachers in school, head teachers felt that male teachers tend to reinforce traditional masculine identities. In doing so they reinforce attitudes and behaviours which contradict the academic ethos of the school. For example, the small numbers of male teachers are clustered in the "traditional male" subjects such as physics and maths and virtually invisible in the arts subjects such as English. Furthermore, male teachers at the schools in the study tended towards perpetuating gender-stereotypical attitudes to subjects. The female head of a rural all-girl school, for example, felt that male teachers, particularly in the sciences, held very rigid views about what constituted men's role in the school:

> I have a young graduate science teacher who will not correct English errors of pupils because he says he is a science teacher and it's not his job. He's not the only one who won't pay attention to language skill because it's a woman's subject. They refuse to use English themselves when they set and mark work. We are having some problems with this right now. So many students and particularly men cannot cope with English when they get to university.

This raises an interesting point in regard to "masculinity" and the teaching role. Connell (1985) writes about the apparent incompatibility between the conventional positioning of femininity and the disciplinary role of teacher, in that authority is associated with masculinity. Leaving aside the issue that authority may not be seen as compatible with femininity, Connell's point is of relevance here because it highlights the fact that the teaching role is not unambiguously masculine. This is because it involves emotional involvement and caring, which is usually defined as women's domain. The classroom, argues Connell, is not designed to cope with emotional ambiguity which may challenge traditional gender roles of men as strong and women as vulnerable and emotional. Equally so, the male teacher role may be resilient to the blurring of gender divisions, divisions which perpetuate the belief that particular educational interests and skills are "women's work".

This point was reinforced by several of the heads that we talked to, who expressed concern that men who were attracted to teaching were not necessarily the most appropriate role models for male pupils; the point is captured by the male head of a rural coeducational school in Jamaica: "Where boys are performing well there's usually a father at home. In theory I think male teachers could be role models but really not all of them are qualified to be role models. Role models who are strong get the best results from the boys." Similarly a male head teacher in Barbados suggested, "We need to be aware of the fact that maybe we are not getting enough male men. That is sometimes they have confusion and problems with their maleness or masculinity. We don't seem to be able to attract enough of that kind of person."

Ironically, while the absence of male teachers is lamented by heads, our data suggest that the teaching role is not compatible with the construction of masculinity to which Jamaican males aspire. Hence male teachers will be unable to supply the role model which teachers feel to be crucial to the educational performance of male pupils.

To reiterate, the debate surrounding Caribbean male educational underachievement has been incorporated into cultural concerns about male marginalization more generally. Because of this, differences between pupils, including class, subculture and colour, have been obscured. These differences are not separate to, but cut across, the experience of schooling. While exploring myths about educational failure, this account recognizes that masculinities and femininities are multiple and diverse and are differentially experienced by pupils within systems of schooling across the Caribbean and elsewhere.

Despite its popular appeal, the notion of the vulnerable black male has not gone unchallenged. Pedro Noguera (1996) takes issue with the usage of terms like "crisis", "at risk", "marginal" and "endangered" to describe the plight of black males in America, Britain and the anglophone Caribbean. While not disputing the broad array of social and economic indicators which may locate many black males in lower socioeconomic categories, he argues that black women are rendered invisible. He asks, "What does this mean for black women and aren't they in crisis too?" As Noguera points out, the term "crisis" suggests a short-term urgency, a temporary and recent state. He disputes whether the problems facing black men are any greater than in the past, or that there are any signs of improvement. On the contrary, both in the United States and the Caribbean available figures suggest that (1) things are worsening for black men, and (2) the hardships they are facing are no more than those facing black women. Despite this, the construction of marginalized man makes an implicit assumption (1) that black males share the same experiences and problems as white males, and (2) that all black men share identical problems.

It is important therefore that issues of educational performance affecting both males and females should be understood in their wider societal context. Unfortunately, the concern about "masculinities", which has currently grabbed the popular imagination, has obfuscated the complexity of the issues involved and served to both perpetuate and add to existing educational inequalities.

References

Bernard, Jessie. 1982. *The Future of Marriage*. New Haven: Yale University Press.

Bernstein, Basil. 1975. *Class Codes and Control: Towards a Theory of Educational Transmission*. London: Routledge and Kegan Paul.

Connell, Robert. 1985. *Teachers Work*. London: Allen and Unwin.

Elliott, V. 1995. "Black Schoolboys Need Male Role Model". *Sunday Telegraph*, 10 September.

Epstein, Cynthia. 1993. "Positive Effects of the Multiple Negative". In *Changing Women in a Changing Society*, edited by J. Huber. Chicago: University of Chicago Press.

Herzog, Elizabeth, and Cecilia Sudia. 1971. "Children in Fatherless Families". In *Review of Child Development Research,* vol. 3, edited by B. Cadwell and H. Ricciult. Chicago: University of Chicago Press.

Klein, Susan, ed. 1985. *Handbook for Achieving Sex Equity through Education*. Baltimore: Johns Hopkins University Press.

Lareau, Anette. 1992. "Gender Differences in Parent Involvement in Schooling". In *Education and Gender Equality,* edited by J. Wrigley. London: Falmer Press.

Leo-Rhynie, Elsa. 1989. "Gender Issues in Secondary School Placement". Gender and Education, Third Disciplinary Seminar. Women and Development Studies Project, Jamaica: University of the West Indies.

Mac an Ghaill, Mairtin. 1994. *The Making of Men*. Buckingham: Open
University Press.

Mickelson, Roslyn. 1992. "Why Does Jane Read and Write So Well? The
Anomaly of Women's Achievement". In *Education and Gender Equality,*
edited by J. Wrigley. London: Falmer Press.

Miller, Errol. 1986. *The Marginalization of the Black Male: Insights from the
Development of the Teaching Profession*. Kingston, Jamaica: Institute of
Social and Economic Research.

————. 1989. "Gender Composition of the Primary School Teaching Force:
A Result of Personal Choice?" Gender and Education, Women and
Development Studies Project, Third Disciplinary Seminar. University of the
West Indies, Kingston, Jamaica.

————. 1991. *Men at Risk*. Kingston, Jamaica: Jamaica Publishing House.

Noguera, Pedro. 1996. "The Crisis of the Black Male in Comparative
Perspective". Paper presented at the Caribbean Studies Association
Conference, Puerto Rico.

Parry, Odette. 1995. "What's Sex Got to Do with It?" *Guardian, 5*
September, education supplement.

Saltzman, Amy. 1994. "Schooled in Failure". *US News and World Report, 7*
November.

Scheifelbein, Ernesto, and Sonia Peruzzi. 1991. *Education Opportunities for
Women – The Case of Latin America and the Caribbean: Major Projects
in the Field of Education in Latin America and the Caribbean*. OREALC
Bulletin no. 24. New York: UNESCO.

Stack, Carol. 1974. *All Our Kin*. New York: Harper Touchstone.

Stanworth, Michelle. 1983. *Gender and Schooling: Study of Social Divisions
in the Classroom*. London: Hutchinson.

Stockard, Jean. 1985. "Education and Gender Equality: A Critical View".
Research in Sociology of Education and Socialization 5.

Stockard, Jean, and J.W. Wood. 1984. "The Myth of Female
Underachievement: A Re-examination of Sex Differences in Academic
Underachievement". *American Educational Research Journal* 21, no. 40.

Whiteley, Peter. 1994. "Equal Opportunity? Gender and Participation in
Science Education in Jamaica". Unpublished Working Paper. Kingston,
Jamaica: University of the West Indies.

World Bank. 1993. *Access Quality and Efficiency in Education*. World Bank
Country Study. Washington, D.C.: World Bank.

CHAPTER 7

History, (Re)Memory, Testimony and Biomythography
Charting a Buller Man's Trinidadian Past

WESLEY E.A. CRICHLOW

There comes a time when silence becomes dishonesty. The ruling intentions of personal experience are not in accord with the permanent assaults on the most commonplace values. For many months my conscience has been the seat of unpardonable debates. And the conclusion is the determination not to despair of man, in other words, of myself. The decision I have reached is that I cannot continue to bear a responsibility at no matter what cost, on the false pretense that there is nothing else to be done.

   – Frantz Fanon, *Black Skin, White Masks*

Introduction: Laying Out Ethical Concerns

The story that you are about to read is not exclusively a story of oppression; it does, however, express a considerable amount of pain and humiliation. The process of articulating so as to ask other men, or bullers,[1] to make public their stories is an attempt to assert and broaden the reality of black male same-sex existence in

Trinidad and Tobago or the Caribbean. In this project the phrase "buller man" will be used to talk about men who have sex with men, for two reasons. One, it is a term I grew up with culturally, hence it resonates a specific set of historical events in charting my past; two, I feel it is necessary to reclaim the term in today's culture to share that past.

Same-gender sex, sex, sexuality and sexual orientation still represent a very taboo subject and area, which too many people in the Caribbean, for far too long, have tried to erase and by proxy avoid. The absence of dialogue on same-sex practices between black heterosexual communities and black male same-sex communities is central to this exploration. Both hooks (1988) and Lorde (1984) have urged dialogue within black communities to unearth black epistemological claims to truth and knowledge. Dialogue, in this case, takes place when bullers and heterosexuals meet to talk about and reflect on their lived experiences and create social ties. Yet dialogue seems almost impossible – at least for now. The assertion and representation of a buller man's existence in Trinidad and Tobago communities are essential to facilitating more humane and human social relationships.

But this chapter will be limited to the history and memory of a buller man's past from the 1970s to the early 1990s. I also recognize that in reading my story of pain and humiliation, the readers may become voyeurs of the exotic other. This process may objectify my life and present my experiences as entertainment. This inevitable danger raises a number of questions: Does the academic and political project of this work justify the public presentation of this pain? How can readers work to overcome the possibility of being voyeurs?

I urge readers to reflect on these questions and to ask themselves consciously how they might be complicit with my story. The problems of voyeurism and objectification become greater whenever someone presents excerpts of their own or other people's lives and codes them into data. The presentation of this material to people who have not experienced how bullers live raises a number of ethical concerns. The researchers and the reader should adopt an ethical stance in their analytical practices and in their reading. They must be willing to analyse critically the ways in which their failures to challenge heterosexist[2] oppressive practices affect the lives of bullers or gay men. All of us should attempt to include an analysis of personal complicity with the oppression that I experienced every day while living in Trinidad or abroad.

Academic writers have an obligation to account for the type of framework that they use. Because of my social location and my professional and personal commitment to social justice, I must as a buller man work for positive change. When we engage in work to which we are personally committed, our academic contributions are more likely to come out of a creative, politically engaged self, one that adds social to academic purpose (Olsen and Shopes 1991, 200). In pondering how to narrate my gay life in Trinidad and how to make connections with others, I decided to engage in a history and memory testimony of my gay youth while in Trinidad, or to employ the framework of Audre Lorde's biomythography. I hope this approach will allow me to elucidate the similarities and differences with other men who share and have shared a similar location, towards the goal of social change. As Trinh Minh-ha has put it, "The place of our/my hybridity is also the place of our/my identity" (1992, 29). Or, our struggles over meaning are also struggles over different modes of being: different identities (Minh-ha 1989). Identity is never fixed; that is, it is fluid and continuously changing, hence suspect. My awareness of the complex issues involved when I make my life public has, I believe, informed my ethical approach to this project.

In Gayatri Spivak's terms, I see myself as subaltern – representing self and relating to other similar, yet unique experiences in a developmental exploration of other bullers' lives and identities. All representation is constructed and hence partial; it will never be virtual, will never fully reproduce "reality". It is always interpreted by a particular system of thought – here, by a heterosexist structure of dominance. Trinidad's nationalistic, hegemonic, heterosexist community contains structures of dominance where heterosexism and morality prevail. Thus as a subaltern I speak from a contested place. This project shows how I made sense of my life within the confines of black nationalism, Trinidad communal living, black families and the church. It analyses how I and possibly others suffer at the hands of a hegemonic compulsory heterosexism that, I argue, is paralysing Trinidadian black and other communities.

The Genre of Biomythography

I am a black buller[3] man, born in Trinidad and Tobago to Caribbean parents. It is from within this ethnically rich cultural heritage – imbibed from grandparents, parents, relatives and friends – that I begin my journey. I use biomythography, as coined by Audre Lorde (1982) – life story, or representation of self – to translate my experiences of hetero-sexist oppression into this project. The genre elucidates Lorde's interest in using her life story to create a larger framework for other zamis.[4] For her the individual becomes the collective, as she recognizes the women who helped give her life substance: "A hybrid group of friends, family, lovers and African goddesses: Ma-Liz, Delois, Louise Briscoe, Aunt Anni, Linda and Genevieve; Ma-wu Lisa, thunder, sky, sun, the great mother of us all; and Afrekete, her youngest daughter, the mischievous linguist, trickster, best-beloved, whom we must all become" (1982, 255). In this sense Lorde enables the move from the singular (I) to the collective (we) in black autobiographical writing. Anne McClintock argues that

> Lorde's refusal to employ the prefix "auto" as the single, imperious sign of the self expresses a refusal to posit herself as the single, authoritative, engendering voice in the text. Instead, her life story is the collective, transcribed life of a community of women – not so much a perfect record of the past as a fabulated strategy for community survival. (1995, 315)

Marlon Riggs too, in his documentary film *Black Is Black Ain't*, links his individual identity with that of his grandmother's "gumbo"[5] – a metaphor for the plurality and rich diversity of black identities. He brings us face to face with black people – grappling with numerous, often-contested definitions of black life, black oral inscriptions and black identities. Identity here is represented as coming to being through black communities.

In a similar vein my sense of writing, as influenced by others in the community, continues the tradition of Lorde's biomythography and Riggs's gumbo. The absence of frameworks for bullers in the Caribbean made it imperative that I incorporate the biomythography as used by Lorde and the gumbo analysis as used by Riggs and by myself as a starting point for this, to assist me in developing a framework to write and talk about Trinidadian gay men's lives. I do not posit myself as a single, authoritative voice. For me biomythography has been invaluable, because I am living proof of some of the experiences that some men in the Caribbean face in coming out and coming to terms with their sexual orientation.[6] To truly "question is to interrogate something from the heart of our existence, from the centre of our being" (Van Manen 1984, 45). As a black intellectual and buller man, I find that this genre provides greater legitimacy to my project in relationship to my community (Gramsci 1971).

Yet the questions that arise are not superficial, nor do they disappear, merely because I am a member of the community, or given space to write about the experience. In Gramsci's sense, an organic intellectual can experience and be experiencing the consequences of living from a certain social position, and can articulate a set of problems associated with the lives of himself or herself and others. Gramsci's essay "The Formation of Intellectuals" describes the organic intellectual:

> Every social class, coming into existence on the original basis of an essential function in the world of economic production, creates within itself, organically, one or more groups of intellectuals who give it homogeneity and consciousness of its function not only in the economic field but in the social and political field as well. (1990, 118)

Quite simply, one must "connect" to oneself, each other and "those others" in order to become, in the Gramscian sense, an organic intellectual (Gramsci, 1971). The organic intellectual is one who is positioned to have experienced – and is experiencing – the particular consequences of living from a certain social position, and has articulated a set of problems associated with one's own life and other people's lives. As a result, one develops a relationship of familiarity with people and has the opportunity to think through issues, in order to effect change in the oppressive heterosexist structures of dominance. For too long the silence of bullers has been deafening in its support of systemic inequalities. Struggle and the repositioning of identities are essential, especially for heterosexuals who have long enjoyed the benefits of homophobia and heterosexism. It is critical to locate myself in this project, to bring into being a self-conscious buller, within a particular set of experiences and social history, to make clear the experiences and ways of understanding that inform my theoretical framework.

There is an integral relationship between myself and other men of similar experiences to those described in this project. According to Lila Abu-Lughod, there is a "discourse of familiarity":

> Others live as we perceive ourselves living not as automatons programmed according to "cultural" rules or acting out social roles, but as people going through life wondering what they should do, making mistakes, being opinionated, vacillating, trying to make themselves look good, enduring tragic personal losses, enjoying others and finding moments of laughter. (1993, 27)

The varied, complex experience of other bullers has inspired my research and provided a forum for articulating the strength, pride and dignity required to negotiate black communal living. In charting my bio-mythography, I locate myself in my childhood memories of schooling and community living, family, religion, popular culture and mass media, sports and trades, and girlfriends. In short, as a young black man in the Caribbean, I found a desperate assurance in my hyper-masculinity through religion, sports, aggressiveness, loudness, having many intimate women friends, and practising occupations or trades constructed as "manly" in my family and the community at large.

Family

I am of mixed race from parents of black, Indian and Chinese ancestral backgrounds, raised in a heterosexual nuclear family with fourteen siblings – five sisters and nine brothers. I am the fourteenth child and the youngest boy. My elder brothers and sisters left home and migrated to North America early in my life. As a result, the youngest five of us formed a close relationship. I grew up with my elder brothers but had very little in common with them. I felt that I could never compete with them in the arenas of sports and masculinity, so I avoided these contexts. I was very close, however, to my elder sisters, as well as to the youngest.

Within my family, discussions on same-sex relationships came up only in private and between adults. My parents raised us to embrace constructs and values that were inherently heterosexist. We were told what "pure and clean" sexuality was and which member of the opposite sex we would marry and go on to form a nuclear family with. My parents would often ask me, during my teenage years, about the girls in my life: "Do you have a girlfriend yet?" "I have never seen you bring home any girls." "Are you okay?" These questions were a way for them to assure themselves that I was "normal", and to signal a warning to me if something was wrong. It was always acceptable for us to talk about having more than one young woman in our lives, but if we failed to mention any young women, our parents would suggest potential girlfriends.

Most of the time our parents suggested girls who were Indo-Caribbean, light skinned and well educated. They often told us that blacks were not a progressive group and that if we wanted to succeed in life we should avoid them. We had a black neighbour and very good friend who would compare blacks to crabs in a pan of pitch oil – as one tries to climb out, the other pulls him or her down. Parents often spoke in parables to pass messages to children, and if we did not know what they meant, they would say, "If you doh want to hear, then you would have to feel."

Needless to say, my parents never once asked if I was interested in same-sex relationships, and would not speak about or allow any other sexual identities or options beyond heterosexuality. This situation imprisoned me within compulsory heterosexuality and constructed same-sex relationships as sinful, traitorous and deviant. Lorde writes, "As a forty-nine-year-old Black lesbian feminist-socialist mother of two, including one boy, and a member of an inter-racial couple, I usually find myself part of some group defined as other, deviant, inferior or just plain wrong" (1992, 47). Within my family the naturalization of heterosexism and its cultural norms about sexuality produced and defined same-sex practices as unwelcoming and unnatural. Caribbean feminist scholar Jacqui Alexander has demonstrated, for example, how the "naturalization of heterosexuality as state law has traditionally depended on the designation of gay and lesbian sex and relationships as 'unnatural' ".

She further points out that there is no absolute set of commonly under-stood or accepted principles called "the natural" which can be invoked def-initionally, except as they relate to what is labelled unnatural (1994, 9).

This typical, unwelcoming family environment, along with the result-ing private nature of homoerotic sexuality, are realities for most bullers in the Caribbean. My family assumed that I, like my father, would marry someone of the opposite sex and have a family and maintain the fami-ly name and identity through paternity, even though I had fourteen sib-lings. As hooks (1992) has argued, black men are expected to reproduce and maintain the black family. Part of this pressure also stemmed from my close relationship with my father and his expectations of me. In many respects my father was like an elder brother to me – he trusted me, and we did a lot of things together.

When I was eight he showed me how to drive his motor vehicles and how to do basic auto repairs, something that he never did for my older brothers. He also taught me basic welding, plumbing and masonry repair, and he would often call on me when repairs needed doing around the house or at the homes of my brothers and sisters. We also had some friends in common and socialized in some of the same places. I accom-panied him to the grocery store, did market shopping with him and paid the bills. He would often let me drive him, and was very proud of me when with his friends. When going places we would talk about local and international politics, social issues and relatives, and each of us had very vocal opinions on most subjects. We played cards together with his adult friends, many of whom I highly respected. In Trinidad and Tobago, playing cards, especially "all fours" at the competitive level, is a popu-lar sport among males, especially on the block (a street corner) or in village competitions. My father and I were often partners at cards. I was only a teenager, and this meant a great deal to me, especially because it helped to disguise the signs of my being a buller.

Overall I thoroughly enjoyed my relationship with my father, and yet there was a sense of shame, betrayal, dishonesty and distance that I felt because I was hiding my sexuality from him, and it caused me great pain. Despite our shared activities I never felt comfortable enough to let him know about my same-sex feelings and desires. This produced a deep ambivalence within me. I grew hesitant about working closely with him and yet had no way of refusing. I also knew that my masculinity was secure when I was with him, because his friends would often say, "Your son is so nice; he will grow into a good man." I felt that the tasks that I performed with him were "manly enough" to hide the signs of my emerging sexuality. Hence I constructed a hyper-masculinized persona within the family to cover up my confusion and remain in the closet.[7]

My relationship with my mother was very different. It mattered greatly to her that we got an education, had three meals a day, and were healthy and happy. She was a very busy woman who listened to everyone's problems and managed the family finances. I would often turn to her for permission to go places or for money to buy clothes or food or to socialize, but she and I did not talk much about other people, political issues or my life. She was very private, very cautious about what she said in front of us, always reminding us that if we could not say good things about someone then we should say nothing. She hated any form of gossip and was always ready to remind us that we should not keep bad company. She had instilled in me a very rigid hyper-male gender prison, which meant that I had a slightly different type of gender-raising structure, and I was often even more cautious around her than around my father. I never wanted to give her any signs or raise suspicions of my same-sex attraction for men, so I acted hyper-masculine to exhibit the persona she expected of me.

It was my mother who would chastise my behaviour when she thought it stereotypically feminine; "Stop acting like a girl," she would say. She had very clearly defined gender roles for her children, which decided the chores that she would assign us. We boys always did the field or yard work, and the girls, the housework. While our mother considered food shopping feminine, her sons had to do most of it, because it meant lifting heavy baskets or boxes of food to feed a large family. Physicality avoided signs of tenderness or femininity. The only "soft" tasks for the boys were polishing and whitening shoes for school, cleaning fish from Saturday market, shelling peas and cleaning sorrel. Such discourses demonstrate how roles in families are always gendered, always already, in Stuart Hall's words, underpinned by a particular sexual economy, a particular figured masculinity or femininity, a particular class identity, and so forth (1992, 31). The term "discourse" is used here to describe how knowledge, behaviour and practices are institutionalized in social policies and in family as an extended institution of the state. Discourses are located within relations of power and organized positions and places in the field of power. In Foucauldian theory, discourse is not just another word for speaking, but denotes historically situated material practice that produces power relations. Discourses are thus bound up with specific knowledges. My family is an example of how social knowledge about gender norms, and attitudes about gays and lesbians as deviant, sick and immoral, are organized through a particular heterosexist discourse.

I always felt that my mother knew that I was a buller and hoped that religion or a heterosexual relationship would cure me, so that I could hide it from her. She was very particular about where I went, who called for me, and my clothes and hairstyle. For her some of these codes were central to defining appropriate male behaviour. I never imagined that I could fool her, and I therefore always felt great pressure in her presence, which reminded me of her religious beliefs and their attitude towards same-sex practices.

Religion

It is sad that we as a church have more often than not turned our back on a significant portion of God's people on the basis of their sexual orientation. We have inflicted on gay and lesbian people the tremendous pain of having to live a lie or to face brutal rejection if they dared to reveal their true selves. But oppression cuts both ways. Behind our "safe" barriers of self-righteousness, we deprive ourselves of the rich giftedness that lesbian and gay people have to contribute to the whole body of Christ.
– Archbishop Desmond Tutu, 20 December 1995

Christianity is the dominant religion of most Caribbean islands, a relic of colonial rule. When community members object to same-sex relationships, they often invoke religious discourse to condemn those relationships as immoral and sinful. In Trinidad and Tobago, Christian congregations have traditionally viewed and continue to view same-sex practices as sinful and, as a result, have sought to regulate these practices.

While growing up in Trinidad I went to church every Sunday, and the pastors often referred to biblical verses condemning same-sex relationships – for example, Genesis 19; Leviticus 18:22 and 20:13; Romans 1:18–32; 1 Corinthians 16:9; 1 Timothy 1:10; and Revelation 21:8 and 15. The passages in Leviticus are the most explicit: "You shall not lie with a male as with a woman; it is an abomination" (18:22), and "if a man lies with a male as with a woman, both of them have committed an abomination; they shall be put to death; their blood is upon them" (20:13). My mother always mentioned these teachings when she saw a buller man or heard about someone thought to be a buller. I was uncomfortable when pastors spoke about marriage and "family values", for they always found a way to talk about men having sex with men. Thus in church services and Sunday school I felt confused and ashamed, because I was aware of my sexual feelings and tendencies. However, I continued to attend services, hoping for a "cure" for my desires.

The sense of duality articulated by W.E.B. Du Bois takes on a particularly painful and specific meaning for bullers who experience powerlessness, rejection, alienation and shame in black communal living. Although Du Bois analysed the concept of "the Negro" in the United States, his ideas are equally applicable to black men who engage in same-sex practices and are seeking agency, acceptance and approval within black and Trinidadian communal life.

Du Bois (1903) wrote about double consciousness, or the two-ness of being – the sense of always looking at oneself through the eyes of others. I always looked to family, the parish priest and friends for approval. As a buller man I found that my double-consciousness hampered my ability to make up my mind on significant issues such as same-sex sexuality, gender construction and identity politics, or to speak out in support of buller men. Du Bois argued that with a strong cultural sense of self and a commitment and connection to African people, blacks would move beyond double consciousness. He urged us to look at the duality of conflict produced by living in an oppressive or racist society. Being both black and a buller meant harbouring "two warring souls":

> A sort of seventh son, born with a veil and gifted with second-sight in this American world – a world which yields him no true self-consciousness, but only lets him see himself through the revelation of the other world . . . . One never feels his two-ness, their unreconciled striving; two warring ideals in one dark body, whose dogged strength alone keeps it from being torn asunder. (pp. 16–17)

The longing to attain self-consciousness, deny my same-sex desires and merge into a heterosexual, sexualized manhood was a source of psychological confusion and moral regulation that existed inside me, two souls forever torn asunder in Trinidad.

Dennis Altman, in his classic text, *Homosexual: Oppression and Liberation,* maintains "that societies impose upon humanity a repressive regime that channels our polymorphous eroticism into a narrow genital-centered, procreative-oriented heterosexual norm" (1971, 74). This confining of sexuality manufactures the illusion of sexual liberation as its social foil. It forces the subordinated to bear the social anxiety concerning repression (Adam 1978, 44). Gayle Rubin calls this the "erotic pyramid" of sexuality, which has heterosexual procreative masculinities at the top:

> Modern Western societies appraise sex acts according to a hierarchical system of sexual value. Marital, reproductive heterosexuals are at the top of the erotic pyramid . . . . Individuals whose behaviour stands high in this hierarchy are rewarded with certified mental health, respectability, legality, social and physical mobility, institutional support and material benefits. As sexual behaviour or occupations fall lower on the scale, the individuals who practice them are subjected to a presumption of mental illness, disrespectability, criminality, restricted physical and social mobility, loss of institutional support and economic sanctions. (1984, 278)

The idea that the sexual impulse exists solely for procreation, not for pleasure, is rooted in the Bible, the Qur'an and the *Bhagavad-Gita,* which have fostered religious interpretations and hegemonic practices that exclude same-sex relationships. Religious debates and the ongoing debate about respectability, cleanliness and decency take on social forms such as church, school, and family on which individuals rely and live their lives through. These institutions mediate the many ways in which people might view sex, sexual practices and same-sex relationships. Within these institutions and discourses, state and non-state organizations control sexuality, sexual identity and communal cultural identity. As Alexander points out, these institutions which narrate and position gay and lesbian sexuality as unnatural also serve to naturalize heterosexuality as an implicit norm (1994, 5–6).

Because of religious and moral regulation of the body and its practices, I always felt that my identity was deployed against the subjective grounds of the dichotomies of good/evil, moral/immoral, sinful/nonsinful. In this scenario the core of consciousness, as espoused by the various black communities in the Caribbean and as instituted by schools, communal living, churches, the state and the black family, erases the realities of gay people's lives.

School and Community Living

School represented a crucial phase for me in dealing with sexuality and coming to terms with manhood. As a teenager I listened as my schoolmates and friends expressed their hatred towards bullers. I can recall conversations with friends, both in school and in the community, that proposed violent acts such as stoning – with the intent to kill – against men whom they suspected were bullers. As Peter Noel writes of violence against batty bwoys in Jamaica:[8]

> hunting batty bwoys is as instinctive as the craving for fry fish an bammy, a national dish. The mere sight of them can trigger the bedlam of a witch hunt. When the toaster rapper (Hammer) Mouth discovers two gay men in a garage – "hhok up an ah kiss like . . . meangy dog" – he hollers: Run dem outa di yard. Murder them, advises another toaster, kill them one by one. Murder dem till dem fi change dem plan. (1993, 83)

Likewise, as a teenager I frequently witnessed verbal and physical harassment of bullers or effeminate men in Trinidad as they walked past gatherings of men standing on the street corner. In Kingston, Jamaica, writes Noel, between 1983 and 1988 many suspected homosexuals were stabbed or shot dead (1993, 84). My friends and others who disliked and targeted bullers often attacked them violently. Witnessing these acts provoked the type of psychological and emotional fear I lived through as a teenager in Trinidad.

I often heard my older brothers, when we had arguments or fights, tell me to stop acting like "ah she or Reginald". Reginald was a man whom many in the community suspected of being a buller. The reference was dismissive and reinforced the obvious fact that I was younger, not quite a man yet, and needed to be warned or policed about what not to become. When his name came up in arguments, it substituted for heterosexist oppressive language, induced guilt, and encouraged shame and emasculation. I consciously resisted arguing with my brothers, for fear that they would call me Reginald in front of my parents or friends.

Anger towards zami queens seldom surfaced, because most people expected women to carry themselves in traditional ways. Women played highly feminized gender roles, raising children, cleaning house, cooking, washing, dressing and behaving in ways that excluded the labels "lesbian", "manly" or "zami". According to Judith Butler gender is a corporeal style, a way of acting the body, a way of wearing one's flesh as a cultural sign (1989, 256). That is, it is a sign, a signifier of an underlying biological sex and a discernible sexual orientation.

Women wearing men's overalls, or doing physical work traditionally constructed as masculine, did not challenge women's traditional gender roles. If anything, some of the clothes that women wore reflected poverty, and it was acceptable to use them until they could afford something new. Here clothes function as visible signs of identity, subject to disruption and symbolic theft, which challenge the role of clothes as a ground for gender. Furthermore, acts such as physical aggressiveness, when a woman was fighting for her male partner, children, girlfriend or a good friend, were reconfigured and represented as very womanly – the act of a strong woman and at the same time a girlish thing to do. Observers never assumed that a woman protecting another woman from male violence had a sexual interest in her, or that women who listened to each other's problems had same-sex attractions. Rather, women supported one another in response to violence and shared communal experiences.

Jacqui Alexander calls this a "gendered call to patriotic duty. Women were to fiercely defend the nation by protecting their honor, guarding the nuclear/conjugal family,[9] 'the fundamental institution of the society' guarding 'culture' defined as the transmission of a fixed set of proper values to the children of the nation" (1994, 13). Or, as patriarchal black nationalists have argued, a woman's role "is omnipresent as the nurturer of Black children, the cultural carrier . . . and the teacher of the community" (Lubiano 1997, 241). Such public practices and gender expectations of black women do not correlate protective or caring behaviour with sexual preference. There are very strong stereotypical roles enforced for women, but they are also blurred for women in ways that they are not for men. Within a Trinidadian community some codes of women's behaviour allowed women to go unmarked, less rigorously policed in terms of a regulated notion of gender behaviour and its connection to sexuality. The notion of what it meant to look and to be zami was not as overtly marked as what it meant to look and act as a buller man.

The stability of a male's sexual identity would be interrogated if he wore the wrong clothes or colours, failed to participate in particular sports, or did not protect his female partner or show an interest in events constructed as "boyish" or "mannish". The sexual identity of men who stepped outside their traditional masculinized or mannish roles was always in question. Yet many bullers had very good relationships with older women in the community. Some women, mostly housewives, had no problem forming close relationships with bullers, as long as the males displayed laughable, gossiping, stereotypical, flamboyant, feminine characteristics, presenting themselves less as maligned than as humorous.

Bullers have been and still are objects of contempt in Caribbean culture. They are part of a communal setting with teachings and practices that involve the policing of same-sex relationships, grounded in religious canons. Today same-sex relationships and homosexuality are still

illegal[10] in most Caribbean islands, subject to the long line of oppressive "-isms" in society. These "-isms" have not created, for Caribbean
folks, any new spaces, but continue in the tradition of oppressive thinking. Heterosexuality or heterosexism, like racism, classism and ableism,
deny people their human agency to be fully who they are. It further creates a hierarchy of heterosexual categories. In essence, heterosexism
operates and starts from a paralysing position that everyone is heterosexual, while denying the human sexual or emotional existence of those
who engage in same-sex practices and identifying these practices as
deviant, sick and abnormal, as well as religiously and morally wrong.

During my teenage life, in an effort to temporarily secure my masculinity or hyper-masculinity and hegemonic heterosexuality, I participated in events such as stealing (sugar cane, cocoa, coffee pods, plums,
mangoes and other fruits), breaking bottles with slingshots or stones on
the street, engaging in physical fights, and "hanging on the block" with
the boys until late at night. These heterosexist hyper-masculinist constructions were ways for me both to assert and test my physical strength
and to attest to my heterosexuality.

During my childhood these physical acts secured my masculinist persona. For me heterosexuality was, as Judith Butler puts it, "a normative
position intrinsically impossible to embody and the persistent failure to
identify fully and without incoherence with these positions revealed heterosexuality not only as a compulsory law, but as an inevitable comedy
. . . a constant parody of itself" (1989, 122). For many of us these
forms of hyper-masculinity were like walking with or having a permanent "hard-on" – necessary performances that bought our way into the
communal construction of a normative masculinity, constructed through
the prism of heterosexuality. Our fights usually indicated an "overt disdain for anything that might appear soft or wet – more 'a taboo on tenderness' than a celebration of violence"(Morgan 1987, 48), a "matter
of learning to identify being male with these traits and pieces of behaviour" (p. 82). Young women aided young black men in maintaining this
form of behaviour, and sometimes ascribed status to them for being able
to do all these things and not get into trouble. Furthermore, these activities demonstrated "power" to parents, women, teachers and friends,

who were proud to see that a young man was not a buller, a sissy or a coward.

In school young men often called me "buller man" if I refused to talk about any sexual encounters with young women, harass young women, laugh at the clothing of economically disadvantaged students, play sports after school, or break *l'ecole biche* (skip classes). My associates saw these qualities as feminine and believed that they had the right to call me a buller. Many days I felt unsafe going to school but was afraid to let my parents know why. Homophobic violence in school and homophobia within my family left me with nowhere to turn for help or advice. On several occasions I left for school but never arrived. Throughout high school I lived in fear of men who wanted to beat me because they thought that I was a buller man. For me, acting macho was a product of what I now see as masculinized resistance, and I presented myself as tough, independent, loud, aggressive and in control – attributes of traditional dominant gender constructions and of their definitions of manhood – in order to erase all signs of being a buller or Shirley.

I negotiated heterosexist violence also by forming relationships with men who had sex with other men, who did not self-identify as bullers or bisexual and who were constructed as heterosexuals in the community. These men were tough, big, masculine and aggressive. No one dared to cross their paths. They were considered heterosexual because of their large frames, their hyper-masculine actions and their heterosexual relationships. They were the "cool guys" on the block. Many young men "hung out" with them when they were going to the movies, smoking pot, going to the river to "make a cook", playing cards on the block, or going to football and cricket matches. Most of these men also had blue-collar jobs in the auto industries, stove and refrigeration industries, or sugar cane factories – showing their masculinity, providing for the family and forestalling questions about their sexuality. Their masculinized fronts made them appear heterosexual – true men and real brothers.

I associated with these men and confided in them in order to avoid or mitigate violence, verbal or physical. My contacts with them secured me against often violent attacks on bullers by gangs of young men, always ready to protect their gender and hyper-masculinity. I often heard my friends talk about the beatings that they had given to men whom they caught at the river during the day, or in the savanna at night,[11] having sex with other men. These acts of violence often had police support, leaving the victims without recourse to state or community.

These men also exposed me to a culture of same-sex sexuality through magazines and books. They confirmed and provided an avenue for my self-recognition and acceptance of myself as a buller. They also told me secrets about other men with whom they had sexual encounters or who they knew were doing it "the other way" or were swinging. My ongoing association with these men reduced my ambivalence by affirming my sexuality, and protected me from heterosexist violence. Yet they were also friends with my brothers, although I never heard my brothers interrogating their sexuality – they perfectly re-presented my brothers' social construction and understanding of heterosexual masculinity. Knowing these men facilitated my understanding of my same-sex sexual desires and made me feel a bit more comfortable. I was not alone.

Despite this enabling self-recognition and my growing knowledge of my sensibilities and possibilities, my constant fear of heterosexist violence prevented any form of public expression. There was an emerging self-identification, as a result of my feelings and understanding and of the way in which other people were naming me and subjecting me to violence. Violence against "queers", argue Bill Wickham and Bill Haver, is "installed . . . in that ideological, lived relation termed daily life itself, as well as in the objectification, thematization and valorization of everydayness" (1992, 36). Compulsory heterosexuality denies many the possibility of positive self-identification. To avoid violence I embraced forms of a heterosexual identity, constructed and regulated within family, school, religion and popular culture. As a young teenager I was able to position myself as a buller but adopted, as I show next, the appropriate heterosexist type of dress to escape violence.

Clothing

The 1960s, 1970s and early 1980s saw rigid gender-based restrictions on clothing colour in Trinidad. As a man I was not allowed to wear pink, red, yellow or any colour that appeared too "flamboyant or bright", for these hues were viewed as weak, feminine, "uncool" – usually worn by women, bullers or white boys. The socially coded buller man's body is stereotyped as "flamboyant", "effeminate", "flashy", "crazy-acting", and in some cases loud and childlike. The flamboyant buller who became friends with older black women could braid his hair, wear headbands and bright clothing, and speak with a feminine voice, as long as he allowed others to laugh at him and make him the village clown. As gay historian Jeffrey Weeks writes:

> The male homosexual stereotype of effeminacy and transvestism has had a profound yet complex impact on men who see themselves as homosexual. No automatic relationship exists between social categories and people's sense of self and identity . . . . The most significant feature of the last hundred years of homosexual history has been that the oppressive definition and defensive identities and structures have marched together. (1981, 117)

Black men who contravened these codes were always marked as bullers within our culture and community. As Eve Kosofsky Sedgwick states in her classic essay in Michael Warner's *Fear of a Queer Planet*: "Indeed, the gay movement has never been quick to attend to issues concerning effeminate boys. There is a discreditable reason for this in the marginal or stigmatized position to which even adult men who are effeminate have been relegated to the movement" (1993, 72).

For black men generally, effeminophobia has always been a real threat to (their) masculinity, while for some bullers it is another way of reclaiming parts of their identity that they were taught to hate and despise. For many bullers effeminacy is "undesirable", "blightful" or "sinful" because black society condemns it. Yet some bullers employ it to challenge misogynist and sexist practices in black cultures, performing drag or cross-dressing to express themselves. Sedgwick writes about appositional forms of sexual self-expression that challenge the traditional norms and values that imprison black masculinity and black communal living. It certainly is dangerous to resist traditional notions of masculinity. As Sedgwick writes:

> A more understandable reason for effeminophobia, however, is the conceptual need of the gay movement to interrupt a long tradition of viewing

gender and sexuality as continuous and collapsible categories – a tradition of assuming that anyone, male or female, who desires a woman must by the same token be masculine. That one woman, as a woman, might desire another; that one man, as a man, might desire another: the indispensable need to make these powerful, subversive assertions has seemed, perhaps, to require a relative deemphasis of the links between gay adults and gender nonconforming children. (1993, 72–73)

It is not surprising, then, that fear of violence, actual or psychological, affects the lives of men who define themselves as bullers. My actions and my fears of communal and family violence emerged from this psychological trauma of same-sex practices, which I attempted to erase through activities such as sports and trades.

Sports and Trades

My involvement in competitive sports such as football and cricket was a means of survival. Sports offered an accepted arena in which young men could exercise their masculinized personhood and erase same-sex suspicion. Parents and teachers strongly encouraged sports. It was common to hear parents and coaches talk about how big and muscular the boys were becoming, and to hear schoolgirls scream at the display of black bodies in competitive boys' sports.

Once while I was playing football in the savanna with my male friends, a young man walked by. My fellow players yelled out, "Look ah buller man, check she how she walking nah. Leh we go beat and kill de man nah." As the young man walked in fear and hope that the harassment would stop, he did not respond. My friends went up to him and insisted that he fight. His refusal led to more name-calling and physical attacks, which left him bruised and alone. I stood and watched and did nothing.

This experience made me question my own safety and wonder how I would publicly affirm a same-sex identity and inform others of it. I started to think about how lonely my life might be if I did inform family and friends about my sexual orientation, and about the potential effects on my family and associates. I did not want to lose my male friends, who would call me "buller" as a put-down, or further risk the violent attacks that I feared in school on a daily basis, so I continuously constructed my gender and acted in a hyper-masculine way to negotiate the homophobic and violent conditions of my daily existence. Here I am reminded of Foucault, who argued that the emergence of the term homosexuality "as a distinct category is historically linked to the disappearance of male friendship. Intense male friendships were perceived inimical to the smooth functioning of modern institutions like the army, the bureaucracy, educational and administrative bodies" (1982, 43).

Even more disturbing for me, there was no protection from the state, nor were there organizations that supported bullers. My friends called me a buller when we played sports. They thought that I put too much emphasis on being clean, on getting home on time and on resisting fights. I also remember the mother whose house stood near where we played cricket in the streets. She would tell her sons and the other young men not to pick me on their team because I did not like to get dirty, would bat and then go home, or was not strong enough, since I was a buller man. If I was selected, I tried to act like a "really tough man" and to avoid her name-calling and her children.

All my older brothers played excellent football and cricket and were very good athletes. I never mastered sports, but immersed myself in them to erase all signs of femininity and possible suspicions about my sexuality. When I played football, men often made fun of me, because I could not kick the ball as hard as my brothers or because I did not score as many goals as they did. I was mostly excluded from playing except as a substitute – a position with which I became all too familiar.

It was useful to learn trades such as welding, plumbing, carpentry and masonry in school, to be able to do basic repairs and simple construction at home. Most communities called on members for help with building a community project or a house. Men would do the physical labour, and women the cooking. The person or group being helped was expected to supply large amounts of food for the workers. Sometimes those who could afford to pay for the work did so, in addition to serving food. For many men, including me, there was pride in having helped a family to build their new house by mixing cement, welding fences or laying bricks. It also allowed men to project their masculinized selves to the community, which earned them popularity. Especially when women were around, men would often show off their strength by hauling heavy loads and comparing their accomplishments to those of others. As Ray Raphael wrote, "Our competitive initiations tend to exaggerate rather than alleviate male insecurity and the greater our insecurity, the more prone we are to overcompensating for our weakness by excessive and aggressive male posturing" (1988, 138).

Sports and trades were – and are – valued by Trinidadian men more than academic achievement. Many young men in Trinidad still argue that academic subjects such as mathematics, physics and English are for bullers and women, while trades are for men. This embrace of a physical form of knowing – displaying dexterity and knowledge of one's own body – was and is a means for young men to graduate into their black male coolness, machismo and masculinity. Hence school, family, male communal pressure and popular culture form and maintain social values. Raphael adds "that macho, or cool, as constructions of masculinity, is just one more indication of insecurity" (p. 3).

Fathers, older brothers or uncles, neighbours, friends and relatives reminded us of how big, strong and tough they were and how hard they worked to provide for and protect their families. They boasted about the many women in their lives. Someone who did not have as many women as they did was "sick", "suspected as a buller" or not "the average young black male". My father, however, never fit these stereotypical constructions of manhood. He was very gentle and never worried about the chores that he did in the home. Nor did he have more than one female in his life. But these stereotypes continue to frame judgments of black men.

Popular Culture and Mass Media

The mostly American movie genre that appeared in Trinidad in the 1960s, 1970s and 1980s typically portrayed violence, stereotypes, a colonial and sexist mentality, and American heterosexual family values. Racist and colonial representations of cowboys and Indians, the black rapist, the black macho stud, or the black comedian inundated the market. Evil was invariably equated with "blackness". We watched television shows such as *Bonanza, The Brady Bunch, Dark Shadows, Days of Our Lives, Lassie, Flipper, The Lone Ranger, Lost in Space,* and *Tarzan* and movies such as *The Million Dollar Man* and *Planet of the Apes.* Then came the "blaxploitation"[12] genre of the 1960s, 1970s and 1980s, depicting black machismo and black language/slang in movies like *Black Belt Jones, The Black Godfather, Cleopatra Jones, Coffee, Held Up in Harlem, Sheba Baby, Shaft Big Score* and *Urban Jungle.* Kobena Mercer and Simon Watney argue: "The hegemonic repertoire of images of Black Masculinity, from docile 'Uncle Toms,' to the shuffling minstrel entertainer, the threatening native to superspade figures like Shaft, has been forged in and through the histories of slavery, colonialism and imperialism" (1988, 136).

Many black Caribbean men imitated the representation they saw in the blaxploitation films, adopting codes of "machismo and Black masculinity" to recoup some power over their conditions. This depiction of manhood, masculinity and hyper-masculinity transformed the ways in which black men in the Caribbean acted and how they treated women and gays. Most of them started to wear big Afro-hairstyles, plaid pants and high-heeled platform shoes, to adopt American and not-so-American accents, and to claim an identity that they interpreted as cool and popular. This adoption of style and politics was also partly influenced by the Black Power movements of the time; again, these were mostly driven by black American male activists. For Richard Majors and Janet Billson, in *Black Manhood,* "cool" is "the presentation of self many Black males use to establish their identity . . . it is a ritualized form of masculinities that entails behaviors, scripts, physical posturing, impression management and carefully crafted performances that deliver a single, critical message: pride, strength and control" (1992, 4)

Parents caught up in the Hollywood dream started to name their children after black movie stars. This seemed to suggest that black male babies would grow up to be bodies without brains, insecure and animalistic, without feelings or compassion. This representation reinforced existing insecurities and racist stereotypes already facing black men in the Caribbean. Slave masters defined, labelled, racialized and sexualized black men and women as "other" without understanding, valuing or respecting them.

In 1970 Trinidadian and Caribbean popular television culture saw the birth of a new form of sexual politics. From NBC's New York studios came the first black male cross-dressing character on television. A black American male named Flip Wilson played the role of Geraldine,[13] in the first successful black-hosted variety show in television history, *The Flip Wilson Show Tonight.* Watching him was painful, for my family and friends directed derogatory and heterosexist remarks at him during the show. Some of my friends said that they wished that they could pull him out of the television screen and "put ah good lash and beating upon him and straighten him out". My parents would caution us about the programme and insist that we not watch it unattended, or would recommend that we do school work while it was on. People would often express disbelief that a buller man was on television and wonder why he would embarrass black people by acting so stupid. This show came at a time when the North American feminist movement was beginning the struggles for women's liberation and at a time when women within the black consciousness movement were questioning their roles and places in society. Forced upon us through American cultural hegemony, popular culture became a contested site upon which the Trinidadian and Tobagonian, through comedy and music, entered, in a more public or open fashion, the gender, sex, sexuality debate and hence the resistance at the time was constructed around social change. Wylie Sypher reminds us that humour or comedy also "reappears in its social meaning, for comedy is both hatred and revel, rebellion and defense, attack and escape. It is revolutionary and conservative. Socially, it is both sympathy and persecution" (1980, 242).

Redd Foxx's big-screen movie *Norman Is That You?* (1976) was a little more controversial, playing with sex, sexuality and the heterosexual sexual revolution. *Norman Is That You?* is based on a Broadway play by Ron Clark and Sam Bobrick, about a young man who is black and gay. Redd Foxx's character after not seeing his son Norman for over ten years, pays Norman a surprise visit. Norman at first hides his effeminate white boyfriend, Garson, who tries to persuade him to tell his father that they are lovers. In Norman's absence, Garson returns to pick up his clothes and opens the closet door by packing a dress in his suitcase in front of Norman's father. The father attempts to convince his son that he is not gay by asking him to walk and to say "Mississippi", and by reminding him that he never dropped the ball when they used to play football. He even tells Norman to go to a physician for help, which is not an uncommon suggestion from many parents who see homosexuality as a sickness.

For the first time a black American movie televised in the Caribbean depicted a same-sex relationship involving a black man, just when most people in the Caribbean were denying the existence of such a thing. For many Trinidadians, however, the decadence of whiteness explained Norman's status as a buller. According to their heterosexist logic, whites infiltrate day-care centres, prisons and schools, turning black males into sissies, bullers and weak traitors to their race.

Many calypsonians, mostly men, sang about Norman that year and the next. It is common for calypsonians[14] engaging in musical competitions to make fun of buller men, village women or public figures. Such music often appropriated sexist, homophobic and misogynist themes in a society where hyper-masculinity is the key to manhood. Calypsonian Dennis Williams (a.k.a. Merchant) captured Trinidadian pop culture with his 1977 hit "Norman Is That You". His calypso launched a debate – in communities, on television and radio, in the broadsheet and tabloid newspapers – about same-sex relationships. Many other calypsonians, especially those without record labels in their calypso tent, continued during Carnival seasons to sing and make fun of bullers in the most hostile and violent way.

That year people started to identify some mas bands as buller-men mas bands[15] and some as heterosexual. Hecklers on the street or within my family would call a male who walked, spoke or acted in a feminine manner "Norman". The graphic, violent and homophobic calypso "Pepper in the Vaseline" – a threatening reference to sexual practices – reflected prevailing attitudes towards bullers and batty bwoys. Another calypsonian's song said, "Come out at your own risk."

Then came calypsonian Edwin Ayoung's (a.k.a. Crazy) popular song titled "Take ah Man", a controversial song that became a private anthem and a way of reclaiming power for many gays in Trinidad, who enjoyed the double meaning of the song. His most empowering words for some bullers were "If yuh cyar get ah wooman, take ah man." Under the cover of discotheques and private parties in Trinidad, this song was loved and played often by bullers. The same experience was played out among Caribbean bullers and lesbians living in Canada.

As a buller, I found the calypso and the debates about the mas bands illuminating. I started to learn about places and people in Trinidad that had a culture of bullers. I discovered how they created their space for survival, their geographies and sites of pleasure. Although I did not attend their events or visit their homes, at least I knew that I was not alone and that there was an emerging culture of bullers that I would be able to embrace someday. If you were an out buller man, everybody called you Norman, Buller, Anti-Man, Panty Man, Shirley or "she", and you dared not respond because physical and verbal violence would follow, with no police protection. Buller men both challenged and confirmed heterosexist norms, but could not offer a transformative challenge.

The movie *Norman Is That You?* became a great concern for pastors. They reminded the congregation about the evils of same-sex relationships. There was a moral panic about men becoming bullers. Our parents warned us not to become a buller like Norman. I saw two options for myself: be silent or join in the slander of bullers. Most of the time I joined in the slander, because it helped me to erase guilt and provided privileged membership in the hyper-masculinized heterosexist club.

There was also a paucity of reading material on same-sex issues. The Bible, traditional psychology and psychiatry, and the local newspaper condemned bullers. Trinidadian weekly tabloids such as the *Bomb* and the *Punch,* and the daily newspaper, the *Express,* slandered men and women suspected of being in same-sex relationships. They would often publish a picture and write about someone in the most destructive and belittling way, sometimes urging that person to leave the community or even the country. The *Bomb* and the *Punch* reported the first known buller-man wedding in Trinidad, in 1982; the reports exposed the names of the two grooms and their families, which forced both men to quit their jobs and move to Canada, where they now live. Through this irresponsible reporting I learned a great deal about other bullers and zamis, and about the violence to expect if I decided to come out. I often hid from family members when I read these stories.

In reading rooms or libraries the subject of homosexuality appeared only in the sections about law, medicine, psychiatry, psychology or sociology, under the topics of deviance, immorality or mental illness. After discovering this pathology I ceased my search for reading material on same-sex issues. Eventually I turned to texts by black writers such as Stokely Carmichael, Eldridge Cleaver, Angela Davis, Bobby Seal and Eric Williams, hoping to find a paragraph or two on black same-sex relationships. Instead, most of the ideologues of the 1960s and 1970s had negative views or had ignored the subject, grounded in the historical and often-virulent presence of racism. For brevity's sake, I will not develop further an analysis of the Black Power movement and its impact on homosexuality in Trinidad and Tobago. However, black literary works, consciousness, ideology and nationalism, and the discourses of black activists, have sought to present the race in the "best light", often depicting blacks with qualities, values and beliefs admired by white, patriarchal right-wing society. Many black writers have felt great anxiety about presenting sexuality, same-sex desire or feminist politics. In the words of bell hooks (1984), black nationalism has been constructed as a "dick thing". Henry Louis Gates, Jr has written:

> that is not to say that the ideologue of Black Nationalism in this country has any unique claim on homophobia. But it is an almost obsessive motif that runs through the major authors of the Black aesthetic and the Black power movements. In short, national identity became sexualized in the sixties and seventies in such a way as to engender a curious subterranean connection between homophobia and nationalism. (1993, 79)

Nonetheless, these texts continue to help shape black culture, communal solidarity and identity.

Girlfriends and Exploring the Erotic

Social pressures and family and community values made me feel that I had to have a few "girlfriends" with whom I was intimate. This pressure was a combination of two forces: the normative prescriptions of family and community, and my own internalized fear and guilt about an attraction to men. Thus I sought out intimate relationships with women. These relationships, I hoped, would cure my same-sex erotic feelings and attach me to the rules of a heterosexist cultural masculinity within family and community. Being intimate with girlfriends, or having multiple sexual partners, was another way to exhibit my toughness and masculinity and to erase public suspicion about my being a buller man. However, my relationships with women did not last long, because I was never fully comfortable or satisfied with the resulting exploration of my erotic, emotional and physical feelings.

I use the term "exploration of the erotic" in a broad sense, as Lorde has defined it: "our deepest knowledge, a power that, unlike other spheres of power, we all have access to and that can lessen the threat of our individual difference" (1984, 53). A form of Caribbean state-ordained nationalism and/or religious hegemonization has discouraged such exploration by creating a "dualism central to [Caribbean/]Western thought, finding parallels in distinctions between good/evil, man/woman and a range of other binarisms, which have shaped the glass through which institutionalized Christianity (religion) has viewed the world: either/or; good/bad; us/them; soul/body" (Sedgwick 1990, 123). It is within these religious binarisms that I judged my same-sex attraction, often leading to a sense of shame, unhappiness, sinfulness and dirtiness, while being torn apart inside.

The gender system (or prison), as Steven Seidman argues in his classic essay "Identity Politics in a Postmodern Gay Culture", "is said to posit heterosexuality as a primary sign of gender normality. A true man loves women; a true woman loves men. Sex roles are a first and central, distinction made by society" (1993, 114). The gender performance, as constructed for black manhood, has been both heterosexist and sexist. Marcel Saghir and Eli Robins state that "a majority of gay people irrespective of race [over half of gay men and more than three-quarters of gay women] have had heterosexual experiences" (1973, 92). This practice is common to many people in the Caribbean, although not unique to that region. Michael Warner calls this heteronormativity "the domination of norms [*sic*] that supports, reinforces and reproduces heterosexual social forms" (1993, xviii). For Warner, a reproductivist conception of the social institutions of heterosexual reproduction, institutions of socialization, and heterosexual hegemony supplements this heteronormativity (pp. vii–xxviii).

As a social construct heteronormativity permeates what Gayle Rubin has called the "sex gender system", which codes everything from social class to race into a particular set of sexualized and gendered identities that constitute and reproduce the social system in which we live (1984). Clearly most bullers have accepted heterosexuality as the norm and have viewed homosexuality as "abnormal, deviant, or different". Perhaps this explains why for bullers, according to Saghir and Robins,

> the most frequently encountered emotional reaction following heterosexual involvement is that of indifference. It is not an aversion, nor a conscious fear of heterosexuality, for most homosexual women and men find no emotional aversion and feel no trepidation in becoming involved heterosexually. The determining factor in the subsequent avoidance of heterosexual involvement is the lack of emotional gratification and true physical arousal with opposite sex partners. (1973, 214)

These norms invade same-sex practices by feminizing some black men who, when engaging in same-sex practices, act hyper-masculine in order to secure their heterosexuality and masculinity. Black nationalist and black individuals embracing stereotypical constructions of masculinity and black self-expression have sought to regulate and control the masculinity and sexual practices of bullers, and thereby to discourage all same-sex sexuality. As bullers, if we attempt to deconstruct and reconstruct the traditional black, nationalist, male, heterosexual gender "norms", we encounter great hostility and in some cases violence. Nevertheless, I resist the myopic definitions of "black masculinity" and "manhood". I do so to free myself from the black gender prison imposed on us by white racist constructions of black masculinity, which go hand-in-hand with the black ideologue's construction of family and black masculinity.

Without Conclusion

> And my brother's back at home, with his Beatles and his Stones.
> We never got it off on that revolution,
> What a drag,
> Too many snags.
>   – David Bowie[16]

For me this debate is ongoing, hence "without conclusion" correctly captures the stage of our struggle for same-sex recognition and equal protection in law. I also want to say that although I have focused on my struggles as a Trinidadian, these struggles are common in other Caribbean islands. For example, according to the International Gay and Lesbian Human Rights Commission (IGLHRC), a homophobia-fuelled protest was staged in Jamaica in anticipation of a concert by the Village People in March of 2002 (their appearance was cancelled). In addition, when the Jamaican government suggested condom distribution in the prisons to the guards and inmates alike, the insulted (and, one might add, homophobic) guards walked off the job, setting off a series of riots in which prisoners killed sixteen of their fellow inmates believed to be batty bwoys/bullers (Amnesty International report 2001). In the Bahamas a cruise ship was turned back by the Bahamanian government when they found out the cruise was filled with gay men from the United States (Amnesty International report 2001). These are just a few examples of recent stories and issues that have plagued other Caribbean islands.

It would indeed be an understatement, from both a historical and a contemporary perspective, to say that Caribbean culture has been unkind to men and women who engage in same-sex practices and relationships. This is obvious in the policing of bodily practices, institutionalizing of hegemonic laws, acts of violence, compulsory heterosexist practices and other borders that set bullers apart from heterosexuals through the denial of our human rights and dignity.

When Louis Althusser (1977, 1) wrote that ideology represents "not the system of the real relations which govern the existence of individuals, but the imaginary relation of those individuals to the real relations in which they live" and which govern their existence, he was also describing exactly, to my mind, the functioning of sexuality and sexual orientation. An engendered space is negotiated within Althusserian Marxism, one of the most humanistic branches of Marxist thought. Here "negotiation" describes the process of including a formerly excluded, taboo, marginalized or policed concern. So if, for example, many in Trinidad and the Caribbean do not see the struggle for same-sex recognition and human rights protection to be an important area for consideration, it is our responsibility who carry the burden and have a stake in social-justice work to always be vigilant, and to speak to issues of human rights concerns for men and women who have and are in same-sex relationships. The failure to do so leaves me to ask myself: Where has the passion for left politics disappeared to, if no one is bringing this struggle to the forefront in Trinidad? Such passion does exist, as has been seen with Black Power movements in Trinidad and Tobago. For example, who ever would have thought that we would have a Black Power revolution in the 1960s and another attempt to overthrow the ruling government on 27 July 1990,[17] shutting down the country for almost two weeks? Change is inevitable, and a sexual revolution is boiling and it will boil over soon, as it has started to boil over slowly in Jamaica.[18] It is hoped that other Caribbean islands, like Jamaica, will gain the confidence and garner the support for social activism on the issue of same-sex protection.

I have always been driven by the desire to serve my community and my people, and I believe that those who live in that community understand its problems. Some of those intelligent, sensitive, understanding and resourceful people are women, buller men and batty bwoys. I am frequently told that I can support and be active in heterosexist black organizations, attend sit-ins and street demonstrations, fight against police injustice, and work with homeless youths and their families. But I must not "flaunt" my "sickness", because it runs counter to black unity, black family values and black collective consciousness.

Positing a split between being a good black person/Trinidadian and being gay can be dangerous, because of the inherent dangers of denying differences within our black communities. As Cornel West concludes in Marlon Riggs's documentary *Black Is Black Ain't,* "We have got to conceive of new forms of community. We each have multiple identities and we're moving in and out of various communities at the same time. There is no one grand Black community or Black male identity" (1995). Stuart Hall, too, has called for a new kind of politics, based on the diversity of the black experience and recognizing black people's historically defined black experiences. Hall's plea for "a new kind of cultural politics" insists that we "recognize the other kinds of difference [those of gender, sexuality, race and class, for example] that place, position, and locate Black people" (1992, 30).

In summary, the lack of support in the Caribbean context for people engaging in same-sex practices; the violent attacks on people who seek same-sex agency or identities; and family, community and religious oppression have made it impossible for people to engage in same-sex practices and be open about it. The Caribbean context has policed desire along lines of good and bad, clean and unclean, and has imposed stereotypical roles and expectations on men and women, hence constructing at all times a heterosexual identity. We did not have a Stonewall riot in the Caribbean to give rise to a black same-sex politics that would support bullers politically, economically and socially. However, I do foresee change in the Caribbean, due to North American hegemony, in this millennium. Just as many things have changed, we will see a change in the policing of peoples' attitudes in the Caribbean, in particular when women[19] join the struggle for sexual liberation, and I do believe that the collective will is there and that the time is soon. State and cultural power will shift in their policing of differences, as Chicana poet Gloria Anzaldúa writes:

> Borders are set up to define the places that are safe and unsafe, to distinguish us from them. A borderland is a dividing line, a narrow strip along a steep edge. A borderland is a vague and undetermined place created by the emotional residue of an unnatural boundary. It is in a constant state of transition. The prohibited and forbidden are its inhabitants. Los atravesados live

here: the squint-eyed, the perverse, the queer, the troublesome, the half-breed, the half-dead; in short, those who cross over, pass over, or go through the confines of the "normal". (1987: 3)

And these borders we will cross!

Notes

1. "Buller man" is an indigenous derogatory epithet that I grew up with in Trinidad and Tobago, used to refer to men who have sex with other men. It is also widely used in some English-speaking Caribbean islands such as St Lucia, St Vincent and Barbados. "To be a bugger; to be (male) homosexual. G – Said that he heard M – say that C – 'bulled his way through the Gold Coast in St James'. G – Said that he understood the word 'bull' to mean to be a homosexual. Thus it is also to gender with the male cow. The word appears to have a different history in Barbados. Sir Denys Williams, Chief Justice of Barbados, stated in a judgement dd 87/06/17 'that the natural and obvious meaning those words [he bulled his way to success] to a Barbadian audience is that the plaintiff engaged in homosexual activity . . . that the plaintiff . . . had . . . committed the offense of buggery" (Allsopp 1996, 120).
2. "Heterosexist" is used to refer to characteristics of an ideological system that denies, denigrates and stigmatizes non-heterosexual forms of behaviour, identity, relationship or community. The end result of this dynamic is oppression, intolerance and daily acts of violence.
3. While I am attempting to use or restore indigenous sexual terms or knowledge specific to Trinidad and Tobago, I am also at the same time echoing Jamaican anthropologist, Charles V. Carnegie, who argues that "as we seek to restore indigenous terms and knowledge systems, we must simultaneously seek to sharpen an 'indigenous' criticism" (1994). Hence the use of the term "buller man" is not without criticism due to North American hegemony in Trinidad and Tobago, but it is important to employ this concept because this move signifies a break with the white hegemony of lesbian and gay politics and the recent development of queer theory. Finally and importantly, when I was in Trinidad it was the term I knew.

4. Lorde, reaching back into the past, remembering her Grenadian mother's history in a small island called Carriacou, tells us that "zami" is a Carriacou name for women who work together as friends and lovers. The word comes from the French patois for "les amies", lesbians. For more on this see Lorde 1982.

5. A traditional Southern black American dish made from a combination of seafood, poultry, meats, sausages and other ingredients. For Riggs, "gumbo" as metaphor expresses who we are as black people: "Some are light skin, dark skin, Christian, atheist, men, women, women who love women, men who love men, a little bit of everything that makes whole Black communities" (Riggs 1995).

6. Sexual orientation, according to Simpson (1994), refers to an individual's predisposition to experience physical and affectional attraction to members of the same, the other, or both sexes. Established early in life, it is the result of a little-understood but complex set of genetic, biological and environmental factors.

7. The metaphorical term "closet" is used to talk about persons who are aware of their same-sex attractions and identities, but choose not to declare them to the public, family, friends, community or work. To "be in the closet" results in others assuming that you are "heterosexual", or repressed and living in social isolation.

8. Batty boy/bwoy/man is a derogatory term indigenous to Jamaica, but it is also commonly used in Antigua and Guyana (Allsopp 1996, 84), to describe sexual practices between men who have sex with other men. I have not been able to discover its etymology as I have been able to do with buller man, but an adequate history of the genesis of the term might help to enable its use in contemporary Caribbean theories in the area of study on sex and sexuality.

9. While the nuclear/conjugal family may be the "ideal", it is not the norm for most in the Caribbean. But some Caribbean parents still push for that ideal to protect class image and identity.

10. In Trinidad and Tobago the Sexual Offences Act or Sodomy Laws of 1986, sections 13 and 16, and the Immigration Act of 1986, article 8 (18/1), prohibit and regulate sexual activity between consenting adults and declare homosexuality illegal in the country.

11. The savannah is the grounds used for sporting, political and cultural activities.

12. "Blaxploitation" films involved black actors being trapped in the racist, stereotypical "other" position, while white actors were cast as heroes and

smart people. Blacks were always thieves, shiftless, lazy and unintelligent; often the first to be killed, they sometimes acted in stereotypically humorous ways to gain acceptance.

13. Geraldine was created, according to Flip Wilson, because while he was working, white men would often come up to him and invoke the age-old racist and sexist stereotype, asking, "Hey, can you get me a girl?" He took offence to this and wanted to erase white society's racist stereotype by creating a proud, independent and dignified black woman, so he created Geraldine (Flip Wilson, interview by Tom Burke, in *New York Times Magazine*, November 1979).

14. Then there was the Mighty Sparrow's "Jean and Dinah".

15. I had many male friends who had sex with other men, who played in mas bands such as Peter Minshall, Wayne Berkley, Stephen Lee Young and Harold Saldenah. They informed me that these were the bands to play with, or that I should attend these bands' launching parties in order to meet other bullers. They also stressed that this was an ideal opportunity to meet tourists who were bullers and who came to play mas – in particular Peter Minshall's band. Minshall's band, they argued, had the most whites (tourists or locals) who were bullers. These bands and mas tents often got my undivided attention, because I saw this as a way to seek out men like myself, but I was afraid to get close to them or let any of my hyper-masculinist friends or family know that I found these bands interesting, or that I liked them. I felt that if I mentioned any of these bands to my friends, it would make me the target of suspicion, a suspicion I could not deal with or defend myself against at the time.

16. Written by David Bowie (1972), performed by Mott the Hoople, *Mott the Hoople Greatest Hits*, CBS, 1976.

17. On Friday, 27 July 1990, at approximately 5:30 p.m., a group of black Muslims, members of the Jamaat Al Muslimeen, took over the nation's parliament at the Red House in the capital city of Port of Spain. Nineteen hostages were captured; among them were the prime minister, members of parliament and other civil servants. For more on this see Deosaran 1993.

18. On 5 June 2002 the Jamaican Forum for Lesbians, All-Sexuals and Gays (JFLAG) made a historic presentation to the Jamaican parliament (the Joint Committee on the Charter of Rights) to make the case for protecting Jamaicans from discrimination on the grounds of sexual orientation (*JFLAG Newsletter*, June 2002).

19. It might be presumptuous of me to assume that the women's struggle in the Caribbean will bring the debate for same-sex recognition closer to the local human rights agenda. But I make this statement as a observer of the feminist struggles in North America that also created an opening for debates about redefinitions of the family, which in turn led to legal discussions about same-sex rights, which eventually became law.

References

Abu-Lughod, Lila. 1993. *Writing Women's Worlds: Bedouin Stories.* Berkeley: University of California Press.

Adam, Barry. 1978. *The Survival of Domination: Inferiorization and Everyday Life.* New York: Elsevier.

Alexander, Jacqui M. 1994. "Not Just (Any) Body Can Be a Citizen: The Politics of Law, Sexuality and Postcoloniality in Trinidad and Tobago and the Bahamas". *Feminist Review,* no. 34 (Spring).

Allsopp, Richard. 1996. *The Dictionary of Caribbean English Usage.* London: Oxford University Press.

Althusser, Louis. 1977. *Lenin and Philosophy.* London: New Left Books.

Altman, Dennis. 1971. *Homosexual: Oppression and Liberation.* New York: Outbridge and Dienstfrey.

Anzaldúa, Gloria. 1987. *Borderlands/La Frontera: The New Mestiza.* San Francisco: Aunt Lute.

Butler, Judith. 1989. *Gender Trouble: Feminism and the Subversion of Identity.* London: Routledge.

Carnegie, Charles V. 1994. "On Liminal Subjectivity". Paper presented at the National Symposium on Indigenous Knowledge and Contemporary Social Issues, Tampa, Florida, March.

Deosaran, Ramesh. 1993. *A Society under Siege: A Study of Political Confusion and Legal Mysticism.* St Augustine, Trinidad: McAl Psychological Research Centre, University of the West Indies.

Du Bois, W.E.B. 1903. *The Souls of Black Folk.* Chicago: National Urban League.

Fanon, Frantz. 1967. *Black Skin, White Masks.* Translated by C.L. Markmann. New York: Grove.

Foucault, Michel. [1989] 1982. "Friendship as a Lifestyle". *Gay Information* 7. Reprinted in *Foucault Live!* New York: Semiotext(e).

Gates, Jr, Henry Louis. 1993. "The Black Man's Burden". In *Fear of a Queer Planet: Queer Politics and Social Theory*, edited by Michael Warner. Minneapolis: University of Minnesota Press.

Gramsci, Antonio. 1971. *Selections from the Prison Note Books*. New York International Publishers.

———. [1957] 1990. *The Modern Prince and Other Writings*. Reprint, New York: International Publishers.

Hall, Stuart. 1992. "What Is This 'Black' in Black Popular Culture?" In *Black Popular Culture*, edited by Gina Dent. Seattle: Bay Press.

hooks, bell. 1984. *Feminist Theory: From Margin to Center*. Boston: South End Press.

———. 1988. *Talking Back: Thinking Feminist, Thinking Black*. Boston: South End Press.

———. 1992. *Black Looks: Race and Representation*. Boston: South End Press.

Lorde, Audre. 1982. *Zami: A New Spelling of My Name – A Biomythography*. Trumansburg, N.Y.: Crossing Press.

———. 1984. *Sister Outsider*. Trumansburg, NY: Crossing Press.

———. 1992. *A Burst of Light: Essays on Sexuality and Difference*. Toronto: Women's Press.

Lubiano, Wahneema, ed. 1997. *The House that Race Built: Black Americans, US Terrain*. New York: Pantheon.

Majors, Richard, and Janet Mancini Billson. 1992. *Cool Pose: The Dilemmas of Black Manhood in America*. New York: Lexington.

McClintock, Anne. 1995. *Imperial Leather: Race, Gender and Sexuality in the Colonial Context*. New York: Routledge.

Mercer, Kobena. 1988. "Imagining the Black Man's Sex". In *Photography/Politics: Two,* edited by Patricia Holland, Jo Spence and Simon Watney. London: Commedia/Methuen.

Minh-ha, Trinh. 1989. *Woman, Native, Other: Writing Post Coloniality and Feminism*. Bloomington: Indiana University Press.

———. 1992. *The Framer Framed*. New York: Routledge.

Morgan, David. 1987. "It Will Make a Man of You: Notes on National Service, Masculinity and Autobiography". *Studies in Sexual Politics,* no. 17.

Noel, Peter. 1993. "Batty Boys in Babylon: Can Gay West Indians Survive the 'Boom Bye Bye' Posses?" *Village Voice,* 12 January.

Olson, Karen, and Shopes, Linda. 1991. "Crossing Boundaries, Building Bridges: Doing Oral History among Working Class Women and Men". In

Women's Words: The Feminist Practice of Oral History, edited by
S. Berger Gluck and D. Patai. New York: Routledge.

Raphael, Ray. 1988. *The Men from the Boys: Rites of Passage in Male
America.* London: University of Nebraska Press.

Riggs, Marlon. 1995. *Black Is Black Ain't.* Independent Television
Service/California Newsreel.

Rubin, Gayle. 1984. "Thinking Sex: Notes for a Radical Theory of the
Politics of Sexuality". In *Pleasure and Danger: Exploring Female
Sexuality,* edited by Carol Vance. Boston: Routledge and Kegan Paul.

Saghir, Marcel, and Eli Robins. 1973. *Male and Female Homosexuality: A
Comprehensive Investigation.* Baltimore: Williams and Wilkins.

Schlatter, George. 1976. *Norman Is That You?* Metro Goldwyn Mayer.

Sedgwick, Eve Kosofsky. 1990. *Epistemology of the Closet.* Berkeley:
University of California Press.

———. 1993. "How to Bring Your Kids Up Gay". In *Fear of a Queer Planet:
Queer Politics and Social Theory,* edited by Michael Warner. Minneapolis:
University of Minnesota Press.

Seidman, Steeve. 1993. "Identity and Politics in Postmodern Gay Culture:
Some Historical and Conceptual Notes". In *Fear of a Queer Planet: Queer
Politics and Social Theory,* edited by Michael Warner. Minneapolis:
University of Minnesota Press.

Simpson, Bonnie. 1994. *Opening Doors: Making Substance Abuse and Other
Services More Accessible to Lesbian, Gay and Bi-sexual Youth.* Toronto:
Central Toronto Youth Services.

Sypher, Wylie, ed. 1980. *Comedy: "An Essay on Comedy," by George
Meredith, and "Laughter," by Henri Bergson.* Baltimore: Johns Hopkins
University Press.

Van Manen, Max. 1984. "Practising Phenomenological Writing".
Phenomenology + Pegagogy 2, no. 1.

Warner, Michael. 1993. *Fear of a Queer Planet: Queer Politics and Social
Theory.* Minneapolis: University of Minnesota Press.

Weeks, Jeffrey. 1981. "Discourse, Desire and Sexual Deviance". In *The
Making of the Modern Homosexual,* edited by Kenneth Plummer. London:
Hutchinson.

Wickham, Gary, and William Haver. 1992. "Come Out, Come Out,
Wherever You Are: A Guide for the Homoerotically Disadvantaged".
Typescript.

PART THREE

Class, Ethnicity, Nation and Notions of Masculinity

CHAPTER 8

Black Masculinity in Caribbean Slavery

HILARY BECKLES

Caribbean academics and public policy planners are engaged in several interactive discourses that concern the ideological constructions, and social effects, of historicized black masculinities. The social representations of these masculinities, and their relationships to the meanings of everyday life, have produced discernible cultural results over time. One of these results is endemic imbalances between males and females in public institutions and social processes. In areas of political power and domestic authority other results are seen, as manifested in the problematized popular behaviours of young black males, now perceived as labyrinths, or laboratories, for detecting the origins of dysfunctional deviance in cultural life (see Bond and Peery 1970; Brod 1987; Brittan 1989; Connell 1987, 1995; Easthope 1986).

One recommendation of the discourse calls for the detection of the historical origins of what is a startling "discovery"; that the postcolonial black male is psychically defeated and socially at risk. It is said, furthermore, that the very notion of "nation" is at risk, subverted, if you will, by socially dysfunctional masculine attitudes and cultural tendencies. Analytical subtleties apart, the idea is aggressively promoted that historically shaped and validated masculinities within the region have been parked by postmodernity in a derelict cul-de-sac as far as the ideologies of community and development are concerned.

All too often in these conversations, seminal moments and critical ideas within the historical contexts, and the perspectives they should yield, are ignored, missed or understated. Critical historical evidence is often set aside, condemned and discredited as an apologetic voice for particular antisocial types of masculinities. Linked to this posture is a suspicion of the traditional historian's craft as a politically supportive ideological activity of patriarchy within the gender order. With keen awareness of these positions, what is proposed here is not an attempt to confront these postures nor to suggest an escape route through historicism. Rather, this intervention is intended to fully open the historical narrative at the primordial juncture of the slave society. The search is for a perspective that may illuminate the historical nature of relations and structures within Caribbean civilization and allow one to comment on the process of social and ideological continuities (see Baker and Chapman 1962). Definitional specification requires that since our concern is with black masculinities, analytic attention should focus on the terms "black" and "male". The proposal here is that we adopt them both at the general level of popular understanding, and take on board the view of Hare and Hare (1984) that recognizes masculinity in terms of a culturally determined tendency to act as a provider and protector.

It is important to recognize that the ideology of masculinity is largely "a socially produced script" on which historical notions of role fulfilment have been coded. This feature of the process dictates that the script is under constant revision; it is therefore unstable, even though the continuity of certain fundamental elements can be discerned. These elements, collectively, constitute the rollers on which masculinities evolve as sites of cultural power within changing social realities. As male role fulfilment changes over time, ideological representations of masculinities are revised, an indication of the interactive nature of ideology and institutional power.

The intention here, then, is to discuss how the masculinity of enslaved blacks was constructed and how it interacted with the hegemonic structures of white masculinity. The principal site of this interaction was property rights cultures (including blacks as capital assets) and the public governance of colonial society. The focus is on differentiated, marginalized, subordinated and stigmatized black masculinity that struggled by violent and non-violent means to develop what Messner describes as an "autonomous positional identity". This dialectical process was driven largely by an intense concern for personal and collective survival, and a general quest for independent power and privileges (Messner 1991). During slavery the right to life and social liberty was denied blacks not on the basis of gender, but by the race inequities of colonial culture. Gender differences, however, and inequalities among males and females served to demonstrate how considerations of race differentiated black and white masculinities. At the same time gender difference provides a lens through which to view attempts by all men to construct and legitimize their domination and control of all women in private and public social relations (see Beckles 1993).

Connell's concept of the "gender order" is relevant and useful. The "gender order" is presented as a turbulent, dynamic process that moves the analysis beyond static gender-role theory and reductionist concepts of patriarchy. It demonstrates, furthermore, how competing masculinities – some hegemonic, some marginalized – interact, particularly with respect to the shared project of the domination of social culture, material resources and women. Not all men, however, consumed equally the produce of this ideological investment – hence endemic contests between masculinities across class, ethnic and cultural lines (Connell 1995).

The enterprise of Caribbean colonization was essentially a white male–owned and –managed project. The construction of agrarian and mercantile systems called into existence the institution of chattel slavery as the mechanism to exploit the labour services of Africans. For most of the slavery period Caribbean businesses displayed a preference for male labour. Establishing infrastructure for large-scale production (land clearance, communications networks and so forth) in formative periods generated a greater demand for muscle power. The slave trade, responsive to this preference, delivered a 65 per cent male "cargo" to the region.

Colonial societies were constructed, therefore, upon the demographic basis of a dominant white-black male encounter. Over time the process of maintaining and reproducing businesses focused on female labour, and despite limited natural growth performance in a few places, failed to equalize sex ratios. In 1800 some 55 per cent of the slaves in the English colonies were situated in Jamaica. There, 70 per cent of them were male. Only Barbados, of all the major sugar economies, achieved a balanced sex ratio. Most territories were never normalized, and males within all so-called races predominated in the populations of rural and urban communities.

In this respect, then, the origins of the institution of slavery can usefully be discussed in terms of the military defeat and subsequent violent subordination of black males by white men. While it is true that the slave trade flourished, in part, as a result of some voluntary commercial exchange between European and African male business elites, the fact of European military conquest and ultimate superiority in most parts of West Africa provides a compelling explanatory context. In most West African societies, during the period of the slave trade, states were constructed and defended by armies drawn mostly from among men. The enslavement in the Caribbean of defeated male warriors, now required to labour on estates, symbolized the achievement of white male triumphalism. While women also participated in the political and military rule of some West African societies, the prevalence of dominant patriarchal formations reinforced the significance of this development (see Law 1977; Law 1991; Hilton 1985).

Black men, therefore, embarked on a Caribbean experience within the context of institutional environments that reflected the conquistadorial ideologies and interests of white patriarchy. Empowered white men ideologically represented their masculinity by reference to the dominant imperatives of their imperial project. Central to these representations was the quest for monopolistic control, ownership and possession of all properties and power in these societies. The monopoly possession of power, profits, glory and pleasure was specified as a core element in the social translation of white masculine ideologies in which enslaved black men were relegated to otherness.

Outnumbered by black men in West Africa and the Caribbean, colonial white men, though "armed to the teeth" with guns, cannons and battleships, privileged the apparatus of mind power over body and appropriated for themselves an iconography of the former while projecting an imagery which associated the latter with black men. The conquest and control of the black male body, and the denial of a mind to it, reside at the centre of the dichotomized masculine Caribbean contest. The managerial culture of empire, established as a function of white patriarchy, fuelled forces that produced a complex apparatus for the ideological representation of black men. The control of the enslaved required it. The survival of colonialism mandated it. Enslaved black men, as the Caribbean social majority, had to be "kept", and kept down, in order to ensure the success of the dominant socioeconomic project (Tiffin 1987; Low 1990; Markus 1990; Fanon 1986).

Imported Africans, and their creole progeny, however culturally understood, shared and actively supported the important tenets of the ideology of masculinity as represented by white men within the colonial encounter. Notions of political authority, economic power and domestic dominance as publicly presented by white elite masculinity were culturally sanctioned by enslaved black men. Similarly, white men's denial of these states of consciousness and experience to disenfranchised and dispossessed white women within colonialism set in place conditions for enslaved black men to assert their physical and social subjugation of black womanhood. But unlike white women, many of the African-born enslaved black males were denied much of the power and status that were personally familiar.

In social relations, the enslaved black male and his offspring were fed, clothed and sheltered by white men whose hegemonic masculinities determined that being "kept" and "kept down" were symbolic of submissive inferiority, and gendered as feminine. The enslaved black male received as "gifts" a number of social concessions, in addition to his subsistence rations and allocations of leisure time. He was denied consumer access to the night by strict regulatory systems and could neither claim nor assert any right beyond or outside those of his owner, in public or private social spheres. According to Patterson (1967), he was natally alienated, his masculinity dishonoured, and his being rendered "socially dead". The condition of being "kept" and "kept down", then, located enslaved black masculinity within white patriarchy as a subform starved of role nourishment, and ideologically "feminized" (see also Patterson 1982, 1993).

Chattel slavery, therefore, an institution built upon private property rights in persons, was thoroughly gendered in its design and functions. Throughout the Americas European enslavers decreed, for example, that the status of an infant at birth should not be derived from that of the father. Slave holders had neither social nor economic interest in black fatherhood. Black children at birth entered into a social relation that was predetermined by the status of their mothers. Legally, it had absolutely nothing to do with the status of the father. Children fathered by free black men or white men were born into slavery if their mothers were slaves. Since white women, by virtue of their race, were not enslaved, their children under all paternal circumstances were born into freedom.

Throughout the West Indies, white women produced free-born children with enslaved, free black, and free coloured men. Slavery, as a sociolegal status, completely marginalized and alienated black fatherhood, and focused its attention upon black motherhood. Estate managers generally had no policy interests in the identity of the fathers of children. The documents on families, for example, are rich and detailed on the maternal dimensions of kinship, but silent on paternity. An excellent way to demonstrate this characteristic is to examine the records of plantations that were known for meticulous documentation. The Newton and Seawell plantations in Barbados were such properties. They were perhaps the best documented eighteenth-century slave plantations in the Caribbean. Both were owned by the absentee Lane family, and the records for Newton, in particular from the 1720s to the 1830s, are a rich source of literature on the black domestic experience. In the 1776 annual report of manager Sampson Wood, for example, he lists all the "matriarchs" on the two estates, and sets out a schedule of their children, grandchildren and great grandchildren.

The paternal evidence is almost completely missing from these records. Take Great Occoo, for example. She has six children and great grandchildren. Her first daughter, Violet, has four children. Nothing is said of fathers, grandfathers or great grandfathers. The same is true for Great Phebe. She had five children and five grandchildren. Her spouse is not recorded, nor is Statira's (her only daughter who had a child). Great Sarcy's family can be shown as follows:

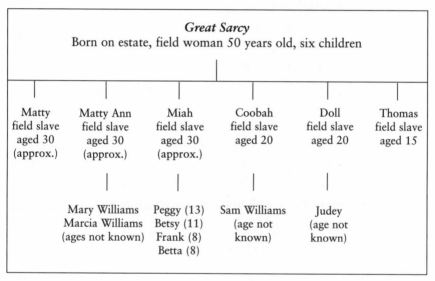

Figure 8.1: Family tree of Great Sarcy

She has six children: four daughters and two sons. All her daughters have children, a total of eight grandchildren. Great Sarcy's spouse is not recorded, nor are the spouses of her four daughters. The records are silent on the fathers of these children. Sampson Wood did not think it important or necessary to list these fathers, husbands and lovers; they remain invisible, outside of history (see Newton Plantation Papers).

Fatherhood as an aspect of masculinity, then, is non-existent within the archival literatures of the estates. Such an issue raises the question of men's greater "invisibility" within historical records, a matter that has been considerably ignored and underestimated. Describing the enslaved woman as essentially a "submerged mother", Edward Brathwaite locates her "invisibility" within the "archival material" and suggests that it is but an "aspect of that general invisibility which haunts [black history]". For him the slave woman, being black and female, suffered a "double invisibility" which in turn promoted an historiography of neglect (Brathwaite 1975, 1984). There is, therefore, a significant conceptual and empirical problem to be tackled with respect to the "invisibility thesis". It has to do with the fact that the archival evidence historians have (over!) used as baselines for social history narratives – deeds, wills, manumission lists, diaries, plantation accounts, managers' reports and so forth – says considerably more about enslaved women than it does about enslaved men. The slave male, in fact, is the one who was rendered largely invisible (Beckles 1995; Brathwaite 1975, 1984).

This characteristic of the evidence has to do with the female-centred nature of the slave system. Its principal concern was with maternity, fertility, the management of white households, and the sociosexual expression of patriarchal power and ideology. More is recorded about slave mothers than slave fathers; more was said about female slave lovers of white men than about male slave lovers of white women. Certainly, in this last regard, enslaved men have been rendered almost completely invisible – though partly, it should be said, for their own safety. The general intimacy of slave women with the empowered agents of the colonial world – white male and female – placed them at the top of the documentary queue (Beckles 1998, 34–38).

This condition, in turn, raises the question of whether modern historians of slavery – mostly male – have contaminated historiographic discourse with the women's "invisibility" thesis, which is really a conceptual borrowing from European historical discourse. Slave owners' fictional literature, where representations of black masculinities were constructed and ventilated, however, used a vocabulary which made reference to the term "infantilization" rather than "feminization". Infantilization was also a central concept used in slave owners' representation and "imaging" of women. The enslaved black male, by virtue of being denied dominant masculine roles and access to recognized institutional support systems on which to construct counterconcepts, and kept in a childlike welfare-subsistence relation, was conceived to have degenerated into a pre-gender consciousness – a condition of nothingness associated with innocence and femininity.

In this literature, furthermore, slave owners coined the terms "Quashee" to represent their ideological characterization of enslaved black men. Quashee was "gay, happy-go-lucky, frivolous, and cheerful". In his 1808 account of Jamaican slave society, John Stewart described Quashee as "patient, cheerful, and commonly submissive, capable at times of grateful attachments where uniformly well treated". He was also "possessed of passions not only strong but ungovernable; a temper extremely irascible; a disposition indolent, selfish, and deceitful; fond of joyous sociality; riotous mirth and extravagant show." Stewart, in addition, was keen on informing his reader that "creole" white women exhibited many of the personality traits of "Quasheba" – the feminine of Quashee (Stewart 1808; see also Long 1774; Nugent 1939).

Quashee, then, was ideologically constructed and fixed within preslavery texts as the "typical" black male in a state of enslavement. Furthermore he was, says Stewart, "docile but irresponsible, loyal but lazy, humble but chronically given to lying and stealing; his behaviour was full of infantile silliness and his talk inflated by childish exaggeration." In addition, his relationship with his master was one of dependence and childlike attachment; it was indeed this childlike quality that was the very key to his being. Slave owners' archives assure us that black males as "a group of atomized, childlike individuals had no means by which to relate themselves to others save the integrative framework provided by the owner's authority. The self-(slave) they allegedly related to was a direct function of the other (owner)" (Patterson 1967).

Congruity in the concepts of infantilization and feminization, as systems of representation of the black male, indicates clearly the direct nature of slave owners' political and ideological intention. As distortions of the relations of everyday life these representations operated as important weapons, with measurable political effects, in that they helped to shape understandings of the encounter between whites and blacks. By fixing reality through language and fantasy, slave owners denied that enslaved black men were "men" in the sense of their ascribed normative characterization of manhood. This discourse, as an apparatus of power, provided slave owners with several privileges – particularly the psychic courage to manage the colonial enterprise.

The slave owning community, considerably outnumbered by subordinated groups, devised systems of governance by which it could reproduce its dominance. Military might was important, but insufficient. The slave owner had to walk among the enslaved, eat what they cooked, and sleep within their physical reach. To function within this environment it was necessary to psychologically "read", "write" and "imagine" subordinated black masculinities as inversions, represented within popularized gender ideology as timid, passive and submissive.

The systems of violent terror used to suppress and punish insubordination – the burning alive, dismemberment, castration, lynching and so forth – were conceived to offer the slave owner a functional degree of comfort in the assumption of success. When we enter the world of Thomas Thistlewood, for example, an English slave manager/planter in Jamaica (1750–86), the language and political effect of this violent power is immediately encountered. Thistlewood records in his diary:

- Wednesday, 28th January, 1756 – Had Derby well whipped, and made Egypt shit in his mouth.
- Friday, 30th July, 1756: Punch catched at Salt River and brought home.
- Flogged him and Quacoo well, and then washed and rubbed in salt pickle, lime juice and bird pepper; also whipped Hector for losing his hoe; made New Negro Joe piss in his eyes and mouth.
- End of October 1766 – A Stout Negro man of Dr Lock's is now gibbitted alive in the Square . . . a resolute rebel.

Actions such as these highlight the contradictory and ambivalent nature of stereotyped representations as major discursive strategies. The physical violence directed persistently against enslaved black men by white men indicates the fact of their recognition of an irrepressible black masculinity, and their inability to fix everyday patterns of behaviour to fantastic ideological constructions (see Hall 1989).

This dis-articulation between social reality and imagination, however, provided the instability needed to constantly reconceive the constituent elements of representations in order to express changing forms of domination. In addition, it contributed to the evolution of complex language forms and perceptions that tracked and targeted the multiple forms and expressions of black masculinities. The thought-leader (sage, priest, obeah man), for example, was stripped conceptually of power within a representation that projected him as childlike, incapable of rational thought and devoid of scientific method. The Ashanti-Mandingo warrior groups were represented as easily tamed and subdued by caring friendship and compassion. Subordinate white males, whose dependent social existence openly subverted from within the ideological texts of white hegemonic masculinity, were driven into colonial outbacks, and their condition accounted for in terms of the degenerative impact of tropical climates and intimate exposure to black culture.

Black men, furthermore, were expected to offer non-violent responses to the social effects of white men's unrestricted sexuality. Colonial mastery, it was understood, demanded as a property right access to the sexuality of the enslaved. Both male and female among the enslaved were sexually exploited by whites who understood their "racial" authority in terms of its power over the life, body and mind of the enslaved. Patterson asserts:

> The sexual exploitation of female slaves by white men was the most disgraceful aspect of Jamaica slave society. Rape and the seduction of infant slaves; the ravishing of the common law wives of the male slaves under the threat of punishment, and outright sadism often involving the most heinous forms of sexual torture were the order of the day. (1967, 42)

An English traveller, during his three-month tour of Jamaica in 1832, was told by a white bookkeeper that he had twelve "negro wives" in six months, and that this was expected of him by his peers. Black husbands or partners who protested, noted Henry Coor, speaking in 1791 before a parliamentary commission on the slave trade, were flogged "under the name of some other misdemeanour" (Evidence of Henry

Coor, House of Commons Select Committee on the Slave Trade, 1790–91, vol. XXXLV, 42).

Non-slave-owning observers of slavery paid particular attention to the impact of white men's sexual culture upon black masculinity. The denial to enslaved black men of the right to family and patriarchal status, and its occasional conferment as a concession for "good" behaviour, meant that they could not expect to assert domestic "authority as a husband and a father". Thomas Cooper noted in 1824 that his wife was the property of another, and her commitment to the owner took privilege over any duty to husband or family. "The net result of all this," Patterson states, "was the complete demoralisation of the Negro male." He concludes:

> Incapable of asserting his authority either as husband or father . . . the object of whatever affection he may possess, beaten, abused and often raped before his very eyes, and with his female partner often in closer link with the source of all power in the society, it is no wonder that the male slave eventually came to lose all pretensions to masculine pride and develop the irresponsible parental and sexual attitudes that are to be found even today. (1967, 167–68)

The anonymous author of an abolitionist pamphlet was explicit on the point: "Patent submission to the lash and manly feelings are incongruous". The pamphlet asked whether slavery had not destroyed any masculine feelings enslaved men might possess, and intimated that white men pursued this objective in several ways – particularly in the sphere of competition with black men for sexual access to black women.

Another visit to the diary of Thomas Thistlewood reveals three issues:

1. Thistlewood's claim of a right to sexual access to all enslaved black women on the estate, and the right to punish enslaved black men who confronted or in any way questioned this right;
2. His right to allocate enslaved black women for the sexual pleasure of his friends, whatever their domestic relations with black men.
3. His right to punish enslaved black men for physically abusing their "wives" or "partners", since this constituted a violation of his property rights on the female.

With respect to the first of these, Thistlewood documents some of his sexual encounters with enslaved estate women during 1751:

8th January,	"cum Phibbah"
9th January,	"Pro. Temp. A nocte. Sup. lect. *Cum* Marina"
10th September,	"About 2 am *Cum* Negrue girl, super floor"
21st November,	"About 1am. *Cum* Ellin, an Ebo, by the morass side, Sup. Terr. Toward the tittle plaintain walk"
1st October,	"Last night *cum* Dido"
11th October,	"Paid Dr Joseph Horlock, for curing me of the clap, £2.75s. 6d – yet am in some doubt if perfect. Was 44 days curing."
3rd December,	"Last night cum Jenny. Jenny continue with me *as noctibus*"
21st December,	"In the evening *cum* Susanah (a Congo negro) Stans, in curinghouse"

In the early part of 1752 he adds Sabina, Phoebe, Little Mimber, Warsoe, Little Lydde and Daphne to the list (Hall 1989).

Many of Thistlewood's enslaved females lived with "husbands", whose protests were occasionally recorded in his diary. Dido's "husband", for example, beat her when he discovered that she slept with Thistlewood. For this he received a flogging from Thistlewood. When Jenny courted a negro man from a neighbouring property, Thistlewood took away a necklace and fine clothing he had given her. When she promised not to see her new lover, he returned the gifts. On 6 March 1754 Thistlewood whipped Quacoo for severely beating his wife, Yara, and on the sixteenth he advised Sancho not to beat his wife Quasheba, but to separate from her, when he found her sleeping with Morris, the estate cooper.

On 2 April, however, Thistlewood did not punish Cobenna for giving London "a good thumping" when he was caught having sex with his (Cobenna's) wife Rossanna. Lincoln, however, was less fortunate; he was severely dealt with by Thistlewood for twice beating his wife Violet after a domestic dispute. When Thistlewood hired Robert Gibbs, a Barbadian, as overseer, he allowed him "use" of Nanny as a "wife", and "matched" Susanah with the Irish overseer, Christopher White, for the same purpose (Hall 1989).

That enslaved black men shared some basic patriarchal values with white men, expressed in terms of an assertion of masculine authority and power over women, seems evident from Thistlewood's and other accounts. Their inability, however, to "live" this ideology outside the jurisdiction of dominant white authority confirmed the subordinated status of their masculinity. There were areas, nonetheless, where enslaved black men were allowed by white men to exercise male power in relation to black women. Moitt tells us that in the French slave colonies, especially Saint Domingue, "Courrir les filles" (girl-hunting) was a popular pastime among enslaved males. They were given leave from estates by overseers and owners to wander through the countryside in search of sex (Moitt 1995).

The rape and kidnapping of enslaved black women was a common enough expression of this activity. When the Barbados Council debated in 1823 a despatch from the Colonial Office which called for an end to the unsupervised flogging of enslaved women by black drivers, Councillor Hamden invoked the interest of black husbands in his opposition to the proposed policy. He told the council, "Unfortunately our black ladies have rather a tendency to the Amazonian cast of character; and I believe that their husbands would be very sorry to hear that they were placed beyond the reach of chastisement" (Beckles 1989, 40).

With respect to Jamaican slave society more needs to be known about the role of kidnapping and sexual exploitation of enslaved women in the formation of Maroon communities. Maroon men did kidnap plantation women in order to secure wives and forced labour; this much also figures prominently in the social history of all colonies that harboured Maroon communities. Little is known, however, of the life experiences of enslaved women who were integrated into the polygynous households of Maroon males. It is entirely possible that some Maroon women experienced at the hands of black men a continuation of the kinds of occupational and resource discrimination, and sexual domination, that typified enslavement on the plantations.

Esteban Montejo, the Cuban runaway slave, for example, expressed views of women and sexual relations in his autobiography that corresponded to the ideological expression of his owner's masculinity, and that of other men within the slave-owning community. Slave owners, of course, knew this, and developed an obsessive interest in the sexual aspects of black masculinity. Terrified in their fantasies about the power implicit in perception of the black male sexual culture, white men developed a range of social attitudes and policies concerning relations between white women and black men. Castration and lynching were placed before black men as a likely response by white males to their sexual access to the white woman (see Craton 1982).

The hostility of colonial power, and the fetishization of black masculine sexuality, were but aspects of a wider discourse that involved the violent responses of enslaved black men in the projection of their own perceptions of masculine values. Violence was the principal social action by which enslaved black men could subvert the security and stability of the slave owner's project. Only violence by slaves could terminate the colonial mission and liberate the enslaved community. Enslaved black men could take away white men's lives and property through violence, and this reality became endemic to the relationship. It was not that enslaved black men needed violence to assert or secure their masculinities, but that the right to take life, which white men held as a constitutional privilege, could also be grasped by black men – hence the function of the subaltern's violence as an ultimate and intimate equalizer.

There was therefore nothing surprising about the manner in which enslaved black men in the Haitian Revolution took hold of the instruments of the independent state in 1804 and effectively marginalized women as second-class citizens, despite women's popular involvement at the leadership and rank-and-file levels. The significance of this political development is widened by the fact that Haiti was the first society in the Caribbean to experiment with the concepts of citizenship and nationhood. Mimi Sheller has shown how, after the violent defeat of slave owners and their imperial allies, "building black masculinity became a central task in the construction of Haitian national identity". The effect of this project, she argued, was the "exclusion of women

from the wholly masculine realms of state politics and citizenship"
(1997, 20).

The "high symbolic" images of the state emerged from the functions
of the military and the organs of national governance, areas white men
had monopolized and defined as masculine space. The feminine space
was considered to be agricultural labour, domesticity and petty commerce. Masculinity was associated with national strength and security. The nation was defined in the first constitution of 1805 as a
"family", headed by the president and his generals, all of whom
became rich landlords employing masses of female subsistence workers. In fact, Article 9 of the constitution was explicit on the matter of
gender and citizenship: "No one is worthy of being a Haitian if he is
not a good father, a good son, a good husband, and above all a good
soldier". The iconography of the black male warrior, the liberator
and protector, was enshrined within the discourse of nation building,
and the woman, despite her revolutionary experience, was set aside as
the "nurturer" of the hegemonic masculinity that emerged with the
new nation.

Haiti's freedom, then, achieved by the struggle of men and women,
resulted in a nation-state that was designed to suit masculinist interests.
Haitian women protested these realities, and much of the anti-state struggles of peasants and urban workers that destabilized both President
Dessalines and King Christophe originated in women's opposition to
exclusion from equal citizenship. This struggle was also violent, and
served to illustrate that oppositional militarism underpinned the politics of men as well as women within colonialism (Sheller 1997).

Colonial masculinities, then, took social form within the context of
a culture of violence which embraced all relations of social living and
consciousness. Violence was the principal instrument of all contending
parties; it held them together and tore them apart. It assumed a quasi-
religious character as groups sought constantly to control the balance
of power and terror. Creole black males were socialized as infants within this crucible of death, blood and suffering. They learned to use it as
it was used against them. This explains in part the enormous loss of life
this region experienced in over one hundred slave revolts, indicating how

relations between the enslaved and the enslavers were characterized by ongoing psychological warfare and bloody battles.

Within the black community other emancipations provided grand opportunities for reconstruction, particularly with respect to the perceptions of masculinity outside of warfare and power conflict over life and liberty. At the same time they reduced the intensity of the struggle for political determination, economic power and cultural self-definition. In most parts of the region white hegemony within economic life, social institutions and ideological discourse persisted. The majority of black men remained marginalized and subordinated; today, the cultural values of these subordinate masculinities seem at odds with new social imperatives, many of which have emerged from the regenerative forces within women's and feminist movements.

Implosive community violence remains an expression of subordinate black masculinities. The seemingly rudderless quest for an inversion of the dominant agenda has left the streets of communities, the language of social discourse, sexual relations, political dialogue and the lyrics of popular music shot through with violence, both virtual and real. That it is socially destructive is evident; that it is new or phenomenal is less obvious. New representations of subordinate black masculinities are taking shape in much the same way today that they were during the slavery period. Now, as then, these constructions are part of a process of subjectification necessary for the perpetuation of forms of discursive and discriminatory power.

References

Baker, George W., and Dwight W. Chapman. 1962. *Man and Society in Disaster.* New York: Basic Books.

Beckles, Hilary. 1989. *Natural Rebels: A History of Enslaved Black Women in Barbados.* New Brunswick, N.J.: Rutgers University Press.

———. 1993. "White Women and Slavery in the Caribbean". *History Workshop Journal,* no. 36.

————. 1995. "Sex and Gender in the Historiography of Caribbean Slavery". In *Engendering History: Caribbean Women in Historical Perspective,* edited by Verene Shepherd, Bridget Brereton and Barbara Bailey. Kingston, Jamaica: Ian Randle.

————. 1998. "Historicizing Slavery in West Indian Feminism". *Feminist Review,* no. 59.

Bond, Carey, and P. Peery. 1970. "Is the Black Male Castrated?" in *The Black Woman Anthology,* edited by T. Cade. New York: New American Library.

Brathwaite, Edward. 1975. "Submerged Mothers". *Jamaica Journal* 9, nos. 2–3.

————. 1984. "Caribbean Woman during the Period of Slavery". Elsa Goveia Memorial Lecture, University of the West Indies, Cave Hill, Barbados.

Brittan, Arthur. 1989. *Masculinity and Power.* Oxford: Basil Blackwell.

Brod, Harry, ed. 1987. *The Making of Masculinities: The New Men's Studies.* Winchester, Mass.: Allen University.

Connell, R.W. 1987. *Gender and Power: Society, the Person, and Sexual Politics.* Stanford, Calif.: Stanford University Press.

————. 1995. *Masculinities.* Oxford: Polity Press.

Cooper, Thomas. 1824. *Facts Illustrative of the Condition of the Negro Slaves in Jamaica.* London: Phillips.

Craton, Michael. 1982. *Testing the Chains: Resistance to Slavery in the British Caribbean.* London: Cornell University Press.

Easthope, Anthony. 1986. *What a Man's Gotta Do: The Masculine Myth in Popular Culture.* Boston: Unwin Hyman.

Fanon, Frantz. 1986. *Black Skins, White Masks,* with foreword by Homi Bhabha. London: Pluto Press.

Hall, Douglas. 1989. *In Miserable Slavery: Thomas Thistlewood in Jamaica, 1750–1786.* Warwick University Caribbean Studies series. Basingstoke: Macmillan.

Hare, Nathan, and Julia Hare. 1984. *The Endangered Black Family: Coping with the Unisexualization and Coming Extinction of the Black Race.* San Francisco: Black Think Tank.

Hilton, Anne. 1985. *The Kingdom of the Congo.* Oxford: Oxford University Press.

Law, Robin. 1977. *The Oyo Empire.* Oxford: Oxford University Press.

————. 1991. *The Slave Coast of West Africa.* Oxford: Oxford University Press.

Long, Edward. 1774. *The History of Jamaica.* London: T. Lowdes.

Low, G.C. 1990. "His Stories? Narratives and Images of Imperialism". *New Formations,* no. 12.

Markus, A. 1990. *Governing Savages.* Sydney: Allen and Unwin.

Messner, Michael. 1991. "Masculinity and Athletic Careers". In *The Social Construction of Gender,* edited by Judith Lorber and Susan Farrell. New York: Sage.

Moitt, Bernard. 1995. "Women, Work and Resistance in the French Caribbean during Slavery, 1700–1848". In *Engendering History: Caribbean Women in Historical Perspective,* edited by Verene Shepherd, Bridget Brereton and Barbara Bailey. Kingston, Jamaica: Ian Randle.

Newton Plantation Papers, M.523 Series. Senate House Library, University of London.

Nugent, Maria. 1939. *Lady Nugent's Journal of Her Residence in Jamaica from 1801 to 1805.* Kingston, Jamaica: Institute of Jamaica.

Patterson, Orlando. 1967. *The Sociology of Slavery.* London: Mackibbon and Kee.

———. 1982. *Slavery and Social Death: A Comparative Study.* Cambridge, Mass.: Harvard University Press.

———. 1993. "Slavery, Alienation and Female Discovery of Personal Freedom". In *Home: A Place in the World,* edited by A. Mack. New York: New York University Press.

Sheller, Mimi. 1997. "Sword-Bearing Citizens: Militarism and Manhood in Nineteenth-Century Haiti". *Plantation Society in the Americas* 4, nos. 2–3.

Stewart, John. 1808. *An Account of Jamaica and Its Inhabitants.* London: Longman.

Tiffin, Helen. 1987. "Post-Colonial Literatures and Counter-Discourse". *Kunapipi* 9, no. 3.

CHAPTER 9

Caribbean Masculinity at the *Fin de Siècle*

LINDEN LEWIS

It is by no means fortuitous that as we enter the new century there is an emerging consciousness revolving around the question of gendered identities and gender politics in the Caribbean. In this regard, and for a variety of reasons, women have been much more reflective, and have become much more politicized by considerations of the sociopolitical construction of femininity and issues of inequality associated with the experience of womanhood. Conversely, until recently, men have paid less attention theoretically, ideologically and intellectually to the issue of our own gendered identities. We have assumed that the male privilege which we enjoy and the hegemony which some of us exercise render considerations of the construction of manhood and masculinity peripheral to our own existential reality. Indeed, masculinity is one of those privileged identities and ideologies which is rarely consciously articulated because it is so often represented as universally applicable, settled and beyond question in its hegemonic influence. We have been finding out rather belatedly, however, that the issue of gendered identity is far from settled, and is subject to social, political and intellectual contestation. Such contestation of power, hegemony and privilege comes not only from women but, as I will argue, should emerge from within the ranks of men as well.

Masculinity as used in this chapter, therefore, refers to a socially constructed set of gendered behaviours and practices of men, which are not frozen in time or culture and which are mediated by notions of race, class, ethnicity, religion, age and sexual orientation, among others. In nonessentialist terms one should of course be mindful that masculinity is not necessarily reducible to men. Such behaviours can be appropriated by women. Note, for example, the claim of Eve Kosofsky Sedgwick: "As a woman, I am a consumer of masculinities, but I am not more so than men are; and, like men, I as a woman am also a producer of masculinities and a performer of them" (1995, 13).

Part of what we understand to be masculinity is manifested through performance (see Butler 1990), that is, the way we act out our maleness. It is in this acting out that we exteriorize the gender-specific behaviours which we have been taught, depending on whether we are boys or girls. Masculinity, however, is not some concrete object that is easily identifiable; it can indeed be objectified in such a way that asexual or neutral objects can be gendered. Masculinity can be variously defined in relation to one's gait, a set of gestures, one's car or the size and aggression of one's dog, for that matter, or in relation to the type of drink one has in a social setting. The list of objectified ways in which masculinity is constructed could be endless, depending on the culture of the society, among other factors.

Why, one might ask, should these issues which are not settled but unsettling gain more salience as we enter the new millennium? The reasons are indeed quite complex. I would like to suggest, however, that there is some precedence for such coalescing at this historical conjuncture. We have all become aware of the fact that the end of the millennium has historically been characterized by periods of ponderous thought. The *fin de siècle* has a tendency to conjure images of decadence and decrepitude of the cultural, moral and political space, which appears to be desperately in need of transformation if apocalypse is to be averted. It is therefore not surprising that at the turn of the century we are learning of the social and economic crisis which Caribbean men are presumed to be experiencing. I will return to this point shortly. As Elaine Showalter argues, the end of centuries seems not merely to suggest but to intensify crises: "The crises of the *fin de siècle*, then, are more intensely experienced, more emotionally fraught, more weighted, with symbolic and historical meaning, because we invest them with the metaphors of death and rebirth that we project onto the final decades and years of a century" (1990, 2).

The above point is worth noting insofar as there is a need to recognize that there is more at stake here than the mere ending of the century and the beginning of a new one, irrespective of its ominous connotations. Rather, the point is that the global, regional and national problems and concerns around such issues as economic restructuring of production, disparities of wealth and income between the developed industrialized countries and the so-called Third World, unemployment, debt, racial and ethnic conflict, environmental degradation and gender inequity, and so forth, have persisted and have seemingly begun to crystallize as we move into the twenty-first century. The end of the century tends therefore to magnify ongoing crises, as the economic expectations of people come up against a global capitalist system driven by the new requirements of accumulation and profit maximization. Eric Hobsbawm, in reflecting on the end of the twentieth century, observes: "The Short Twentieth Century had been one of world wars, hot or cold, conducted by great powers and their allies with increasingly apocalyptic scenarios of mass destruction, culminating in the, fortunately avoided, nuclear holocaust of the superpowers. This danger had clearly disappeared" (1996, 559). Hobsbawm concludes: "In short, the century ended in a global disorder whose nature was unclear, and without an obvious mechanism for either ending it or keeping it under control" (p. 562).

This historical period has also reopened a discourse on the politics of "endism" in neoliberal democracy. The politics of endism was gaining currency even before Daniel Bell precipitously declared the end of ideology (1960). In more recent times, however, Francis Fukuyama (1989) has reintroduced the discourse on endism with his declaration of the end of history. Indeed, the end of one epoch and the beginning of another is commonly indicated, or at least implied, by the plethora of scholarly articles and books containing the prefixes "post" and "beyond". The concern here is that as we move into the new century, the politics of endism is accompanied by fears, real and imagined, of social and gender crises. I would like to focus briefly here on the nature of economic crisis.

It is worthy of note that at the end of the nineteenth century the social and gender troubles which engulfed Europe and the United States were occasioned by a series of economic crises of multiple origins, which began with the crisis of 1873 and continued well into 1895 (see Beaud 1983, 117). Michael Beaud notes, for example, that in France in 1898 the Metals Company and the company responsible for the construction of the Panama Canal both went bankrupt (p. 119). This situation was accompanied by credit crises, stock exchange problems, economic depression and the rise of protectionism. In Britain there were problems associated with banking, while economic conditions worsened as a result of reductions in trade in such places as the United States (p. 119). Beaud notes that for the United States, "the stock exchange prices for railroads securities collapsed and 491 banks failed. The depression grew worse in 1894 with more unemployment and an effort to reduce wages" (p. 119). Such restructuring within the social relations of production and the concomitant social dislocation occasioned by these changes resulted in an early exploding of the myth of the male breadwinner, and not only represented a loss of status for bourgeois men but was perceived as very threatening to some forms of masculinity. However, although this myth might have been shaken somewhat, it did not die. The myth of the male breadwinner has proven to be quite resilient, for it is deeply rooted in culture and constantly reinvents itself to exploit differences between men and women and to structure the sexual division of labour.

Regenia Gagnier, who is cited by Showalter, comments that there was "a crisis in the 1890s of the male on all levels – economic, political, social, psychological, as producer, as power, as role, as lover" (1990,

9). What is remarkable is that, globally, similar variables currently affect or are believed to have affected some men in precisely the same way. There are those, such as Abigail Solomon-Godeau, who argue that masculinity, however it may be defined, operates in much the same way as capitalism, "always in crisis". For her the important question is "how both [capitalism and masculinity] managed to restructure, refurbish, and resurrect themselves for the next historical turn" (1995, 71).

Elizabeth Badinter (1995), drawing on the work of Jacques Le Rider, and being a bit tongue-in-cheek in her comment, suggests that the end of the nineteenth century was marked by a virulent antifeminism: "Not only philosophers but also psychologists and biologists, as well as historians and anthropologists, evinced an extremely violent antifeminism. All set out to demonstrate, with success, woman's ontological inferiority" (p. 16). Badinter surmised that the feeling at the time led to the position that only "the reestablishment of the sexual boundaries would free men from their anxiety over their identity" (p. 17).

The Caribbean in the Nineteenth Century

The closing years of the nineteenth century in the Caribbean represented a set of altered economic and social circumstances. Emancipation from slavery, having finally arrived in 1838 in the former British West Indies after a period of apprenticeship, was characterized by what the Caribbean novelist George Lamming (1996) has described as the region's first structural adjustment measure. The closing decade of the nineteenth century in the Caribbean was marked by the loss of international commercial appeal. By 1897 the British West Indies sugar industry was essentially bankrupt. Commodity production was on the decline; sugar – the main agricultural export crop – had encountered serious competition from European beet sugar, while labour control proved to be increasingly problematic (Scarano 1989, 52).

With the change in the mode of production from slavery to free labour came changes in the social relations of production. As free labour replaced slave labour, wage labour began to eclipse indentured or contract labour. Reddock argues that with these changes emerged the foundations "for the long-term process of proletarianization, and its eventual corollary, 'housewifization', which were finally established" (1994, 69). Toward the end of the nineteenth century in the Caribbean the economic situation became increasingly volatile, as suggested above, with conditions which were conducive to riots and protests. In Jamaica, for example, riots broke out at Cumberland Pen in 1894, ostensibly the result of police arrest of a young man for illegal gambling at the races (Bryan 1991, 269–70). At this time, though there is as yet no formal mechanism of redress for workers, there is an emerging working-class consciousness which begins to manifest itself in the form of strike action. Strike action occurred in May of 1895, among wharf workers in Kingston. It was not only in Kingston that such tensions emerged; in Montego Bay there emerged increasing problems associated with unemployment in 1895 as well. In short, labour was in the throes of negotiating a new type of social relationship with capital, in ways which proved to be problematic for the latter.

The trade union movement which was to emerge subsequently was an important site of the construction and articulation of masculinity for both middle- and working-class men. Labour organizing and the establishment of trade unions provided an institutional mechanism through which mainly men, ably assisted by women, contested colonial authority and the existing wage-labour relationship. Indeed, the trade union as an organization proved to be an important institutional locus of power for men in the Caribbean. It merged rising nationalist concerns with political ambitions, both of which were refracted through the social ontology of labour. The trade union as a crucial site of patriarchal power in the Caribbean remains largely unexamined, despite the voluminous literature on its economic, industrial and political contribution to the region.

According to Richard Hart the end of the nineteenth century represented the first wave of labour organization in the English-speaking Caribbean (1988). These first efforts took place in Trinidad and Jamaica. The Trinidad Workingmen's Association was established in 1897. In Jamaica, the Carpenters, Brick Layers and Painters' Union was organized in 1898. In addition, Walter Rodney (1981) has noted that 1884 represented a new dimension of violent labour confrontation on the estates of Guyana. He pointed to thirty-one "strikes and disturbances" occurring in 1886, fifteen in 1887 and forty-two in 1888. Although apparently occurring with much less frequency between 1889 and 1890, major disturbances again surfaced between 1894 and 1895, "and for another ten years thereafter" (p. 154).

One of the factors explaining the dominance of men in the early wave of labour organizing is related to their predominance in the skilled trades. This feature, however, should not lead one to conclude that there was a lack of involvement or interest on the part of women in labour mobilization. Women participated in these processes. Indeed, women were seen as playing crucial roles in the subsequent waves of labour organization in the Caribbean; however, they did not receive the rewards they had expected for their contribution to such struggles.

> The marginalization of women within the trade union movement came therefore not from a lack of involvement and militant participation in labour struggles but from their absence and exclusion from the most powerful and concentrated sectors of working-class employment and from the impact of male-supremacist and increasingly petty bourgeois frames of reference and forms of leadership on the mass labor movement. (Green 1994, 163)

The end of the nineteenth century in the Caribbean, therefore, was marked by bleak economic prospects, a reordering of the social relations of production, and efforts at labour organization and mobilization. In all of these changes Caribbean men began to appropriate the new opportunities for leadership which were emerging and became actively involved in contesting certain aspects of the established economic and political order of the day. In the end, freed and formerly indentured men in the Caribbean at this historical conjuncture began to negotiate new routes which would eventually lead to their control over much of the public domain. In short, by the end of the nineteenth century the transition from colonial male domination to indigenous male ascendancy had already begun.

Millennial Change

One must note, of course, that the economic restructuring which characterized the end of the nineteenth century is qualitatively different from that which marked the end of the twentieth century. In the first instance, the technological developments of the twentieth century in the areas of production, medicine, information, telecommunication, robotics, photonics, fibre optics, business and finance are much more global in their impact and complex in their operations. In addition, such advances have done more to transform our entire way of life: the way we travel, work, communicate with each other and essentially view the world. In short, the technology has altered our conception of time and space in fundamental ways.

The fact that, towards the end of the twentieth century, some of the problems of the nineteenth century still seem to persist is testimony to the failure to address and resolve some of these issues within the present system. However, it is precisely this systemic nature of the problem which is overlooked in many academic discourses of gender. Rather than contextualize the nature of the problem faced by men and women in terms of structural determinants, many reduce the problematic to the level of the individual or the collectivity, so that the issue becomes conceptualized as pathology to be corrected without reference to wider social considerations. It is within this context that ideas of Caribbean male social and economic crises have to be reconceptualized.

Men and Crisis

At the present conjuncture it would appear as though Caribbean men face two interrelated types of crisis, one economic in orientation and the other social and gender related. The economic crisis is the result of global restructuring of capitalism which has the effect of reducing and displacing significant segments of the labour force and engendering fear and insecurity among workers. The social crisis is related to the problems experienced in civil society, itself the product, at least in part, of the economic restructuring. Here unemployment coupled with bleak prospects of future work, dwindling chances of realizing the goal of home ownership, for example, and a growing recognition of one's powerlessness to control one's own social reproduction, among other things, have tended to dislocate familiar gender roles for men, leaving them groping for ways to negotiate this new territory.

I have been arguing for some time now that men do not experience crisis in a social vacuum (see Lewis 1990, 104–12). If Caribbean men are in crisis then women, children and families, along with other institutions within civil society, must of necessity also be in crisis. This latter point is not based on any presumption of men's pre-eminence in society around which everything else revolves, but rather on the nature of social interaction among individuals in any given social environment. It means, therefore, that to understand the problems which men and women face as we encounter the challenges of the new century, we must begin to come to grips with the restructuring of the social relations of production at the global, regional and national levels. Coming to terms with these issues means developing a broader understanding of the reconfiguration of certain functions of the neoliberal state, which after all plays an instrumental role in fashioning the terrain of gendered identities; it means comprehending the complexities of the nature of the crisis of civil society, partly the result of the impact of the first two factors; and recognizing the historical and psychosocial forces at work which coalesce around these issues. As we investigate the complexity of gender in the Caribbean we cannot afford to ignore its corporeal or social reality. Failure to ground one's investigation in these considerations truncates the analysis of gender relations, rendering it ludic if not entirely banal.

One further point about the nature of the crisis which is presumed to be visited upon Caribbean men should not go unmentioned here. Talking about the focus on black men as embattled and endangered in the United States, feminist social critic bell hooks argues against claims of the uniqueness of the pressure placed upon men as opposed to women. Her point would be equally valid, I believe, in the context of the Caribbean. hooks, while not negating the social and economic difficulties faced by black men, points to the fact that black women were also daily threatened, in perhaps different ways, by sexism, misogyny and violence. She elaborates:

> The assumption that black men suffer more or are more endangered is rooted in sexist thinking: the idea that the pain of men is always more important than that of women. From a sexist standpoint, black male concerns will always, always be seen as more in need of attention than those of black females. (hooks and Marable 1994, 40)

hooks's point is well taken: the educational performance of boys *vis-à-vis* girls in the Caribbean, the apparent aimlessness of young men, their high drop-out rates from school and their consequent high unemployment have become overwhelming concerns of governments and regional institutions. What is important here is that these problems, whether real or imagined, are presumed to be of the highest priority when they involve men; there seems to be an all-consuming interest in addressing and resolving these issues immediately. Hence hooks's comment about the pain of men appearing to be more important than that of women.

However, hooks seeks to explain away the problem in terms of sexist thinking. In fact, this sexist thinking should be considered along with the social psychology, sociology and political economy of the class, identity and status of men, if one is really to understand the nature of this feeling of male marginality. Put differently, it is not only a matter of sexist thinking, although this is a point worth stressing. It is also the case that such attitudes and behaviours are fundamentally rooted in the material conditions of existence of certain classes of men.

As the Caribbean moves into the twenty-first century, those of us who study and try to understand masculinity should be mindful of avoiding the pitfall of the exceptionalism of men's suffering in a changing national and regional context. To the extent that male marginalization exists at any level, not only would it be mediated by factors of race, class, age and sexual orientation, it would also be the product of changing socio-economic and political considerations and not of wilful intent to penalize working class men – the ones who seem to feel most affected. In short, capitalist restructuring – which is the source of much of their alienation – is concerned with its own reproduction, and not particularly respectful of any gender which gets in the way of its drive for accumulation. Having stated the above, one must hasten to add that it is difficult to conceive of a situation of male marginalization in the Caribbean, when the structure of patriarchy seems so firmly in place in the region.

Shifting Terrain of Gender Relations

It is becoming increasingly clear that part of the social impact of the process of economic restructuring mentioned above is the dislocation of gender roles. Given the scope and intensity of change taking place at all levels, it is entirely foolhardy to expect that gender relations would somehow be immune from transformation of some kind. It is precisely in the interstices of this process that considerable gender trouble engulfs the contemporary Caribbean. At the core of these troubles is the exploding of the myth of the male breadwinner, the persistence of unemployment and the feminization of some aspects of manufacturing and of certain jobs in the region.

The concept of a male breadwinner is, for many men, at the core of the construction of masculinity. It is clearly not the only criterion of masculinity, but it inhabits an important space in the masculine imaginary. Defining men as principal wage earners asserts and maintains male control over women and their reproduction. This control is in turn tied to men's ability to appropriate the domestic labour of women in the household, as well as their capacity, depending on the relationship in which they stand to the means of production, to exploit women's labour power outside of the home. To the extent that the above is possible, it would suggest that the role of the male breadwinner is ideologically contingent on the vicissitudes of capitalism and patriarchal practices.

In her most recent work, *The Myth of the Male Breadwinner: Women and Industrialization in the Caribbean* (1995), Helen Safa argues that the concept of the male breadwinner is becoming a myth as women worldwide become increasingly important contributors to the household economy. Safa clearly demonstrates how in Puerto Rico, the Dominican Republic and, for somewhat different reasons, Cuba, economic necessity associated with the new rhythms and requirements of capital has led to the feminization of forms of manufacturing. Sylvia Walby was careful to warn of this issue of women's work:

> The attempt to subordinate women in the labour market is not new, but part of a continuing dynamic in the interrelationship of gender, class and ethnic structures and practices. It is partly in response to the successes that women have won in terms of entry to the labour market and elsewhere that this new round of restructuring is taking the form that it is. (1997, 76)

As more women become employed at lower wages than those traditionally offered men, and as the latter become economically marginalized, the myth of the male breadwinner begins to explode, opening up opportunities in the process for feminist contestation of and resistance to this role. What is true of the Hispanic Caribbean is equally true for the English-speaking, Dutch and French Caribbean, where export processing zones and offshore assembly and data processing companies mainly employ women. This has become an effective strategy of reordering the social relations of production in the interest of transnational capital. Green (1994) has observed that the growth of female employment in certain sections of manufacturing has been occurring at a time of economic decline in those traditional areas of male industrial labour-force participation such as sugar, oil and bauxite. These are the areas most affected by processes of mechanization (for details see Green 1994, 167). What is often missed in this apparently increased employment of women is the volatility of the employment, given the nature of the informal sector which employs many women: the export processing zones and the off-shore industry. Although some might be able to point to a few very successful micro-entrepreneurs within the informal sector, the majority of women who find work in that sector merely eke out a living, often living on the margins of society. Furthermore, as some economists have reluctantly begun to recognize, a lot of what passes for self-employment is really disguised unemployment. In addition, companies in the off-shore sector are notorious for their mobility in the face of what they perceive to be unfavourable conditions of operation.

In the present global economic climate, information processing has become crucial to manufacturing and the service industry. Key to this process is the digital rendering of information. According to Davis and Stack (1996) as the process of digitization proceeds, the need for labour diminishes. "So entire layers of human labor are evicted from production, warehousing, transportation and sales" (p. 5). The digital rendering of information is not constrained by considerations of location, since products can be transmitted via telecommunication networks. This being the case, such locations as Barbados, St Lucia, Trinidad and Jamaica become attractive sites for the establishment of these off-shore industries.

The economic advantages are quite compelling and include low transport costs, reduced labour costs and resource efficiency, among other considerations. Of particular importance here is the fact that these industries exploit difference between men and women for their own advantage. They argue, rather naively, that women are less industrially militant, their labour is cheaper, they bring greater dexterity to such processes as data entry operations, are less likely to engage in industrial sabotage and are more dependable. It is for some of these reasons that women enjoy more employment in these areas of manufacturing and services in the growing off-shore industry.

In the middle stratum of management in the private and public sector in many Caribbean societies, middle-class, educated men who have always been employed, and who have always "brought home the bacon", are also finding their jobs made redundant and their employment terminated. (This phenomenon perhaps does not occur as frequently as within the ranks of the working class.) Always a tenuous stratum and arguably a contradictory location, the middle class in the Caribbean is ever more shaky and in dire fear of sliding back into the bowels of the working class from which it has emerged. In some cases, however, these middle-stratum men have to make a greater adjustment than their working-class counterparts, since they have hitherto enjoyed security of employment. The fact of the matter is that security of employment can no longer be guaranteed for anyone who is forced to sell her or his labour power.

In short, then, the concept and reality of the male breadwinner has been under severe stress in the closing years of the twentieth century, largely as a result of the process of economic restructuring and chronic unemployment in the Caribbean. R.W. Connell, writing in another context, speculates that the concept of the male breadwinner will come under greater pressure "when it becomes impossible for men to win the bread" (1995, 9). Cornwall and Lindisfarne framed the problem more poignantly when they asked the rhetorical question: "And, if a man fails to do 'what a man's gotta do', does he cease to be a man?" (1994, 12). It is the search for answers to this and related questions that should commend itself to future research agendas on the construction of Caribbean masculinities.

To date, adjusting to the shifting terrain of gender relations in the Caribbean has been quite intriguing. For some men the loss of job, the challenge to their positions of authority, privilege and status, or the academic and intellectual observation of such occurrences, has ushered in a new consciousness about the construction, existential reality and dislocation of masculinities. Part of this response constitutes a genuine attempt to understand a rapidly changing social and economic milieu. Part of the response, however, represents an irrational fear of redundancy and feelings of inadequacy, inspired not only by loss of status but by the possibility of relinquishing the control over women which is part of the folklore of the masculine imaginary.

For some men in the Caribbean the dislocating and uprooting of some gender roles may provide an opportunity to "escape from their own sexual burdens" (Showalter 1990, 11). Put differently, subordinated forms of masculinity in the Caribbean, which under normal circumstances find little room to express themselves without severe penalty or sanction, may actually welcome whatever respite is made available from the strictures of hegemonic forms of masculinity. In short, the shifting terrain of gender relations may not only reveal problems and antagonisms between men and women, but may also illuminate as well as problematize the tensions, conflicts and contradictions among men over rigid constructions of masculinity.

Mostly, however, the shifting terrain of gender relations has been causing some Caribbean men, from Puerto Rico to Guyana and from Barbados to Trinidad, to throw up their hands in frustration over how to act, how to perform and how to behave under these new and politicized circumstances. It is in this performative space that many Caribbean men seem most confused. Is there a point at which sensitivity can be construed as weakness? Or, in the words of the calypsonian Penguin, as "soft" or as "a soft man"? Can the sexual economy of desire be exhausted within the parameters of monogamous relationships? With respect to the sexual economy of desire, we need to be addressing some pertinent questions here. Given the plurality of sexual relationships into which Caribbean men and women enter, it should become evident that not all such relationships are occurring within the context of monogamy. We need therefore to investigate the extent to which such desires are being satisfied within and outside of monogamous relationships. We need to begin to investigate how sexual desire is constructed through the culture and history of the region. We need also to investigate how this desire reproduces heterosexual practices, while simultaneously marginalizing, if not deliberately suppressing, non-hegemonic forms of desire. As Mark Figueroa, the Jamaican economist, said to me in a personal aside, "We need also to explode the myth of female monogamy in the Caribbean."

What does it mean to be a real man? Can the desire for respect as a strong man be realized without the assertion of hegemony? What do Caribbean women really want and realistically expect of men? Do women really understand that "liming with de boys" is an important psychic and gendered space in which masculinity is constructed, negotiated and contested? Understanding the male "lime"[1] is not a matter of men seeking permission from women to spend time with their male friends, or using the male bonding experience as an excuse to be away from the home – to shirk domestic responsibilities – or to establish parallel relationships. It is understanding that the "lime" is a liminal space for Caribbean men and an important, though not exclusive, site of male socialization. In short, the point is that Caribbean men are groping for ways of adjusting to these changed and changing gender circumstances. What is remarkable is that rather than developing new modalities, many men, particularly younger men who ignore these changes at their peril, are asking of society that it provide a blueprint, a set of signposts on how to proceed. Unfortunately, no such blueprint is available for men or women. In the absence of such a gender map, some men are receding into the temple of the familiar. They hark back to an imagined era in which their fathers, uncles or older male friends served as principal role models, and were all "strong men" who "laid down the law", and "did not put up with nonsense from women". In short, this position is similar to that which was noted earlier in relation to European men at the end of the nineteenth century, who were in search of the re-establishment of sexual boundaries. This type of thinking is what Etienne Balibar, writing in another context, describes as a retrospective illusion (Balibar and Wallerstein 1991). Such sentiments are commonly expressed on the editorial pages of many Caribbean newspapers, in barber shops and increasingly in public fora, where elite men in the region have begun to give voice to such views. Rather than pursue this intellectual cul-de-sac, men could more productively explore the possibility of learning to navigate the new terrain of gender relations. We must be cognizant of the fact that mistakes are possible, but may ensure against repeated error. Most importantly, men must understand that gender was never meant to be considered as stable and unchanging, "rather, gender is an identity tenuously constituted in time" (Butler 1990, 140).

Cultural Nationalism and Masculinity

As the Caribbean embarks on the new millennium, it finds itself desperately fighting off the encroachments of foreign influences which are cultural, political and economic. Given the process of globalization discussed above, seemingly stable features of society such as the state, sovereignty and national boundaries are increasingly subject to contestation. If, for example, we acknowledge the ability of finance capital, goods and services, and information to transcend national boundaries, it becomes easy to understand the extent to which the impact of developments in the logic of late capitalism affects the national interests of peripheral economies such as those in the Caribbean. It should be noted that these transnational flows are not intended simply for the malicious destabilization of small societies, but rather to ensure that an appropriate environment is created within which capital accumulation can be realized globally.

Throughout the contemporary Caribbean there is a growing concern with the issue of cultural sovereignty. There is a familiar lament in the region about the Americanization of the Caribbean as a result of over-exposure to cable television, Cable News Network (CNN) views and perspectives, American advertisements, fashion trends, gossip tabloids, music videos, satellite dishes and films. These foreign cultural practices are believed to contaminate the region, misdirect Caribbean youth and promote values and morals which are not only alien to the area but detrimental to its cultural integrity.

The above position is fundamentally a culturally nationalist one. It is designed to protect and privilege those elements at the national level which are believed to constitute a collective identity or community, a national bond among all a country's citizens. It is, in the final instance, a search for a cultural essence. Moreover, the need to defend and protect the cultural integrity of the region implies two related assumptions: (1) that what is being protected is in fact pure and unaffected by outside influences in the process of its own constitution, and (2) that the foreign influence is itself pure and uncorrupted by other cultural forces. Both of these assumptions are fundamentally flawed in their conceptualization. Both Paul Gilroy (1993) and Homi Bhabha (1994) have been, in their different ways, at pains to point out the itinerancy of culture. Culture is never pure but always hybridized; that which we celebrate as Caribbean culture has long since been borrowed and adapted mainly from Africa, Asia and Europe, and creatively fashioned within the region. In short, Caribbean people have never been able to seal off their culture from foreign influence and are not in a position to do so at this historical conjuncture.

The search for cultural essence is part of a broader attempt to control and protect boundaries as social, economic, ideological and political practices become destabilized and reconfigured in the passage through the new millennium.

In periods of cultural insecurity, when there are fears of regression and degeneration, the longing for strict border controls around the definition of gender, as well as race, class, and nationality, becomes especially intense. If the different races can be kept in their places, if the various classes can be held in their proper districts of the city, and if men and women can be fixed in their separate spheres, many hope, apocalypse can be prevented and we can preserve a comforting sense of identity and permanence in the face of the relentless specter of millennial change. (Showalter 1990, 4)

Of particular concern here is the fact that nationalist currents, whether cultural, political or racial, have tended to be unmindful of the rights of women. Indeed, as Mosse (1985) notes, such nationalist currents have historically had a special affinity for male society. Nationalist currents are the modalities within which particular forms of hegemonic masculinity reside. Anne McClintock has pointed out that all nationalisms are gendered and, at some level, represent relations to political power and to certain forms of violence (1996, 260). Like Mosse, she argues that the interests of the nation are aligned with the goals of men, which constitute a form of male national power, based "on the prior construction of gender difference" (p. 261). Students of Caribbean gender relations should carefully examine the extent to which the articulation of cultural nationalism, which has been gaining currency in the region, carries the seeds of a specific brand of masculinity, which is oppressive both to women and to men in subaltern classes and sexual categories.

This type of masculinity can be discerned by its promotion of the assertion of men as the "rightful" heads of households, organizations and the state. It is threatened by the social mobility of women, and yearns for their return to the household and their exclusive responsibility for child rearing and domestic services; it is convinced of the existence of a masculine essence which is applicable to all men irrespective of race, class, age or sexual orientation; and it is simultaneously embarrassed by, and hostile to, men who "deviate" from the heterosexual ideal. If the Caribbean intends to move towards a position of gender equality, the above type of masculinity is hardly the vehicle through which such an ideal could be realized.

Conclusion

As the Caribbean embarks on the new millennium, its people at all levels of society should begin to examine new visions of masculinity and femininity. Given the focus on masculinity in this chapter, it would seem incumbent that the region begin to recognize that masculinity is not a homogeneous category but a complex and nuanced, socially constructed one. Although the point may seem elementary, it is remarkable the way in which precisely such a misconception is often articulated and expectations of behaviour premised upon it.

It is important that those of us who study Caribbean masculinity envision this social category as dynamically constructed. Conceptions of masculinity change over different historical periods, but also within the life cycle of the individual man. To this extent, research in the region on age and the definition and practice of masculinity seems worthy of further pursuit. What is important to note here is that masculinity is constantly being negotiated and contested in different times, places and under certain circumstances in the Caribbean, in ways which remain largely untheorized.

In re-visioning Caribbean masculinity as we enter the new century, it is also important that this phenomenon not only be seen as a social category which is defined in relation, or in opposition, to femininity, but also with respect to relations among and between men. Masculinity is not merely about how men relate to women, but about how men relate to other men, how they seek the approval, honour and respect of other men, and how they weigh and ponder the sanctions of other men.

In addition to the above, a specific research agenda for Caribbean masculinity in the future should investigate the following areas. There is a certain urgency to examine the relationship between masculinity and the state in the Caribbean. Moreover, we need to know a lot more about the relationship between masculinity and the whole complex of social institutions as important and crucial sites of power for men. It is not merely a question of the numbers of men in this or that institution or arena but, more importantly, how this institutional presence of men is finessed, manipulated and used to consolidate themselves within the apparatuses of power in Caribbean society.

Much more research needs to be done on the relationship between masculinity and labour in the Caribbean. We must begin to understand the full implications of the real impact of unemployment on gender relations and particularly on men, especially since this social problem has become chronic in the region. By impact I am not simply referring to indices of material impoverishment, but to issues of self-worth and psychic trauma, among other consequences. We need to know whether these altered states lead to suicide and other social-psychological manifestations by men. In short, we need to be investigating how men handle stress in areas of their lives that we assume are under control. A look at these issues might provide some insight into whether men seek help for their problems or convince themselves that they are capable of handling them without social-psychological intervention.

Finally, it is crucial to theorize the issue of power in relation to gender studies. Caribbean masculinities cannot escape such scrutiny. In constructing a theory of power it is worth noting that masculinity is not inherently about power, but that power is inscribed in the political processes of the social construction of masculinity. The fact of the matter is that, generally, men still continue to control the apparatuses of power in the Caribbean, and although women have experienced some mobility and increased status over the years, these advances do not represent a diminution of male power in the region. What the changing status of women means for men in the Caribbean is that some sort of adjustment has to be made to accommodate the presence of women in hitherto exclusively male areas, and the sooner men realize the need to make this adjustment, the better social and gender relations will become.

The end of one century and the beginning of another may hold no particular significance for some. For others, however, the event is imbued with symbolic significance of hope, or ominous foreboding, or both. In the case of Caribbean men it may be fruitful to approach the new millennium with new insights and vision and a new commitment to understanding the collective and individual project of equality and human liberation. The cold reality is that however we explain the forces of

change which have been unleashed on Caribbean society, gender relations will never again be the same. The sooner men come to terms with
this reality, the better will be our adjustment to the new social dynamic. The twenty-first century is full of challenges and possibilities, one
of which is for men and women to establish new social relationships
based on respect and equality. Failure to construct such a new demo-
cratic environment will only lead to a continuation or exacerbation of
the existing tensions between feminist assertion and patriarchal power.
Caribbean masculinity at the dawn of the new millennium should not
be about reclaiming past glories, but about fashioning a genuinely dem-
ocratic alternative pattern of gender relations.

Acknowledgements

This chapter was originally a paper presented at a symposium entitled "The
Construction of Caribbean Masculinity: Towards a Research Agenda", sponsored by the Centre for Gender and Development Studies, University of the West
Indies, St Augustine, Trinidad, 11–13 January 1996. A revised version of the
paper was later presented at the Twentieth Annual Conference of the Society
for Caribbean Studies, held at the University of North London, England, 3–5
July 1996. In addition, I would like to thank Karen Morin for drawing my attention to some important points, and Hilbourne Watson for his generous comments and suggestions on this paper.

Notes

1. To "lime" in the Caribbean is to "hang out", to congregate or to pass
    the time in some location. This activity is not restricted to men; women
    can also lime. Liming can also be a pastime which is shared by a mixed
    group of men and women, depending on the circumstance or occasion.

References

Badinter, Elisabeth. 1995. *On Masculine Identity.* New York: Columbia University Press.

Balibar, Ètienne, and Immanuel Wallerstein. 1991. *Race, Nation, Class: Ambiguous Identities.* London: Verso.

Beaud, Michel. 1983. *A History of Capitalism, 1500–1980.* New York: Monthly Review Press.

Bell, Daniel. 1960. *The End of Ideology.* Glencoe, Ill.: Free Press.

Bhabha, Homi. 1994. *The Location of Culture.* London: Routledge.

Bryan, Patrick. 1991. *The Jamaican People, 1880–1902.* London: Macmillan Education.

Butler, Judith. 1990. *Gender Trouble: Feminism and the Subversion of Identity.* New York: Routledge.

Connell, R.W. 1995. *Masculinities.* Oxford: Polity Press.

Cornwall, Andrea, and Nancy Lindisfarne. 1994. "Dislocating Masculinity: Gender, Power and Anthropology". In *Dislocating Masculinity: Comparative Ethnographies,* edited by A. Cornwall and N. Lindisfarne. London: Routledge.

Davis, Jim, and Michael Stack. 1996. "The Digital Advantage". *Left Curve,* no. 20.

Fukuyama, Francis. 1989. "The End of History?" *National Interest,* no. 16 (Summer).

Gilroy, Paul. 1993. *The Black Atlantic: Modernity and Double Consciousness.* Cambridge, Mass.: Harvard University Press.

Green, C. 1994. "Historical and Contemporary Restructuring and Women in Production in the Caribbean". In *The Caribbean in the Global Political Economy,* edited by Hilbourne Watson. Boulder: Lynne Rienner.

Hart, Richard. 1988. "Origin and Development of the Working Class in the English-Speaking Caribbean Area, 1897–1937". In *Labour in the Caribbean,* edited by Malcolm Cross and Gad Heuman. London: Macmillan.

Hobsbawm, Eric. 1996. *The Age of Extremes: A History of the World, 1914–1991.* New York: Vintage.

hooks, bell, and Manning Marable. 1994. "Breaking Boundaries: A Dialogue with bell hooks and Manning Marable". *Race and Reason* 1, no. 1.

Lamming, George. 1996. "The Role of the Intellectual in Post-Colonial Societies". Lecture given at Bucknell University, Pennsylvania, 1 April.

Lewis, Linden. 1990. "Are Caribbean Men in Crisis?" *Caribbean Affairs* 3, no. 3.

McClintock, Ann. 1996. "No Longer in a Future Heaven: Nationalism, Gender, and Race". In *Becoming National: A Reader,* edited by Geoff Eley and Ronald Grior Suny. New York: Oxford University Press.

Mosse, George. 1985. *Nationalism and Sexuality: Respectability and Abnormal Sexuality in Modern Europe.* New York: Howard Fertig.

Reddock, Rhoda. 1994. *Women, Labour and Politics in Trinidad and Tobago: A History.* London: Zed Books.

Rodney, Walter. 1981. *A History of the Guyanese Working People, 1881–1905.* Baltimore: Johns Hopkins University Press.

Safa, Helen. 1995. *The Myth of the Male Breadwinner: Women and Industrialization in the Caribbean.* Boulder: Westview.

Scarano, Francisco. 1989. "Labour and Society in the Nineteenth Century". In *The Modern Caribbean,* edited by Franklin Knight and Colin A. Palmer. Chapel Hill: University of North Carolina Press.

Sedgwick, Eve Kosofsky. 1995. "O Gosh, Boy George, You Must Be Awfully Secure in Your Masculinity". In *Constructing Masculinity,* edited by Maurice Berger, Brian Wallis, and Simon Watson. London: Routledge.

Showalter, Elaine. 1990. *Sexual Anarchy: Gender and Culture at the Fin de Siècle.* New York: Viking.

Solomon-Godeau, Abigail. 1995. "Male Trouble". In *Constructing Masculinity,* edited by Maurice Berger, Brian Wallis and Simon Watson. London: Routledge.

Walby, Sylvia. 1997. *Gender Transformations.* London: Routledge.

CHAPTER 10

Globalization, Migration and the Shaping of Masculinity in Belize

LINDA M. MATTHEI and
DAVID A. SMITH

During the 1990s perhaps no other city in the world evoked as strong an association with violent crime and street gangs as Los Angeles. Tales of drugs, guns and violent gangs in the "City of Angels" became daily fare, and terrifying images of "drive-by shootings", "crackhouses" and "carjackings" filled the media and shaped perceptions around the world of life in urban America. Currently, however, the United States is enjoying a decline in violent crime rates – even in Los Angeles – while countries in the Caribbean basin struggle to gain control of a crime wave that is seemingly sweeping the region.

At first glance Belize (population 239,000) seems a most unlikely place to find Los Angeles–style urban problems. It is a land of rainforests, coral reefs and tropical agriculture. The country is sparsely populated and still mostly rural; its only sizable urban centre, Belize City, has a population of only about 55,000 (Government of Belize 2000). The tiny country is at first glance so unlike Los Angeles, in fact, that it gives the impression of a "rural Mayberry, an oasis of peace at the edge of Central America" (Darling 1999, 1). Despite its bucolic appearance, however, Belize is experiencing a serious crime problem. The proliferation of criminal activity currently plaguing the country includes cross-border trafficking of drugs, guns and stolen automobiles. At the centre of these emergent criminal enterprises are young men with ties to US-based urban gangs, especially the "Crips" and "Bloods" of Los Angeles (Farah and Robberson 1995). Armed with high-powered weapons illegally imported from the United States, by the early 1990s the gangs brought the same sorts of wanton violence to the streets of Belize City that have plagued Los Angeles for years:

> More than 80 people were arrested in a week-long drive against drug-related gang violence last month; they were charged with possession of drugs, arms and ammunition. Members of the Belize Defence Force were brought in to patrol streets in Belize City. Several people have died in recent shooting incidents attributed to drug gangs. (*Caribbean Insight* 1992)

Another report in the mid-1990s portrays similar imagery:

> Following months of increased gang violence in Belize City, including three gang-related murders in one eight-day period in May, police . . . began "Operation Gang bang" in an effort to take back city streets. They detained and then released some two hundred alleged gang members. (*Belize First* 1995)

Unlike Los Angeles, where gang violence has abated somewhat, the violence in Belize continues. During a holiday weekend in 1999, for instance, three men were killed and two wounded in seemingly trivial disputes over a bottle of stout and a stolen bicycle (*Reporter Daily News* 1999). Between August 1998 and July 1999 there were fifty-six homicides in Belize; thirteen of these were believed to be drug or gang related, and guns were the murder weapons in twenty-two of the murders (*Belize First* 1999). By US standards the figures seem infinitesimal, yet given Belize's small population they represent a crime rate almost three times that of the United States – and this tiny nation is ill-equipped to deal with it. Although a youth curfew was implemented in 1999 and periodic police sweeps for guns and drugs are widely reported in the Belizean media, neither strategy seems to have had any real impact.

Our objective in this paper is to offer an explanation for the apparently paradoxical (and for Belizeans very unwelcome) transformation Belize is undergoing. We argue that the proliferation of crime in Belize is related to particular patterns of international labour migration to the United States which involve the country's two Afro-Belizean ethnic groups, the Garifuna and Belizean Creoles.[1] Second, we argue that in migration-sending nations like Belize, youthful identities are increasingly shaped by forces which transcend family and locality. Among young males, in particular, identities are profoundly affected by a complex array of transnational linkages created through migration, markets and the global media. Increasingly, we argue, Belizean masculine identity formation occurs at the intersection of complex local and global forces.

Our story must begin with an understanding of international migration conceptualized in terms of Belize's historical role in the global political economy, but migration is also a social and cultural process in which the "distinct voices" of "class, gender, and ethnicity" should be heard (Lie 1995, 305). This chapter highlights the voices of the Garifuna as they pursue their lives and livelihoods in an increasingly globalized world. Although the Garifuna comprise only a portion of the Belizean migrant population and identify themselves as a distinct ethnic group, they share many cultural similarities with Belizean Creoles and settle in the same neighbourhoods in the United States. We believe, therefore, that their experiences are similar to the larger Creole population.[2] The chapter is based on ethnographic research in the Garifuna diaspora community in South Central Los Angeles and in a Garifuna migration-sending community in Belize (Miller [Matthei] 1993).[3]

Garifuna Ethnohistory and Labour Migration

As an ethnic group, the Garifuna are a product of European colonization of the insular Caribbean.[4] Their exact origins are shrouded in various myths and legends (Taylor 1951), but they emerged as a distinct ethnic group during the eighteenth century. Essentially a Maroon society, they are descendants of escaped African slaves who lived among, and adopted the language of, the indigenous Caribs on the island of St Vincent. British colonizers eventually expelled the Garifuna (to whom they referred as "Black Caribs") from the sugar-producing islands; by 1800 the Garifuna had migrated to the Central American coast where they settled horticultural and fishing villages from present-day Nicaragua to Belize.

Soon after their arrival on the Central American mainland, Garifuna men became an important source of labour in the British colony's mahogany and logwood operations, where they supplemented slaves who were always in short supply. Seasonal movement to the logging camps and later to the plantation economies of Honduras and Guatemala eventually gave way to more permanent migration to the United States. During the 1940s Garifuna men joined migrant workers from throughout the Caribbean to replace US males serving in the military.

With few opportunities available to them in Belize's forestry and agricultural enterprises, Garifuna women also eagerly embraced wage labour migration when, during the 1960s, economic restructuring in the United States gave rise to an increased demand for female labour in the low-wage service and manufacturing sectors. In fact, women quickly overtook men, and have outnumbered them in migration to the United States for the past several decades.

Los Angeles is a key destination for both documented and undocumented Garifuna because of its relative proximity to Belize and historically strong immigrant labour market. While the demand for male workers has declined as a result of de-industrialization, unskilled jobs for immigrant women in local garment factories, assembly plants, hotels, hospitals and private homes are plentiful. In fact, Garifuna women are often able to arrange jobs through friends before ever leaving Belize (Miller [Matthei] 1993).

While the United States has been a powerful magnet for Garifuna men and women who enjoy few opportunities in Belize, there are also significant drawbacks associated with migration – not the least of which are the significant social problems which besiege the South Central Los Angeles neighbourhoods in which most settle.

The Garifuna Immigrant Community in South Central Los Angeles

Like their West Indian counterparts from the insular Caribbean, most Belizean immigrants arriving in California in the 1960s and 1970s settled in largely African-American South Central Los Angeles.[5] By the 1980s, however, the city's rapidly growing population of Mexican and Central American immigrants began expanding into the area, while middle-class African Americans began to move out to suburban areas of the city. By 1990, according to the Census Bureau, South Los Angeles (which includes the South Central area) was only 49 per cent black, 44.8 per cent Latino, 3.6 per cent Anglo, and 1.8 per cent Asian or Pacific Islander (Silverstein and Brooks 1991).

By the mid-1970s, economic restructuring was also transforming the Los Angeles labour market. Between 1978 and 1982 the metropolitan area lost some 75,000 mostly unionized, relatively high-wage manufacturing jobs to plant closures and indefinite layoffs (Soja 1987, 182). The rapid decline of the industrial sector devastated the South Central area, where the "median family income fell by the late 1970s to $5,900–$2,500 below the city median for Blacks" (Silverstein and Brooks, 1991).

In the aftermath, crime rates – especially those associated with gang violence and drug trafficking – soared. In 1987 the Los Angeles Police Department's 77th division, in the heart of the South Central area, reported 155 homicides, "a per capita murder rate higher even than Washington, D.C., the nation's newly proclaimed murder capital" (Morrison 1989, 1). By 1990 the local NBC television affiliate began to refer to the South Central area as the "land of the drive-by shooting".

Given the dismal economic situation and the proliferation of crime in their neighbourhoods, few Garifuna residents were surprised when riots erupted in the spring of 1992.[6] In fact, interviews in the community in 1990 often revealed fear and frustration with the worsening conditions in their neighbourhoods. In reply to a survey question, for example, which asked what respondents disliked most about living in Los Angeles, thirty-four of fifty-one individuals (two-thirds) identified

gangs, drugs and drive-by shootings as their primary concerns. In informal interviews they often spoke at length about their fears. This excerpt
from an interview with a woman in her fifties is representative:

> They [gang members] don't have no respect, that's why I'm afraid of walkin'
> up and down on the street. Because that's when the drive-by shootin' – when
> the gangs are out there – that's when the opposite ones – because in this area
> they are the Bloods, you see – and the Bloods shoot up where the Crips are,
> and the Crips come and shoot up where the Bloods are. There's certain colours
> you can't even wear. You can't wear red in this area because we're in the
> Bloods over here . . . . I don't go out in the night. And I don't open the door.
> I don't open the door for *nobody* after dark – not even my own brother.

Even locked doors do not always ensure one's safety in South Central
Los Angeles, however:

> The year before last I have a roommate, and he was standin' close to one of
> the wall and a bullet came through. He was makin' tacos. He didn't eat no
> tacos that night! A man that time – a man was goin' to the store and he got
> shot when the bullet came through my wall. It was an innocent man goin'
> to the store, and he got shot.

Oppositional Identity Formation in South Central Los Angeles

Conditions in South Central Los Angeles are of serious concern to everyone who lives in the area, but bringing up children in the city is especially daunting. Hoping to insulate youngsters from the temptations of
the streets, members of the Garifuna middle class work to instil a strong
ethnic identity and achievement motivation in their offspring. Those who
are financially able enrol their children in private Catholic schools like
those they themselves attended in Belize rather than the notoriously
violent public schools in South Central Los Angeles. The preferred school
is staffed by the same order of nuns who taught many Garifuna in Belize.
Parents note that in addition to providing the discipline lacking in public schools, some of the nuns speak the Garifuna language and encourage the students to learn it. At the very least, the nuns insist that students

speak "proper" English and not the "street language" that Garifuna immigrants associate with lower-class African Americans. Several organizations also focus on the "preservation" of various aspects of Garifuna culture, offering Garifuna history lessons, language classes, and singing, dancing and drumming lessons.

An annual "Garifuna Career Day" organized by a small group of middle-class men and women grew out of efforts to reduce school dropout rates and delinquency among Garifuna teenagers. The event, which is held on the campus of a private Catholic university, features a panel of speakers from the community who recount their own successes and failures, mistakes and achievements while dispensing practical advice about educational options and careers. Each in their own way also cajoles the mostly middle-class teenagers to spend their time in wholesome pursuits rather than "hanging out" on neighbourhood streets.

Community efforts notwithstanding, working-class and poor Garifuna families find it difficult to insulate their children from the crime and gang activity in their neighbourhoods. A significant proportion of Garifuna families in South Central Los Angeles are headed by women who have few employment skills and, as often as not, lack legal immigration papers (Miller [Matthei] 1993). With few formal employment options available to them, many take jobs in private households as housekeepers, babysitters or companions to the elderly, jobs which require extended absences from their own homes and children. Community members often cite a lack of parental authority in single-parent homes as a factor in youthful delinquency:

> Some people they get these sleep-in jobs, you know, where they have to stay at the job. Well, then the kids are home by themselves. They say they don't have any choice – they have to work. And because that's the only kinda work they could do, they do that. And the kids once they are thirteen or fourteen, they're allowed to take care of themselves – maybe an adult will go check on them now and again. They're on their own. They really have access to go out and do what they want to do.

Nuclear-family households are not necessarily immune from the problems posed by residence in US inner-city neighbourhoods. Families in which both mother and father must work long hours in order to make ends meet may also find their children straying. Monica, a young woman who joined her parents in Los Angeles when she was eight, describes her experiences and those of her siblings in Los Angeles:

> Up to today, my grandmother would say that the United States ruined us, because we had no focus once we came. Our parents were always working, which left us to do whatever the hell we wanted to do – including being a part of a gang, smoking marijuana, drinking. You name it, we did it – at an early age at that!

Recent studies of children of working-class and poor immigrants in the United States indicate that they do not simply assimilate to the dominant culture and values, nor do they necessarily share the ethnic identity of their parents (Portes 1995; Zhou 1997). Instead these "second generation" immigrants – many of whom live in racially segregated inner-city areas – typically identify more closely with the racial and ethnic minorities of their own neighbourhoods than with either dominant US culture and values or those of their hardworking parents (for examples see Zhou 1997; Portes 1995). Having watched their parents work hard and yet achieve little or no success, the second generation becomes aware of the level of racial discrimination in the United States and, like their US minority peers, often adopt an adversarial identity which is oppositional to dominant group values (Bourgois 1989; Portes 1995).

While Garifuna youths of both sexes may adopt oppositional stances, the gendered nature of identity tends to place girls at much less risk than their male counterparts. Although parents may complain about their daughters' occasional rudeness or lack of motivation, one rarely hears of any serious trouble among Garifuna daughters. Despite her recollection of youthful rebellion, for example, Monica was at the time of her interview a student at a highly ranked Los Angeles university.

In her recently published study of West Indian immigrants in New York, Mary Waters (2000) suggests that because boys are more often the targets of racism in the United States, they tend to be more militant in their rejection of dominant group values. Anyone who has spent much time in central city neighbourhoods is likely to have witnessed police harassment of black males. In Los Angeles ongoing investigations of police corruption have brought to light a pattern of serious abuses of African-American and immigrant males in inner-city neighbourhoods, ranging from evidence tampering to illegal deportations and even suspected homicides. Such experiences, we believe, must certainly increase young men's mistrust and hostility towards the dominant authority structure.

Parents worry about the safety and welfare of all their children, but traditional child rearing and socialization patterns in Belize, which give boys a good deal more leeway than girls, also place them at greater risk. A certain amount of "cheekiness" is condoned and even encouraged in boys, while girls can expect to be scolded severely or even lashed soundly for relatively minor offences. Boys also enjoy a longer tether than girls, and therefore more opportunities to go astray: "Unlike their sisters, who as a rule occupy most of their hours out of school with household work, boys spend a great deal of the day away from the household. As their mothers frequently complain, they devote most of their free time to 'drifting' about with male peers . . ." (Kerns 1977, 151–52). While relatively harmless in the villages of Belize, on the streets of Los Angeles the customary freedoms granted to boys can have grave consequences.

Although Garifuna immigrants are understandably reluctant to talk about crime and gang involvement among their offspring, most acknowledge that there is a problem. And even a casual observer would find it difficult to overlook the distinctive clothing and the hand signs which proclaim young men's gang affiliations at Garifuna community gatherings. It is impossible to estimate how many Garifuna youths actually belong to gangs or actively engage in criminal activity, but there is disturbing evidence.[7] According to a local community leader at least ten young Garifuna men were killed as a result of gang or drug-related activity (or both) during a two-year period. And since the mid-1990s when US immigration officials began targeting immigrant gang members, on average two Belizeans have been deported per week as "criminal aliens" by the Immigration and Naturalization Service because they have been convicted of felonies in the United States.[8] Unfortunately at least some of the deportees who have been implicated in the proliferation of gang violence in Belize are Garifuna (O'Connor 1998).

Migration and the Dilemmas of Parenting

Hoping to avoid the potential risks associated with rearing children in US inner cities, many Belizean parents leave their youngsters behind with kin when they seek work in Los Angeles. Reliance on child fostering is a long-established cultural tradition among the Garifuna, as it is throughout the Caribbean region (Clarke 1957; Sanford 1971; Soto 1987). For generations Garifuna women have temporarily placed their children in the care of kin (usually maternal) in order to take advantage of the limited income-earning opportunities available to them in Belize (Taylor 1951; Kerns 1983). With this childcare system already in place, Garifuna of both sexes are able, with minimal fuss, to participate in labour migration to the United States. Women and men who seek to migrate rarely have difficulty finding a relative or friend to care for their children. With few employment opportunities available locally, non-migrant women in Belize seek every opportunity to forge ties to kin in the United States. Fostering the children of migrant kin not only ensures a regular flow of cash remittances, it also builds a network of potential support in the United States should they or a member of their household decide to migrate. Therefore, sisters and mothers of migrants often compete for the opportunity to provide childcare. As a woman in Belize explains, "Even a little job in the States can support two families" – one in the United States and another in Belize.

During the 1960s and 1970s, child fostering arrangements were typically temporary. Parents left their children in Belize for a year or two until they were well enough established to send for them or until the children were old enough to attend school in the United States. However, as crime rates began to soar in Los Angeles over the past decade or so, more and more families began to extend the length of their children's fosterage. Today, a persistent daughter may convince her parents to bring her to the United States once she reaches an age where she can help with household chores, but few see any advantages to bringing sons, given the dangers that lurk in the streets of US inner cities. Unfortunately, since many, if not most, parents lack legal US immigration documents, they are wary of risking trips to and from Belize. So actual visits home to see children left behind are rare; letters, gifts and occasional telephone calls must replace face-to-face contact between parent and child.

Not infrequently, teenage boys who have spent most of their lives in the United States are sent off to kin in Belize "under punishment" because they have become unruly at home, gotten in trouble at school or become involved in gangs. Still others are sent to Belize (as noted above) not by parents but by the US government – deported as "criminal aliens" after serving sentences in juvenile or adult prison facilities. Reared (and in some cases born) in the United States, these young men find it difficult to adjust to their "exile" in Belize and to life with relatives who are often complete strangers to them. Moreover, the Belize that they return to is not the idyllic one that their parents remember. During the past two decades the kinds of crimes that are so characteristic of US cities have found their way to Belize, too. In Belize City, but also in more remote settlements, crack cocaine has largely supplanted marijuana as a popular and readily available street drug, and international theft rings operate with relative impunity, bringing a steady supply of stolen automobiles and high-powered weapons to Belize's own burgeoning criminal class. Thus, despite the good intentions of their parents and their Belizean kin, the boys who are sent to Belize for rehabilitation are often lured back into the behaviour patterns that got them into trouble in the United States.

Globalization and Black Masculinity

Although globalization is perceived as a late-twentieth-century phenomenon, networks of trade and migration between the United States and Belize were already well established long ago. As early as 1935 the British governor of Belize noted a substantial – though perhaps exaggerated – US cultural presence: "The whole colony is . . . largely influenced by the comparative proximity of the U.S. and the people as a whole are more Americans than British in their outlook" (quoted in Educational Task Force 1984, 64). Trade and the back-and-forth movements of immigrant workers certainly brought glimpses of the United States over the years, but more recently global technology has inundated Belize with images from the North.

There are eight privately owned television stations in this nation of some two hundred thousand people; each station relies almost exclusively on intercepting satellite-relayed programming from US broadcasters, and 80 per cent of all household electricity consumers have television sets (US Department of State 1996; Lent 1989). In Belize City sixty cable channels from all over the world are available (Darling 1999). Even in outlying towns viewers can watch CNN, ESPN, HBO, Black Entertainment Television (BET) and even the local NBC affiliate from Boulder, Colorado. Researchers suggest that US programming has created an unparalleled demand for US goods (Wilk 1990; Lent 1989). Although the actual relationship between television and buying habits is difficult to measure, the US Commerce Department (1994) reports that Belize is the highest per capita importer of US consumer-ready food products in Central America.

The US cultural influence appears to have the greatest impact among teenagers and young adults. Like their counterparts elsewhere in the Caribbean, Garifuna youths listen to American rap music along with their own punta rock, wear the baggy jeans and shirts favoured by US hip-hop artists and, it seems, anything else they can find emblazoned with the logos of companies like Nike and Tommy Hilfiger. Despite parental resistance many, if not most, view migration as a rite of passage and enthusiastically tell anyone who will listen about their plans to go to the United States – "With or Without Papers", as a punta rock song's lyrics proclaim. A survey of Belizean youths suggests that the US media influence youthful migrant dreams. In the study, two-thirds of a sample of Creole and Garifuna youth reported watching television, with US programmes dominating their lists of favourite shows, and 45 per cent expressed a desire to live in the United States (Snyder, Roser and Chaffee 1991).

Noting the global reach of US media and consumer items, Ruben Rumbaut asserts that "many immigrants (and for that matter non-immigrants) these days are already 'Americanized' to varying degrees in the countries of origin before they even set foot in the United States" (1997, 494). But to which America do they assimilate? The images beamed into Belize and the rest of the world hardly present the United States in all its complexity; rather they are at best "strips of reality" from which distant audiences are left to construct "imagined worlds" (Appadurai 1996, 35). The black men that US television and movies project onto the global screen are not hardworking family men or university students; instead the models of black masculinity that Belizean youngsters see and emulate are those of "super athletes" and "super criminals" – aggressive, cold, menacing men who are imminently capable of violence (Ross 1998). At least one police official in Belize blames US television for introducing gang warfare to Belize:

> The kids gravitate to what they see on T.V., a and they see America as the leading country. It's like following a role model, but in this case, the role model was bad. The worst thing for us was when the movie *Colors* was shown on T.V. in April 1989; that's when the kids got the gang idea. (Katz 1991, 1A)

In Honduras, which is even farther removed from US influence than Belize, young Garifuna men draw heavily on media-generated images of African-American masculinity:

> From dreadlocks to shaved heads, baggy pants to backward caps, basketball jerseys to Nike high-tops, Garifuna fashion displays a self-conscious black aesthetic. The music they prefer includes soul, reggae, dancehall, and hip-hop and some of their favorite films, often sent by video from relatives abroad, depict the lives of inner-city African Americans (such as *Boyz 'N the Hood*, *Menace II Society*). (Gordon and Anderson 1999, 291)

Ironically, the characters in the movies and the music videos, and the clothing they wear, are mostly produced and disseminated by whites who profit from the sales at the same time that they perpetuate negative stereotypes and potentially harmful images of young black males (Seelow 1996).

Remittances and Absentee Parenting

For decades remittances have formed a vital economic link between Garifuna migrants and their kin who remain in Belize. A Garifuna community leader and a local social worker estimate that 80 per cent of households in one Garifuna town receive some form of remittance (cash, material goods or both) from relatives and friends in the United States. Although a substantial portion of cash remittances provide basic economic support for elderly parents and dependent children left behind with local kin, the flow of remittances from "absentee parents" also fosters unhealthy desires, according to local residents. In order to compensate in some measure for their extended absences, some migrant parents send spending money directly to their children, along with expensive clothing and other consumer goods. A Garifuna official, himself a former US migrant, provides his assessment of the disruptive influence of this recent trend:

> Now, some parents stop sendin' used clothes to their kids. They begin to send new clothes, expensive clothes. Now, if these are school children, they're goin' to the same school, we in the same class. Well here we are, your mother and father in the States, my mother and father in the States. You wearin' those things. Look at what I'm wearin'. That has its psychological effect . . . they don't feel happy, they look at it as neglect. Okay, so they hurriedly destroy [the used items], and they write their parents personal letters. And the next thing you know that the parents with this thing fresh in their minds they'll send new clothes, new outfits for a period of time, and stop. Then that create a new problem. Then, uh, this boy or this girl begin to feel something is not correct . . . If it's a boy reaching that age . . . he see that quick dollars are passin' from some other friend who is not goin' to school anymore by probably selling a few stick of weed for that man over there. Then he begins to think of start makin' his own money. Then that develops from sellin' it to usin' it, until that boy becomes worthless . . . . It also happen to people [whose parents] do not go, who do not travel. These same children begin to see that other children are usin' expensive and good things.

Members of the immigrant community in Los Angeles are reminded by kin back home and by visiting Belizean dignitaries that they share significant responsibility for the social problems currently facing their homeland, and that they must share in efforts to resolve them. In 1990 the mayor of a Garifuna town in Belize spoke to a large crowd celebrating the Fourth of July in Los Angeles. In her speech, the mayor expressed empathy for the immigrant parents in the audience, but urged them to make "a re-commitment" to their Belizean communities and to the children they had left behind:

> One serious factor posing a continuous threat to the stability of our families and our community is the great percentage of absentee parents . . . and our society is beginning to reap the bitter rewards . . . . I am aware of the problems that confront parents who are forced to seek a better life here in the United States and are forced at times to leave their children behind. Given the circumstances of life for some parents in the United States it is sometimes difficult for these children to be with their parents. My appeal to you my dear people is to communicate with your children – not through clothes and other material goods which seemingly have become a replacement for our love for our children, but to write to them and let them understand that you are close to them in your hearts. It will not be the answer to their problems but they will understand that there is a mother or a father who means more than a brand new pair of Adidas, Levis, and a stereo system.

Garifuna immigrants in Los Angeles are deeply concerned about the disturbing changes occurring back home. And few would dispute that the social problems impacting Belize are related to their own migration to South Central Los Angeles. They identify as members of a transnational community, and make substantial contributions to development projects in towns and villages that they continue to view as their own. They also recognize, however, that there are no easy solutions to the social problems overtaking Belize. Migration – and the erosive effects of absentee parenthood – are likely to continue as long as parents must choose between staying home to raise their children in poverty and exposing them to the crime-ridden neighbourhoods of South Central Los Angeles.

Acknowledgements

Linda Miller Matthei gratefully acknowledges research support provided by the National Science Foundation and by a Rockefeller Foundation postdoctoral fellowship at the Institute of Latin American Studies, University of Texas at Austin, 1992–93.

Notes

1. Creoles, who comprise 30 per cent of the population, are descendants of Belize's slave population.
2. We cannot be sure, however, because to our knowledge no study of Creole migration patterns to the United States exists.
3. The primary field research upon which this chapter is based was dissertation research carried out by the first author (Miller [Matthei] 1993). However, Linda Matthei continues to maintain relationships with Garifuna informants in Los Angeles and in Belize.
4. Shoman (1994) provides a recent, detailed history of Belize, stressing the impact of British colonialism and US imperialism. Elsewhere the authors have provided a fuller account of the historical-structural context of Garifuna international migration and the incorporation of women into these flows (see Matthei and Smith 1996, or especially Miller [Matthei] 1993).
5. In 1970, when many Garifuna settled there, the population of South Central Los Angeles was 79 per cent black (Palacio 1982, 15).
6. Although it is difficult to know if any Garifuna participated directly in the riots, several families lost their homes to the fires which swept their neighbourhoods. Despite the violence the riots seem to have had little impact on the continued flow of new migrants from Belize. Explaining why Belizean Garifuna continue to come to South Central Los Angeles, despite the warnings of kin already there, a woman in Belize stated simply, "You have to compare hard here, to hard there."
7. Crime data in the United States do not reflect the ethnicity of those arrested. Thus, Garifuna arrestees would simply be reported as black or African American.
8. Personal communication with staff of the Belizean consulate in Los Angeles; US Immigration and Naturalization Service 2000.

References

Appadurai, Arjun. 1996. *Modernity at Large: Cultural Dimensions of Globalization*. Minneapolis: University of Minnesota Press.

Belize First. 1995. "Belize Police after Gangs". 2, no. 2. <www.turq.com/belizefirst/vol2e.html>.

———. 1999. "New Study: Belize Had More than Fifty Murders in the Past Year". August 26. <www.turq.com/belizefirst/vol2e.html>.

Bourgois, Phillippe. 1989. "Crack in Spanish Harlem: Culture and Economy in the Inner City". *Anthropology Today* 5, no. 4.

Caribbean Insight. 1992. "Belize: Briefly". 15, no. 6 (June).

Clarke, Edith. 1957. *My Mother Who Fathered Me: A Study of Family in Three Selected Communities in Jamaica*. London: Allen and Unwin.

Darling, Juanita. 1999. "Serial Killer is Stalking the Oasis". *Los Angeles Times*, 22 October.

Educational Task Force. 1984. *A History of Belize: Nation in the Making*. Belize City: Sunshine Books.

Farah, Douglas, and Tod Robberson. 1995. "U.S. Style Gangs Build Free Trade in Crime". *Washington Post*, 28 August.

Gordon, Edmund T., and Mark Anderson. 1999. "The African Diaspora: Toward an Ethnography of Diasporic Identification". *Journal of American Folklore* 112, no. 445.

Government of Belize. 2000. National Population and Housing Census. <http://www.belize.gov.bz/features/cs0_welcome.html>

Katz, Gregory. 1991. "Crack Violence Spreads to Belize: Gangs, Addicts Crop up after Colombians Bring Drug to Once-Tranquil Nation". *Dallas Morning News*, 1 July.

Kerns, Virginia. 1977. "Daughters Bring In: Ceremonial and Social Organization of the Black Carib of Belize". PhD diss., University of Illinois, Urbana-Champaign.

———. 1983. *Women and the Ancestors: Black Carib Kinship and Ritual*. Urbana: University of Illinois Press.

Lent, John. 1989. "Country of No Return: Belize since Television". *Belizean Studies* 17, no. 1.

Lie, J. 1995. "From International Migration to Transnational Diaspora". *Contemporary Sociology* 24, no. 4.

Miller [Matthei], Linda. 1993. "Bridges: Garifuna Migration to Los Angeles". PhD diss., University of California, Irvine.

Matthei, Linda Miller, and David A. Smith. 1996. "Women, Households and Transnational Migration Networks: The Garifuna and Global Economic Restructuring". In *Latin America in the World-Economy,* edited by R. Korzeniewicz and W. Smith. Westport, Conn.: Greenwood.

Morrison, Pat. 1989. "In the 77th It's Life at Mach 2: City's Danger Zone". *Los Angeles Times,* 14 May.

O'Connor, Anne-Marie. 1998. "American Threat to a Proud Heritage". *Los Angeles Times,* 4 April.

Palacio, Joseph. 1982. "Garifuna Migrants in the Los Angeles Area: Process of Social Change". Centre for Afro-American Studies, University of California, Los Angeles. Manuscript.

Portes, Alejandro. 1995. "Children of Immigrants: Segmented Assimilation and Its Determinants". In *The Economic Sociology of Immigration,* edited by Alejandro Portes. New York: Russell Sage Foundation.

Reporter Daily News (Belize). 1999. "Tenth Weekend Marred by Violence", 17 September.

Ross, Marlon B. 1998. "In Search of Black Men's Masculinities". *Feminist Studies* 24, no. 3.

Rumbaut, Ruben. 1997. "Paradoxes(and Orthodoxies) of Assimilation". *Sociological Perspectives* 40, no. 3.

Sanford, Margaret. 1971. "Disruption of the Mother-Child Relationship in Conjunction with Matrifocality: A Study of Child-Keeping among the Carib and Creoles of British Honduras". PhD diss., Catholic University of America.

Seelow, David. 1996. "Look Forward in Anger: Young Black Males and the New Cinema". *Journal of Men's Studies* 5, no. 2.

Shoman, Assad. 1994. *Thirteen Chapters of a History of Belize.* Belize City: Angelus Press.

Silverstein, Stuart, and N. Rivera Brooks. 1991. "South L.A. Shoppers Need Stores". *Los Angeles Times,* 24 November.

Snyder, Leslie, C. Roser and S. Chaffee. 1991. "Foreign Media and Desire to Emigrate from Belize". *Journal of Communication* 41, no. 1.

Soja, Edward. 1987. "Economic Restructuring and the Internationalization of the Los Angeles Region". In *The Capitalist City: Global Restructuring and Community Politics,* edited by Michael Smith and Joe Feagin. New York: Basil Blackwell.

Soto, I.M. 1987. "West Indian Child Fostering: Its Role in Migrant Exchanges". In *Caribbean Life in New York City: Sociocultural*

Dimensions, edited by Constance R. Sutton and Elsa M. Chaney. New York: Centre for Migration Studies.

Taylor, Douglas. 1951. *The Black Carib of British Honduras.* New York: Wenner-Gren Foundation.

US Department of Commerce. 1994. *Belize Country Commercial Guide FY 1993.* Washington, DC: Department of Commerce.

US Department of State. 1996. *Belize Human Rights Practices, 1995.*

US Immigration and Naturalization Service. 2000. *Statistical Yearbook.* Washington, DC: Department of Justice.

Waters, Mary. 2000. *Black Identities: West Indian Immigrant Dreams and American Realities.* New York: Russell Sage Foundation.

Wilk, Richard. 1990. "Consumer Goods, Cultural Imperialism and Underdevelopment in Belize". In *SPEAReports 4: Second Annual Studies on Belize Conference.* Belize City: Society for the Promotion of Education and Research.

Zhou, Min. 1997. "Growing Up American: The Challenge Confronting Immigrant Children and Children of Immigrants". *Annual Review of Sociology* 23.

PART FOUR

Popular Culture and Literary Images of Masculinity and Femininity

CHAPTER 11

Under Women's Eyes

Literary Constructs of Afro-Caribbean Masculinity

PAULA MORGAN

"Is a pen a metaphorical penis?" This now famous question was posed in 1979 to introduce Gilbert and Gubar's exploration of the manner in which patriarchy and its texts have sought to imprison women in silence. *The Madwoman in the Attic* unveiled the subtle strategies employed by nineteenth-century female writers to deconstruct the existing cultural paradigms of femininity. Indeed, a major concern of feminist theory has been to expose the collusion between the ideology of dominance, which underlies the social construction of gender, and the cultural practice, which governs our day-to-day interactions.[1] And literary critics have been particularly concerned with what Greene and Khan term "the collusion between literature and ideology, focusing on the ways in which ideology is inscribed within literary forms, styles, conventions, genres and the institutions of literary productions" ([1985] 1991, 5).

Today women writers of the postcolonial world have successfully
brought female subjectivity from periphery to centre; they have interrogated ideological assumptions of dominance based on gender as well as
on ethnicity and class; they have inscribed in their literary discourses
new gender ideologies which are filtering into cultural practice. The
pen can no longer be perceived exclusively as a metaphorical penis. But
a related issue emerges. Now that women have, by dint of struggle,
acquired the didactic and hegemonic mantle of the story-teller, what
manner of man is being generated within the literary womb of the
woman?

A characteristic which Caribbean women's writing shares with the
fictions of African-American and African women is its predominantly
negative portrayal of men and male-female relationships. In 1975 Mary
Helen Washington introduced a selection of African-American short narratives with the observation that in many stories

> the relationships between black men and black women are often deadlocked.
> In the past there was much fighting and knocking of heads (the woman's usu-
> ally), these antagonisms being brought on, for the most part, because of the
> economic and political powerlessness of the black family. The literature of
> black women strongly implies that in the future the black woman will more
> and more choose to be alone. (1975, xxvii)

Mordecai and Wilson, in their introduction to a 1989 anthology of
women's writing from the Caribbean, contend that the portrayal of male-
female relationships in the writing "from the earliest work to the most
recent augurs ill. Almost invariably the man regards the woman as an
object, neglects, abuses, ill-treats and diminishes her" (p. xiv). In 1993
O'Callaghan, also pointing to the predominant negativity of these portrayals, suggests that some female writers display the understanding that
the men are victims of the "social and historical factors that sanction
male tyranny" (p. 5). In 1994 I also concluded a cross-cultural study of
a substantial cross-section of African, African-American and Caribbean
women's novels with the comment that, for the most part, they deliver
a devastating judgment on their male characters. A substantial cross-
section is depicted as weak or blindly egoistic; if they are strong, they

are inclined to be vicious and cruel or complacent, authoritarian and unwilling to listen, or vain and foolish. Perchance the isolated man may be a caring companion; he nevertheless remains faceless or a trifle unconvincing.[2]

This paper takes a closer view of selected portrayals of male characters in women's writing, and poses the following questions: Does gender create an alien and alienating barrier which cannot be breached? Are the portrayals of men merely superficial, displaying no in-depth understanding of the inner feeling of what it means to be a man? Do women possess the sensitivity and the intuitive understanding to get beyond the petty barriers to understand the other? Do differences in gender – and, for that matter, in race, class and sexual orientation – create islands in the imaginations which limit the perceiving eye/I to encountering the other only via stereotypes or external portraits of greater or lesser detail and accuracy?

Some may take issue with this line of enquiry, or perhaps more so with its timeliness. To borrow term, it is "morning yet on creation day" in terms of literary representations of womanhood. The process of dismantling stereotypes and cultural paradigms is intricate and takes generations to come to fruition. Especially in a multiethnic Caribbean framework, the interlocking impact of gender, ethnicity and class makes the task of defining a female identity infinitely more complex and therefore, one might argue, deserving of maximum attention. True. But I question whether we will be able to adjust existing paradigms of womanhood unless we also adjust existing paradigms of manhood. The shift in emphasis from women's studies to gender studies and the increasing interest in investigating masculinity affirm this.

The representation of male characters can be approached in several ways, the most obvious being their centrality in the text. Sybil Seaforth (*Growing Up with Miss Milly,* 1988) and Velma Pollard (*Karl and Other Stories,* 1994) have written of male development, with emphasis on maternal interactions with the emerging man. Paule Marshall has penned four stories using adult male characters and dealing with the awakening of emotionally impoverished men (*Soul Clap Hands and Sing,* [1961] 1988).[3] Patricia Powell has explored male homosexuality within

Jamaican society in a novel which examines social reactions and the homosexual's dealing with the devastations of illness and death (*A Small Gathering of Bones*, 1994). However, the majority of female-authored texts in Caribbean literature overtly or tacitly question the male-dominated literature in which female representation is largely stereotypical, marginal or both.

I will begin the detailed analyses with an examination of a male character who impacts our dreaming and waking reality in a most fearsome manner.[4] What accounts for the making of the criminal as a young man, who becomes younger with each passing day; who possesses no notion of private ownership, unless it is of his right of enjoyment of that which he has stolen; who has no respect for life, unless it is his own – a young man who would effectively complete a robbery and then hang around to just "pop one" (murder a man) for the fun of it? What crucible has created the monster who makes hitherto vexing literary issues, such as the motiveless malignity of an Iago, seem puerile?

In "Country of the One Eye God" (1986) and in "The Dispatcher" (1989a) Olive Senior examines the nature of Jack Spratt:

> People who say
> overpopulation is the greatest
> curse of the nation should
> give medal to Jack Spratt
> for what we over-produce
> Jack Spratt will reduce
> with efficiency and dispatch
>   (1989a, 107)

Jack Spratt, to all intents and purposes, exemplifies an antiheroic view of pure manhood. His is the culturally enshrined fairy-tale transformation of the pauper into the prince. He is the poor, ignorant country boy, who starts with no resources but comes to town and makes good. He affirms the assumption that hard work, efficiency and diligence create success. In a society in which the pursuit of power is an extremely desirable heroic objective, he becomes a repository of personal power and representative of institutional power – public servant, contractor, poten-

tial medal-winner. He is set on a clearly demarcated and well-travelled
fast track, and shows every indication of arriving at the upper echelons
of the criminal world with his characteristic dispatch. Moreover, as the
central authority figure, the supreme signifier of his world, he has apparently attained an ultimate human quest objective – the power over life
and death:

> . . . Jack Spratt
> have the might and the right
> to decide who sleeping
> in tonight and who outside
> in Hope River bottom
> or in cold Sandy Gully
> (1989a, 107)

The musicality generated by the internal rhyme "might" and "right" and
the initial rhyme "in" and "in" ironically affirms the sense of the appro-
priateness of the order created by Jack Spratt and his machinations.

The strength of the poem is the extent to which Senior introduces the
ironic sense of normalcy into the deviant criminal world. The exploits
of Jack Spratt are related dispassionately with a flat ironic detachment,
as if they represented a communally recognized and accepted success
story of an eminently powerful man. Surely this must stand as an indictment against a society which measures manhood based on the size of
one's car and bank balance, the number and attributes of one's women,
and the extent of personal and institutional power one is able to wield.

"Country of the One Eye God" focuses more closely on this antiheroic type within the family group. Here Jack Spratt, with his name
now reduced to its diminutive, Jacko, has fallen into adverse circumstances; he returns to his Grannie seeking money to escape from the
police. Senior presents multiple perspectives which can account for his
making. As far as Jacko is concerned his outcome is natural and logi-
cal, given his upbringing. As it is written of Jack Spratt, so it is with
Jacko:

> his grannie
> did beat him
> with supple jack cant done

boy so tough
never cry
Grannie say
is bad seed
       (1989a, 106)

The child is nurtured on a steady diet of licks to beat out the bad blood, and rejection based on the hope (deferred year after year) of his parents, who have migrated to the promised foreign land, sending for him. The outcome is a man who recognizes no constraint of morality or religion, love or duty, decency or social order. His criminal actions of robbing and conceivably killing his grandmother for the burial money which she jealously guards on her person are framed in his mind as reciprocity for the abuse and maltreatment which he received in the name of an upbringing. The effectiveness of dispensing corporal punishment in the home, in the absence of affirmation of love and clear moral and ethical direction, comes into question. For Jacko the constant beatings merely manifested his outsider status.

Yet Ma B's consistent beatings of all her children to eliminate bad ways were proffered out of concern and ignorance of more viable child-raising techniques. Senior intentionally problematizes the situation; had child abuse been sufficient cause, Ma B would have raised a generation of criminals, not just one. Hence, she searches further afield into her lineage for a cause: "She had coldly cast her mind back to every thing she knew about every single member of the family to discern if there was something hidden in her tribe that betokened this ending, and she could find nothing that warranted such a hard and final cruelty." Moreover, she searches the range of circumstances successfully confronted by her antecedents and her generations: "they had faced deaths starvation hurricane earthquake cholera typhoid malaria tuberculosis fire diphtheria and travel to dangerous and distant places in search of work" (1986, 16). Here, too, she draws a blank, for at no time in the past has this series of adversities produced a hardened criminal. If these characters had sat down to dialogue in a masculinity symposium, the criminal would have posited nurture – that is excessive punishment, rejection, poverty and adverse circumstances – as the main causative element. And the primary nurturer would have posited nature – "bad seed" and pre-destination; it is written that the youth raise up "the ways of their destruction" (p. 19). Each of these may be a contributing factor, but neither of these is sufficient enough to nullify the individual's power of choice.

A focal point in the story and the poem is the formulation of life's objectives, and particularly the personal and culturally shared correlations between representation and desire. For Jacko, and unfortunately for a substantial cross-section of Caribbean islanders, "foreign" represents the culmination of wealth and well-being – it represents the home and comforts that he has never had, the parents for whom he has longed in vain. Even with his impressive credentials as a professional "thief, a murderer, a hired gunman, a rapist, a jailbird, a jail breaker, and now, at nineteen, a man with a price on his head" (p. 16), he is poised to shed his grandmother's blood to facilitate his much-longed-for home-coming:

"What? Yu plan to go foreign?"
"What else? Don't I have mother, don't I have father in foreign?" (p. 21)

The irony is that he shares with Ma B an essentially irrational response to a life of poverty and deprivation. As she has become disillusioned with life's goals, she too has found a focal point for her hope, so intense that she is prepared to die in defence of the money saved to give her an ostentatious burial. In the interaction between the two, Senior uses third-person omniscience to parallel the workings of a criminal, irrational mind with the skewed but innocuous thinking of a well-meaning old woman. Both see, in her guarded cache of money, their future and fulfilment of their greatest quest objects. He is portrayed as coldly, method-ically fighting for life without a clue of what life signifies; for him it is the dream-space of "foreign" from which he was excluded. Similarly, despite the grandmother's apparent intimacy with God, her dream-space remains earth bound. For her the epitome of life, the final triumph over poverty, smallness and meanness, is the resplendent coffin in which she will lie in state to receive tribute to the wealth, beauty and order which she had never acquired in life. Even as she prays desperately "don't let him get my burial money", he levels the gun at her and reasons, "Ma B, for the last time, give me the money. Yu soon dead and lef it yu know. What you want money for? Let it go nuh. I have the whole of my life still in front of me" (p. 25).

The encounter also represents a shift in power alignment from an ageing rural-based matriarchy to an emerging urban-based counter-hegemonic masculinity. In the exchange Jacko reverses the traditional social structure, which privileges respect for the authority of age and for the mother figure, based on allegiance and gratitude for her sacrificial acts on behalf of kin. Despite his fear and anxiety as a wanted man running for his life, he retains the (albeit illusory) stance of a masterful, threatening authority figure holding over her the power of life and death. She, who treats her excitable seventy-year-old nephew as a child because he had never acquired her calm, is constrained to bow to the evil life force in Jacko: "In the pale light, Ma Bell wondered how such a little boy could suddenly grow so huge as to fill all the spaces in the room. She felt shriveled and light, compressed into the interstices of space by his nearness" (p. 23). It is from this position of power that he presents his own reasoning, logic and rationale: the issue of justice is subverted for him by the essential injustice of the world. Note that although he is unable to deny the existence of God, he reasons that God is a one-eye God who has aligned himself with the unjust power structure: "Him no business with ragtag and bobtail like unno. God up a top a laugh keh keh keh at the likes of you" (p. 24). Ironically, like his grandmother, he is a man of faith. Since all power and meaning is vested in the material world, he in turn vests his belief in a God of the materially prosperous, which leaves him free to create his own alternative existential reality as sovereign over a counter-order – a dog-eat-dog world, in which he can affirm his masculinity as top dog.

The irony is that, as Jacko's birth parents have rejected him, the only place of belonging he will ever possess is in the heart of the grandmother who, despite her intimate knowledge of his reprobate nature, rejoices when in his flight from the police he answers the call of blood and returns to her sheltering. He ruthlessly desecrates and despoils the only home that he will ever have, a place in the heart and loyalty of this mother-woman.

Clearly, in the face of unrelenting social adversity and unachievable economic aspirations, the metropolis beckons as a dream-space in which this nebulous, successful manhood can be sought. It is in "foreign" that we encounter the second character which I have chosen for analysis: Deighton Boyce of *Brown Girl, Brownstones* (1959), Paule Marshall's study of the popular stereotype of the black West Indian male, who is unable to prosper materially and wastes his substance on ostentatious clothing and mistresses. The petted and pampered son of a refined, deserted mother, he repays his mother's sacrifices and high hopes for his future with promiscuity and irresponsibility. His aspirations are constantly being flouted. His personal limitations, insufficient mastery of his current project and racial bias in society combine to exclude him from material success. Although he is presented as crippled from youth by the white-controlled Barbadian economy, which distributes jobs and material prosperity on the basis of race and colour rather than merit, racism functions as yet another disguise for his impotence. Labelled by his wife as "always looking for something big and praying hard not to find it", Deighton has come to accept that rejection is his lot, and he is even more fearful of success than of defeat (p. 174).

In drawing this character Marshall pierces the façade of the black dandy obsessed with his fancy clothes and his women. A new image is superimposed on the perfumed and bedecked "sweetman". In his daughter Selina's memory the picture of Deighton leaving for his weekly visit to his concubine survives as a man "stumbling in defeat down Fulton Street – the Saturday crowd engulfing him as the sea did later" (p. 268). He inarticulately longs for simpler times when male self-image rested on brute strength and sexual prowess – the ability to flash a knife and bed a whore. The narrative voice frames on his behalf the puzzle which he is unable to crystallize: "But what of those, then, to whom these proofs of manhood were alien? Who must find other, more sanctioned, ways?" (p. 38). Bewildered, weak and vain, his enduring sense of hope is his greatest virtue.

Deighton retains antiheroic qualities because he refuses to embrace the prevailing notion of self-worth based on material acquisition; however, he lacks a valid basis of self-perception as an alternative. Whereas chances are that Deighton would have survived in the gentler, slower-moving Caribbean society, he is unable to deal with transplantation into the urban, capitalist environment. Mechanization and the forces which fuel modern industry emerge as an implacable enemy in Marshall's fiction. Man is portrayed as dwarfed, reduced to enslavement in service of the machines which he has created. In the massive war-production factory, the roar of the machine robs man of his power of expression, a key marker of his humanity. Moreover, mechanization divorces him from the natural world which is the wellspring of his spiritual well-being. The necessity for continual, back-breaking labour also causes the individual to lose touch with his inner being. The new society which is powered by gigantic and impersonal machines is inimical to Deighton's life force. While Silla's formidable force matches the ugly grandeur of the colossal machine with its frenetic life beat, symbolically and in actuality Deighton is eaten in its maw which "sucked in his arm as it sucked in the metal to be shaped then spewed it out crushed" (p. 155).

Together, Deighton and Silla represent a reversal of concepts which are traditionally associated with masculinity and femininity. It is Silla who carries the burden of association with machine, will to power, material productivity, conquest, all of which are traditionally associated with the male quest. Indeed, the grimness of the economic environment, coupled with her husband's rejection of this role, necessitates the sublimation of her softness and femininity, until she even appears to lose her human status and to assume the mantle of deity. On the other hand, Deighton is associated with an imperfect mix of the opposing elements – music, freedom, imagination, dreams – which are usually associated with femininity.

Indeed, in the eyes of her husband and children, Silla assumes the role of a terrible mother-goddess. Deighton's favourite retort to his wife's many diatribes is "You's God; you must know" (p. 26). Fleeing in terror from his own failure and from the shy, expectant bride who has been transmuted into a raging, implacable goddess, Deighton eventually seeks the comfort of a non-threatening man-made god – short, brown, innocuous Father Peace who possesses none of the terrible grandeur of Deighton's wife and who teaches,

"The mother of creation is the mother of defilement. The word mother is a filthy word. When a person reaches God he cannot permit an earthly wife or so-called children to lead him away. God is all!" Deighton leaped up from his seat of recognition, trembling, the perspiration coursing past his blind eyes. "So true!" He cried. "So true. I am nothing!" And his arms flew out in a gesture that did, indeed, cancel his entire self. "God is everything. Need you, Father, need you." (pp. 168–69)

Deighton finds in the Father Peace cult a negation of the concept of the mother (which is how Silla is referred to throughout the narrative) and a justification of his own failure as patriarch, ruler of the home and family, and within the wider commercial sphere. His religion does afford a sense of community, but it is a false community which involves abdication of human responsibility to the extent of denying paternity of his children and transferring his personal bid for immortality unto union with Father Peace. Moreover the Father Peace cult, modelled on the actual Father Divine Movement, is in fact intensely materialistic and egotistical. Father says, "So here I stand with everybody adoring, adoring me. So much adoration is worth more than two million dollars. So much adoration you cannot put a price on it" (p. 169). Father, preying on failures, wreckages, casualties of the American dream, substitutes a new version of the religion of wealth, showmanship and adoration which can be attained by those whose wills have been broken and purpose shattered. He represents the subsuming of individual will, the surrender of purpose to the supreme destiny of worshipping Father who brings Peace. Then, shorn of individuality, family commitment and all but basic needs, the devotee is free to put his or her labour at the disposal of father's kingdom and his commercial ventures.

Father Peace's creed is diametrically opposed to all that Silla represents: the assertion of individual will towards the accomplishment of material success. It represents a force which lures her husband away from her and displays her failure to control him. It provides Deighton with an aura which makes him immune to her attack. Indeed, each venomous onslaught simply affirms his adorable worthlessness and nothingness, his abject sinfulness and the absoluteness of his surrender to Father Peace. Her spiteful betrayal, which leads to his deportation as

an illegal immigrant and his suicidal leap from the ship, becomes a fulfilment of her earlier prophecy that she would kill him. It is intended to
rob him of his immunity, his kumbla/cocoon, the triumph of his
benumbed peace, his retreat into nothingness and final flight from
responsibility. Just as the acceleration of their bitter struggle coincided
with the beginning of the world war, its culmination in death is marked
by the cessation of global armed conflict. On the domestic front, there
is no victor.

In closing, I will examine the male characters from Merle Hodge's *For
the Life of Laetitia* (1993). This didactic children's novel gives literary
representation to a paradigm of manhood extant within the working-
class Afro-Caribbean framework, the visibility of which, Hodge argues,
has been obscured by the existing concept of male marginality and the
assumption that the ideal family grouping is the nuclear family.

Arguably, Senior presents a worst case and Hodge a best case of a
similar scenario – the parent migrates to the metropolis to seek better
economic prospects, resulting in children being left with grandmothers
who raise them with varying degrees of support from the absent parent.
Mammy Patsy, despite her physical absence, has left in the minds of her
family no question as to her love, devotion and sacrificial labour on their
behalf. Her rootedness in the Caribbean environment is reflected in the
ambition to stop mopping hospital floors in America as soon as her
financial commitments permit, and to return to her garden. Moreover,
she deconstructs in her children's minds the popular myth of "foreign"
as a coveted dream-space when she writes, "This place they call New
York is not fit for people, far less for people's children" (p. 12).

How are the domestic situations different? Although the power of
veto within the family is vested in Ma, Pappy, with his philosophical orientation, is crucial to the decision-making process which also incorporates Uncle Leroy, the physically absent Mammy Patsy, and Uncle Jamsie
and Tantie Monica who live away from the family home.[5] This pattern
of decision making affirms for Laetitia that family interactions based
on reciprocity and mutual respect are more desirable than the acquisition of things and even the contents of the inevitable barrel from abroad,
and this notwithstanding the poverty, the limited diet, the smallness

and meanness of their home and possessions. This is not to imply that
Hodge glorifies poverty and eschews self-advancement. Indeed, Laetitia's
high school attendance is looked upon as a long-term investment for
the welfare of the entire family.

Most significantly in Hodge's scenario, there is the active participation of men in the full range of familial functions. Pappy and Uncle
Leroy, both responsible, caring, family-oriented men, are revisionary
portrayals of the role of the Afro-Caribbean male within the family
network.[6] Uncle Leroy is pictured in the bosom of the maternal family unit, providing economically for all by his work in the family plot.
A male counterpart to mother-women, he nurtures, cares for and
imparts values to all the children of the family group (including his
own daughter, Charlene, when she comes to visit), bound together by
blood and other linkages. He is variously stern taskmaster, instructor,
provider, cook, joker, confidante and friend. One of the most memo-
rable scenes of the narrative portrays Uncle Leroy dispensing evil-
smelling worm oil, and later preparing for the thoroughly purged and
half-starved children an enormous coconut bake with smoke herring
and *baigan choka*.[7]

Demonstrating that biological parenthood does not necessarily equal
paternal care, Laetitia's father, Mr Cephas, is presented as a foil to Uncle
Leroy. The point is made decisively that the existence of the nuclear family does not automatically lend to its participants the security and sense
of well-being which human beings need to flourish. In fact, there is an
implication that the male breadwinner–female caretaker model which
obtains in many nuclear families can entrap the male in empty postures
of authoritarianism and dominance, as readily as it can entrap the female
in repetitive, unrewarding domestic chores, boredom, and lack of human
companionship. Although Mr Cephas's home is fairly prosperous and
based in the town, it is desperately lacking in any central core. Frequently
absent, he swoops in to exert "headship" by futile acts of patriarchal
dominance. Mr Cephas holds to a rigid, gender-based division of labour,
and is so paranoid about masculinity that he is convinced that washing
dishes will somehow permanently impair his son's manhood. He maintains no real understanding and meaningful communication within the

family. Wife and son alike are desperately insecure, and Laetitia desires nothing more than to escape this loveless, imprisoning domestic enclosure.

The text is a fictional representation of Hodge's belief that a more complete portrayal of kinship interactions indicates that men portrayed as delinquent and absentee fathers in relation to their own progeny can and do play an active role in the care, nurturance and economic provision for children within the kinship group. In the process, she deconstructs the notion of working-class Afro-Caribbean male marginality within the family network. In an unpublished interview (Hodge 1998), she elaborates:

> This notion of male marginalization is related to the whole misconception about what family is. As long as you insist that the only arrangement you can call a family is a man, his wife and his biological children, then of course you would see men as marginalized, but if you recognize what the Caribbean family really is, then you would realise that men have a very large role indeed. Men feel more loyalty to their maternal family than to their women. They often don't see a woman as their family. They see the children as her family, but men are very active and functional in their mother's house, among their sister's children. There is also that phenomenon of not splitting off from the biological family as soon as we reach seventeen. A lot of grown people live in their maternal homes, like I do. We all travel all about the world and return to our mother's house. And we bring our children with us.[8]

Hodge achieves in this novel a much-needed corrective to the traditional, patriarchal, Euro-centric paradigm of the family, the limitations of which are reflected in the teaching aid's kinetic image of the blond, smiling, happy family, which despite the best efforts of the teacher keeps falling down. This critique of the devices used through the education system to entrench dominant cultural aspirations parallels Toni Morrison's deconstruction of the *Dick and Jane* introductory reading primer used as a framing device for *The Bluest Eye* (1970). Such devices dictate that for black, working-class children in North America, to enter into literacy is to imbibe unreal cultural paradigms and iconography; moreover, to read is to read themselves as written out of the text and into invisibility. I agree with Rahim's conclusion:

The Afro-Caribbean man has seldom appeared in positive nurturing roles. Hodge makes visible a dimension of Caribbean manhood that has been little examined, or in many instances has been subject to sweeping generalizations. The irresponsible, philandering black, working class man is absent in this novel. Pappy and Uncle Leroy in particular are characters that subvert the negative stereotyping of their race, class and sex. Hodge also embraces the wider and even tragic ramifications of misconceived manhood. She exposes the evil of patriarchal oppression in the character of Mr Cephas, as well as Anjanee's chauvinistic father and brothers. Indeed the injustice of sexism traverses races and cultures. (1994, 11)

But I have a reservation. Female writers have explored the stereotype of the irresponsible male at length. Hodge's exploration speaks authoritatively to a particular omission in their literary constructs of Afro-Caribbean masculinity. It is concise, effective and fulfils the fictional contract of its genre – didactic children's literature. Nevertheless, perhaps it is the simplicity and clarity acceptable within this genre which allow it to credibly create silences of its own. Whereas Morrison goes on in *The Bluest Eye* to portray with brutal frankness the weaknesses within her fictional family, Hodge's text can read as an idealized, unidimensional view of a complex sociocultural scenario. It de-centres the issue of the man's relationship to his lover and mother of his children. Indeed, it introduces only oblique mention of tensions encountered by Charlene's mother, and it frames these in terms of ethnicity and mother-daughter conflict: Maharajin's initial desire to throw out her daughter, who is making a child for a "kilwal" man. For the moment, the exploration of the nurturing, caring father/lover/provider in all of his multifaceted dimensions remains on hold.[9]

Let me return, then, to the questions posed at the beginning of the chapter. There are undoubtedly female-authored Caribbean fictions which marginalize men or portray them in unfavourable stereotypical profiles. But the fictions examined here do not support the assumption that gender is an alien and alienating barrier which cannot be breached. Rather, even when the portrayal of the male character is negative, Senior risks sympathetic and compassionate authorial identification with a most hateful man, a criminal who threatens to brutally murder his grandmother in cold blood. Hodge, in her effort to recuperate the vilified, working-class Afro-Caribbean male, de-centres the potentially problematic dimensions of male-female expectations and aspirations in the interest of displaying, within the family network, what Rahim terms "a manhood stripped of chauvinism" (1994, 11).

By deconstructing negative stereotypes of the sexually irresponsible, economically impotent Afro-Caribbean man, Hodge alerts the reading public to alternative, submerged cultural paradigms of manhood, which have hitherto remained obscure. On the other hand, Paule Marshall engages precisely this stereotype, but she does so with such sensitivity that one comes to understand this manner of man, with all his charm and frailty.

Notes

1. White feminists have not been as quick to explore how dominance based on ethnicity and gender has shaped cultural practice. The title *The Madwoman in the Attic,* drawn from Bronte's *Jane Eyre,* is based on the character of Bertha Mason, the Jamaican creole heiress assumed to be racially tainted. Naming *Jane Eyre* as a cult text of western feminists, Spivak (1985) cites Gilbert and Gubar's failure to read the text of Bertha's positioning in the "axiomatics of imperialism" as an example of their tacit complicity with the system of imperial dominance. She argues that the function of Bronte's native subject is "to render indeterminate the boundary between the human and animal and thereby weaken her entitlement under the spirit, if not the letter, of the law" (p. 247).

2. My reading of the situation was also qualified by the proviso: "To the extent that the novels locate the formative experience within the dynamics of the plantation economy and the vicissitudes of neocolonialism, they invite one to survey the wreckage of human relations created by this sociopolitical scenario and to celebrate the power of self-determination which is able to interrupt the downward spiral" (Morgan 1994, 274).

3. In this collection Marshall experimented with the possibilities of a woman writer truly exploring male sensibilities. She sought to pierce that facade of emotional imperviousness and inviolability which, to these

men, is the essence of their masculinity. These ageing protagonists are awakened from their lives of spiritual and emotional paucity, to grasp in vain for life and sustenance from vibrant black women and (in the case of British Guiana) from a young black man. Senior's "View from the Terrace" (1989b) has a nearly identical story-line and dénouement.

4. The portrayal of the young male criminal is fairly common in female-authored fictions, perhaps as a measure of the sense of vulnerability and the widespread fear which each gory and explicit account of crime strikes in the hearts of women, concerned for themselves and their families.
    As in literature, so in life. I recall my own sense of horror and violation when, in the wake of the brutal murder of a housewife in Santa Margarita, Trinidad, who was preparing a meal for the gardener even as he was preparing to murder her (1993), I read again Michelle Cliff's *No Telephone to Heaven* (1978). In this text, the handyman brutally slaughters an entire family in post-independence Jamaica. The gross, gratuitous violence is an outgrowth of the decadent, insensitive extravagance of the upper class and the seething, explosive violence of the lower class.
    At the same time, I encountered Jean Rhys's "Our Gardener" (1986; the last creative work published in her lifetime), a grim poem in which a child witnesses the brutal murder of her parents by the gardener. It begins: "I thought Ken a nice man / Ken was a pal". And the poem culminates:

    People came running
    Ken didn't look round
    He laughed as he was striking
    Mum on the ground
    Went on laughing
    And this is what he said
    "White flesh, white flesh"
    Talking to my Mother, dead.

These fictional portrayals, juxtaposed in my mind with the Santa Margarita murder, brought into focus the warped complexity of race and class relations in the Caribbean; the reasons why even in the mid-1990s, the object of white/upper class animosity and distrust is likely to be the male rather than the female servant; and most chilling of all, the way in which the latent violence seems more prone to erupt where there is some measure of social interaction – cordiality and even acts of kindness – exchanged between criminal and victim.

5. This raises the issue of the coping strategies employed by the transnational family to remain a unit, given the role which migration has played in the social and economic life of Caribbean people. One area for further research is the role played by the absentee male in the transnational family.

6. Leroy displays a mature version of nurturing functions incipient in Mikey in Hodge's earlier novel *Crick Crack Monkey* (1970).

7. *Baigan choka* is a food of Indo-Trinidadian origin, consisting of eggplant roasted on an open fire to which spices are added, along with the hot oil in which they have been fried.

8. The issue of male marginality has also faced substantial revision at the hand of sociologists and other researchers. Rodman, in his study on "friending" relationships in Trinidad, identifies "marital shifting" as an answer to the man's economic inability to maintain a household and "childshifting" as the answer to the woman's subsequent childrearing problems (1977).

    Another perspective is that the male's absence from the familial home and the dissolution of the relationship with his child's mother does not automatically add up to marginalization. Senior makes reference to the fact that fathers who have been separated from their families through migration retain financial responsibility and consequently are perceived and respected as the heads of their households, despite long-term physical absence. Pulsifer, seeking to account for the propensity of males in traditional West Indian yards to display greater involvement in the child-care of the offspring of their female relatives than in their own children, suggests a tenuous link between this practice and matrilineal descent rules (Pulsifer 1993).

9. The visiting relationship is quite complex. It is not expected to be permanent, yet despite its casual, makeshift appearance it is governed by firm social expectations. Rodman's (1971) study of five hundred friending relationships in Trinidad attributes the impermanence of the union, in part, to the attitude of mistrust generated by low levels of male supervision and control, combined with the expectation of financial support for any child of the union.

References

Cliff, Michelle. 1978. *No Telephone to Heaven.* New York: E.P. Dutton.

Gilbert, Sandra M., and Susan Gubar. 1979. *The Madwoman in the Attic: The Woman Writer and the Nineteenth-Century Literary Imagination.* New Haven: Yale University Press.

Greene, Gayle, and Coppelia Kahn. [1985] 1991. "Feminist Scholarship and the Social Construction of Woman". In *Making a Difference: Feminist Literary Criticism,* edited by Gayle Greene and Coppelia Kahn. Reprint, London: Routledge.

Hodge, Merle. 1970. *Crick Crack Monkey.* London: Andre Deutsch.

———. 1993. *For the Life of Laetitia.* New York: Farrar, Straus and Giroux.

———. 1998. Interview by Paula Morgan. University of the West Indies, St Augustine, Trinidad, June.

Marshall, Paule. 1959. *Brown Girl, Brownstones.* Chatham, N.J.: Chatham Bookseller.

———. [1961] 1988. *Soul Clap Hands and Sing.* Reprint, Washington, D.C.: Howard University Press.

Mordecai, Pamela, and Betty Wilson, eds. 1989. *Her True-True Name.* Oxford: Heinemann Educational Books.

Morgan, Paula. 1994. "A Cross-Cultural Study of the Black Female-Authored Novel of Development". PhD diss., University of the West Indies, St Augustine, Trinidad.

Morrison, Toni. 1970. *The Bluest Eye.* New York: Washington Square Press.

O'Callaghan, Evelyn. 1993. *Woman Version: Theoretical Approaches to West Indian Fiction by Women.* London: Macmillan.

Pollard, Velma. 1994. *Karl and Other Stories.* Essex: Longman Caribbean.

Powell, Patricia. 1994. *A Small Gathering of Bones.* Oxford: Heinemann.

Pulsifer, Lydia Mihelic. 1993. "Changing Roles in the Life Cycles of Women". In *Traditional West Indian Houseyards: Women and Change in the Caribbean,* edited by Janet H. Momsen. Bloomington: Indiana University Press.

Rahim, Jennifer. 1994. "Fatherhood: A Silence Explored in Hodge's *For the Life of Laetitia*". *Trinidad and Tobago Review* (9–11 July).

Rhys, Jean. 1986. "Our Gardener". In *The Penguin Book of Caribbean Verse in English,* edited by Paula Barnett. London: Penguin.

Rodman, Hyman. 1971. *Lower-Class Families: The Culture of Poverty in Negro Trinidad.* New York: Oxford University Press.

————. 1977. "Affluence, Poverty and the Family's Future: The Case of Trinidad". *Studies in Comparative International Development* 17, no. 1 (Spring).

Seaforth, Sybil. 1988. *Growing Up with Miss Milly.* New York: Calaloux.

Senior, Olive. 1986. "Country of the One Eye God". In *Summer Lightning and Other Stories*. London: Longman Caribbean.

————. 1989a. "The Dispatcher". In *Voiceprint,* edited by Stewart Brown, Mervyn Morris and Gordon Rohlehr. London: Longman Caribbean.

————. 1989b. "The View from the Terrace". In *Arrival of the Snake Woman and Other Stories*. Essex: Longman.

Spivak, Gayatri Chakravorty. 1985. "Three Women's Texts and a Critique of Imperialism". *Critical Inquiry* 12 (Autumn).

Washington, Mary Helen. 1975. *Black-Eyed Susans*. Garden City, N.Y.: Anchor.

CHAPTER 12

Calling All Dragons
The Crumbling of Caribbean Masculinity

KENNETH RAMCHAND

Tiger had never smoked. He had only seen his father and the others. But he had decided that he was not going to appear a small boy before his wife. Men smoked: he would smoke. He would drink rum, curse, swear, bully the life out of her if she did not obey him. Hadn't he seen when his father did that?

– Sam Selvon, *A Brighter Sun*

Of course, in all the games we played I was always given the lesser part. If we played knight and dragon, I was the dragon; if we played discovering Africa, he discovered Africa; he was also the leader of the savage tribes that tried to get in the way of the discovery, and I played his servant and not a very bright servant at that; if we played prodigal son he was the prodigal son, and the prodigal son's father and the jealous brother, while I played a person who fetched things.

– Jamaica Kincaid, *Annie John*

Now at twenty-two, his whole ambition was to be noticed. It was not enough that he had made his presence felt and feared in the house. It was not enough that his father, his mother, his two elder brothers and their wives stood in awe of him. He wanted to be looked upon with awe by the whole village. He hankered to be popular, but to be popular in a spectacular way. He wanted people to point at him and whisper, "See that fellow going there? He is Gurudeva, the bad-john."

This fancy of Gurudeva was born mainly of the stories that old Jaimungal often told on evenings of the dare-devil exploits of dead and gone bad-johns.

– Seepersad Naipaul, *The Adventures of Gurudeva*

He could feel himself wasting, marking time, the strength in his arms and the quickness in him that he tried to throw off-balance in his crawl, flowing up against his thighs, pressing against his armpits, his own strength stifling him. He wanted to burst out of himself, to fly out and become himself. He walked into one club after another, seeking the battle that would free him; but all he met with were old bad-Johns, warriors who had seen their time and lived now on their fame, their very names forgotten by everyone outside a small circle of acquaintances, and some younger fellars, mediocre men who had no class nor name and who would acquire neither, were satisfied to live out their promise in sullen corners of night clubs, at the side of some whore they owned, brandishing a knife or a razor they claimed they could use.

– Earl Lovelace, *The Dragon Can't Dance*

The main purpose of this chapter is to relate a number of literary texts, including Earl Lovelace's *The Dragon Can't Dance* (1979), to the original conference theme: constructions of Caribbean masculinity. There are some necessary preliminaries. In the first place, the term "construction" poses a problem. It can sound mechanical and calculated. It might suggest too much optimism about the capacity of human beings to understand and direct the complex combinations of forces (some of them quite nebulous) that are involved in social formation. And it might find little use for the exploratory procedure of works of art. What I am trying to get at is to be seen in Jamaica Kincaid's *Lucy* (1990).

This iconoclastic and seemingly cynical work turns out to be a novel about the construction or invention of self, and it points at the end to the need for a tentative and provisional approach that is not mechanical and does not pride itself on working with a formula. After a year in America during which the protagonist rebels against every formative influence and person in her life the young woman, Lucy, arrives at this realization:

> I understood that I was inventing myself, and that I was doing this more in the way of the painter than in the way of a scientist. I could not count on precision and calculation; I could only count on intuition. I did not have anything exactly in mind, but when the picture was complete I would know. (p. 134)

Lucy makes a distinction between the way of the scientist and the way of the painter, but the real distinction highlighted by the novel itself is that between the approach of the artist and the approach of the social scientist. This is a chastening distinction for commentators.

The term "construction", nevertheless, is not without virtue. At least it restores the notion of human agency, of someone doing the constructing, and allows us to conceive of personal responsibility – the deliberate and conscious part we can play both in the process of making-over or reconstructing ourselves and in the shaping of concepts and images that influence behaviour and attitudes. The term might also imply the guilt and responsibility that certain interests must bear for establishing, or for acquiescing in, "constructions" of persons not justified in nature, and of social arrangements disadvantageous to particular groups and classes. It is convenient and appropriate to use the term "construction", then, so long as one does not lose the perspective that it refers to only one part in a more comprehensive and unpredictable drama of social (and psychological) formation.

The second preliminary is obvious enough but can bear restatement. It would be impossible in any country to examine the construction of masculinity or femininity by itself since these take place in relation to each other, and it would be unsatisfactory to treat either as a new problem generated by the given moment. The case is more emphatic in Caribbean countries, which have a history of enslavement, indenture and colonialism. Here the constructions of both masculinity and femininity have been ordered by the imperatives of organized systems of oppression and exploitation. Here the struggle of the obscure or obscured person to emerge as a self, to become visible and make a mark in the world, the necessity to find the true self, exists for male and female alike.

This does not absolve us from recognizing the oppression, within the common oppression, that is endured by the female at the hands of the male in her group. Nor should we act as if it were not true that power relations and the status quo in most societies play a foundational part in the establishment and interiorization of certain limiting attitudes concerning the role and the possibilities of the female. After the demise of the oppressive regime, moreover, they continue to give privilege to the interests of the male. In *Annie John*, Jamaica Kincaid's radical novel of 1985, the roles appropriated by the boy Mineu in the games he condescends to play with Annie reflect an early assumption of male superiority (see second epigraph).

Kincaid links this attitude to another masculine ploy. The novel shows through Mineu the male's early fixation with and denigration of the female body. At the climax of a game he has improvised for the occasion Mineu falls to the ground laughing, kicking the air with happiness after he succeeds in getting the compliant Annie to take off all her clothes and sit on a red ants' nest where she is stung in her private parts. The teenaged Annie recalls this childhood episode when she meets four boys including Mineu on the street, and she feels ashamed of her body because "I saw him glancing at them out of the corner of his eye, smiling in a knowing way and then looking back straight at me, a serious look on his face" (p. 100).

In another incident in the same novel the controlling Mineu accidentally tightens a noose about his own neck and hangs choking to death from a gate, while his riveted playmate neither moves from the scene nor calls for help. The innocent Annie's reflection after Mineu is rescued by a neighbour with a cutlass is "I didn't know what to make of my own behaviour, and I could not explain myself" (p. 99). A reader would be justified in taking it into his head that the episode reveals Annie's wish for ultimate revenge, and that the novel is in this way intimating the female's outraged sense of male injustice and exploitation. The moral of this story is that however masculinity has been constructed in the past, it must check up on itself or be hung with its own rope.

Some Versions of Masculinity

Notions of masculinity in the island of Trinidad are historically linked with the figure of the bad-john. The term itself has early and strong associations with the yard, the ghetto and lower-class Afro-Trinidadian life. Allsopp seems to imply this in his *Dictionary of Caribbean English Usage* (1996), although the dictionary is not forthcoming about the origin of the phrase. If it was formed by analogy with other combinations ending with "John" (a common male name, applied to anyone the speaker does not consider worthy of individual notice), it is possible that it was first used to indicate persons repeatedly flouting colonial attempts to regulate and civilize them.

The phenomenon is explored extensively and on the other side of the sociohistorical façade in the work of Earl Lovelace. In the 1982 novel *The Wine of Astonishment* the bad-john Bolo is projected as a Christ figure sacrificing himself for the resurrection of community. In the prologue to *The Dragon Can't Dance* the bad-john appears variously as Maroon, as a figure of resistance and as African warrior. These imaginative projections are not inconsistent with a proper sociocultural understanding. In all the Lovelace novels the bad-john is the extreme case of the person wanting to be seen or acknowledged as a person. Lovelace's revisionary treatment does not seek to excuse the violence of the bad-johns and their versions of masculinity, so much as to speculate imaginatively and compassionately about what lies beneath the surface manifestations.

The will towards understanding seems to operate in Seepersad Naipaul's collection *The Adventures of Gurudeva* ([1943] 1995) as well.

Given the date and given the community being written about, it is a little surprising that the word "bad-John" appears in Seepersad's text, but
it does: we are told that Gurudeva is entranced by "the dare-devil
exploits of dead and gone bad-Johns" as related on evenings by the village elder, Jaimungal. We make out from the reportage that the figures
Seepersad's text refers to as "bad-Johns" (p. 35) are heroes of the race,
champions of the culture, and figures of defiance against the authorities
in the new land. Not surprisingly, Gurudeva longs to join their ranks.
Seepersad's comment on Gurudeva's yearning to be a bad-john forces
us to recognize the longing that Bolo and Gurudeva have in common
although they are separated by forty-six years:

> Now at twenty-two, his whole ambition was to be noticed. It was not enough
> that he had made his presence felt and feared in the house. It was not enough
> that his father, his mother, his two elder brothers and their wives stood in
> awe of him. He wanted to be looked upon with awe by the whole village.
> He hankered to be popular, but to be popular in a spectacular way. He
> wanted people to point at him and whisper, "See that fellow going there? He
> is Gurudeva the bad-John!" (p. 35)

Although Gurudeva is a wife beater and domestic tyrant, Seepersad
exposes these deformities without obscuring the character's struggle
against nonentity and nothingness in spite of his limitations. Lovelace
goes further with Fisheye in *The Dragon Can't Dance* (1979). He beats
everybody in the house, according to his stepson Basil, and he takes his
violence out into the community. Lovelace's treatment is so balanced,
however, that when Fisheye sees himself as a general in a steelband army
or a bandy-legged, two-gun cowboy with a walk like Henry Fonda's, the
reader is unable to ignore or dismiss the character's bottled-up yearnings to stand out from the mass and to be part of a community.

The bad-john behaviour of Fisheye is first described in chapter 4, "The
Bad John", and Lovelace's omniscient narration does not hesitate to tell
us that

> the truth was that he wanted nothing but to live, to be, to be somebody for
> people to recognize, so when they see him they would say: "That is Fisheye!"
> and give him his space; and when they see someone who concerned him, to

say: "That is Fisheye woman! That is Fisheye friend," and not to fuck around either of them to make him turn beast. (p. 59)

Lovelace uses the character of Fisheye to trace a number of stages in the history of the figure of the bad-john, and this is done against the background of a changing social environment. At first Fisheye revels in his standing as a warrior in the battles that take place between the bands. Then, at a suggestion from his woman, he becomes champion of the idea that the bands should form themselves into an army to take power away from their oppressors. He opposes the coming of sponsorship and soon turns his violence against his own band for selling their integrity to the sponsors. Finally he leads a small group into an armed uprising that threatens for awhile but then peters out, because the uprising had no purpose that could make it anything more than yet another demonstration. During his sojourn in jail, however, the one who at the critical moment stood up like Achebe's Okonkwo for lost glory accepts that the "enemy" is too strong:

> I know now that you have to have real power, and if you don't have it man, you have to survive with them that have it. It's a joke, man, this business of being bad, a bad John. That is a old time thing. That gone out with the biscuit drum and the three note boom. Now a man have to learn how to live. (p. 190)

The cynicism and surrender in Fisheye's "a man have to learn how to live" can be measured by the novel's demonstration of how Aldrick learns to live.

"Aldrick, you growing old, boy. You getting soft."

Lovelace's careful unfolding of the stages through which bad-johnism passes is interesting for its own sake, but it is also complementary to the treatment of the main character, Aldrick, in whom there are elements of the bad-john. It is mostly through Aldrick that the author exposes some of the ruling constructions of masculinity and points towards a viable reconstruction. Through Aldrick's attachments and activities

Lovelace's novel examines gender relations, responsibility to community, the presentation of self in society, and every person's need to come to terms with the inner world of their thoughts and feelings.

I have demonstrated elsewhere (Ramchand 1986) that Lovelace's uninhibited use of the omniscient technique to render the thoughts and feelings of all his characters corresponds with the author's attitude that each of his characters is a centre of interest. Since what is writ large and extensively in the case of the main character exists by implication and in vivid shorthand in all the other characters in the book, it may be impossible to discuss Aldrick without bringing in some of the other characters. And we can hardly ignore Pariag, because the parallels between Aldrick and the Indian character are part of the overall design of the book and of its statements about masculinity.

The phrases and clauses in the long periodic sentences of the prologue march with sensuous oral logic through a summary account of African marronage in the period of enslavement and outright rebellion or sly sabotage on the plantations. They halt in triumph at the refusal of many in the postemancipation period to participate in an economic system in which they would still be no more than tools and implements:

> And when they could not perform in space that escape that would take them away from the scene of their brutalization they took a stand in the very guts of the slave plantation, among tobacco and coffee and cotton and canes, asserting their humanness in the most wonderful acts of sabotage they could imagine and perform, making a religion of laziness and neglect and stupidity and waste; singing hosannahs for flood and hurricane and earthquake, praying for damage and pestilence: continuing it still after Emancipation, that emancipated them to a more profound idleness and waste when, refusing to be grist for the mill of the colonial machinery that kept on grinding in its belly people to spit out sugar and cocoa and copra, they turned up this hill to pitch camp here on the eyebrow of the enemy, to cultivate again with no less fervour the religion with its Trinity of Idleness, Laziness, and Waste. (Ramchard 1986, 10–11)

Aldrick is a proud aristocrat in this tradition. But if the prologue celebrates the resistance of the formerly enslaved to a socioeconomic system that devours the self, we should not allow that part of the tone to deafen us to another note. The prologue insinuates that, while this tradition had a function in the period of enslavement and in the century before universal adult suffrage, it is now outmoded, an inherited stance, "a pass-key whose function they only half-remembered" (p. 10). The philosophy of non-possession may have saved them from another form of slavery, but living in the material world requires participation and taking on responsibility for worldly things. "All we thinking about is to play dragon. All we thinking about is to show this city, this island, this world, that we is people, not because we own anything, not because we have things, but because we is. We are because we is. You know what I mean?" (p. 111). Aldrick's masculinity is shaped by the old tradition, but when the novel opens this masculinity is already punctuated with evasiveness and uncertainty in the face of social change.

It is useful to begin with Aldrick's misgivings about non-participation and non-possession, and his questioning of the roles he plays on the Hill and on Carnival days. The misgivings are first clearly articulated when Guy, the rent-collector, and Miss Cleothilda, who runs a small parlour, urge Aldrick to take bad-john action against the Indian outsider, Pariag, and defend the Hill against the newcomer. Pariag has bought a bicycle and is setting up as a small businessman, and according to Guy and Cleothilda, the Indian is flouting the Hill's philosophy of non-possession. Aldrick finds he is unable to resent Pariag's honest attempt to make a living in the world (p. 105) for he realizes that all around him things are changing and many of the inhabitants of the Hill, none more than Guy and Cleothilda, are in fact abandoning the philosophy of non-possession while seeming to subscribe to it. The resentment Guy and Cleothilda show when Aldrick refuses to destroy Pariag's bicycle drives Aldrick into himself and leads to this confession to his friend Philo:

> You see me here, I is thirty-one years old. Never had a regular job in my life or a woman or nutten. I ain't even own a house or car or radio or race-horse or store . . . they killing people in this place, Philo. Little girls, they have them whoring. And I is a dragon. And what is a man? What is you or me, Philo? And I here playing a dragon, playing masquerade every year, and I forget what I playing for, what I trying to say. I forget Philo. Is like nobody remembering what life is, and who we fighting and what we fighting for . . .

everybody rushing me as if they in such a hurry. I want to catch a breath, I
want to see what I doing on this fucking hill. Let the Indian buy his bike.
Guy and Cleothilda ain't fooling me. The Indian is a threat to them, he ain't
no threat to me. (p. 110)

It is worth pointing out right here that the terms in which Aldrick
questions himself are similar to the terms used by Pariag in his own
self-questionings, Pariag who had left the sugar estate to experience the
larger world and become somebody in the city, but who had lost something in his progress to being a successful shopkeeper:

What it is you doing? What you doing? What you doing? Questions which,
while they touched the sorest centre in himself, he had allowed himself to
neglect, seeing that the shop in which he was ceaselessly at work had the
appearance of an answer the whole world would understand, if not applaud.
Now, it settled into him, this sense of loss and aloneness, as a pain no one
knew of, but one that he was sometimes grateful that he could still feel, as a
nostalgia for the earlier purpose that had moved him out of the bosom of his
family and New Lands to encounter men like Fisheye and Aldrick in Port of
Spain. (p. 206)

The novel's revisionary promptings and Aldrick's troubles begin with
his consciousness of the young girl Sylvia. Aldrick's crumbling is a fore-
gone conclusion in the novel, and one of Lovelace's achievements is to
render concretely the twistings and turnings of the diehard:

To him she was the most dangerous person on the Hill, for she possessed, he
suspected, the ability not only to capture him in passion but to enslave him
in caring, to bring into his world those ideas of love and home and children
that he had spent his whole life avoiding. So he had watched her swing back
and forth in the yard, not even wanting to meet her eyes, keeping his distance, not even trying to get her into his bed, for he knew that she could make
him face questions that he had inoculated himself against by not working
nowhere, by not being too deeply concerned about anything except his dragon costume that he prepared for his masquerade on Carnival day. (p. 31)

On her way to an assignation with the rent-collector, Guy, who has
promised to pay for her Carnival costume, Sylvia pauses at Aldrick's
window. In the emotional skirmish that follows it is obvious that with

the slightest encouragement from Aldrick, Sylvia would be willing not to grant Guy the role of buying her costume. But the dragon cannot bring himself to change his lifestyle for the love of a woman, and he turns from the window to let her go her way. A few days later Sylvia renews her promise and challenge by saying to a comprehending Aldrick "I ain't get my costume yet".

In the silent scene that follows (pp. 43–45), with Aldrick not replying and Sylvia waiting, Lovelace's reportage of the character's thoughts and feelings makes concrete to the reader all the hesitations, alarms and conflicting emotions of Aldrick. He feels doomed; he cannot escape her this time; he thinks of making a joke or trying a smile or finding a hole to escape through; he swings back and begins to stumble towards repeating his earlier benediction that she is a princess. But masculinity reasserts itself and Aldrick switches back again, arguing to himself that to compliment Sylvia now would be to make a proposal, and even to offer to buy her costume would "contradict the very guts and fibre of his own living" for he was a dragon, a hustler, a man who worked nowhere, a man whose only responsibility was to play the dragon on Carnival day. Just as he seems to have regained his composure, however, the word "Sylvia" comes out of his mouth and he does not know what he is about to say. He is rescued, if only for the moment, by the arrival of his brother in masculinity, the calypsonian Philo.

In the days and weeks that follow, Aldrick agonizes over Sylvia and reveals to his now apprehensive friend Philo the ways in which thoughts about Sylvia are undermining his cherished freedoms, including his freedom from responsibility:

> "You know, I use to say to myself: 'Aldrick, you living the life. If it have one man in the world living the life is you – no wife, no child, no boss, no job. You could get up any hour of the day you want to, cuss who you want. Anywhere you go people like you. You is a favourite in the world. Anybody will give you a dollar just so. And for Carnival you's the best dragon in the whole fucking world' . . . and now this little stupid girl, this girl . . ."
>
> "Have your head on," Philo said, suddenly quite grave. "I . . . I thought it was just the costume you wanted to give her."
>
> "Tain't nutten, she just have me thinking, that's all."

"Have your head on," Philo said softly, as if he was more than a little afraid (p. 101)

Aldrick accuses himself of growing old and getting soft (he tries to protect the little boy, Basil; he begins to acknowledge the Indian man, Pariag). He upbraids himself for grinning and spinning and not being able to answer a question from a girl (p. 111). He watches Sylvia hardening into the role of kept woman and regrets the decline of the princess into the fate of all the women on the Hill, but the hard shell of masculinity refuses to crack until that Carnival day when he sees Sylvia in her slave costume dancing in the band (pp. 127–28). Although Lovelace's novel is not about gender identity, his theme of selfhood depends for its working out on a dismantling of the prison of inherited notions of masculinity and femininity. In this scene the selfhoods of both Sylvia and Aldrick are at stake, and the novel's argument about mutuality, about the role of male and female in helping each other to find self, begins to declare itself.

Aldrick interprets Sylvia's dancing as a cry for her true self. She is dancing "as if she wanted to leap out of herself into her self, a self in which she could stay for ever, in which she could *be* for ever" and he sees her both "rejoicing in a self and praying for a self to live in beyond Carnival and her slave girl costume". He wants to join her in this tall, rejoicing dance "and lose himself and gain himself in her". It strikes him now that his dragon threat was small beside this girl's life-affirming scream:

> He could threaten. He had to learn how to live and how to give life; this flash came to his brain, humbling him. And suddenly, he wanted to touch Sylvia, to tell her in his touching what had just been revealed to him. He found himself moving towards her, gliding through the spaces between dancers to her side. "Sylvia!" He reached out to touch her, to receive her blessing and to bless her, to cheer her and to be cheered by her. And then she saw him, saw his awkward hand reaching to her, and in one movement she spun out of his reach and turned to face him in a tall, sweeping disdain.
>
> "No, mister!" she said. "I have my man!" (pp. 127–28)

Aldrick grows from the rejection he has suffered, from his participation in Fisheye's Black Power uprising, and from the five years in jail that he turns into years of introspection and self-education. From this moment, which occurs about halfway through the novel, Lovelace also engages with Sylvia, tracing her inner growth and outward stasis, registering her disappointment in the young men through whom she hoped to escape the deadening relationship with Guy, making us feel the pity of her apparent loss of hope and the wrongness of her decision to settle for respectability and marriage to Guy, who is now a minor political figure. Her decision, as she announces it to Cleothilda, is an indictment of impotent masculinity: "Is time for me to settle down, make something of my life, have children. I ain't getting younger, you know. And I tired with these fellers I offer myself to. I tired listening to them talk, and can't see nothing" (p. 201). Aldrick himself wonders whether "she had not so much chosen Guy as refused the impotence of dragons" (p. 203).

Aldrick has returned from prison with the self-appointed task of giving Sylvia back her self, and at the end of his valedictory conversation with her he urges that she does not need the cover of a bourgeois establishment. The male author has brought his masculine dragon so far that Aldrick goes on to assert that this female does not need to think of herself as dependent upon any sheltering man: "You don't want nobody to take care of you, to hide you, to imprison you. You want to be a self that is free, girl; to grow, girl; to be, to be yourself, girl" (p. 202). Aldrick is terrified that Sylvia might marry Guy, but he lives up to his own precepts by having faith in her:

> In truth, he felt to rush back to her and hold her in his hands and lift her up and carry her away with him; but, he had come to Sylvia, not to claim her, but to help her claim herself; and he felt the need for the strength and the faith, the love, to allow her to make that claim for her own self. (p. 203)

The significance of the episode is twofold. It essays towards a new construction of femininity. It also registers a major breakthrough in the reconstruction of masculinity: Aldrick has grown to the point where he can recognize Sylvia as a person in her own right. He can see the female as needing to refuse to surrender her individuality for the care and protection of any man, and he can want to help without doubting her capacity to make her own way.

The novel's preoccupation with mutuality between male and female and with the envisaging of a new masculinity in conjunction or collaboration with a new femininity is mainly worked out in relation to Aldrick and Sylvia, but it is echoed significantly in Lovelace's presentation of the Indian couple, Pariag and Dolly. Throughout the novel Dolly is a shadowy but supportive figure to her husband and is the stereotype of the traditional Indian wife. At the end, however, when Pariag is regretting that he had not gone out and spoken to Aldrick as he passed the shop, and when he is resignedly equating what one is with what others see, he is surprised by his wife's strong interjection: " 'You is more, Boya. More than what you show them. I is more than what I show you not so?' " Dolly goes on to agree with Pariag that he should have gone out to Aldrick, but at this point the episode is taking a different turn:

"I see now", Dolly said. "You shoulda talk to Aldrick in truth".
But he was thinking of something else, seeing something else.
"We have to start to live, Dolly, you and me."
"Me and you ?" Dolly asked, her voice choking. "Me and you?"
What did he know of this woman? She had tears in her eyes and she was looking at him with a kind of astonishment and respect, the same way she had looked at him when he had said, "You going to have to live in Port of Spain." (p. 212)

Lovelace's novel ends with Sylvia drifting back to Aldrick so that both their growths may be completed, and with Pariag and Dolly on the edge of the unexpectedly new experience of getting to know someone nearer home, someone "who know you too long and don't know you at all" (p. 212).

It has been apparent following the death of the federation and the failures of independence that the old preoccupations with national identity, with constitutional advances, with different forms of social adjustment and other issues of an outward nature have been compromised by insincere professions, cynicism and self-seeking. According to the Brathwaite poem, "O Dreams O Destinations", political leaders are now blind "to that harsh light and vision that had once / consumed them", and the "supporting poor, famished upon their simple / politics of fish and broken bread" find themselves reduced again to "beaten spirits trapped in flesh" (1967, 61–62).

One broad consequence is that nationalism has taken the form of cultural nationalism, and in literature the heady political themes of the 1950s and early 1960s have given way to themes of cultural recuperation and the liberation of the person from imposed images. Lovelace's novel is part of this new thrust towards cultural and personal self-knowledge. In *The Dragon Can't Dance* self-knowledge is related to cultural assertion (see Sylvia's dancing as interpreted by Aldrick) and to something not often emphasized in West Indian literature – an acknowledgment of the inner life and an embrace of feelings still despised as soft, weak and feminine. In Chinua Achebe's *Things Fall Apart* the protagonist's downfall is connected with his disparagement of artistic expression and the tender emotions as womanish and likely to undermine manliness and warriorhood.

In the West Indies, admission of such feelings has not been regarded as consistent with survival throughout the series of brutal and shape-shifting regimes that began with the reduction of the aboriginal Indians, continued with enslavement and indenture, and continues still as the sanctification of market forces and a bowing-down before a footloose capitalism that demands dowries and incentives but reserves the right to move on. All of these regimes place a premium upon the skills necessary for survival and advancement, and regard humane feelings as a handicap. All of this gives saving relevance to Aldrick's final succumbing to the need to take off the armour of uncaring and teach himself to feel.

Aldrick's reflections on his rejection by Sylvia lead him to put it chidingly to himself that throughout his seventeen years in the Hill community he has been playing dragon symbolically on Carnival days without attempting in his day-to-day life to fulfil the promise proclaimed by the dragon. He realizes too that he has been living by rules of masculinity according to which it is wrong to admit to being hurt or touched by anything at all:

He had reached home last night with the phrase "I have my man" hammering in his brain, hammering at his whole self , torturing him so that if he had

been able to he would have cried, if he could have felt the extent of feeling
that it called forth, he would have been happy to let himself be soaked by
pain. And he said to himself in anguish: "I have to learn to feel."

And he was thinking this again now, standing at his open door, watching
the shacks stacked like medieval shields of a disassembled army, realising that
he had never really lived here on this Hill, never embraced this place as home,
never felt it to himself, to his bones. He had been living in the world of the
dragon, avoiding and denying the full touch of the Hill. He had been cheating himself of the pain, of the love, of his living . . . . (p. 131)

Few West Indian prose writers have written about the relationship
between men and women, or about the subtle movement of thought and
feeling, with the lyricism and convincingness or with the revisionary
intentions of Lovelace. To Aldrick, acknowledging his long-repressed
feelings is a homecoming and an arrival:

She have her man. He couldn't laugh at that. No, sir. But this morning he
felt humble before his own feelings, and not so afraid of them. He wanted
to call them to him, to feel them. He felt a great distance from himself, as if
he had been living elsewhere from himself and he thought that he would like
to try and come home to himself; and even though it sounded like some kind
of treason, he felt that at least it was the only way he could begin to be true
to the promise of the dragon to which he felt bound in some way beyond reason, beyond explanation, and which he felt had its own truth. (pp. 131–32)

This is a new note in West Indian literature, and an important one,
because it has fundamental implications for the ways in which we come
to understand ourselves as persons and consequently for the way we
think about masculinity and femininity. It gives new resonances to the
themes of exile, alienation, voyaging and discovery that dominate West
Indian writing.

References

Achebe, Chinua. 1958. *Things Fall Apart*. London: William Heinemann.

Allsopp, Richard. 1996. *Dictionary of Caribbean English Usage*. Oxford: Oxford University Press.

Brathwaite, Edward Kamau. 1967. *Rights of Passage*. London: Oxford University Press.

Kincaid, Jamaica. 1985. *Annie John*. New York: Farrar, Straus and Giroux.

———. 1990. *Lucy*. New York: Farrar, Straus and Giroux.

Lovelace, Earl. 1979. *The Dragon Can't Dance*. London: André Deutsch.

———. 1982. *The Wine of Astonishment*. London: André Deutsch.

Naipaul, Seepersad. [1943] 1995. *The Adventure of Gurudeva*. Reprint, London: Heinemann. (First published as *Gurudeva and Other Indian Tales*. Port of Spain, Trinidad: Guardian Commercial Printery.)

Ramchand, Kenneth. 1986. "An Approach to Earl Lovelace's Novel through an Examination of Indian-African Relations in *The Dragon Can't Dance*". *Caribbean Quarterly* 32, nos. 1 and 2 (March–June).

Selvon, Samuel. 1952. *A Brighter Sun*. London: Allan Wingate.

CHAPTER 13

I Lawa
The Construction
of Masculinity in
Trinidad and
Tobago Calypso

GORDON ROHLEHR

This chapter is a preliminary enquiry into how masculinity in Trinidad and Tobago has been defined, reflected, contained, revealed, constructed, deconstructed and reconstructed in the Trinidad calypso. The calypso is a living tradition of overwhelmingly, though not exclusively, male discourse about everything under the sun, including masculinity, femininity, work, sport, politics, ethnicity, race, nationalism, male and female sexualities, and social, political and domestic conflict. This discourse is conducted through songs that may be philosophical, flippant, grotesquely comic, gravely serious, gaily celebratory or satirical. All the stereotypical notions of gender and gender roles are there, sometimes openly enacted and illustrated, at other times subtly encoded and masked in thousands of calypso fictions over almost a century of recorded commentary. The calypso, then, constitutes a useful basis for research, analysis and eventual theorizing about a masculinity that it simultaneously masks and unmasks, employing modes of self-perception that are at once aggressively confrontational and defensively evasive.

We begin with a quotation taken from one of the calypso's root origins: the stickfighting tradition of martial encounter, heroism, rhetorical self-celebration and boasting song. Our quotation is a short, self-confident boasting speech which a Trinidad stickfighter made to Daniel Crowley, the famous anthropologist of Carnival:

> I Lawa (French Le Roi) with stick,
> with fight, with woman, with dance,
> with song, with drum, with everything.
> (Crowley 1959, 64)

This boast, as much a part of heroic rhetoric as any speech by Beowulf or Hotspur, tells us something about how masculinity was constructed among the pastoral and urban folk of Trinidad. Masculinity was associated with a notion of kingship and attendant notions of controlled territory, turf or province. Kingship was not inherited but won, asserted and maintained through the skill, courage and dominance necessary to the challenging worlds of "stick" and "fight". Kingship was the ultimate reward of triumphant warriorhood.

The stickman's bois or poui constituted his primary medium for illustrating skill, self-assertion and dominance within the community of males. Metaphorically the stick represented the phallus. It was the batonnier's rod, staff and sceptre of dominance, the ultimate symbol of his kingship. Hence Crowley's stickman, Lawa, next mentions woman as a central part of his territory of conquest, control and dominance. Woman was the greatest ornament in the realm of the stickman/warrior/king. Often, as the stickfighting legends disclose (Pearse 1956, 250–62), woman was the prize for whom the champions fought, and some of these women, so prized, were themselves fierce and violent in their defence of their claim to the men who had won them in battle.

The connection between masculinity and the complex of warriorhood, conquest, control of territory and acquisition of woman became such a prominent feature in the formation of Trinidad for the first six decades after emancipation that it was carried over into the twentieth century as a deeply inscribed and virtually immutable pattern. This pattern was reproduced in the rivalry that existed between steelbands over the first two decades of the steelband's evolution, when violent clashes sometimes occurred on Carnival days between parading steelbands. Territoriality and rivalry in musical skill, or over whose pans were better tuned, were the major causes of these Carnival battles, while several of the fights which broke out between steelbandsmen outside of the Carnival season were said to have involved rivalry over women.

If the stick, bois or poui was transmuted from batonnier's staff into phallic symbol, the woman was transmuted from being the passionate prize of flesh and blood which crowned triumphant warriorhood into property, ground within which the phallus made its play, or antagonist against whom the male-as-rampant-penis fought out the battles that tested, affirmed and reaffirmed his masculinity. Such metaphorical linkages would generate in the calypso a consistent tendency to represent sexual and general intercourse between males and females as forms of martial rather than marital encounter, in which all of the ritualistic elements of the stickfight are reflected. Such elements include the rhetorical boasting and exalted self-celebration common to male heroic traditions worldwide; the glorification of the bois, reduced in the calypso to the penis (or the glorification of the penis exalted to the size, potency and durability of the bois); the representation of the sexual act as a stiff battle between male and female sexualities: that is, between the very nature of "manness", as novelist Earl Lovelace (1979) terms it, and "womanness".

The calypso that best illustrates how the stickfight became a metaphor for male-versus-female sexual confrontation is Zandolie's (Sylvester Anthony's) "Stickman", composed in the early 1960s and revived nearly three decades later. "Stickman" tells of a "stickfighting" contest between protagonist Zandolie and "a female stickfighter named Winnie living in Sangre Grande". The contest is fought out in three phases. In the first round Zandolie, too eager to vanquish Winnie, loses control, attacks too impetuously and has his bois broken after only four strokes. This evokes contemptuous, mocking laughter from Winnie, who is unaf-

fected by such a brief attack and such premature "breaking" (ejacula-
tion) of the stick:

> I fell on meh knees and I charge she the first bois
> Under she belly
> She break the bois and she back back
> Watch me fixed in meh eye and laugh
> I get delirious and I charge she three in succession
> Meh wood break in half
> > (*c.*1994)

This battle between male and female sexualities is described entirely in
stickfighting imagery of "carray" (squaring off), "charge" (thrust of
penis), and "break(ing) the bois" (parrying or accepting and containing
the thrust). There are the mocking eyes and the laughter of the female
which goad the male into a rashness that brings about his early downfall.

Ashamed at his own poor performance and consequent loss of "fame"
– the reputation that is inseparable from masculine warriorhood, that
crowns kingship – and stung by Winnie's scornful laughter, Zandolie
tries his best to repair his broken wood by the incongruous device of a
piece of string. His second foray, desperately aggressive, is more successful than the first in that its fury evokes not laughter but a loud bawling
from his opponent. Retreating, he stumbles and falls on his back in a
drain that runs alongside the alley where the stickfight is taking place.
Winnie, seizing the advantage, charges and assumes her stance above the
now prone Zandolie, who from his position on his back and in the drain
"charge she a bois to dig out she liver / Meh wood break again".

The stickfight has, so far, lacked spectators. But the performance of
masculinity requires the applause and acclaim of spectators if it is to
bestow the kingship which is its ultimate objective. The third round is
therefore fought before a gathering crowd. Here fantasy outdoes itself
when Zandolie replaces his twice-broken wood with one borrowed from
"an old stickman named Joe Pringay". One can either read this as a
breakdown of the metaphorical design of the calypso – since it is impossible for one man to borrow the penis of another man, however desper-

ate the need – or as a comic enhancement of the marvellous and magical elements of the fable. For Zandolie's "Stickman" lies in the tradition of the fabulous: the folk-tale; the trickster narrative; the gross, earthy
fabliaux narrative that in its emergence from North Africa was appropriated by Boccacio then by Chaucer; the erotic narratives of what Leo
Frobenius named *The Black Decameron* (Frobenius 1971). In the tradition of the fabulous, the sudden restoration to potency of a badly broken and ruined bois is entirely possible.

Thus equipped with Joe Pringay's legendary and magical – probably
"mounted" (charmed) – bois, Zandolie becomes the inheritor of the masculinity of all ancestral warriors. He becomes rampant maleness itself,
total invincible phallus, bearing a wood that seems capable of outlast-
ing not only this present encounter, but time itself. Retreating before this
new assault, it is Winnie who begs quarter:

> Now I charging like if ah crazy
> and she only backing from me
> She say "I don't know you coulda play stick so
> Oh meh Lard oh, beg pardon Zando."
> Now she scramble on meh bois
> with she two hands playing tug-o-war
> I say "leggo, leggo, leggo woman,
> whe yuh doing dat for?"
> Well, it slipped out she hand
> and she fell in agony, begging me to stop
> I say "Wood make you fall, wood make you bawl,
> is wood to make you get up."
>   (*c*.1994)

This is the climax of Zandolie's narration of a primal, a central dream-
fantasy of the male imagination: the fantasy of a lasting triumph of the
phallus over the threat of an emasculating female sexuality. While Winnie
is ashamed at having lost face in public and is forced to resign from the
stickfighting competition, she takes comfort from having twice broken
Zandolie's wood: "She say she know she get bois but she ain't mind /
She break meh wood twice so she could resign." Curiously, Winnie never

questions whence Zandolie derives his third and unbreakable bois, the phallus that neither loses its potency nor experiences the satisfaction of orgasmic release. Zandolie, for his part, is far more concerned with having – by whatever trickster stratagem – won the contest, gained public acclaim, and received the token of his kingship: ". . . a ring they put on meh wood / with a medal marked 'woodman of the year' ".

There is snide laughter in the fact that the "chairman of the competition", who genuflects, shakes Zandolie's hand, and crowns his wood with ring and medal, is "a Chinee doctor from – [of all places] – Barbados". The triumph of stereotypically phallic African masculinity is, obviously, all the sweeter for its being enacted in the presence of the stereotypically "deficient" Chinese male, whose gesture of reverence – he genuflects before he crowns Zandolie's astounding bois – suggests that not just kingship but divine omnipotence has been achieved through success in the stickfight.

Crowley's batonnier also claimed, as part of his province of kingly attainment, supremacy in the more aesthetic qualities of song, dance and drum. Such supremacy also featured in the early construction of masculinity. The kalinda chantwel, descendant of griot and praise singer and perhaps of bard and balladeer, needed to possess oratorical and poetic skill, power over words, rhythm and melody. Song involved violent conflict in rhetoric, picong and demeaning insult. Like "stick" and "fight", song was a medium for the fierce assertion of ego, and the chantwels, as much as the batonniers, claimed and commanded territory. One was the chantwel of a particular band in a particular area, sharing in the honour won by the batonniers. Some chantwels combined the roles of "stick" and "song", as Crowley's batonnier seemed to do.

Few features of the calypso tradition have been more deeply inscribed than the notion of the singer as a protagonist in an intense contest through which skilled males measure their masculine worth one against the other. This contest is perennial, though it is usually more intense during eras of transition between the waning of an old king and style and the legitimation of a new one. Hence Executor, the unrivalled king of the oratorical period of the first three decades of the twentieth century, finds himself in the late 1930s defending not just his song but his very

identity as bard, warrior, shaman, king and man. His "They Say I Reign
Too Long" (1938) is simultaneously a "signification" through rhetorical recollection of his past achievements, after the style of epic heroes,
and a warning to contemporary challengers not to measure their skill
against the ageing warrior-king:

> They say I reign too long
> Forgetting that me constitution is strong
> Instead of glorifying me long years' reign
> They making plots to break down me name
>
> They say I reign too long
> Forgetting that me constitution is strong
> The Lord Executor can hold his own
> Tell them in Calypso I'm the cornerstone
>   (Lord Executor 1938)

Comparing his own performance to that of Queen Victoria, Jack
Hobbs, old wine and the nearly 120-year-old *Port of Spain Gazette,*
Executor, who in 1938 would have had almost forty years' experience
as a calypsonian, establishes that kingship has in significant cases been
enhanced by years of experience in dominance. He next provides three
examples of his own successful warriorhood over upstart calypsonians
who have challenged him in the past: Boldavia, King Pharaoh and Black
Prince. The first challenger turns tail, lacking "the courage to prolong
the war". The second, "King Pharaoh, the bravest of all", has the
courage but lacks the "strength in his arms to gain the prize". The third,
Black Prince, is punished for the hubris of his attempt to usurp Executor's
throne:

> Then came Black Prince with his armour on,
> Boastful, antagonistic and full of scorn,
> And in chains of bondage the villain was bound
> And cast in a dungeon far underground.
>   (Lord Executor 1938)

In spite of this last, awesome demonstration of his kingship in calypso singing, Lord Executor is forced to contend with myriad, nameless
nonentities who challenge him from time to time:

Then all over the colony
I found pretenders waiting for me
But when I, Executor, draw nigh
Man and beast and insect must die
              (Lord Executor 1938)

The singer here is shaman, magician of word and melody, omnipotent controller of not only the kingdom of calypso but the natural order of the cosmos. A phenomenal carnivalesque masking is employed in this construction of masculinity, which resembles the rhetoric of the Midnight Robber or the African-American "signifier". Calypsonians fully understood the difference between the assumed mask of power and the reality of impoverishment, joblessness and powerlessness that confronted them in their daily lives. A considerable amount of calypso laughter has emerged out of the space between the power of the mask and the absurd futility of daily existence. Yet calypsonians have continued to play mas with their identities by seeking a phenomenal kingship, the elements of which have changed only slightly over the six decades since Executor buried his opponents.

One has only to consider the mid-1940s contestation between Young Brigade and Old Guard singers; the Sparrow–Melody picong series of over twenty calypsos which enlivened the late 1950s and early 1960s; the sometimes ill-humoured contestation of Sparrow and Kitchener from the mid-1960s to the mid-1970s; the challenge of Shadow from the early 1970s onwards; and the ongoing polemic as to what constitutes authenticity in the calypso. Song remains a battlefield of sometimes violent contestation, at the centre of which issues of identity, masculinity, warriorhood and kingship are still being contested. Some of these issues have crystallized in the debate about whether equal recognition should always be given to patriarchs of the art form such as Sparrow and Kitchener, in terms of the symbols through which their different claims to kingship might be made visible: Sparrow's University of the West Indies doctorate; the statue of Kitchener; Sparrow's Chaconia Gold; Kitchener's insistence, reinforced by Delamo's "Trinity Is Still My Name" (1994), that he deserved and would accept nothing less than the Trinity

Cross; more recently, the proposed statue of Sparrow to counterbalance, one senses, the Kitchener statue that commands the entrance to St James.

While such issues of seniority and hierarchy continue to preoccupy an older generation, the contemporary era is characterized by a plethora of song forms and musical market trends, each of which seeks its own competition and monarch. The gender-specific masculinist kingship of the past has, since Calypso Rose in 1978, been replaced by the still male-dominated but now gender-inclusive "monarchy" of the 1980s and 1990s. In 1999 both the Calypso Monarch (Singing Sandra) and the Road March Monarch (Sanelle Dempster) were women. In 2003 this feat was repeated by Singing Sandra (Calypso Monarch) and FayeAnn Lyons (Road March Monarch). This does not mean that the calypso has ceased to be a text that holds clues to the construction of masculinity in this era. It means, rather, that for the first time this masculinity has been forced to take account of critical quasi-feminist and feminist/womanist perspectives, which have the potential of challenging constructions of masculinity in even more radical ways than each new generation of males has in the past oedipally challenged the structures of warriorhood and kingship that have barred and determined its entry into full manhood.

Along with his proficiency in stickfight and song, Crowley's Lawa claimed kingship in *drum* and *dance*. Drum and dance were intimately linked in the complex of performance skills which stickfighting demanded. The drummer was the link between the dancer and the orisha at one level, and at a more mundane level the controller of the whole martial game, through the medium of rhythm and coded message. The dancer had to marry rhythm to graceful, sliding, subtle movement. Dance in the context of the stickfight was not so much a softer skill as the means whereby, as in fencing or karate, the batonnier slid into the most advantageous position for attack or defence. Out of dance, however, would emerge a variant heroic type: the dandy or saga boy, celebrated in scores of calypsos of the "Papa Choonks" (1941) variety long after the stickfight had retreated to the provinces or the jagged edges of the city. Dancing frequently functioned as a metaphor for the sexual act in the mildly risqué calypsos of the 1930s.

So far, then, it is apparent that the stickfighter prototype contained many of the elements out of which Trinidad masculinity was later constructed. The society's first real folk hero was a warrior. Earl Lovelace glorifies this figure in his novel *The Wine of Astonishment* even as he chronicles his waning. Errol Hill structures his play *Man Better Man* (1964) on stickfighting legends. Willi Chen, painter, sculptor and author of short fiction, is also preoccupied with the figure of the batonnier: his ethic of honour, skill, violence as test, man-to-man encounter without quarter, *sans humanité* (Chen 1988). He is there in Ismith Khan's portrait of Massahood in his novel *The Obeah Man* (1964). Clearly a romantic figure in the society's consciousness, the stickfighter with his defiant boasting song or speech provided the calypso with prototypes for its later rhetoric of bravado. Chalkdust's "Stickman's Lament" laments the disappearance of the stickman from his formerly central place in the development of Carnival and calypso (Liverpool 1996). One might compare Lancelot Kebu Layne's location of the figure of the Djab Molassi at the centre not just of Canboulay and Carnival, but of a tradition of heroic defiance and resistance within which the society's instinct for freedom has been deeply rooted (Layne 1983).

The figure of the warrior-king is also evident in calypsos which deal with sport. Games, particularly violent contact sports, have traditionally been recognized and accepted as an integral part of the process whereby the young male is separated from the gentler ethos of the mother's early weaning and nurture and initiated into the environment of "proper" manhood: the tough, masculine world of constant testing, measuring, squaring off, facing up, asking and giving no quarter, delivering and enduring blows "like a man".[1] Although there have been oral accounts of formidable female stickfighters, particularly during the Jamette era of mid- to late-nineteenth-century Port of Spain (Pearse 1956, 250–62), the stickfight was a game indulged in mainly by males, who regarded it as a crucial test of their manhood.

The social and political dimensions of this measuring of manhood became evident in the 1880s when stickfighters squared off against mounted and armed police officers in the Canboulay Riots of 1881 and in the 1884 protests against the Peace Preservation Ordinance. According to one account (Hill 1993, 36–39), Captain Baker wielded a sword, while his men were armed with balata sticks and bayonets; the stickfighters confronted the police with only their staves and pots on their heads to ward off blows. "Thirty eight policemen were injured in the melee, eight of them seriously" (pp. 36–39). It was the manhood of the batonniers versus that of Baker and his officers, the game of stickfight reverting to its origins as a martial art. Confrontation between policemen and batonniers would continue to be a regular feature of post-1884 Carnivals, and would last well into the twentieth century.

Out of such grim man-to-man confrontations have emerged a number of tendencies: the tendency on the part of "straight" society to nurture race and class stereotypes of entire segments of the urban underclass; the tendency of the police – acting on behalf of the ruling elites – to criminalize the underclass, whom they regard, presume to be and treat as criminals; the tendency of the criminalized underclass to construct masculinity in terms of resistance, rebellion, aggressiveness, toughness, and the style and reputation that are inseparable from any ethic of violent masculine performance.

Following in the wake of the stickfight, other games played by males became, in the context of colonial Trinidad, not only tests of the players' manhood but arenas for social, racial and ultimately political encounter. The best account of this process exists in C.L.R. James's seminal *Beyond a Boundary* (1963). Calypsos from the 1920s to the present also provide us with a chronicle of how the gladiatorial, embattled attitudes of the stickfighter were passed on to other categories of sportsmen. African-American boxers were adopted by Afro-Trinidadians as fellow-soldiers in the same fight against the barriers of racism and oppression, and celebrated in calypsos of the 1930s and 1940s as well as throughout the era of Muhammad Ali (Rohlehr 1990, 194–200). In Eric Roach's poem "The Fighters" (1992, 106–7), Henry Armstrong and Joe Louis become metaphors of the diasporan African freedom struggle, offering hope to a poet whose poetic testimony, "I Am the Archipelago", represents diasporan African masculinity as a bruised, bitter and broken thing, betrayed and betraying blood and race and woman, yet reclaiming all of its lost ancestral ground, its history of unrewarded labour, its submerged primal energies, for a rage which the poet prays will never be unleashed in genocidal revenge against its historical enemies. The African-American boxers in that late colonial period gave this rage a shape and a direction within the gayelle of the boxing ring, and within the structure of rules and decorum which alone separates sport from the warfare for which it is a recognized surrogate.

It is, of course, also depressingly true that black rage, avoiding or afraid to confront its enemy, has been redirected towards an intestinal and self-destructive warfare. Black masculinity throughout the ghettoized diaspora has tested, measured and proven itself most consistently on black masculinity. This too has been the concern of a large number of calypsos; Stalin's "Black Man Killing Black Man" (1996) is offered as an example of this type of calypso.

The West Indian cricket team, which David Rudder describes in "Legacy" as "affirming and reconfirming my Caribbean energy", replaced the boxers as the manifestations of Ogun, the spirit of energy, rage, defiance and freedom, honed to the demanding skills and controlled by the complex laws and structures of the game and the discipline which the game requires. Rudder's great naming and praise song provides a clue about how masculinity is being perceived and constructed in this time:

> I thank God in my life and time I have known these men
> Affirming and reconfirming my Caribbean energy
> Striding to the centre with their beautiful arrogance
> Every blur of red, every flashing blade
> Means so much to you and me
> And even as I speak a child is born in our islands
> With shoulders so broad they have to take him out by
> the way of Caesar
> A frightening thought to those bewildered knights who stand in the way of
> our destiny
> Today if they think it's hard, well, tomorrow is harder
>   (Rudder 1995)

What "Legacy" celebrates is masculinity as kingship. The great West Indian batsmen, culminating in Trinidad's Brian Lara who had the

previous year broken both the test and first-class records in batsman-
ship, are heroes whose achievements challenge the old colonial order of
authoritarian control and undermine the ancient stereotypes and fixed
negative assumptions about the potential of the Caribbean man. Lara,
"the prince who promised so much, is now monarch of all he surveys"
(Rudder 1995). There has been a redefinition of the terms upon which
aristocracy and royalty may be achieved. Rudder identifies the attributes of the hero: "arrogant beauty", forceful self-assertiveness, "a fire
in his eyes and the cool of a champion's swagger". The cricket team provides, for a Caribbean riddled with dissension and divisiveness, an example of a central idea around which the islands might unite to their
advantage. The idea is that of "legacy", a recognition of common history, heritage, struggle and achievement. The pathfinders, the patriarchs,
Headley, the three Ws (Sir Frank Worrell, Sir Everton Weekes and Sir
Clyde Walcott) and Constantine, have left a passage through which the
ever-lengthening line of their descendants have walked and must continue to walk towards their "destiny".

It is sad that such a great song of praise and faith should have come
in the very year that the West Indies commenced their rapid slide down-
hill after nearly two decades at the top of world cricket. This has not in
any way reduced the power and truth of the song which is, if anything,
even more relevant to this era of decline, when both the region and its
cricket team need a central unifying idea in which people can invest their
faith.

Over the past six decades there have been many calypsos celebrating
cricket and eulogizing cricketers as warriors and emblems of Caribbean
masculinity.[2] Less obvious, but actually far more copious, have been
the scores of calypsos – forty in 1999 alone – about the steelband, another male-dominated institution. Although it may not be immediately
obvious, every calypso about pan is indirectly a celebration of Trinidad
masculinity in the form of the skill, patience, discipline, devotion and
creativity that this new musical invention has required for its nascence
and now its full-fledged growth. The link between the emergence of the
steelband and male heroism is made explicit in the Mighty Terror's
"Steelband Jamboree" (1966), which celebrates the triumph of pan over

jazz and other popular forms of music, and bestows on panmen the acco-
lade of "heroes":

> Ah hear the heroes are:
> Desperadoes
> All Stars and Tokyo
> South Symphony
> Renegades and Sun Valley
> Pan Am North Stars
> Tripoli and a band from Tunapuna
> Ah don't know, ah was only told
> These are some panmen who toured the world
> The heroes!

The pattern here is the same as in the stickfight and in the calypso,
whose greatest exponents in the 1920s and early 1930s used to be
referred to as "the heroes". The representative champions of a new
music, pan, have confronted and defeated other rival musics, in the
process winning space and popular acclaim. The panmen's victory is particularly sweet because "the heroes", once despised by the older jazz and
brass bandleaders, are now the popularly acclaimed purveyors of a totally indigenous new sound. There is more pride and triumphant amuse-
ment than sympathy in Terror's tone as he observes,

> Well this ehn [ain't] no joke
> Pan put jazz musicians outa work
> Some of them with tears in dey eyes
> They looking for work in Custom Excise
> Some a dem join the Police Force
> To lock up some of the panmen, of course
> But this is what the public declare
> Is only the steelbands they want to hear.
>
> (Mighty Terror 1966)

Heroic masculine performance needs always to be crowned by popular
acclamation.

Queh-Queh and the Phallocentric Muse

The stickman as phallic hero, dancer and boasting celebrant of his own prowess metamorphosed into the saga boy and the cocksman, a prominent figure in post-1945 calypso. "I'm the cock / Of the rock", boasts the Mighty Duke (1975), continuing, "Is not luck / Is good [that is, hard] wuk." Sparrow and the former "Love Man", Lord Shorty, would construct their own stage personae, and perhaps their masculinity as well, on the phallus. Relatively early Sparrow calypsos such as "The Village Ram" (1964a) and "Mr Rake and Scrape" (1960) celebrate the presence of a hero who is a sexual anarchist from the *demi-monde,* whose mission is to offend the prudish and the respectable. The Village Ram is a cock for hire. He is inexhaustible, aggressive, even violent, and describes his sexual performance in imagery taken from wrestling and boxing:

> I'm the champion without a doubt
> I never lose a bout
> And ah fight them in every class
> Don't ask who come last
> All meh fights is fifteen roun'
> If you ain't in shape don't come
> Every time this champion connect
> The power of the punch always get respect
> (Mighty Sparrow 1964a)

Masculinity is here, as elsewhere, associated with championship. Its ethos is that of the gladiator. Love-making occasions are bouts, fights; the penis is powerful fist, its thrust has the force of a knock-out punch. Yet, "not a woman ever complain yet" against this species of violence. All and sundry have left satisfied.

All this boasting – made more obvious through the protagonist's repeated denial that he is boasting – is done not only to attract the woman, but to rile and triumph over rival males who, presumed unable to satisfy their partners, are mockingly invited to engage the services of the Village Ram:

The girls that they have in town
They so big and strong
And Lord look at confusion
They ain't fraid no man
So, in case of emergency
If you eh able with she
And you find yourself in a jam,
Send for the village ram.
>   (Mighty Sparrow 1964a)

The performance of masculinity, according to Rosalind Miles (1992), is done to establish the subject's superiority over the threatening male other. The female, often impersonalized, may be the ground, the territory over or upon which fierce battles are fought, yet, strangely, the conflict remains one of the male ego, which seems doomed to have to prove and affirm itself perennially through rituals of aggression performed in the presence of other males.

This reading of the performance of masculinity seems applicable to Sparrow's "Village Ram". One would, however, want to recognize other dimensions of this calypso which was in part Sparrow's defiant response to critics of the day who, hypocritical about their own love for the bawdy, were condemning his public and open celebration of it in his songs. There is something about the extremity of songs like "The Village Ram", "Mr Rake and Scrape" and "The Congo Man" (1965) that suggests a conscious and defiant transgression of the imposed bourgeois canons of good taste, moral virtue, decency and respectability. There is something aggressively carnivalesque about the grossness of image through which Sparrow represents naked appetite and lust. In "Mr Rake and Scrape" he is a sexual scavenger – not the man who heaves the bag of rubbish onto the truck, but the man who scrapes up the remnants of garbage that have escaped the diligence of the main scavengers. In "The Congo Man", he is a sexual cannibal.

The annual condemnation of phallocentricity and overtly indulged sexuality in the contemporary calypso conceals older and deeper dimensions of discourse about how male and female sexualities have weathered the peculiar history of this Caribbean space. I choose Guyanese queh-queh songs for my first example of such ancestral discourse. Queh-Queh songs were, and in a few areas of rural Guyana still are, sexual advice passed on by members of a senior generation to young couples on the verge of marriage. Afro-Guyanese women play a central role in the performance of these erotic queh-queh songs. Indo-Guyanese and Indo-Trinidadians possess a similarly ancestral institution in the form of matikor. Such sexual advice as is passed on in queh-queh and matikor via song, dance and gesture is frank and explicit. The special festive space afforded by the queh-queh was probably the only time that the senior generation would have open discourse with the younger on the highly censored subject of sexuality.

According to Kean Gibson the older women describe to the prospective bride the shape, nature and function of the male sexual organ, and instruct the presumably inexperienced young woman on her role in the sex act (1998, 163–98).[3] One of their songs says:

Move a path let cocki walk
Move a path let pokey talk
Move a path let cocki play
Move a path let pokey laugh.[4]
          (Gibson 1998, 170)

A probable translation of this is:

Move aside: allow the penis to walk
Move aside: allow the vagina to talk
Move aside: allow the penis to play
Move aside: allow the vagina to laugh.

Such journeying, such conversation, such play and such laughter of delight are the most ancient, the most primal known to man and woman, and in the sexual instruction via song and dance that queh-queh is lies a frank recognition that no barriers should stand in the way of the journey and "play" (that is, both game and subtle movement) of the penis and the co/responding conversation, movement of the labia and laughter of the vagina.

The fragment of queh-queh advice quoted suggests that under the heavy overlay of puritanical prudery that has been part of Caribbean male and female socialization lay, and perhaps still may lie, an openness of acceptance by men and women of each others' bodies, each others' genitals and their modes of functioning, that was healthy, genuine and deeper than all social taboos, deeper than the ethic of decency and respectability that controlled both sexuality itself and discourse about it.

While Trinidad and Tobago is a different country from Guyana and calypso miles away from queh-queh, which is itself of limited currency among Afro-Guyanese, song forms such as calypso and chutney (Constance 1992), and the special spaces in which both used to be enacted, performed functions of secular ritual that were essentially similar to that of queh-queh. The calypso outwitted censorship and spoke about sexuality behind its thin mask of metaphor, thus maintaining a tradition of primal discourse even as it emerged from the controlled spaces of gayelle and tent into the "moral light" of the public forum, where overt acknowledgment or celebration of sexuality has long been censored.

The calypso, like the Scottish ballad, the songs of Robert Burns's *Merry Muses of Caledonia* (1966) and the genuine English folk song, celebrates a beleaguered earlier tradition which ran and runs counter to the demonization of human sexuality that has been central to Puritanism. Fertility, male potency, intercourse as intense conversation of male and female bodies, sex as the interplay, journey and laughter of the genitals: these are some of the major themes of this earlier sensibility. So that in the context of this primal, ancestral tradition, masculinity has been unashamedly phallocentric and femininity gynocentric. There are literally scores of metaphors for the penis, the vagina and the sexual act in the calypsos of the last seven decades.

Calypso images for the phallus – and this is a short list – include snake, wood, devil, brush, plantain, banana, fig, bamboo, hardwood, steel, iron, needle, bull pizzle (or pistle), electric plug, pole, wire, knife, stick, watering hose, black pudding, roast corn, cock, prick, picka, fork, billiard cue, cane, totee, toto, boy, son, cricket bat and whip. The sexually rampant male has been represented as donkey, mule, horse, dog, bull, doctor or dentist administering injections, roast-corn vendor, cannibal, ramgoat, scavenger cleaning up every variety of garbage, dancer doing the fox trot, the Volga boatman, the soca, the jam and wine, computer technician, gardener forking up the land or watering the garden, athlete running a race and bursting the tape (that is, taking a woman's virginity or "devirginizing" her, as Buchi Emecheta might have termed it), town man (tongue man), vampire, demon, Barnabas, black-pudding vendor, iron man (that is, percussionist in the steelband) and, dream of dreams, bionic man or cyborg who as "a mixture of human and machinery" can "work all night and never tire" (Maestro 1977).

The female genitalia have not been under-represented in fanciful calypso imagery. Words such as pussy and cat, coming straight out of British folk speech, have been beaten to a frazzle. There have also been euphemisms such as "Miss Mary", and folk words such as tooney (two knee), tun tun and coon coon. Rose used palet and "the iced milky lollie". There have been pum pum (poom poom); kangkalang; mango vert/long mango (Sparrow [1959]: "If you eat it right the hair won't stick in your teeth"); nanny/nani/nanie; business; property; craw; hole; and all the puns on "cunt" that one can imagine – country, mudda country, contents, yuh mudder come, and so forth; food; honey (sometimes as a mask for "cunny"); pork; meat; beef; saltfish; bag of sugar; sawmill; purse (as pun on "puss"); sports page (Duke in "See Through" [1969]: "You could see she old age / You could read she sports page"); ID card; and joy bottle.

These are only short lists of the elaborate representations of sexual organs and the sexual act, but they should serve to illustrate the extent to which ancestral modes of perceiving male and female sexuality are alive in the contemporary calypso. The construction of masculinity around the *poteau mitan* of the phallus, and of femininity around the vagina and womb, is a continuation of ancient modes of centring life in fertility and reproduction. Such modes were undoubtedly intensified in colonial slave societies that were literally founded on genocide, extremes of violence, the constant and wanton destruction of African lives and, after the abolition of the slave trade, the necessity that faced the planter class for the local workforce to regenerate itself with some regularity (now that genocide was no longer economically viable). In this period the fertile stud must have been an important element of the declining plantation economy, the phallus rising as the planter class fell.

Ancestral phallocentricity and gynocentricity existed in the face of or, more appropriately, beneath the heavy weight of a superimposed and countervailing moral imperative articulated by the numerous Christian denominations, as well as other major religions that arrived later to inherit a New World swept and garnished through genocidal European conquest. Phallocentricity was challenged by such prophets of the predominant capitalist system as Malthus of the nineteenth century and Mouttet and Morgan Job[5] of contemporary Trinidad and Tobago who, noting the relationship between excessive fertility and persistent poverty, have proclaimed the sound economic wisdom of old-time Miltonic puritanical restraint, responsibility and the necessity for controlling desire via work and economic productivity. Phallocentricity in all of its dimensions has also been the target of a vast amount of feminist discourse, which has been concerned with how phallocentred constructions of masculinity have led to fixed ascriptions of gender roles, particularly of the roles of childbearing and child rearing through which women's identities and social and human functions have been prescribed. One reggae song of the early 1970s took the form of a chorus of female voices wailing in unison, "No more, no more, nuh gimme no more pikni. Nuh gimme, nuh gimme, nuh gimme no more pikni." A change of some sort was being demanded.

Constructing and Deconstructing Masculinity

It is therefore necessary to return to our vast body of calypso texts in order to determine the extent to which the calypso celebrates, and the extent to which it may in fact simultaneously elevate and deflate, the ideal of phallocentric masculinity. Calypsonians, like their ancestors the queh-queh singers, the matikor singers, the Scottish bawdy balladeers, were socialized in the radically contradictory spaces of gayelle, rum shop, cook shop and tent, on the one hand, and temple, church, Sunday school, classroom and women's room, on the other. These singers have therefore been inscribed with conflicting moralities which are reflected in the presence of a large body of moral, socially responsible calypso texts, alongside the vast corpus of fertility and celebratory songs. Every year there is debate related to the problem of ascribing moral, social or aesthetic value to both modes of expression. And while on the whole the two types of calypso are promoted by different types of singer, it is quite possible to find major singers who have tried their skills at both modes of song, and who have seemed to reconcile the conflicting moral universes contained in the ancestral folk mode and the superimposed imperial mode of church, school and plantation.

Phallocentricity and its corollary, phallic potency, become topics of self-mockery and reductive humour in several calypsos, suggesting that phallus worship, such as appears to be happening in calypsos like the Puppet Master's 1998 hit, "The Greatest Love", is largely a mask worn by calypsonians because of tradition, but equally mocked by them because of its disconnection from reality. The latest in a long line of phallocentric calypsos, "The Greatest Love" is ostensibly about a man's yearning for a son to bear his name. When, after several daughters who seem not to count, this precious only-begotten son is born, his father nurtures him with a solicitude that exceeds even maternal tenderness.

Concerned that his "boy" should be weaned on only the best foods, he buys him all the things he has seen advertised in the media, as well as everything local that has acquired a reputation in the folklore for its power to nourish and strengthen. Thus, the years from birth to early boyhood see a diet of "high protein soya milk", "mixed cereals", "Seven Seas Cod Liver Oil with malt and tonic", "Ovaltine, Milk, Klim, Lasco, Frico, Quik". There is such overkill in this list of fine advertised foods and in the massive quantities that he purchases that one begins to feel sorry for his son, who must eat, endure and live through it all in order to fulfil the expectations of his doting father.

As his "boy" grows, the foreign designer commodities – Sanatogen, Centrum, Vitara, Ginsana – are steadily supplemented with more sold and more natural local foods, such as "Good fish broth with young fig for iron . . . / Pacro soup with fresh ground provision" (Puppet Master 1988). These lay the foundation for vigorous youth and the father, who has nurtured his "boy" on the best nutrients of both worlds, begins to dream of an athletic career for his son. His "boy", properly fed and trained, might achieve the eminence in sport of an Ato Boldon or a Dwight Yorke, or he might develop differently into a world-champion calypsonian such as Sparrow or Grandmaster Kitchener, who are examples of mature and ageing masculinity while Boldon and Yorke manifest youthful athleticism.

However this is only the external and ostensible plot, the mask of innocent narrative that conceals the real theme of the calypso: a man's doting care and worship of his penis from cradle to grave, an obsession so extreme and all-consuming that the penis, part of the body, assumes a human personality and identity of its own. In a sense, the man has become his penis, a walking, perpetually upright phallus, the archetypal *homo erectus*. The protagonist's final ambition, for his "boy" to emulate Dwight Yorke or Sparrow, is fired less by the desire for eminence in sport or musical performance than by admiration or envy of Yorke's tabloid fame and Sparrow's self-advertised reputation as sexual athletes and champion cocksmen/lovers. All the foods, foreign or local, are chosen for the reputation they have gained as stimulants of male sexual potency. "To strengthen mih boy", the objective of all the protagonist's efforts, is to fuel both the male sexual drive and the capacity for its sustained fulfilment: sustainable development of male phallic propensity, one supposes.

When the protagonist's wife objects to his narcissistic obsession with his "boy"/penis as an unhealthy kind of deviance, he refutes her diagnosis on the ground that she, as a woman, cannot truly understand the dilemma of the male condition:

> Wifey say, "Your behavioural pattern stray
> Playing with your boy whole night and whole day
> Boy chile obsession ha you gigiree
> On your boy you spending all yuh money."
> I say "My boy's importance you don't understand
> Is my boy does make me feel like a man
> If mih boy dead now, Oh God, I will grieve.
> You and all might pack up yuh grip and leave."
>   (Puppet Master 1988)

Gigiree, according to Allsopp,[6] means nervous or uneasy. In this context it may also mean insecure, for it is insecurity that the wife discerns lying beneath her husband's centring of his masculinity in the penis. The wife's voice can be taken to represent the contemporary feminist intervention in traditional masculinist discourse. Such an intervention has of necessity been diagnostic, deconstructive and deflationary.

The male protagonist of "The Greatest Love" senses this and is on his guard against it. First he warns his wife that the solicitude that he showers on his "boy"/penis is for her gratification as much as his. The boast of being able to satisfy "Woman" was, as we have seen, a crucial part of Lawa's self-signification. Satisfying Woman sexually remains a major part of the masculine project and, consequently, a major area of male insecurity. It is the fragile spot in masculine self-construction, and it needs the greatest shoring up, the most intense psychic reinforcement, the most powerful boasting rhetoric and the most elaborate masking.

This is why the protagonist desperately redoubles his efforts "to strengthen mih boy" after his wife's criticism. Now his bizarre diet includes

> Arrowroot, linseed, coconut water
> To strengthen mih boy
> Sanatogen, Centrum, Vitara, Ginsana
> To strengthen mih boy
> Boil up goat milk with bay leaf and corn meal
> Why? To strengthen mih boy
> Ah get some dhal an ah fling in some cow heel
> To strengthen mih boy
> (Puppet Master 1988)

No wife is going to deter him from this crucial project. A life-threatening accident that he survives only reinforces his resolve or obsession, his sense of the peril that surrounds his boy and that can strike at any time. His care, in this triumphant version of the phallocentric fable, pays dividends. Erection becomes permanent (note the similarity here to Zandolie's "Stickman"), much to the dismay of the protagonist's wife – "My boy always up in the night / An to wifey that is problem left and right" – who is at a loss for a means of putting the boy to sleep and so winning some ease for herself, respite from the now insatiable demands of "mih boy". Clearly a caring husband, he suggests to his wife an easy method for soothing her insomniac son to sleep:

> Ah tell she, "Don't fret, dou dou, use your tact
> Either pat he head girl or rub 'e back"
> But she say how she auntie tell she
> To get mih boy to sleep put brandy in 'e tea
> She try the brandy ting; in no time she stop
> More brandy he get more mih boy wake up
> (Puppet Master 1988)

It may well be this inability of his wife to satisfy his "boy's" appetite that generates in the protagonist a desire to prepare his "boy" for the international world of sport. Such an extraordinarily well-nurtured talent deserves exposure outside the home. The calypso ends with the happy image of a well-creamed, sweetly scented, well-fed and vigorous youth whom "women always want to hug up and kiss". The wife, by this time, has disappeared from the picture. Again a parallel may be drawn between this ending of the phallocentric fable and the ending of Zandolie's "Stickman" where Winnie loses the contest, begs pardon of Zandolie, and disappears from the text while the triumphant and still erect "wood" of the male batonnier is crowned with ring and medal by the awestruck and genuflecting Dr Kim Lau. (In the folklore of phallo-centricity, the ring was worn by men with oversized tools in order to indicate the point beyond which it would be unsafe to insert the penis into the vagina.)

From the above analysis it would seem that "The Greatest Love" is no more than a clever and witty affirmation of the reconstructed masculine myth of a phallic potency capable of overwhelming and defeating the antagonist: female sexuality. The elaborate listing of phallus-sustaining foods is a warning to men that it requires eternal vigilance and effort, constant strategizing, to keep the enemy at bay and finally drive her out of the gayelle. Yet there is just a suspicion of satire here, of the slightest distance between the obsessed protagonist who narrates the calypso and the calypsonian, the toothless Puppet Master, who composed and who performed it. Is there satirical laughter at the gross extremes to which the protagonist goes just "to strengthen mih boy"? Is there covert affirmation of the wife's diagnosis of her husband's behaviour as aberration, sickness and obsession? What about the gap between the phallocentric fantasy that is the calypso's subject and the sentimental love song, "The Greatest Love", whose chorus is perversely parodied in the calypso's refrain?

In performing the calypso, Puppet Master illustrates the obsession of the doting father by making a number of sounds and indulging in the sort of baby talk that is generally associated with mothers. He is, in fact, borrowing from Composer's hilarious satire on baby-talk, "Child Training" (from the early 1970s). One doesn't know what Puppet Master intended, but one of the things that he did achieve was to show how the male, in his enactment of the phallocentric fable, ironically "effeminizes" his performance. The difference is that while the mother expends all her devotion in the nurturing of a whole child, a separate being, the effeminized male expends his intense care on himself, or an extension of himself, the phallus, to which he has limited his entire psyche. The fact, too, that he has fixed on this tumescent and all-important protuberance the title of "mih *boy*" may be an indication that he has allowed himself to become trapped in a kind of infantilism. When he tells his protesting wife, "Is my boy does make me feel like a man", is this not an unwitting recognition on the protagonist's part of an arrested psychic growth? His wife certainly sees this when she diagnoses: "Boychile obsession ha you *gigiree*."

The latent critique of male phallocentricity here, however, is overwhelmed by the calypso's enthusiastic celebration of the same principle. This makes the Puppet Master's calypso true to its tradition. One saw the same tension between celebrating and satirizing phallocentricity in the calypsos of Kitchener, Sparrow, Shorty and Duke, with the greater emphasis by far falling on the tendency to celebrate masculinity as the province of the warrior-king-cocksman and the sign of "I Lawa". Kingship in calypso has always required the incumbent to assume the mask of phallic potency. This was true of the Roaring Lion in the 1930s, when he developed the reputation for entering a tent surrounded by a bevy of his "lionesses" and composed songs like "I Can Make More Love Than Romeo" (1939) that advertised his "sweet man" image.[7] The youthful Kitchener took the calypso world of the late 1940s and the 1950s by storm with compositions such as "Mount Olga" (1947), "Ah Bernice" (1951) and "Kitch Take It Easy" (1952) all of which celebrated his prowess as lover. A long list can be added to these from his compositions of the 1960s and 1970s.

Sparrow, from his earliest years when he sang sexual fantasy songs such as "Sailing Boat Experience" (1957), "Lucy Garden" (1961) and "Mae Mae" (1960), right into the 1990s of "Both of Them" (1992) and "The More the Merrier" (1993), has worked indefatigably to sustain the warrior-king-cocksman mask over four decades of performance. Shorty, who in the decade from the mid-1960s to the mid-1970s sought to rival Sparrow's kingship with his own "love-man" persona, sustained ruined fortunes, rebirth in the Piparo forest and reincarnation into Ras Shorty I, elder, father figure, moralist and preacher-man – an entirely different construction of masculinity from the model and archetype that we have so far been exploring. The bitter exchange in the mid-1990s between Sparrow ("Both of Them" and "The More the Merrier"), Ras Shorty I ("That Ain't Good Enough" [1992] and "Latrine Singers" [1994]), Iwer George and Tigress ("Kneel" [1997] and "Ent You Love Kaiso/We Getting the Kaiso We Deserve" [1996]) centred on this changing construction of masculinity and the correspondingly different definition of artistic responsibility and commitment that has been evolving over the past two or three decades.

As a male singer ages his ability to perform the macho mask of warrior-king-cocksman-lover wanes. The Sparrow who in "Both of Them" (1992) sang of his protagonist's simultaneous accommodation of two sisters won the monarchy that year, but was less convincing in the role than the leaner, lither Sparrow of 1966 or 1976 would have been. In the argument that ensued between him and Ras Shorty I, who in press interviews and songs admonished that a senior citizen and calypsonian should demonstrate a moral responsibility commensurate with his age, Sparrow made no distinction between himself and the persona in the song. He rather expressed outrage that Ras Shorty I, the former "Love Man", should be casting aspersions on Sparrow's sexual ability, and declared that he was (still) "very capable", all the more so for having followed the instructions so generously articulated since 1973 by Ras Shorty I himself in "The Art of Making Love".

This curious failure or reluctance on Sparrow's part to distinguish between self and mask, actor and role, is an indication of the power of the mask of masculinity, both as ancestral archetype visible in the shape of contemporary calypso fables, and as transmitted social construct inscribed on the calypsonian's consciousness by generations of repeated performance. The mask eventually will, like the Puppet Master's "boy", assume its own personality, and begin to play the singer. Confronted with the trauma of the collapse of the life he had constructed for himself, Shorty broke free of the power of the mask of masculinity and worked towards the construction of a new and different public image. Driven by the desire to sustain or renew his kingship in the face of the calypso's perennial shape-shifting, Sparrow recycles or updates old modes of performance.

In spite of this, Sparrow has at times questioned and even discarded the mask for something closer to lived reality. An early calypso like "Everybody Washing Their Mouth on Me" (1959), in which he defends his right to love and marry whomsoever he pleases, reveals for one brief moment the hurt man beneath the brash surface of picong, braggadocio and violent self-assertiveness that he so fervently promoted in those days. A little later, in "Man Like to Feel" (1965), where he advises women on how to control and "tie-up" their men, Sparrow achieves a devastating unmasking of masculine illusions about self and image:

> I am outlining a simple plan
> How every woman could tie up their man
> I am outlining a simple plan
> How every woman could tie up their man
>
> A man like to feel big although he small
> A midget does want to feel ten feet tall
> So you could keep him under your heel
> Just let him feel what he want to feel

A man like to feel he is a big wheel
Big in every way
And he like to feel that he girlfriend feel
He greater than Cassius Clay
But I feel that when bad feelings step in man does feel like hell
A man don't mind he girl make him feel how he look
But don't make him feel how he smell

2

Man like to feel that he's superior
And feel woman should feel they are inferior
He feel he should talk things he ain't know 'bout
And feel very hurt if you box he mouth
So when he feel to lie and feel he fooling you
Let him feel that you feel what he say is true
Always let him feel he is your ideal
And anything he feel let the damn fool feel
Ugly man does feel that he beautiful
When pretty girl is near
And always does feel other people feel
They will make such a lovely pair
He will never feel that the woman nice
And she should feel like a queen
Instead he feel he in paradise
And feel she is a wahbeen.

3

He feel that he possess so much charm
Women must feel to be in he arms
This time the woman feel he's a clown
But he feel to feel they running him down
On pay-day he feel like a millionaire
And feel he should be living in St Clair
Or feel to sleep out so he gone all about and spree
And feel he wife can't feel for no one but he
Some o dem ole but they feel they young
This I must reveal
Some o dem weak but they feel they strong

This is how they feel
But if they want to feel silly
Do not object, just play it cool
You know you dealing with a stupidy feeling
That is felt by a foolish fool
(Ah wanta fall!)

4
If every woman could see with me
She man and she must live in harmony
He give you clothes, give you house and meal
So whe de hell you care how he feel?
If you feel your man must always be near
Let him have the feeling that you ain't care
If he run around the girls and lose all he zeal
Tell him you have a sweet man and see how he feel

A man like to feel woman is he slave
He feel he is boss
He ain't know that he digging he own grave
Better change he course
This feeling man get for fooling woman
And does make him feel like a champ
He ain't know that the woman get a nasty feeling
'Bout he and think he's a scamp
(How you feel? Hah! Hah!)
                    (Mighty Sparrow 1965)

"Man Like to Feel" is an unmasking calypso in which Sparrow pur-
ports to teach women how to demolish or at least see through several
masks of masculinity, including some that have appeared unchallenged
in other Sparrow calypsos. Among these are the mask of
hero/fighter/warrior, here suggested by the men's illusion of exceeding
the achievements of heavyweight champion Cassius Clay. Other patriarchal attitudes ridiculed in "Man Like to Feel" include men's assumptions about a natural male superiority over woman and notions of
mastery and control over women's lives and labour, which are condemned as wrong and dangerous. The calypso maintains that any man

who seriously believes in any of the popular constructions of masculinity, from the warrior-hero to the dandy, lover, saga boy, cocksman and domestic slave-master, is a fool living in a world of illusion. Throughout the calypso the words "feel" and "feeling" convey ambiguous connotations of sentiment and emotion, on the one hand, and illusion and self-delusion, on the other. A sensible woman, the calypso argues, can easily control a self-deluded man, by contemptuously abandoning him to his illusions and ruthlessly pursuing her own desires.

"Man Like to Feel" recommends for women not overt confrontation of male self-centred delusion, but rather a trickster-like pragmatism which allows the woman to humour and play along with the "stupidy feeling" and foolish foolishness that constitute the greater part of how masculinity is constructed. The fact that such a calypso has been sung by one of the greatest celebrants of machismo that the calypso world has seen is a warning to the researcher that calypsos, as products of the carnivalesque frame of mind, are concerned with ceaseless masking and unmasking, in which stereotypes may be simultaneously celebrated and demolished.

Thus, if a sizeable number of calypsos seem to be products of male fantasies, dreams, high ideals and illusions, there has always existed a smaller body of calypsos about unheroic or even antiheroic male protagonists who can fulfil none of the roles through which masculinity is measured and determined. There have always been the old men who cannot pretend (any longer?) to be stickfighters, athletes, hero-kings, saga boys and cocksmen. There have always been also the cuckolds whose control over their women-as-property has slipped beyond retrieval. There are the good husbands whose sexual vitality has waned, and whose machismo has shrivelled to a sad contemplation of the dignity of downfall.

Such figures – and they constitute, if truth were told, a considerable number – generate mild or deep mockery, depending on how seriously they might attempt to maintain their self-delusion or restore their mask of men-in-control. Terror's "Callaloo Tonic" seems unequivocally to celebrate the restoration of phallic potency in a middle-aged male protagonist recently returned from the United Kingdom where, he says, he lost it through his consumption of unhealthy, devitalizing English "food". It is your phallocentric calypso *par excellence,* in which at one point the persona portrays himself as lost in awe at the hardness of his own erection:

> For when ah eat callaloo and ah drink mih rum
> Ah strong like Cassius Clay and Sonny Liston
> And when I lie down relaxing
> Ah feel like a lord when ah watch mih skin
> How it look so stiff and admiring.

The audience is asked to participate in this infantile self-admiration of the resurrected and sustainable phallus:

> Well if you think ah grandcharging
> Come by me and just feel mih skin
> Ah was soft before but now I prepare for war
> The Terror was soft before but now he prepare for war
> 　　　　　(Mighty Terror 1979)

In "Callaloo Tonic" ageing is not confronted. Instead, a male strategy which I have termed ego-retrieval (Rohlehr 1990, 231, 236–37, 276) is employed, through which the mask of phallic potency is restored and the phallocentric hero reconstructed and re-equipped with phallic superpower for new and quite incredible encounters with Elaine and her mother – both of them – or indeed any female or even fly that might be passing by. In reconstructing the hero as warrior and cocksman, "Callaloo Tonic" employs the traditional imagery of sexual intercourse as encounter, contest, warfare, stickfight. Yet beneath this mode of representation one senses a certain comic self-mockery in the very grossness, the very outrageousness of the imagery and ideas, something legendary, fabulous and excessive in this reborn Osiris who is willing to fecundate anyone and anything: Elaine, her mother, his own sister if she comes too close, any other male that seeks to rival him in hardness of phallus, or any fly that alights on his navel. We are in the realm of Bakhtin's carnivalesque here, and we should at least entertain the possibility that more than one voice is speaking in Terror's text, and that at least one of the voices is baiting the audience while another is laughing in the face of impotence, of collapsed masculinity.

Pretender's "Move Yuh Foot Leh Mih Pass" is even more devastating in the triumphant scorn that it pours on ageing:

> Ah know it ent nice
> Fellas ah bound to give this advice
> (Take it or leave it)
> Ah know it ent nice
> As man ah bound to give this advice
> Just face facts and know yourself
> You ain't got to hide on top a shelf
> Ah say to live like sensible men
> And you know how to move round the girls and them.
>
> *Chorus*
> I know, them gals nowadays ain't business with me
> Ah must respect mih age
> I think it pays and I'm sure you'll agree
> Ah got to keep quiet at this stage
> Well look ah done old mih ole
> Me ain't rude, me ain't fast
> Ah don't want no friendship to last
> (Not me). So is darling hold on to this
> Move yuh foot leh mih pass
> (Lord Pretender 1969)

This is the opposite of Terror's attempted restoration of the phallic hero. No such pretence for Pretender, older than Terror by a decade and his senior in the calypso tent by nearly two. Contrary to his soubriquet, Pretender does not pretend. He faces reality and enjoins other fellows to do the same. He was a hero, saga boy and cocksman in the 1940s and 1950s:

> When Preddie was young
> Lord, I was a hero all over town
> A real hot boy all over the place

With mih sweet ole talk an mih pretty face
But since mih grey hairs start to grow
All dem girls want to make me pappyshow
You could tell them for Pretender
They can't give me no tabanca.
                    (Lord Pretender 1969)

Now he is no more than a target for mercenary and mocking young women looking for a sugar-daddy. Retaining the traditional misogyny and mistrust of women typical of the calypsonian of the 1930s that he has never ceased at heart to be, Pretender knows that he can expect no love in a relationship, and openly says that he wants no friendship to last. Relationships must now be kept at a strictly commercial, professional level. The woman, paid for her professional services ("so is darling hold on to this") becomes merely an obstacle in the path of the departing customer.

There is nothing there, total void: no pretence at, not even the ghost of sentiment. In a way this is as bleak a situation as any in, say, Jean-Paul Sartre's *Nausea*. Yet, in all its dryness, there is a clear, cynical laughter which is less at "them gals now-a-days" than at himself and the process of time that has brought him to this pass. Such harshly seen reality is the very opposite of masking and ego retrieval. In the first stanza the calypso offers itself as unpalatable advice to older men, to lay aside their masks and "Just face the facts and know yourself." So what Pretender claims to be offering in this dry, antiheroic confessional is self-knowledge, plain and acrid, and in the face of such withering self-knowledge, concerns such as the construction of masculinity lose their relevance.

A recurrent factor in all of these calypsos is that all explorations of masculinity seem automatically to imply a corresponding vision of a competing, contesting and opposing femininity. Pretender's persona, in fact, recognizes two types of female opponent: a young predatory type and an ageing female whose sexuality seems to have become as obsolete as that of her male counterpart. In the final stanza he explains:

Just as them young girls ain't business with me,
Well me ain't meddle with no ole lady

You make a date with them you bound to regret
They will tell you they coming, they can't reach yet
                    (Lord Pretender 1969)

Thus, while he has only a commercial relationship with the younger women, he has no relationship at all with the senior sorority. He declares in one chorus that "Mih flag flying at half-mast," beautifully blending the ideas of impotence and death, which are one and the same thing to the phallocentric mind. But, like Camus's Sisyphus, he eventually arrives at the consolation of a scornful laughter which can surmount all fates.[8]

Pretender's dry, rare, grotesque comedy, his laughter that verges on grimness, is almost matched in spirit by Duke's "Woop Wap", a calypso that mocks at the absurdly unequal contest of inadequate male and insatiable female sexualities:

Women are always ready
From the day they born
But a man has to get energy
When he has his task to perform
Go ahead, my friend, kill yourself with them
Pat your back and take all the praise
But then later on when you want your fun
You can't get your hand to raise
Not me!

Chorus
I'm a woop wap man and I done
I'm a woop wap man, next one.
Any woman that I meet
My love does be short and sweet
Woop! Wap! And I gone.
So long.
I getting mih pleasure
Just like everyone
But ah have mih measure

After that ah done
I know some men claim
They does get their fame
By the length o time they could stay
But look, that ain't true
Is the things you do
For the little time that you're there

Chorus
These thoroughbred women
We got here in town, (Good Lord!)
When you see you meet them
You got to make them feel that they young
But not me and dat
I does tell them flat
"Gal, watch me carefully
Because when I done
Duke ain't holding on
And waiting for nobody."

Chorus
Some men are so silly
They does boast and say,
"Ah had in some whisky
Ah nearly kill a girl yesterday."
But if they only know
That it can't be so
They put that talk on the shelf
The woman get more strong
And they ain't breaking down
So they only killing theyself.

Chorus
(Mighty Duke *c.*1960s)

"Woop Wap" deconstructs the image of the durable phallic hero, capable of fighting fifteen rounds with undiminished virility, which emerged from Sparrow's "Village Ram" (1964). Comparing the third stanzas of the two calypsos, one finds Sparrow's protagonist willing and able to service the big, strong and fearless city women with such success that he is now advertising for extra emergency work, while Duke's "woop-wap man" refuses to engage with the same posse of thoroughbreds. The persona of "Woop Wap" does not quite reject the phallus as a yardstick for measuring manhood, but he recognizes a futility in the uneven sexual contestation of man and woman, a vast difference in the nature of the two sexualities, and views as folly the attempt by men (like Sparrow's Village Ram) to triumph in the sexual battle. Male sexual excess, the narrator of "Woop Wap" maintains, will eventually lead to impotence while female sexuality, it assumes from line one, is inexhaustible. In the face of such devastating and emasculating "truth", Duke's protagonist recognizes the impossibility of a phallic heroism and chooses instead the cynical, antiheroic prudence of the trickster.

Duke's task in this calypso resembles Sparrow's dilemma in "Ten to One" (1959). In both instances there is the necessity to present as heroic a situation in which the great warrior turns tail and escapes from the field of battle. Both narrators achieve their objective by showing the prudence, the "smartness", of the course of action they have adopted. Duke's protagonist, moreover, celebrates the pleasure that he selfishly enjoys in his short, sweet and – so he says – effective occupation of the crease. The Village Ram's major criterion – durability – is rejected out of hand by a protagonist who, like Pretender's in "Move Yuh Foot", harbours no illusions about the limits of male sexuality. In both calypsos the protagonists recognize the absurdity of phallocentricity: the older man because he is no longer possible to perform, the younger one because male performance is viewed as inadequate in the face of female voracity. In neither calypso is the woman acknowledged or validated as a person: in both she is contemptuously nullified and discarded. And both calypsos, with their hard laughter, are typical expressions of how this vulnerable, stoical, dried-out and resilient masculine sensibility has learned to cope with its many inadequacies, not the least of which has been its inability to satisfy not only female sexual appetite but also its own impossible criteria for heroism.

Female Calypsonians and the Masculine Myth

If the calypsonians of the 1930s and 1940s operated in a context where
female singers were few – Lady Trinidad, Lady Baldwin, Lady Beginner,
Lady Iere, Peggy Daniels – and virtually incapable of providing a critique of the hundreds of chauvinistic songs pouring out of the men's
room, the calypsonians of the 1960s and 1970s, whose works have just
been analysed, were functioning in a steadily changing context. By the
early 1970s, Sparrow, Duke, Shorty and Kitchener were sharing the stage
with Calypso Rose, Singing Francine, Calypso Princess, Lady Excellence,
Singing Diana, Lady Divine and a few other female singers whose presence, though still relatively small, was significant. What were the women
saying while the men were recycling their ambiguous versions of the
phallic myth? What impact did their presence have on the construction
of masculinity in calypsos?

Calypso Rose won her first Calypso Monarch title in a Virgin Islands
competition in 1963 where, she says, she defeated eleven male competi-
tors with her composition "Cooperation" (Ottley 1992, 6). She sang in
Kitchener's tent in 1964 and joined Sparrow's Young Brigade in 1967.
She entered the calypso arena on the terms of encounter that were dic-
tated by the dominant male singers of the time. Patterning her performance style on Sparrow, she presented her songs with similar gusto and
bounce. She also sang on similar themes, acting as counterpart to the
male singers, and was in those early days dubbed the "Queen of Smut"
by the *Trinidad Guardian* and *Evening News* (Ottley 1992, 5).

If Sparrow celebrated the triumphant and rampant sexuality of
"Lawa", the warrior-king-cocksman-lover archetype, Rose responded
by singing songs such as "You Must Come Back to Rose", "The
Wrestler", "The Sweet Nest" and "What She Go Do", all of which celebrated female appetite and mocked at male sexual inadequacy. A summary of the plots of some of Rose's early calypsos should illustrate how
thoroughly she created the persona of warrior-woman who pits her
sexuality against that of male antagonists. In "You Must Come Back to
Rose", this persona presents the male-female sexual encounter from the
point of view of that stock figure of male calypsos, the "ugly" woman

who, sexually exploited by males, learns a kind of obeah by which she ensnares the desire of the male protagonist. Rose's persona declares that she "ain't got no beauty, money or property", the conventional catalysts of male desire, but she has her own magic which makes her desirable:

> When ah take a piece of mih clothes
> And boil it up in spice and clove
> And ah pass the scent by your nose
> You bound to come back to Rose
> > (Calypso Rose 1969a)

Rose's persona triumphantly accepts and celebrates the role of Sparrow's much-despised Melda of "Obeah Wedding" (1966), or of the protagonist of Nap Hepburn's famous "Marriage Recipe".

"Rosie Darling" (1969) is an early protest against the sort of men who would, in Singing Sandra's classic statement two decades later, come to be known as "sexy employers". Rose's persona applies for a job and receives the reply: "Come tonight, I will give you work." In "Lemme Lone" (1969) she dismisses a male companion who beats her, with the command: "Reprobate, get out from me gate." In "The Wrestler" the persona is a female wrestler who delights in squeezing the life out of her male opponents. Like male warrior-lovers, she has her boast – "What goes up it bound to come down" – and advertises her credentials as she flings out her challenge:

> If you strong like a lion
> And I hold you, you bound to bawl
> You could be strong like a concrete wall
> You got to fall
> > (Calypso Rose 1969b)

All of these songs appear on the same album alongside the even more risqué "Palet" and a defence of her calypsos, "What Is Smut". Similar themes recur on other albums. Where her male counterparts sing about their many simultaneous affairs, Rose counters with "A Woman Must Have an Outside Man" (or "Whe She Go Do?"). Women, Rose argues, get respect only when they rebel. No one man can really satisfy a woman sexually, and any woman who has to contend with male impotence or weakness should supplement her diet with an outside man.

If male calypsos reify women and view them as a list of body parts, Rose reverses the tendency in "Flesh by the Waist":

> If they cutting up a man's body
> Just like a piece a steak
> What part o dat body
> A woman should take?
>> (Calypso Rose 1973)

Rose's choice, in this grotesque calypso where a man is reduced to flesh, pure and simple, is the man's penis. It is instructive to read this calypso against Sparrow's "Congo Man" (1965) of a few years earlier and Puppet Master's "The Greatest Love" (1998), which was sung nearly three decades later. Read against "Congo Man" Rose's calypso reverses the representation of woman's body as so much meat to be devoured by a cannibal, by substituting the body part that is most celebrated in the phallocentric calypso. In the process the phallus is not valorized, as it will be in Puppet Master's "Greatest Love", or as it was in Sparrow's "Cockfight" (1969). It is reduced and isolated by the mocking scrutiny of a woman's eye.

Repeatedly, Rose's calypsos of the late 1960s and early 1970s deconstruct macho notions of masculinity by portraying men as weak, impotent, parasitic and brutal. "Bend Down Low" protests against awkward positions in love-making and the brutality of some macho men:

> As soon as ah reach home
> I had to rub myself wid Sloan
>
> These men too advantageous
> They want it by brutal force
>> (Calypso Rose 1972a)

In "Don't Go" the female persona is portrayed in the act of leaving a man who drinks heavily and mistreats her. In "Rose You Leave the Man" she declares, "Me and Duncan couldn't agree / So ah leave him immediately" (Calypso Rose 1972b).

In "How the Bed Break Down" (1972) she reacts to signs of her companion's infidelity by putting him out of the house. Here the woman is the breadwinner, whose job involves lengthy periods of absence from the island. The price she exacts from her sweet-man lover is the one that most reduces his image in the eyes of other macho men: faithfulness to one woman.

Rose, whose discourse on sexuality offended the prudes as much as did that of the male calypsonians whose every theme and image she contested, had to face the same condemnation. In an interview with Keith Smith (*Express*, 27 February 1977) she stoutly defended the vigour of her stage performance:

> These days they saying I too vulgar. Vulgar, mih foot. When I get on that stage and I hear the bass-pedal drumming and the bass strumming, I does just start to move. I tell yuh I find myself doing some steps on that stage that I swear I know nothing about. The music just takes over mih body and Rosie on the move.

Performance, then, is spirit-possession, the manifestation of the orisha in and through the body of the celebrant. Sex is, likewise, a supreme instance of this same flow of energy. As Keith Smith explains,

> Rose has this thing about "voices". A strong Spiritual Baptist, she nearly killed me once by declaring that "[she] dedicated every single one of her tunes to the Lord – even mih sex songs". At that time she had said: "So sex ent natural? The Bible say 'be fruitful and multiply.' So how we go multiply without sex? God made Adam and Eve – so how you think the next generation come? You really believe is an apple dey eat in truth? There is a time and a place for everything. They say you mustn't sing and you mustn't dance and you mustn't wine. But who more hypocritical than them?
>
> "If you read the 150th psalm, it says: 'Praise the Lord with timbrels and songs and dances and trumpets and horns.' That kind of bad-john God they talking bout now, I ent in that, nuh. You ent see even the big churches want to bring steelband and calypso in church? Long-time they had people in the dark ages but now the people see the light."

Rose defends herself by firmly rejecting the "bad-john God" of both Protestant and Catholic asceticism, the joyless, cold patriarch of

Calvinism that so deeply irked the poet William Blake, who invented names for him such as Urizen and Nobadaddy. While Rose never identifies "they" or "them", the reader recognizes Rose's critics as the same people whom Sparrow in "The Outcast" termed "society", and whom he accused of "false pride", explaining his use of the term thus:

> The reason why I say "false pride" is simply thus:
> They enjoy the song, they enjoy the music, but still they so damn prejudice
> And they bracket you in a category so low and mean
> Man, they leave the impression that your character is unclean
>   (Mighty Sparrow 1964b)

Rose does not only attack "them", her critics from straight society, but she also claims and affirms an alter/native way of encountering and celebrating the rhythm and energy of life that she sees as natural to and inherent in human sexuality, and whose pulse she feels in the rhythm of calypso. The God of fertility, renewal, reproduction and replenishment that she acclaims is African, even though he wears a Judaic mask and speaks to her through the words of the book of Genesis. He is the spirit whom we identified in queh-queh songs as indicative of something deeply ancestral beneath the hard crust of imposed European attitudes, systems and beliefs. What Rose terms her "sex songs", therefore, are as much offerings to this creator-god, Olodumare, as her more conventionally religious songs such as "If You Want Pardon" (1972), "Navidad" (1972) or "Hold on to the Balance Wheel" (1982).

There is a clear parallel between Rose's firm rejection of what she terms a "bad-john God" of cold authoritarianism who censors human desire, for a more "natural" ancestral god who accepts human joy in sexuality as an affirmation of his presence, and her persistent rejection of a succession of bad-john lovers who drink heavily, beat women, indulge in a rough sex that is close to rape and, in addition, exist like parasites off the earnings of the working woman. In both instances Rose is attacking masculinity as the self-obsessed imposition of male will on the human, and especially the female, capacity for delight and pleasure. Both bad-john God and bad-john Man are indifferent to the female response. Or rather, bad-john God is positively hostile to it, while bad-john Man ignores it (as Duke and Pretender recommend that it should be ignored) in the interest of his own self-fulfilment.

Rose is, however, a celebrant of the female response. Hence, in "The Pudding", Rose, with a frankness reminiscent of queh-queh songs, proclaims her relish for black male sexuality:

I just had to listen
When the pudding man bawling puddin
He does come right in front me door
And I getting the hot pudding ever more
Is the sweetest I ever get
And up to now I never regret

Chorus
Every morning, every evening
The pudding man passing
And I only eating
If you see the man
With the pudding in he hand
Pudding all round he waist
Is the sweetest I ever taste
                    (Calypso Rose 1968)

Having eaten pudding before from Chinese, Indian and Portuguese men, Rose has developed a preference and an uncontrollable craving for black pudding:

I stop eating sausage
From the time pudding in the village
And I could be sick in bed
As I hear "Pudding" I open me bread.
                    (Calypso Rose 1968)

While this calypso at first glance seems to be no more than a female version of phallus worship, it is different from male phallocentric calypsos in its focus on a woman's response. Its mask is simple and thin, almost no mask at all, yet the calypso works, making perfect sense on both the literal and figurative levels. It also teases the listener with its use of the "eating" metaphor, with the phrase "He does *come* right *in front me door*" and the near perfect final line, "As I hear 'Pudding' I open me bread."

Having succeeded with the pudding metaphor, Rose turned to that of the "palet". This time it is female persona "Rose" who is the vendor of palets or iced milk lollies, and it is her joyful cry that is heard in the chorus as she invites customers to buy and suck her palet. If "The Pudding" hints at fellatio, "Palet" is suggestive of cunnilingus. The two calypsos are connected by the word/idea of "sweetness", an apt taste-metaphor for the feeling of sexual gratification that Rose is seeking to convey. It is only when one considers the enormous pressure that was placed on the evolving Sparrow in the 1956–66 decade, when he spear-headed the sexual revolution in calypso, that one can appreciate the degree to which Rose, as a woman, was treading on forbidden ground. For not only was she bringing female response and female desire into the open, but she was also singing on the tabooed subject of oral sex at a time when this was regarded as the sort of "nastiness" that only pros-titutes and pimps indulged in.

Oral sex, although a covert theme in calypso for decades, was con-sidered to be a vehicle of male effeminization. Celebrated in Sparrow's "Sixty Million Frenchmen" (1968) as a novelty in Trinidad, it had already been hinted at in Kitchener's "Ah Bernice" (1947) nearly two decades before, and in Sparrow's "Mango Vert" (1959) and Melody's "Michael" (1958) of the same era. But the classic male calypso about sex, as has been illustrated above, was about the erect phallus and its ability to outlast the sexual act. The Village Ram turned heavyweight boxing champion of the world must still remain standing after fifteen gruelling rounds. "Mih boy" is an insomniac who gets up in the night and cannot be easily put to sleep. There was no room in these calypsos for either the reified woman or her response. Sparrow's "Mae Mae/May May" (1960), "Wood in the Fire" (1968) and "Sixty Nine" (1962) are possible exceptions here. Shorty – "The Art of Making Love" (1973) – and Brigo, too – "Play with Your Woman" – place the woman's response at the forefront in their instructional calypsos.

Rose's "Palet" was taken by one calypsonian, the Mighty Spitfire, to be a lesbian challenge to male machismo. "Palet" was, after all, a call for softness and sweetness that ran counter to the traditional male emphasis on stiffness, hardness and even the sadist's ability to inflict pain. (See, for example, Sparrow's "Sa Sa Yea" [1968], in which a pretty Martiniquan girl is reduced to "moaning and groaning in pain", and his "Cockfight" [1969], where his champion cock, fed on red-hot guinea peppers, is ready to cut and slash "like Jack the Ripper".) Spitfire, taking up Rose's challenge to her customers to purchase and lick her palet at ten cents a suck, introduced himself as a roast-corn vendor in "Roast Corn for Rosie". His chorus was a grim warning:

> Sell your palet, Rosie,
> I selling roast corn
> Darling when you miss me
> Is St James ah gone
> I goin lick out she palet
> Sparrow tell me it sweet
> But ah hope she don't break she teeth
> When ah give she roast corn to eat
> > (Spitfire n.d.)

The erect and unbendable penis as a roast corn-cob has that hint of sadism that is never far removed from the phallic fable. If Rose's cunnilingus will effeminize the male, Spitfire's fellatio promises/threatens to be painful castigation for the woman who dares match her softness against the corn-cob's hardness.

Among the female calypsonians who responded to the challenge of male machismo was Calypso Princess, whose first encounter with the entertainment world had been as a belly dancer. In 1972 Princess was advising women to "horn your man", in the calypso of the same name. Five years earlier, in "I Want a Good Husband", she had described her futile quest for a dark, handsome, broad-shouldered, two-hundred-pound man capable of satisfying her sexual appetite. She is prepared to pay for the services of such a man, with both her own weekly salary from the calypso tent and that of her husband, the calypsonian Blakie – the reputed "warlord" of calypso who had gained a reputation for violence. While the unfaithful woman was a recurrent stereotype in the calypso, the era of the 1960s was perhaps the first time that the demeaning stereotype had been appropriated by the woman as a vehicle for her rebellion against restricting patriarchy.

In "We Jamming" (1977), Calypso Princess assumes the mask of a Carnival reveller who seeks the freedom of absolute abandon in her masquerade style. Alluding to Kitchener's social and aloof middle-class masquerader, Mrs Harriman, who, bound up in racial and class snobbery, lacks the ability to enter the spirit and surrender herself to the passion of the mas, Calypso Princess pronounces her own manifesto for Carnival/sexual performance:

> I want a man to hold me tight from behind
> And keep jamming all the time
> While ah shaking meh body line
> I must be coming backwards
> And he must be coming forward
> I am a masquerader
> I ain't playing sailor
> And fraiding powder
> I must be winin
> And he must be chucking, chucking
> While the music jamming
> Nobody ain't digging
> He chucking and ah wining, he chucking, ah wining
> He chucking, he chucking, he chucking, he chucking
> (Calypso Princess 1977)

Here again is the female counterpart to the sexually aggressive male of the age of Sparrow, and her manifesto of desire is an open challenge to the warrior-king-cocksman. The same challenge was being issued by Lady Excellence, whose "Master Johnny" (1972) is a complaint against men who cannot satisfy their women:

> Anytime you feel you is a townman
> Don't worry with countrywoman
> Countrywoman hard
> They will work you right round they yard

When sleeping time come
Remember is you wha gone
        (Lady Excellence 1972)

The town (tongue) and country (cunt-ry) pun would resurface a decade later in Poser's "Town Man" (1982). In "Master Johnny" the female persona seems to harbour the same reservations as her male counterparts about males who practice oral sex in preference to vaginal: that is, males who in the calypso's straightforward code are more interested in town than in country. It is also possible that Lady Excellence's real complaint is against males who demand fellatio, then lose the potency necessary for fulfilling their women's extensive appetite and desire to be penetrated: "Man you begging, wake up Master Johnny / Johnny done dead already." "Master Johnny" is not the name of the man, but of his penis to which he is reduced, after having constructed his masculinity around that organ.

There is evidence in the remainder of this loosely constructed calypso that Lady Excellence has no real objection to male tenderness or to cunnilingus. Her real target is the self-deluded lover who simply frustrates a woman while pursuing his own phallic fantasy. In stanza two she enumerates three types of lover, of whom the expert town/tongue man is clearly the most satisfying:

Some of them so old and squingy
But still they want to join matrimony
They looking for young girl at fifteen
They don't know is they own self they killing
Some of them so rough
They don't know how to treat a girl soft,
Some of them, they strong
But still they know how to use they tongue
Some of these men, they are really good
They use their tongue as a piece of wood
And when they hit you, you boun' to bawl
You know from your eyes the water must fall
        (Lady Excellence 1972)

Clearly there is confusion here in how the woman conceives her ideal lover. Part of her construction seems to be phallocentric in that it valorizes the conventional cocksman, while another part, a seemingly truer part, abandons the amazonian mask of hard country woman, and succumbs in tears, or at least in water, to the probing penis-like tongue ("They use their tongue as a piece of wood") of a lover who blends the strength of the conventional macho man with the gentle consideration of the female response that machismo is programmed to scorn.

It is not clear whether the pressure of these women had any immediate effect on how the male singers constructed masculinity. It is possible that the women's aggressive response to the phallocentricity that they encountered both reinforced machismo and set it at bay. Certainly, a warning is sounded in Sparrow's "Don't Back Back", the Road March of 1983, which sounds like an answer to Calypso Princess's taunting challenge, "I must be coming backwards / And he must be coming fowards." Baron's "The Jammer", Duke's "Thunder" (the 1987 Road March), Scrunter's "Ah See Yuh" (1986), Beckett's "Teaser" (1991), Rudder's "Carnival Ooman" and "Winin Season" (1995), among other songs, all acknowledge the power and the presence of this new, self-confident and sexually aggressive woman who, in her most advanced incarnation as the Carnival Ooman, is a bacchant filled and strengthened with the adrenalin of Carnival. Thus possessed, this woman retaliates against her violent spouse with an even greater violence, sends him "straight to Casualty", then dons her jeans for Panorama.

Rudder's chorus acknowledges the freedom of this woman, who begins her celebration by defeating the warrior-king at home and continues it by unleashing her sexual energy against hapless males at the fête:

Now you're a Carnival Woman
Can't stop the baby, can't stop the girl
Carnival Woman, freest of women in all the world
I hear how you fling it, you cock, it, you throw it, you jam it
Then you wheel and tumble down
But woman it's yours
Then you jam a man against the wall

And you start to give him pound
The crowd bawl "Advantage"
That's a Carnival Woman
Man, you dealing with a Carnival Woman
And the rest of the women telling she
"Make him pay, sister, make him pay
Turn him, twist him, give him pepper"
(Rudder 1996)

The Carnival Ooman is being played and possessed by the mas of her own suppressed rage. It is a rage that begins in her domestic situation as victim, hostage of her spouse's transferred aggression. She then becomes spirit and medium of the collective rage of her sisters at the fête, while the anonymous male becomes their scapegoat/victim.

The Carnival stage is restored to what it always has been since the time of "I Lawa": a gayelle for the contestation of identities via successfully negotiated space. The Carnival Ooman's womanist mission of vicarious revenge is not fulfilled in the confrontation with the man. She next turns on a youth:

I hear you leave him home to mind all the children
Now in the fete you explode a young boy's mind
You wine on the boy and make him hot like a pepper
And when the smoke start to come out he ears
You say, "that is fine. Go home now."
Play with all you Carnival woman
(Rudder 1996)

The Carnival Ooman is represented as the archetypal emasculator unmasked, and the final line of the calypso is filled with dreadful omen. This woman who in the 1970s became visible in Shadow's "Shift Your Carcass" and "I Come Out to Play" (1974), or Twiggy's "Take Your Hand Off Mih Property" or Explainer's "Don't Touch Mih Ras", simply as a person demanding her space and her right to the privacy of her body, metamorphized by the end of the 1980s into Tambu Herbert's frenzied posse of "No, No, We Eh Going Home" (1990), whose desire "to mash up the place and blow up the city" is articulated through military imagery and costume.

Already latent in Singing Francine's "Runaway" of 1979, this rebel woman, from the late 1980s into the 1990s, appeared in several guises: as the workplace protestor of Singing Sandra's "Die With My Dignity" (1989); as the retaliator against domestic abuse of Singing Sandra's "The Equaliser" (1998; see Rohlehr 1999); as the sexual rebel of Denise Belfon's "Kakalaylay", the United Sisters' "Donkey Dance" (1993) and, more recently, Natalie Yorke's "Do What You Want". Whether she masks as protestor or rebel against male sexism or as a confident celebrant of her own sexuality, the millennium woman is now open in the challenge she poses to the old patriarchal structures. "Do What You Want" intimidates the cocksman-lover by offering him full freedom to do what he wants with woman's body, while at the same time promising or threatening to provide a running report on the quality of the performance: "If it not long enough – ah go tell you / If it not strong enough – ah go tell you" (Yorke c.2001). What phallus, however well-inflated or intentioned, would not quail beneath such withering and contemptuous scrutiny? Normally the mission of the phallic hero is one of conquest and dominance in an encounter that is represented as warfare, stickfighting contest or boxing, cricket or wrestling match. By offering the phallus uncontested freedom of city and citadel, the woman has undermined the entire mission of conquest/control/dominance. By assuming the superior role of critic and overseer of the experience, the female subject objectifies, "others" and reduces her lover to observable specimen, winning the fight even before it has started.

New Man, New Woman, New Kaiso

Sex, violence and their progeny, violent sex, have long been resident in the calypso, in masked metaphorical disguise or in their naked form. Two major developments occurred during the 1960s and 1970s, the decades when masculinity as constructed by Sparrow, Shorty, Duke and others came under attack from the openly challenging voices of Rose, Princess and, to a lesser extent, Francine: the masks adopted by calypsonians became progressively thinner, and the reggae/dub/dancehall continuum emerged as a major and successful competitor for the attention of young people in the Caribbean. No tradition of masking had informed dancehall, where sex was unequivocally represented as sex and violence as violence. So that when the unmasking calypso began to interface with the nakedness of dub/dancehall, the result was a plainer, less subtle, and at times almost witless hybrid that has dominated the airwaves from the mid-1980s into the 1990s.

One always suspected an element of grandcharge in a calypso such as Kitchener's "Trouble in Arima" (1954), where the protagonist, threatened by a gang of thugs, waits for them round the corner with his cutlass; or in "The Bull" (1969), where Kitchener threatens to "kill a steelbandman". One felt that one was still in the era of the ritualized man-to-man violence of the stickfight. Even Sparrow's famous "Ten-to-One" (1959) and his other "bad-john" calypsos "Don't Touch Me" (1960), "Renegades" (1962), "Royal Jail" (1961), "Hangman's Cemetery" (1962), "Rebel" (1966) or "Bad Johns" (1973), most of which grew out of real occurrences, wear an aura of legend, of the ancient ritual testing and contestation of manhood. What was grandcharge up to the late 1960s became a serious thing in the 1980s where, untempered by wit, picong, or the ritual boasting of the past, violence played itself out in the wasteful, pointless maiming and murders that have continued to be the order of the day and are, in some circles, the new criteria for measuring manhood.

A similar metamorphosis could be observed in the calypsos whose theme was sex. By the 1980s the witty "Sixty Million Frenchmen" of the 1960s had become Crazy's "Suck Me Soucouyant" – simple, straightforward and stripped down to the naked thing itself. In less than a decade the United Sisters moved from Singing Sandra's moving rendition of Tobago Crusoe's "Die with My Dignity" (1989) and Lady B's winning Caribbean Song Festival composition "En Bataille La Woman" to the "Donkey Dance" (1993) and "Four Women to One Man" (1994), in which these four substantial sisters flaunt their sexuality in the face of some mookish, mawkishly reduced male. This is simply Rose's "Palet" unmasked, the flipside, too, of Sparrow's celebration of inexhaustible male sexuality, the village ewes emerging as the final response to the Village Ram.

After Kitchener brought Audrey's posterior into focus in 1979 with "Sugar Bum", there was no stemming the flood of Bum Bum, Boom Boom, Bam Bam, Bambalam, Boombooloom songs. "Four Women to One Man" was not only a direct response to Sparrow's challenging "The More the Merrier" of the previous year (1993), but also an omen of the revenge of the Bum Bum over the much celebrated and vaunted Big Bamboo. But "Four Women to One Man" was mild stuff when compared with dancehall queen Lady Shabba's declaration in "Hold Him and Wuk Him" of her intention to corner some hapless male and grind him to death in bedroom, bathroom and on the roof-top, declaring at the end of each round, "He think me done?" In Lady Shabba's version the woman assumes the role of the male rapist while the male becomes the cowering feminized victim, whose pleas for mercy serve only to stimulate the aggressor into even greater extremes of sexual violence. Lady Shabba's version celebrates the illusion of female sexual empowerment in much the same way as Sparrow's "Sa Sa Yea", "Cockfight", "Village Ram", "Congo Man" and "Mr Rake and Scrape" had, from the 1950s to the 1970s, celebrated the illusion of male sexual dominance.

A truer sign of the growing empowerment of women was the emergence in Calypso Rose's songs of the figure of the female breadwinner. This truly independent female controls her subservient man through the major contribution that she makes to the domestic economy. It is she who owns the house or pays the rent, she who leaves for a year to fulfil contracts abroad, she who dictates when the man can come visiting and when he can spend the night; and it is she who dismisses him as an expendable object when she is through with him. Calypsos in this vein are "Lemme Lone", "Rose You Leave the Man", "Duncan", "How the Bed Break Down" and "Don't Go". In these songs we sense a closeness between singer and persona that is as real as the closeness that Sparrow has sought to maintain between himself and the heroic protagonists of his calypsos. Rose had, in those early years of the 1960s and 1970s, begun to construct her version of the female hero, deconstructing in the process the prevailing masculine version of both the cocksman-lover and the noble breadwinner. The men of Rose's calypsos were drunkards, tricksters, crooks and women beaters, whose violence was a sign not of control at all but of compensation for the dreadful uselessness of their lives.

The man, thus unmasked and unmanned, had no place of refuge. The spirit of *sans humanité,* now appropriated by the emergent woman, pervaded the male support systems; the boys, the lime, the picong-throwing, the all-male sports club, the team, the all-fours, dominoes, draughts and whappie sides, and the calypso tent – an arena, if one can believe Boyie Mitchell in "The Way to Go" (1991–92), that is bedevilled with conflict, rivalry, pettiness, foul superstition and underhand practice. The wounded male abandoned by the matador woman was likely to become the laughing-stock of other males. Sympathy, compassion, the desire to bind up the broken hearted, are not the sort of responses that thrive in a world constructed on the rhetoric, fantasies and self-assertiveness of male egos in competition with each other.

The deepest humiliation is reserved for the man whose spouse has "horned" him "for people to see" (Prince Valiant *c.*1970s) thus making public his failure as a man in control of his "property". The impotence of such a man soon becomes public knowledge within the lime, where the tabanca-ridden lover learns that his pain is interpreted by "the boys" as evidence of his vulnerability. Sparrow's "Papa Jack" (1966) and Maestro's "The Show Must Go On" of the mid-1970s are both evidence of this, as is Tambu Herbert's "Yes Darling" (1986). In "Papa Jack" the narrator pretends to sympathize with his friend's sexual inadequacy and the threat that this poses to the survival of his marriage. (Jack's wife has been announcing to the world her deep dissatisfaction with Jack's sexual performance.) Beneath the surface of the narrator's response there is no sympathy, only a pitiless laughter which is directed at both his friend's waning male and the wife's unfulfilled female sexuality which, in spite of evidence to the contrary, is finally condemned as excessive and unnatural:

If was me and she keep carrying on this way
Making me romance look like child play

I'd tie a jackass in she bedroom for she birthday
          (Mighty Sparrow 1966)

In Maestro's "The Show Must Go On" the situation for the hurt male is even more desperate, to the point of his eventually contemplating murder. Yet his friend can offer no more than smug philosophizing and covert laughter at his plight:

He was crying
He was sighing
He start saying
He wife cheating
So I tell him, "Man don't complain
Just say, Girl, don't do that again"
You could always swallow your pride
Leh she do it till she satisfied.

Ah say, "Man the eternal problem
Is friends cutting against friends
The strong folks pushing the weak down
All going on so long
Long before you born
The show must go on."

2
He looked feeble
Like a weeble
"Are you able,"
I asked Noble?
The man tell me, "Don't be crazy"
How he loaded with energy
All the time she talking bout fight [words unclear]
How he does hackle [words unclear] she in the night

3
He was weeping
He ain't sleeping
Morning and evening
He drinking
The boy pants falling off he waist

Tabanca showing in he face
I had to tell him, "Man don't skylark
Chop in water don't leave no mark."

4

Then he tell me
He will kill she
But the baby
He does study
When she tell him the time is due [words unclear]
He come asking me what to do
Ah tell him kneel down in front o' she
Say, "Dou dou, horn me but don't leave me"
     (Maestro *c.*1975)

It is, of course, possible that the narrator's complacent, snide laughter conceals a fear; that his smugness is really a mask for his inability to empathize, since to empathize is to admit the possibility of the same thing happening to him. But there is a tragic pathos in this calypso, whose situation occurs every week in today's Trinidad. A man slowly disintegrates in front of a friend whose advice, as was Iago's to Othello, is salt rubbed in the raw wound of his emotions. What good does it do to the cuckold, who from the second line of the chorus ("Is friends cutting against friends") we conclude to have been horned by one of his friends, to be told that he is not the first cuckold in the history of mankind; that he should take his horn philosophically; that the misdeed of his spouse is as trivial and transient as a cutlass chop in water; and that he should kneel before and humbly submit to the woman who has horned him and is bearing his friend's child, since clearly he cannot live without her?

Man's Work

In Tambu's "Yes Darling" a man loses his job and becomes a house husband, dependent on his wife's salary. His wife uses her position of economic power to inflict on Tommy the same daily humiliation that he had formerly – as man – inflicted upon her. Tommy's friends "kicks off", that is, jest at his expense. "Yes darling", Tommy's servile response to each of his wife's demands, is the mark of his emasculation. Beneath this calypso lies the assumption, the stereotype, of marital relationship in the Caribbean as relentless conflict in which men and women struggle for power and control – what Chaucer termed *maistrie* – in the domestic politics of their lives. In such a situation the man who loses control and power is open to both the revenge of his spouse and the mocking laughter of his male support group, for whom his anguish is merely "kicks".

If, as Andrew Tolson asserts in *The Limits of Masculinity,* "in Western, industrialized, capitalist societies, definitions of masculinity are bound up with definitions of work" (1977, 12), then Tommy's loss of his job has undermined the very foundation on which his masculinity is constructed. Neither Tommy nor his "kicksing" friends regard the domestic chores that he now has to perform as "real" work, that is, men's work, work at a job somewhere outside the home, work that affirms the male (of straight society) in his masculine role of breadwinner and controller of human and financial property. Part of Tommy's humiliation is clearly his feeling that somehow, the work that he is now doing has effeminized him.

This fear of "effeminization" runs deep in calypso culture. As far back as Atilla's "Women Will Rule the World" (1935) a calypsonian was predicting that men would find themselves baby-sitting and performing domestic chores if they did not "assert control" over their ambitious spouses. In 1973 Lord Coffee, a Guyanese calypsonian who had from the 1950s been singing in calypso tents in Trinidad, composed a calypso entitled "A New Life with Yuh Wife", in which he explored what he presented as the absurdities that would attend men doing "women's work" and vice versa:

> Since ah small ah hear from creation
> After man they create woman
> Since ah small ah hear from creation
> After man they create woman
> But now things change up entirely

How yuh don't know my girlfriend want to rule me
So ah told her last week Sunday
I plan a new kind of living for me and she

Chorus
Ah told she, "You work and pay the rent
I go wash the wares;
You buy the groceries
I clean upstairs
Ah doing all the housework, ah wouldn't bawl
And ah even carrying out Miss Mary and all."

2

Ah then told the young lady
She even got more shirt and pants than me
She watch me and started to groan
Ah said, "Even your hair and all cut like my own."
She said "That is the style what you scratching for?
It seems to me as if you looking for war."
I said, "I ent warring with you honey
You know ah always like to see [us] live happily."

Chorus
An ah told her, "You pay the light bill
Ah go cook the food
Ah go do a day's work when I'm in the mood
Ah scrubbing out the house, keeping the place tidy
Ah even washing out yuh buy one and get one free."
              (Lord Coffee 1973)

The aim of this calypso was to trivialize women's work, even when,
as in a later stanza, it involved waking up early on Sunday mornings
to go to market then "hurrying back home quick, quick to make tea"
(that is, prepare breakfast), present her husband with the Sunday newspapers and begin the preparation of the normally elaborate Sunday
lunch. Among the more "demeaning" chores enumerated by Coffee
were the carrying out of Miss Mary (the chamber pot/*pot
chambre*/po'/posie) and the washing out of his wife's "buy one and get

one free" (her panties). The laughter which greeted this last suggestion in the tent was probably the result of the absurdity perceived in this proposed reversal of gender roles. Washing, and worse, publicly hanging out the panties of one's wife, was deep, deep emasculation. The very suggestion was preposterous. Lord Coffee couldn't be serious. One notes the curious touch of Victorian prudery in Coffee's choice of euphemisms for chamber pot and panties, the suggested moral recoil from the ideas of defecation and sexual intercourse, or perhaps from the anus and the vagina.

This relationship between men's work and the construction of masculinity is all the more fascinating coming from a sector of society in which unemployment has always been chronically high. One reaction to the emasculation that derived from unemployment was a face-saving celebration of that very state. "I ain't working no where / Yet ah walking 'bout in mih silk and satin" used to be the boast of the old-time saga boys, survivors who lived off of women's labour and tried to represent such parasitism as the success of the trickster-hero. Adding insult to injury, the parasite then devalued the woman's labour on which his very survival depended. Such work he connected with the woman's magical power to emasculate. Thus, even when one seems to be dealing with a paradigm of masculinity that is far removed from the issue of male sexuality, one somehow returns to the phallus and to male castration fears; male *testeria,* as one woman has termed it.

Nowhere is this more evident than in Penguin's extremely popular "Soft Man" (1983):

Meh partner in a quandry
He willing to settle down in life
But want to get the recipe
As how to treat and to keep a wife
Ah tell him just treat them kind
And they would love you till death
But one thing he got to bear in mind
And never never forget.

Chorus

Woman doh like

Woman doh like *(twice)*

Woman doh like soft man

They want a man and not a worm

Responsible and concerned

A man who lays down his terms

A man who can stand up firm

Woman doh like

Woman doh like

Woman doh like soft man.

2

A woman would try to rule you

And if you sit down and take it calm

She mamaguy you and fool you

And say you are such a loving man

She spend every cent you make

Without consideration

And when you ain't have no more to take

She gone with a macho man.

Chorus

Woman doh like

Woman doh like *(twice)*

Woman doh like soft man

A man is supposed to lead

Supply all his woman's needs

Never let his yard get weeds

Dig the soil and plant the seeds

Woman doh like

Woman doh like

Woman doh like soft man.

3

Some men does play namby pamby

They sticking up in the house whole time

Cooking, cleaning, washing nightie

And fraid to go with the boys and lime

But as the years travel on
Dem same men women does hate
For woman does always treat with scorn
A man they emasculate.

Chorus
Woman doh like
Woman doh like *(twice)*
Woman doh like soft man
Not a man who does curl their hair
And put earrings in their ear
Very quickly say, "Yes dear"
When she frown, they shake with fear
Woman doh like
Woman doh like
Woman doh like soft man.

4

A man should be like a tower
Protect his household at any cost
He got to show strength and power
And show that he fit to be the boss
His children he must control
Doh make his woman look small
And if he live to a hundred old
She wouldn't leave him at all.

Chorus
Woman doh like
Woman doh like *(twice)*
Woman doh like soft man
You could be a little wild
But with discretion and style
Doh use too much tricks and guile
You is a man, not a child
Woman doh like
Woman doh like
Woman doh like soft man.

Soft man – would never get
Soft man – women's respect
Soft man – everybody
Does call him stupidee
Soft man – look like a fool
Soft man – get ridicule
Soft man – Aye! Look at he!
Softee! Softee!
Soft man, soft man, soft man
Soffee, Soffee, Soffee, Soffee
                    (Penguin 1983)

Penguin received the inspiration to compose "Soft Man" one after-noon in St Eustatius after a conversation with a waitress on male-female relationships. He says:

> She was very talkative on the topic. She said she couldn't stomach the num-ber of "sorf man" around and by "sorf men" she stressed she meant men who lacked will-power. She expressed total disgust with the situation and deeply regretted that men were not as strong in will as in the days of her father. (*Sunday Guardian*, 24 April 1984)

The main content of the calypso's four stanzas grew out of the inspira-tion he received in that conversation. The choruses, he says, were a sum-mary of several other conversations he held with female friends, all of whom he asked to provide their definitions of a "soft man":

> So I went around to them and asked some what their concept of a "sorf man" was. I asked others to tell me what their concept of a macho man, a real he-man, was. Thus the chorus of "Sorf Man" is made up of the responses I received from my lady friends. This is one of the reasons I am so annoyed when people see purely sexual connotations in the calypso. In the responses I got, only one woman mentioned the sexual aspect of being a "sorf man". Most of them simply interpreted the term to mean the man had a serious per-sonality defect. (*Sunday Guardian*, 24 April 1984)

It is enlightening to know that these constructions of the soft man are all based on the responses of Penguin's female friends, and that the soft man is being read against his opposite, the "macho man", the "real he-man". Penguin's 1984 audiences certainly did seize on the ambiguous connotations of the word "soft" which on the one hand suggested "gentle, mild-mannered, weak" and on the other "flaccid, impotent, sexually incapable". Both connotations are skilfully built into the calypso to allow the calypsonian room to proffer the more "innocent" interpretation; room that Penguin obviously needed for his "defence" of the calypso from those who censured him for having composed it.

Certainly the metaphor of the man keeping his yard free of weeds, soil well dug-up and planted with seeds is advice – and quite conventional calypso advice – about man's sexual responsibilities. It is advice that locates the phallus at the centre of the marital relationship. Such advice has been public wisdom and can be heard in the youthful Stalin's "Women Love" (1972) as in old Pretender's "Recipe for Harmonious Living" (1975) and mature, forty-year-old Sparrow's "No Kinda Man at All" (1975). "Soft Man" can be located in this tradition of "counselling" calypsos, where the calypsonian functions as a wise man transmitting the received folklore and wisdom of the tribe to a younger or less experienced generation. The text of "Soft Man" is meant to be advice to a man, the narrator's close friend, who is thinking of getting married and seeks "a recipe [for] how to treat and to keep a wife".

At its "innocent" – that is, non-phallic – level, the level at which Penguin seems to want his listener to read this calypso, softness is equated with male domesticity, a willingness to do housework, a choice of the home over the male lime with "the boys". Curiously, the real man is one who will protect his home at any cost, although, apparently, it is more manly for him to do this from the precincts of the lime. Cooking, cleaning, washing nightie is namby-pamby behaviour and no part of how either this calypso constructs or the women whose opinions are contained in it construct masculinity. Masculine qualities are, in order of appearance:

1. *kindness* in how one treats a woman, although not so much kindness that the man might appear to be soft;

2. *responsibility, firmness* and a certain *authoritarianism* by which the man will lay down his terms (little or no discussion is implied here; such might be interpreted as unmanly);

3. *the ability to stand up firm*: presumably, to hold firmly to a position or opinion that one has adopted; or to stand up against wrong, injustice or anything that fails to meet one's standards (in addition, this criterion implies the less innocent and thinly concealed meaning of phallic potency, a criterion that Penguin says was stated by only one woman: he did not ask Lady Excellence or Calypso Princess, the latter of whom, in "I Want a Good Husband" [1967], had specified strength, height, physique, condition, good looks, a size commensurate with her own "circus horse"–type dimensions and the ability to make her bawl when he squeezed her, in a way that her "short and small" companion, Lord Blakie, could not);

4. *an implied refusal to be ruled, mamaguyed or fooled* by a woman's pretence that softness and timidity in a man are really evidence of his loving nature (a man should not allow himself to be taken in by the feminist text or interpretation of behaviour);

5. *sexual competence, fertility*: a constant watering of the garden (or Sparrow's "Lucy Garden" [1961] or Shadow's "The Garden Want Water" [c.1989]);

6. *the ability to be a leader and provider;*

7. *the refusal to become emasculated* (Penguin's word) by woman's work and fixed role (indeed, the calypso implies that the woman is responsible for such emasculation, even though it portrays as soft a male who clearly chooses and loves domesticity over that world outside the home that has conventionally been regarded as the domain of both men's work and men's play, and has therefore been of far greater importance than the home in such men's construction of their masculinity);

8. *refusal to give into her desires, to be a yes man*: a man must "lay down *his* terms," not listen and submit to those of his spouse;

9. *strength, power* and *the ability to protect* and defend his household;

10. *control over children;*
11. *respect for his wife;*
12. *discretion* in the commission of small indiscretions.

A man, then, must choose between two equal and opposite models for male performance: he could be a soft man and total fool, or a real man – a man-in-control. No other calypso provides as full a delineation of the patriarchal mind-set: its hard, cynical, worldly wisdom in which, according to Penguin's account of the origin of this calypso, women fully acquiesce; its authoritarian narrowness (which is certainly reflected in the leadership styles of a succession of political figures); its fear of effeminization which, like masculinity, it defines in the narrowest of stereotypical terms. What "Soft Man" is saying, in essence, is that women love men who can dominate them sexually and otherwise and scorn men whom they can dominate. Relationships between men and women are recognized to be about power. It also implies that men, despite the assumed naturalness of their right to dominate, also scorn the women they dominate, but call that scornful dominance by another name: love. And if scorn is the single genuine factor in such relationships, then men who find themselves in the "aberrant" and "unnatural" situation of being dominated by women must have a deep scorn of themselves.

Homotextuality in Calypso

This brings us to another issue: the possible connection between rigid constructions of masculinity, male fear of effeminization and homophobia. Given a corpus of several thousands of calypsos – between four hundred and six hundred new songs are composed each year now – the number of songs on the theme of homosexuality has been relatively small. I can think of about twenty-five, and in some of these the theme is barely implied through metaphor. Killer's "Cobo and the Mule" (late 1940s), sung by Melody as "Seagull and the Mule", where the cobo (corbeaux) or seagull affixes itself to the anus of the mule, may be a gross caricature of male homosexual intercourse. Atilla's "Donkey City" (1944–45) involves in its obscure imagery two animals: a mule and a donkey. "And the mule said to the donkey, 'Saga boy don't tarry behind me, donkey Whoa!'" again implies homosexual intercourse, or its unwelcome imminence.

The theme kept popping up in the early songs of Sparrow: "Family Size" (1957) and "John and the Goat" (1956) which, like Wonder's "Ramgoat Baptism" (1947), is about bestiality rather than homosexuality. The two ideas are, however, fused in the folk imagination. "Family Size" deals with buggery and sadistic anal rape that was occurring in the mid-1950s. Melody's "Reply to Sparrow" (1958) contains the lines, "Sparrow walk like a girl / And his hair always press and curl", lines that imply homosexual tendencies. The point is that this was a picong calypso, and one of the most humiliating insults that could be employed to demolish the image that Sparrow had already begun to construct of warrior-king-cocksman-lover was that of "homosexual". Melody, too, "slicked" his hair in this period, in imitation of African-American singers and entertainers Cab Calloway, Nat Cole or Billy Eckstein. But picong easily converted the slicked hair conditioning into a sign of homosexuality.

Another Melody song in this picong series, "Sparrow Melody Horse Race" (*c*.1957), is worth mentioning. While on the surface this calypso seems to be about two race horses which had been named after these two popular calypsonians, Melody's narrative converts the horse race into a homosexual encounter in which he (Melody) plays the role of male and Sparrow that of female ("Sparrow is the she and I is the he"). Again, this is a picong response to Sparrow's devastating attack on Melody in his "Reply to Melody" where, citing Melody's "ugliness" and unhygienic habits, Sparrow refutes Melody's claim of having attracted more women than he:

> You wouldn't try some toothpaste once in a while
> To whiten your teeth and brighten your smile
> So when you say you have nice girl that ain't true
> Is only Gateway Elaine and them for you
>   (Mighty Sparrow 1958)

Among other representations of Melody in the calypso were those of fowl thief, cow impregnator, pickpocket, dracula, gossip-monger, liar, garbage and pimp.

In "Lucy Garden" Sparrow works as a gardener for a rich Jamaican woman. He waters her garden so well that her husband returns to find him still at work. The final line of the calypso sheds light on both why Lucy needed a "gardener" (that is, a lover) and why the husband was not enraged to have caught Sparrow in the act: "The husband want me to water he garden too." Anal sex, if not homosexuality, surfaces in "Elaine, Harry and Mama" (1964), where the insatiable Harry is expelled from the family for practising on Elaine. Mama sends him to "look for Hinds", a reputed homosexual, in order to satisfy his appetite.

Rose's "Man Doing It Too" is the first calypso by a woman on the male homosexual theme. Here the male homosexual is angrily condemned for "disgracing humanity" by "changing to female sex". The homosexual is viewed as a competitor for male attention: "It have some men playing women / Women getting hell to get a man" (Calypso Rose 1970). Rose resents the fact that the homosexuals in the city are mimics who imitate women in dress, coiffure, make-up, gait, gesture and speech, and agrees with the law that says they should be jailed.

Blakie's "Something Wrong" (1969) regresses to the Sparrow/Melody era in its employment of the homosexual tag as insult in a picong attack on Young Killer and Composer. Blakie charges that the reason why these two relatively junior singers were chosen to represent calypsonians at Expo '68 was because of homosexual relationships between themselves and members of the selection committee. "Homosexual", then, was a term of abuse sufficiently elastic to serve any grudge between one man and another. The rhetorical institution of picong still allowed men to test and measure their masculinity one against the other. Young Killer answered Blakie with the cruellest form of picong: that which is based on truth. He cited Blakie's many collisions with the law, including two terms in jail for theft, and concluded, "Something wrong with he!" No selection committee could risk choosing such a character to represent the country as the cultural ambassador that the calypsonian abroad had long seen himself as being.

Apart from Rose's "Man Doing It Too", the 1970s saw Emperor Selassie's "Two Man Friend" (1971), a "scandal" calypso about the extreme grief of one male parting from his male lover. Bomber's "Ma Ma Men" (1973) is a comic portrayal of "Ma Ma men confusion in Woodford Square". These Ma Ma Men have begun to fight over calypsonians, the calypso claims. "Shorty does tell me pass through he back door", claims one Ma Ma Man. Shorty, whose Love-Man image had been constructed in rivalry with Sparrow's, had become a target for mild picong. As had happened with the Melody/Sparrow picong contest of more than a decade earlier, the best way of attacking and reducing the macho-man image of a mocking pretender was via the homosexual taunt.

The homosexual male, clearly becoming more visible in the early 1970s, was caricatured in calypsos as a figure to be ridiculed and feared. The ridicule, indeed, was a mask for the apprehension calypsonians had begun to feel at this new openness of the gay presence and performance in the city. Cypher's "Who Is Who" (1973) sees Trinidad as being caught up in what was a current that was running through the whole world:

> You can't make out woman from the man
> Same pants, same kinda shoe
> They have you in hell to know who is who
>
> If a man see a woman take she for a man
> I can understand
> But if a man see a next man and take he for a woman
> That is confusion
> I'm sure some one will have to screel
> When steel start pointing at steel
> That will be bacchanal
> If it happen for the carnival

Cypher ends by issuing a warning to calypsonians to

> Try and keep out of jam session
> Let the public do their own thing
> Our duty is to make song and sing.
>   (Mighty Cypher 1973)

Calypsonians, celebrants of machismo and scoffers at softness as a sign of femininity in men, were almost uniformly intolerant and frequently contemptuous of homosexuals. Yet the recurrent and accusatory picong as well as the warnings against homosexuality suggest that some calypsonians had begun to recognize the symptoms of gay sexuality within their fraternity. Picong served as a vehicle for social control within the fraternity, but Funny's "Bowling Alley" (1974) hints, if there is any truth at all in its laughter, at the spread of both male and female homosexuality among calypsonians. New York affords them a freedom to play themselves not yet accessible on the more limited Trinidad stage. Funny names three prominent calypsonians along with fourteen other of "de boys and dem up by me" among the bowlers (bullers) who frequent New York bowling alleys. He, however, turns down all invitations to join their company:

> Imagine dey want a man like me
> To join de Bowling Alley
> But with dem big bowlers in town
> I can't make with my background
> De only indoor game for me
> Is Elaine and Emily
> I love me cricket and football
> Not me and bowling at all
> (Funny 1974)

This was also the era of Young Creole's "Sissy" (c.1975), another depiction of homosexual performance in the avenues and city squares. In this calypso a gay male expresses resentment at the teasing he receives from other – presumably heterosexual – males:

> Like is cuss you want me to cuss
> Take care a buss yuh face wid mih puss [purse]
> You too blooming fas' to psoots at me when ah pass
> (Young Creole c.1975)

Duke, named by Funny as one of the frequenters of New York's bowling alleys, would himself return from the United Kingdom with the marvellous news that "It's true what they say / London gay" ("London Gay" [1973]), and Merchant at the end of the 1970s would create his own narrative out of the then popular movie *Norman Is That You*. There, the stimulus to homosexuality is again the metropolitan city, which changes Norman utterly from what he was before – "a jack of all trades and a very good sportsman" – into another one of Trinidad's drag queens. Was Merchant singing his own life here? In the calypso he is the straight man who is deeply concerned about what has happened to his "good partner". Merchant would later contract AIDS and die in 1999 after a long, courageous struggle.

The least malicious anti-gay calypso was probably Dougla's "Man Nicer than Woman", of the 1963–64 period. Here a gay male argues with his straight friend that "it ain't got no woman in this world nicer than man at all". The noisy argument leads to both men's arrest by a female police officer and trial before a female magistrate. The gay man sticks to his position:

> Well he tell she,
> "Man nicer than woman, my honour,"
> The man still insist,
> "Saying 'woman nicer than man'
> That is stupidness."
> The magistrate then turn and tell him
> "Well ah think it would be only right
> Take six months in jail for having good sight
> You going to sleep with men every night"
>   (Mighty Dougla c.1964)

Here Dougla captures both the defensive anger of the straight male who seems to have no convincing response to his gay friend's claim that the male of any species of bird or beast is always more splendidly adorned by nature than his female counterpart. The straight male can only respond with loud invective, a sign that he is losing the argument. Dougla also depicts the malice and resentment of the two women, the policewoman and the magistrate – a phenomenon evident in Rose's contempt in "Man Doing It Too". The magistrate is the spokesperson for the society's desire to relegate the homosexual to the margins of society. As woman she enacts Rose's resentment at the homosexual male, an unwanted trespasser on the terrain of femininity and, by that token, an exile also from the society of "real men". The last line, "You going sleep with men every night", conveys the sexual revenge of spurned womanhood at this anomalous male who houses an imitation of the sensibility of a woman within the body of a man.

Young Exposer's "Pepper in the Vaseline" (1984) demonstrates how much contempt of gays had intensified in two decades. The sadistic imagination behind this song is unmistakable. The gay here is victim and scapegoat of straight society's rage and fear, a terror so deep that it attacks the very seat of gay sexual pleasure with the blistering pepper of retribution. There is no escaping the gloating joy of the narrator/voyeur, whose relish of the discomfiture of the two gay lovers proves him less healthy in mind than he assumes he is. Similarly, Cro Cro's "Lambie's Funeral" (c.1987) extracts a grotesque and macabre humour from the spectacle of "big big men" crying at the funeral of a murdered and reputedly homosexual concert singer and radio announcer, but justifies itself as a serious warning against the danger of AIDS:

People seeing this song as only bacchanal
But this song is also educational
I am teaching the young men of this nation
It could be fatal to get intimate with a man
We just lose Rock Hudson and Liberace
Ah don't want to see this thing spread through the whole country
AIDS is a serious disease, it ain ha no cure
I trying to help so why they gi'ing Cro Cro pressure for?

The City Council should start to clean up the Square
Remove all them Sodom and Gomorrah men from there
And all them boys who does walk with ring in their ear
Get a good insecticide and spray
You see we have to do something to stamp out this curse
Or else good good men like me going to have to walk reverse
So all you come out and help in the clean-up campaign
So ah wouldn't have to sing in them macomere clothes again

Having sung and performed the ultimate homosexual "bacchanal" calypso, one in which he dresses the part and caricatures the spectacle of men crying for their dead companion, Cro Cro presents his apologia for his performance. It is, he says, his small effort towards the AIDS awareness campaign and is directed at the young men of the nation whose existence he regards as a particularly endangered one.

As with Sparrow's attacks on prostitution in the mid- to late-1950s, when the dreaded diseases were syphilis and gonorrhoea, Cro Cro proposes a scheme for eradicating the disease by eradicating its carriers. If in Sparrow's clean-up campaign ("Keep the City Clean" [1959–60]) the targets were Marabunta Jean, Stinking Toe Doreen and Picky Head Eileen, in Cro Cro they are "all them Sodom and Gomorrah men". Both calypsos are infused with the spirit of scapegoating, Cro Cro's more desperately so since his antagonist is AIDS, an incurable (so far) killer disease, one that had by the late twentieth century achieved the same demonic status and evoked the same paranoia as had tuberculosis in the nineteenth and cancer in the earlier part of the twentieth century. Behind the bacchanal and the burlesque of "Lambie's Funeral" resides the spectre of Cro Cro's and the society's paranoia, and it is paranoia that inspires the clean-up campaign in which homosexuals, equated with vermin or disease-bearing insects, are targeted for eradication with insecticide. One is not far away from those songs of the 1990s in which a small but significant number of popular performers – General Grant, Buju Banton and Shabba Ranks among them – called for the murder of male homosexuals.

Anti-gay paranoia has on occasion masked itself as moral righteousness, with calypsonians assuming the patriarchal roles of prophets, warners and spokesmen for the same "straight" society that they more normally unmask and demolish with their reductive laughter. Thus Delamo, in "Sodom and Gomorrah", places homosexuality near the head of a long list of signs of apocalyptic disintegration taking place in contemporary Trinidad. What Delamo perceives, in essence, is that honest and responsible patriarchy has collapsed. Hence the politician; the minister of religion; the businessman large and small, white, Syrian, black or Indian; the officers of law and justice – all of them, ideally, exemplars of responsible patriarchy – have degenerated into agents of "avarice, greed and corruption". Read as sexual perversion and immorality, homosexuality is simply the worst of these signs of masculinity gone off track, deviating from the normal and natural and heading towards chaos. As the males in society lose sight of their divinely ordained roles of leadership, their women too, like Lot's wife, become pillars of salt, their eyes turned backwards on the perversions of the dying, burning city, not the least of which is its perverted sexuality.

> An Angel of Death visited Abraham
> way back in the scripture
> And said, "I would visit death and destruction
> to Sodom and Gomorrah
> But if in the city I find but ten
> righteous men there,
> Peradventure, my spirit would be pacified:
> both cities I would spare."
> But if that very Angel should come visiting
> here in my country
> Tell me if it could find but ten
> men of integrity
> Because avarice, greed and corruption
> is in control of this blessed land
> Social ethics forgotten, modesty downtrodden;
> the Angel may not find *one* man
> [in this whole island]
>
> *Chorus*
> For we are living in this modern
> Sodom and Gomorrah
> And very soon an Angel go visit we here
> in the near future
> So if your wife turn a pillar of salt
> I want you know that it is your fault
> And if the fire and brimstone fall down on we
> I know we are all guilty

2
If we would be judged also by our
standards of morality
Some ministers of religion and politicians would invite
damnation, most certainly
For they indulge in schismologies and bizarre
acts of homosexuality
Exploitation of our womenfolk in return
for meagre acts of charity
But then, men shall be lovers of themselves,
is what the scripture say.
That's why sodomy and acts of buggery
being more and more rampant today
In the past, if a man was on this scene,
of this evil he would be ashamed
But now, boldly to the forefront, these people are "gay"
and proud to carry that name.
They playing the skin game

Chorus
                (Delamo 1981)

Patriarchs and Role Models

Cro Cro's "Lambie's Funeral" and Delamo's "Sodom and Gomorrah"
are both concerned with the interface between sexual and national politics and the ways in which both dimensions of politics are related to
constructions of masculinity. The warrior-hero of the stickfight devolved
not only into the sportsman/boxer/athlete/footballer/cricketer, or the
lover/saga boy/cocksman/phallic hero/sexual athlete, or the singer/
artist/popular performer, but, as politics developed, into the figure of the
rebel, the political leader, the man-in-power. Other father figures are
the male head of a household, priest, pastor, schoolmaster. The calypso
does recognize and at times celebrate the leader, the rebel and the father
and, more often than not, these figures manifest qualities of masculinity that are quite similar to those of the warrior-hero. Penguin's "real

man" we saw, was quite an authoritarian figure in his household. He needed to be a sort of king, strong willed and in control of spouse and offspring.

There is a large body of political calypsos concerned with the quality of leadership and the figure of the patriarch. There are over one hundred and fifty devoted to the figure of Dr Eric Williams, first prime minister of Trinidad and "Father of the Nation," and there are hundreds more that focus on his twenty-five years of kingship. It should be relatively simple to extrapolate the theme of masculinity from these political texts. Other prime ministers – Chambers, Manning, Robinson, Panday – have come under constant, close and at times caustic assessment from calypsonians since 1981. The bulk of calypsos about Williams were involved in a rigorous and reductive criticism of his performance (Rohlehr 1998, 849–88). The pessimism of Delamo's "Sodom and Gomorrah" had something to do with the decline of the 1956 movement, as Williams gradually lost control over the process of postindependence politics.

Just weeks before Williams's death, during the 1981 Carnival season, Delamo had, in "Apocalypse", virtually predicted his demise. Sung in 1982 although recorded late in 1981, "Sodom and Gomorrah" resonates with the uncertainty and shock that Williams's death had engendered even in a poet who had foretold it. It was the unravelling of the fabric of twenty-five years of patriarchy, of kingship, of benevolent dictatorship, of arrogant masculinity in action. This is why "Sodom and Gomorrah" presents its pessimistic portrait of the time in terms of a collapsed masculinity. Politics and priesthood, national security, law and business were all major areas of men's dominance. Political rulership and moral leadership were masculinity in action. The decay of these domains between 1970 and 1980, so graphically chronicled year after year by Chalkdust, Stalin and Valentino (see Rohlehr 1992), was a decay in masculinity. Thus, the tendency of the post-Williams era has been less to celebrate the kingship of the leader than oedipally to attempt the erasure from historical record of one's political predecessor. Gomes had essayed the erasure of Cipriani and Butler; Williams had negated Gomes and relegated Butler to a footnote in the history of modern Trinidad;

Robinson had been accused of seeking to obliterate Williams's achievement. Manning had begun his truncated reign with the shutting down of major National Alliance for Reconstruction projects, and the present United National Congress regime (1995–2001), in the July 1999 local government elections campaign, focused a substantial part of its energies on the demolition, through picong and caricature, of the leadership profile of Patrick Manning. Politics as masculinity-in-action has proved to be little different from the traditional stickfight.

There is, however, one respect in which contemporary politics in Trinidad varies substantially from the stickfight paradigm. Loyalty and honour, a support of one's band to the death if necessary, were important values among stickfighters. Politics in the post-Williams era has been characterized by crossings and recrossings of the floor, and frog-hopping from party to party. This tendency has led calypsonian Chalkdust to conclude that there is little difference between "this thing called PNM" and "this thing called UNC" (Liverpool 1998). There is today far more loyalty among gangsters and criminals than among seekers and finders of high political office.

Thus, while it is still possible to hear the occasional praise-song for a great or significant political leader – Williams, Mandela, Shaka Zulu, Martin Luther King – one is more likely to hear songs such as Watchman's "No Heroes" or Duke's "No Role Models" (*c.*1998) or Chalkdust's "It Ain't Have No Man Again" (1985) or Rudder's "Another Day in Paradise" (1995), "Madman's Rant" (1996) and "The Savagery" (1998). Collapsed and dishonest patriarchy is the target of 3 Canal's "Talk Your Talk" (1999). In the midst of this widespread vision of a society without heroes, of men without qualities, of politics as a savage smash-and-grab game in which crime and law operate by the same value system and police are indistinguishable from thieves, the ancient cry of "come out in the road, warrior" (Chantwell 1997) is a note of hope, though as yet not strong enough to inspire either the restoration of the old archetype or the engendering of a new man for these new times.

Notes

1. Such male initiating rituals have received harshly deconstructive criticism in recent texts such as Miles 1992 and Macbride 1995.
2. For a close analysis of some of these cricket calypsos, see Rohlehr 1994.
3. Queh-queh, or kwe kwe, is described by Richard Allsopp (1996) as being of uncertain Afro-Guyanese origin. Gibson identifies several of the words used in kwe kwe songs as being of Kikongo origin.
4. There are variant versions of this verse, such as:

   Move a pah
   Mek cacki walk
   Move a pah
   Mek pokey talk.

   This version was shown to me by University of the West Indies linguistics lecturer Ian Robertson. I cite it because I am not certain that "pah" and "path" are really versions of the same word. Gibson's "path" could well be a correction towards a probable English equivalent of a totally differ-ent word.
5. This refers to two Trinidad and Tobago personalities, Mouttet and Morgan Job; the former is a business man and former president of the Trinidad and Tobago Chamber of Commerce, and the latter is a politi-cian representing a Tobago constituency.
6. Gigiree: jumpy, uneasy, nervous (Allsopp 1996).
7. This phase of calypso history is fully explored in Rohlehr 1990, 213–77. The Roaring Lion eventually fathered twenty-one children.
8. "The lucidity that was to constitute his torture at the same time crowns his victory. There is no fate that cannot be surmounted by scorn" (Camus 1955, 97–98).

References

Allsopp, Richard. 1996. *Dictionary of Caribbean English Usage*. New York: Oxford University Press.

Burns, Robert. 1966. *The Merry Muses of Caledonia: A Collection of Bawdy Folksongs*. Edited by James Barker and Sydney Goodsir Smith. London: Panther.

Caesar, Eugene (Puppet Master). 1998. "The Greatest Love". *Kaiso Gems 1998: Kitchener's Calypso Revue*. Crosby's Carotte, CD 28C.

Calypso Princess. 1977. "We Jamming". In *Calypso 1977*, edited by Leroy "Fathead" Williams. N.p.

Calypso Rose. 1968. "The Pudding".

———. 1969a. "You Must Come Back to Rose".

———. 1969b. "The Wrestler".

———. 1970. "Man Doing It Too".

———. 1972a. "Bend Down Low".

———. 1972b. "Rose You Leave the Man".

———. 1973. "Flesh by the Waist".

Camus, Albert. 1955. *The Myth of Sisyphus*. Translated by Justin O'Brien. London: Hamish Hamilton.

Chantwell. 1997. "Come Out in the Road, Warrior". *Street Party 2*. Rituals '97 Release, LP 2197.

Chen, Willi. 1988. *King of the Carnival and Other Stories*. London: Hansib.

Constance, Zeno. 1992. *Tassa, Chutney and Soca: The East Indian Contribution to the Calypso*. San Fernando, Trinidad: Zeno Obi Constance.

Cro Cro (Weston Rawlins). *c*.1987. "Lambie's Funeral". Lyrics transcribed from performance at 1988 King of Kings competition.

Crowley, Daniel. 1959. "Towards a Definition of Calypso". *Journal of the Society for Ethnomusicology* 3, no. 2 (May).

Delamo (Frank Lambkin). 1981 (performed in 1982). "Sodom and Gomorrah". B's Records, BRS 1014.

Frobenius, Leo. 1971. *The Black Decameron: Forty Erotic Tales from Central Africa*. London: Sphere Books.

Funny (Donric Williamson). 1974. "Bowling Alley", in *Trinidad and Tobago Carnival '74 Calypsos*.

Gibson, Kean. 1998. "An Analysis of Traditional Kwe-Kwe Songs". *Kyk-Over-Al* 48 (April).

Hill, Donald. 1993. *Calypso Calaloo*. Gainesville: University of Florida Press.

Hill, Errol. 1964. *Man Better Man*. In *Three Plays from the Yale School of Drama*, edited by J. Gassner. New York: E.P. Dulton.

James, C.L.R. 1963. *Beyond a Boundary*. 2d edition. New York: Vintage.

Khan, Ismith. 1964. *The Obeah Man*. London: Hutchinson.

Lady Excellence. 1972. "Master Johnny". In *Calypso '72*, edited by Walter Annamunthodo et al. San Fernando, Trinidad: Unique Services.

Layne, Lancelot. 1983. "Jamballasie Dance". *Kamboulay*. Tambu Bambu.

Lord Coffee. 1973. "A New Life with Yuh Wife". *Original Regal Calypso Hits '73*. Regal Calypso Tent, Port of Spain.

Lord Executor (Philip Garcia). 1938. "They Say I Reign Too Long". *Trinidad Loves to Play Carnival: Carnival, Calenda and Calypso from Trinidad 1914–1939*. Matchbox Calypso Series, MBCD 302–2.

Lord Melody (Fitzroy Alexander). 1958. "Reply to Sparrow". Balisier HDF 1003. Also known as "Sparrow Ugly Too". Cook 914.

Lord Pretender (Ulric Farrell). 1989. "Move Yuh Foot Leh Mih Pass" (1969). *The Living Legend: The Great Honourable Pretender*. Riddum Distribution Network, RDN 1256.

Lovelace, Earl. 1979. *The Dragon Can't Dance*. London: André Deutsch.

———. 1982. *The Wine of Astonishment*. London: André Deutsch.

Macbride, James. 1995. *War, Battering and Other Sports: The Gulf Between American Men and Women*. Atlantic Highlands, N.J.: Humanities Press International.

Maestro (Cecil Hume). *c*.1975. "The Show Must Go On".

———. 1977. "Bionic Man". *Anatomy of Soca*. KH Records, KDS-2014.

Mighty Chalkdust (Hollis Liverpool). 1996. "Stickman's Lament". *Best of Straker's: Ah Feel to Party*. Rounder Records CD 5066/67.

———. 1998. "Too Much Party". *Kon Kon Sah*. Strakers Record World, GS2399.

Mighty Cypher (Dillary Scott). 1973. "Who Is Who", in *Trinidad and Tobago Carnival and Calypsos*.

Mighty Dougla (Cephas Ali). *c*.1964. "Man Nicer than Woman". *Independent Trinidad and Tobago: All-Time Calypso Hits 1963–1964*. TELCO, TLl 5019.

Mighty Duke (Kevin Pope). *c*.1960s. *Woop Wap*. National Record Company, NSP 031.

———. 1969. "See Through". *Calypso "All Night Tonight"*. MCA Records MAP-S-1890.

Mighty Sparrow (Slinger Francisco). 1958. "Reply to Melody".

———. 1959. "Mango Vert". *Sparrow in Hi-Fi*. Balisier HDF-1009, Cook 1126.

———. 1964a. "The Village Ram". *The Outcast*. National NLP 4199.

———. 1964b. "The Outcast". *The Outcast*. National NLP 4199.

———. 1965. "Man Like to Feel". *Congo Man*. National Recording Co., NLP 5050.

———. 1966. "Papa Jack". *The Calypso Genius*. National Recording Co., NLP 8420.

————. 1975. "Cock of the Rock". *Cock of the Rock*. Camille LP 9038.

Mighty Terror (Fitzgerald Henry). 1966. "Steelband Jamboree". National Recording Co., NSP093.

————. 1979. "Callaloo Tonic". *Best of the Golden Voice, Terror*. MNE–001.

Miles, Rosalind. 1992. *The Rites of Man*. London: Paladin.

Ottley, Rudolph. 1992. *Women in Calypso*. Port of Spain, Trinidad: Rudolph Ottley.

Pearse, Andrew. 1956. "Mitto Sampson on Calypso Legends of the Nineteenth Century". *Caribbean Quarterly* 4, nos. 3 and 4 (March–June).

Penguin (Sedley Francis Joseph). 1983. "Soft Man". *Touch It*. Barbados: IBIS 003. Performance Carnival 1984.

Prince Valiant. *c.*1970s. "Benjamin".

Roach, Eric. 1992. *The Flowering Rock: Collected Poems 1938–1974*. Leeds: Peepal Tree.

Rohlehr, Gordon. 1990. *Calypso and Society in Pre-Independence Trinidad*. Port of Spain, Trinidad: Gordon Rohlehr.

————. 1992. *The Shape of That Hurt and Other Essays*. Port of Spain, Trinidad: Longman Caribbean.

————. 1994. "Music, Literature and West Indies Cricket Values". In *An Area of Conquest: Popular Democracy and West Indies Cricket Supremacy*, edited by Hilary Beckles. Kingston, Jamaica: Ian Randle.

————. 1998. "The Culture of Williams, Context, Performance, Legacy". *Callaloo* 20, no. 4.

————. 1999. "Working Towards and Then Beyond a Balance of Terror". Typescript.

Rudder, David. 1995. "Legacy". *Lyrics Man*. Lypsoland, CR 023.

————. 1996. "Carnival Ooman". *David Rudder: The Gilded Collection 2, 1990–1993*. Lypsoland CR024.

Spitfire. N.d. "Roast Corn for Rosie".

Tolson, Andrew. 1977. *The Limits of Masculinity*. London: Tavistock.

Young Creole. *c.*1975. "Sissy".

Yorke, Natalie. *c.*2001. "Do What You Want".

Zandolie (Sylvester Anthony). *c.*1994. "Stickman". *Raw Kaiso: Zandolie and Black Prince with Blakie in Concert*. Lypsoland, COTT CR022.

CHAPTER 14

Uniform and Weapon

CHRISTOPHER COZIER

E quipment for the "hard man" . . . son of Django, admirer of Clint . . . disciple of Wang yu and Bruce . . . .

An art action, a verb rather than an object/noun?

Because of Carnival and our other street festivals, I see the history of our creative desire and expression as coming from an alternative location to those who are concerned with "ART" and who, for example, are seeking validation by perpetually touting nineteenth-century paintings of property and native types. I think that objects and actions have and continue to function with equal agency within and in response to the defining and constructing of a visual language space in the Caribbean.

The Shirt-Jac

With all these questions about, I found myself sitting on a red chair, the hot seat if you would like, talking to a shirt-jac suit, in early 1991. Was

Henry Hamlet

Figure 14.1: *Shirt-Jac* perform-
ance. Aquarella Galleries,
Port of Spain, Trinidad, 1991.
Promotional still.

this our "Post-Utopian" phase, after the political turmoil in Trinidad, Guyana and Grenada in the 1970s[1] and another serious dose of politi-cal violence in 1990,[2] and the return of the conventional European suit as the uniform of the power circuit?

I had at that time become wary of making any more objects. The art market on the island was avariciously touting and defending yet another generation of "nostalgic" and "pastoral" picture makers. Calling oneself an artist was becoming increasingly shameful under these cir-cumstances. I became more interested in working with things co-opted from everyday life, towards understanding their status as signs or sym-bols.

I found this shirt-jac suit in the cupboard of my parents' home. It was given to me when I was about sixteen years old. With the shirt-jac I wanted to understand how our wish to be official and to be formal was

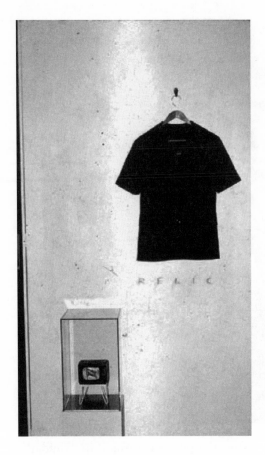

Figure 14.2: Relic, 1990: installation of *Shirt-Jac*. Small sculpture at left: *1962* or *Gift to the Nation*. Trinidad Art Society, November Exhibition, Central Bank lobby.

constructed. Personally, I could not wear a shirt-jac anymore. Consequently, I felt like a snake that had shed its skin. I felt that the shirt-jac was someone else's.

This now quaint (?) and not so virulent navy blue "shirt-jac suit" with short sleeves and military bush-jacket pockets made of European blazer coloured polyester, symbolized the gentlemanly aura of the English royal family simultaneously with the revolutionary "hard man" seriousness associated with Che Guevara and the Cuban Revolution. This object/icon now appeared to be in retreat. It was now seen more at the university, on school teachers and in the civil service, as symbolic of a passing era.

I first exhibited the suit in a Trinidad Art Society's November Exhibition which was held in the lobby of the Central Bank. The suit was simply hung on the wall on an old wooden hanger; I left the moth-balls in the pockets. On the wall below it I wrote the word "relic". I was anticipating the audience for that kind of event and what they might be wearing. For me, eventually, talking to this garment was like talking to your father while he read the newspapers. It was a way of defining the relationship of people of my generation to the discourses of the nation-alist agenda, with its ideas of social responsibility and its cultural con-ventions such as a romance with revolutionary languages and/or stances. It also addressed the issue of "respectability versus reputation": the self-consciousness of an educated middle-class ascendancy and privi-lege against its desire for "grassroots" populist viability, the much sought-after "badness" (machismo?).

There was much debate when shirt-jacs first tried to enter the Red House[3] in the mid-1970s. This came back to me to me while I was fol-lowing the media commentary in 1990 after an invasion of the same site. I wanted to ask the suit why everyone was being so evasive and cau-tious. All my life, almost every week, people were calling for revolution or warning of social upheaval.

But then something actually happened and there was violence and chaos and people "did dead". Were our "positions" (reputations?), the way we had brokered our selves in the media and towards having polit-ical influence or popularity, in danger of being undermined or shown up as just talk? Did our commentators become "mocking pretenders" in the political gayelle? Were we not interested in any kind of truth about the situation we had found ourselves in? So . . . like the looters in the city, we salvaged what we could, regardless? These were the questions that raced through my head.

I asked the shirt questions about how violent we had become . . . I asked it what had happened between Bernard Coard and Maurice Bishop in Grenada, Forbes Burnham and Walter Rodney in Guyana, Randolph Burrows and Guy Harewood in Trinidad? Why was the space between our dreams, aspirations and ability so violent? Was there no middle ground between those previous generations and points of view? Was there no space to "reason" or "rap", to use the terminology of that time? Did one always have to conform, defer or be "fucked up"?!

I also wanted to say things that could not be said within the structures that define the acceptable social/civic space (the art space?) and its protocols. I wanted to investigate the capability of an art work/action to do so. In other words, I wondered if there is an obsession with form and protocol to the point of absurdity where there is only form and protocol and no real discussion. I was wondering if we were merely enacting associative signs of order, of government, of art, of culture and so on.

The shirt-jac seemed to express that inner conflict and desire. It was simultaneously a symbol of hope and failure . . . promise and deception.

Together we conspire, together we deceive?[4]

During the performance I measured myself and then I measured the suit and recorded the differences . . . are we/me bigger than that now? The actual suit was a Sidney Shim shirt-jac given to me by my parents to wear to a graduation in the late 1970s. A previous generation of another class consciousness would have procured a blazer. I measured the expanse between myself and the object on the wall to arrive at a comfortable distance. I was defining formal distance for such an encounter.

It was my intention to do this and to walk away and then wait to see if there would be a response . . . perhaps a discussion afterwards or a review in the papers later in the week. However, the response was immediate. Members of the audience both in Trinidad and in Barbados began lining up to speak to the shirt. Astonished, I found myself on the side becoming integrated back into the audience – watching and listening to their conversations.

An artist in Barbados, a woman, measured the most appropriate distance for herself : "Six inches?" she asked. Another woman asked if she could touch the shirt and put her hand inside it to feel if there was a heart. One young artist in Trinidad complained about the books he had to read and the music to which he was required to listen to be "committed" and to become "conscious".

I began with, "You know we really need to talk . . . ." I did not rehearse. I did not have a fixed statement to make. Unlike my predecessors coming out of another social era of debating societies and so on, I had no skill in oratory, in wedding speeches and public speaking or even in "robber-talk". A rawness and remarkable discomfort and inarticulateness manifested itself. Even though there was a point that I wanted to make, I had no skill or art in that way. I had set myself up, but I wanted my discomfort to be evident.

My back was to the other people in the room. The room was dark and only the shirt was lit. My hands were behind my back, as if tied. I am still a bit confused as to why people from the audience began talking to the garment as well. Was it some kind of inherent theatrical tendency in the society derived from Carnival, or was it that the work anticipated participation? The majority were responding to an alleged

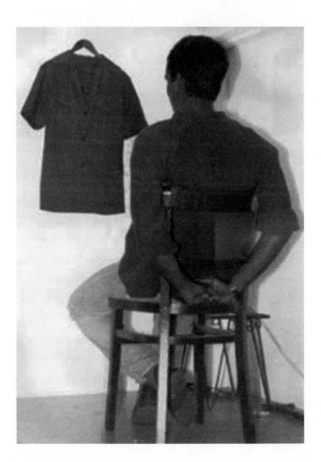

Figure 14.3: Actual *Shirt-Jac* performance, 1991. Cross Over Design Space, Port of Spain, Trinidad.

Figure 14.4: Actual *Shirt-Jac* performance, 1991. Member of the audience talking to the shirt.

Afro-nationalist hegemony and to the civil servant/politician as a kind of bogeyman. It gave me a lot to think about.

The Whip: "Analysis of a Tamarind Rod"

The first time I showed the whip/tamarind rod I called it *System of Organization,* just like the shirt-jac. It was a real object transferred from our everyday-life space into the art space. I stole it from a friend who was teaching in one of the primary schools in Port of Spain. Transferring these objects brought home for me the idea of the conflict between the world of art and that of the life of our society. To me, it was part two of my shirt-jac work.

When I did the performance with it, I referred to "stroke-play" and cricket: the elegance of the gesture, the form, and how the style provided entertainment. I referred to the design of the object. How the branch was cut to be lighter on one side and heavier on the other and to have a slight curve. I spoke about how it facilitated the delivering of a stroke and I marvelled at its creole-ergonomic inventiveness.

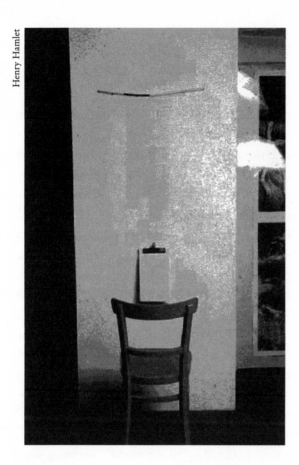

Henry Hamlet

Figure 14.5: The whip/
tamarind rod: *System of
Organization.* Aquarella
Galleries, Port of Spain,
1991.

I spoke about the secret place in the teacher's desk, similar to where
the Sacrament is kept behind the altar in a Catholic church. I recalled
the Irish priest who had trained his dog to do tricks and who gave displays during catechism quizzes when I was a boy. The privilege to bring
the tool/whip was given to certain boys. I enacted asking my classmate,
the class prefect: "Why does your behaviour change when you are told
to watch the class when 'Sir' has left the room? Why do I know that
you would report me to him?"

I spoke about how to take one's blows/strokes. Some boys would
march to the rhythm of the strokes in a circle while looking forward
rigidly, causing "Sir" to pivot so as to keep a good angle. Some boys
would wriggle and fall to the floor like James Brown, twisting and falling
and frustrating "Sir". Some would stand still, looking down at the

ground with their jaws locked, then turn and return to their desk angrily, in a military manner, and others would "bounce"[5] as if "cool".
However, if they appeared to be too defiant they would be recalled for
a "second round/dose".

I often wondered, even if the teacher was "black" and even if the teacher
often preached about how industrious the "black man" must be, and so
on, why did he beat the darkest and poorest boys the hardest and the
most? It was as if he had to beat something out of us or himself. Or was
it that he felt that he had, as we might say, "more license" over them, or
that he felt some anxiety for them, or some responsibility and concern?

I never thought of this until I saw the paddles in the Afro-American
fraternities in the United States many years later. I recalled how sending
for the whip and then selecting the ideal one was a performance/ritual. I
spoke about how the whips had names as well as different sizes and
weights. Names like "George" or "Elizabeth", shortened to "Bess" or
"Betsy", and always connected in some way to the English royal family.

Of course, there is also the idea of "wood" and "bois",[6] in calypso
and stickfighting, as a phallic symbol. There are many songs dedicated to
this subject. I also referred to how the following terms were used in our
social and political discourses in various islands: "the rod of correction",
used by Manley in Jamaican elections in the 1970s; "the big stick", a col-
loquial term to mean force or authority; "to get wood", meaning something like to receive a hard lash or to be tricked or duped in some way (to
be screwed, also). "Heavy manners"[7] was reputed to be a term from the
Grenada revolution which shifted to "manners", as in "to manners someone", or to show them a form which indicates a correctional mode, and
so on; then there was "to get fix" or "to get straighten out".

My intention in creating these works was to begin using artistic means
and methods to talk about my/an experience – to tell a story. I wanted
to shift people's attention away from the usual conversations in Trinidad
about who could draw and paint and what the ideal subject was for the
artist – things about which we spend too much time asserting and pro-
fessing. To me these kinds of conversations and these kinds of ways of
working had converted artists into nothing more than propagators and
decorators of nationalist myths.

The Three Ps

The Three Ps were presented as part of a larger exhibition entitled Blue Soap, representing authority and respectability in small places: priest, police and politician in charge of the soul, the body and the mind, in that order. I began to wonder about the relationship of the artist to society and how ideas of statehood were constructed.

All of these people were the "bogeymen" of the social order who had the "big stick" and who wore the shirt-jacs and who spoke for an alleged "us", or who would come and get you if you had strayed too far away.

Postscript

After doing these perfomative works in the early 1990s, it occured to me that I was developing some kind of video installation or larger performance work that would involve working collaboratively with others. One can say it was a part three. The drawings that I was doing were looking more and more like story boards. I was building a world in which these co-opted objects, the whip and the shirt-jac, operated. In my video installation *Blue Soap* (1994) I wanted to embark upon an investigative narrative about "independence" and what it meant to me at the time. Ideas of order and disorder and the acceptance of my Caribbean experience, in contrast to the kind of conflict and horror that occurs in other societies between people of varied ethnic and religious identities, were on my mind. Blue soap is used to clean things, to keep them white, to wash the tongues of rude children or to bathe a mongrel. Its colour is also related to spiritual cleansing/protection. To bathe oneself with blue soap is either punishment or cleansing. My intention was to bring up feelings about morality, spirituality, the status of the creative person and also of people mixed ethnic identities, like myself. To me, this work discusses "New World" challenges in contrast to "Old World" concepts or ideals. By bathing myself with blue soap I was thinking of the status of the artist in society as a rude tongue. Maybe this is

Figure 14.6: Police from Blue Soap exhibition (mixed media drawing on paper). Aquarella Galleries, Port of Spain, Trinidad, 1994.

Figure 14.7: Priest from Blue Soap exhibition (mixed media drawing on paper). Aquarella Galleries, Port of Spain, Trinidad, 1994.

Figure 14.8: Politician from Blue Soap exhibition (mixed media on paper). Aquarella Galleries, Port of Spain, Trinidad, 1994.

Figure 14.9: Production still from *Blue Soap* installation.

best summarized by Pat Ganese, in the catalogue to the Blue Soap exhibition in Cuba in 1994, when she wrote:

> The black man, seeking acceptance and respectability, dresses himself in the ill-fitting suit of the departed colonisers, takes up their rod of correction, recites their rules, mimics their methods, seeking control. He does not succeed. The woman, locked in her own circle of grasping rapacious hands, wants more than anything else to be free to "be herself". The night is very dark. There is no light at the end.

Acknowledgements

This text is edited from notes made in 1995.

Relic and *1962* (Figure 14.2) and *Police* (Figure 14.6) are in the collection of Dr Ulrich Fiedler, Cologne. The production still from the *Blue Soap* installation (Figure 14.9) is in the collection of the University of Iowa Museum of Art.

Notes

1. This refers to the Black Power disturbances of 1970 and the guerrilla movement of the early 1970s in Trinidad and Tobago.
2. This refers to the 1990 attempted coup of the Jamaat al Muslimeen in Trinidad.
3. The Red House is the building in which the national parliament of Trinidad and Tobago meets.
4. This alludes to the national motto of Trinidad and Tobago: "Together we aspire, together we achieve."
5. A gesture between two persons where each touches the other's closed fist.
6. The bois is a fighting stick used mainly in the pre-Carnival season of stickfighting.
7. This term really developed in Jamaica and spread throughout the region, and was popular during the Grenada revolution [ed.].

Contributors

Rhoda E. Reddock is Professor and Head of the Centre for Gender and Development Studies, University of the West Indies, St Augustine, Trinidad. She is a former associate lecturer in the Women and Development programme at the Institute of Social Studies, the Hague, and lecturer in the Department of Sociology, University of the West Indies. She is an activist in the Caribbean women's movement and a founding member of the Caribbean Association or Feminist Research and Action. Her publications (single-authored and edited collections) include *Women, Labour and Politics in Trinidad and Tobago: A History* (1994), which was named a CHOICE Outstanding Academic Book for 1996; *Ethnic Minorities in Caribbean society* (1998); *Plantation Women: International Experiences* (1998), co-edited with Shobhita Jain; and most recently, *Caribbean Sociology: Introductory Readings* (2001), co-edited with Christine Barrow. In 2001 she was awarded the Vice Chancellor's Award for Excellence in Teaching and Administration, Research and Public Service from the University of the West Indies and in 2002, she received the XII CARICOM Triennial Award for Women.

Hilary Beckles is Professor of History and Principal, University of the West Indies, Cave Hill, Barbados. He has published widely on a range of subjects including Caribbean slavery, women and gender, and cricket. He has also co-edited (with Verene Shepherd) a series of history textbooks which include *Caribbean Slavery in the Atlantic World* (1999) and *Caribbean Freedom: Economy and Society from Emancipation to the Present* (1993). Recent publications include *Centering Women: Gender Discourses in the Caribbean Slave Society* (1999).

Christopher Cozier is an artist and writer living and working in Trinidad and Tobago. He has participated in a number of exhibitions in the Caribbean and internationally, all focused upon contemporary art. Since 1989 he has published a range of essays on related issues in a number of catalogues and journals. He is on the editorial collective of *Small Axe, A Caribbean Journal of Criticism*, and serves as a nominator and curatorial adviser to the international residency program at CCA7 in Port of Spain, Trinidad. He is an editorial adviser to *BOMB* magazine for their Americas issue (Fall 2003). He has taught at various institutions and works in collaboration with a number of younger developing artists, designers and illustrators. His work has consisted of multimedia projects, involving sound, video, live performances and installations, including drawings, constructions and appropriated objects.

Wesley E.A. Crichlow is Associate Professor in the School of Justice Studies, University of Ontario Institute of Technology, Oshawa, Canada. His research interests are social inequality; theoretical and legal approaches to the study of race; racial profiling; social justice; and moral regulation; critical appraisal of youth restorative justice; lesbian and gay rights; judicial reform; Section 15 criminal law charter challenges; anti-poverty as a charter challenge; and criminal justice reform. His publications include the introduction to *Understanding Policing*, edited by K. McCormick and L. Visano (1992), and "Bullermen and Bwaty Boys" in *Queer Country: Gay and Lesbian Studies in the Canadian Context*, edited by Terry Goldie (2001).

Aviston D. Downes is Lecturer, Department of History, University of the West Indies, Cave Hill, Barbados. His areas of research interest include the cultural history of the Americas in the nineteenth and twentieth centuries and the construction of masculinity in fraternal organizations and religion. His work in progress includes colonial education, sport, paramilitarism and the construction of masculinity.

Mark Figueroa is Lecturer, Department of Economics, University of the West Indies, Mona, Jamaica. He has published in the areas of economic theory, environmental economics, and gender and social capital. Recent publications include "Gender Privileging and Socio-Economic Outcomes: The Case of Health and Education in Jamaica", in *Gender and the Family in the*

Caribbean, edited by Wilma Bailey (1998), and "Making Sense of Male Experience: The Case of Academic Achievement in the English-Speaking Caribbean", in *Men, Masculinities and Development: Politics, Policies and Practice*, edited by Andrea Cornwall and Sarah White, *IDS Bulletin* 31, no. 2 (April 2000).

Linden Lewis, a native of Barbados, is Associate Lecturer and Director of the Race/Gender Centre, Bucknell University, Pennsylvania, Philadelphia. A sociologist, he has published increasingly in the area of gender studies. Recent publications include "Masculinity and the Dance of the Dragon", *Feminist Review*, no. 59 (Summer 1998), and "Nationalism and Caribbean Masculinity", in *Gender Ironies of Nationalism: Sexing the Nation*, edited by Tamar Mayer (2000).

Linda M. Matthei is Associate Professor of Anthropology and Sociology, Texas A&M University–Commerce. Her research interests include gender and migration in the English-speaking Caribbean, gender and transnational networks, and the transnationalization of crime. Her publications include "Gender and International Migration: A Networks Approach", *Social Justice* 23, no. 3, and "Belizean Boyz in the Hood: Garifuna Labour Migration and Transnational Identity" (with David A. Smith), in *Transnationalism from Below*, edited by Michael Peter Smith and Luis Eduardo Guarnizo (1998).

Patricia Mohammed is Senior Lecturer, Centre for Gender and Development Studies, University of the West Indies, St Augustine, Trinidad. She has published in the areas of women's and gender studies and increasingly in masculinity studies. She is the co-editor (with Catherine Shepherd) of *Gender in Caribbean Development* ([1988] 1999), editor of "Rethinking Caribbean Difference", the special issue of *Feminist Review*, no. 59 (Summer 1998), along with many others. Her latest publication is *Gendered Realities: Essays in Caribbean Feminist Thought* (2002). Her current work is centred on art and iconography in the Caribbean.

Paula Morgan is Lecturer, Department of Liberal Arts, University of the West Indies, St Augustine, Trinidad. Her research interests are in literary theory, African diaspora women's literature and Caribbean literature. Her doctoral dissertation was "A Cross-Cultural Study of the Black Female-

Authored Novel of Development" (University of the West Indies, 1993); and she is co-editor (with Roanna Gopaul and Rhoda Reddock) of *Women, Family and Family Violence in the Caribbean: The Historical and Contemporary Experience, with Special Reference to Trinidad and Tobago* (1996), and author of " 'Like Bush Fire in My Arms': Interrogating the World of Caribbean Romance", Working Paper no. 5, Centre for Gender and Development Studies (2002).

E. Antonio de Moya is Professor, Instituto de Sexualidad Humana at the Universidad Autónoma de Santo Domingo, Dominican Republic. His research interests include sexuality, masculinity and HIV/AIDS. His publications include "Three Decades of Male Sex Work in Santo Domingo", in *Men Who Sell Sex: International Perspectives on Male Prostitution and AIDS*, edited by Peter Aggleton (1998), and "AIDS and the Enigma of Bisexuality in the Dominican Republic", in *Bisexualities and AIDS: International Perspectives*, edited by P. Aggleton (1996).

Keith Nurse is Senior Lecturer, Institute of International Relations, University of the West Indies, St Augustine, Trinidad. His research interests include globalization and international trade, and the economics of Caribbean culture. His publications include *The Development Efficacy of Export-Oriented Industrialization in the New International Division of Labour: The Case of CARICOM Countries* (1993).

Odette Parry is a former research fellow at the Institute of Social and Economic Research at the University of the West Indies, Mona, Jamaica. She is currently based at the Research Unit in Health and Behavioural Change at the University of Edinburgh, Scotland. A related publication is *Male Underachievement in High School Education in Jamaica, Barbados and St Vincent and the Grenadines* (2000).

Kenneth Ramchand, now retired, was Professor of West Indian Literature, University of the West Indies, St Augustine, Trinidad. He is a leading scholar in literary theory who has published widely in the areas of Caribbean literature, literary theory and the West Indian novel. His publications *The West Indian Novel and its Background* (1970), and *West Indian Narrative: An Introductory Anthology* (1966) are considered classics.

Rafael L. Ramírez, now retired, was Professor of Anthropology, University of Puerto Rico. He is currently Research Associate of the Centre for the Study of HIV/AIDS at the University of Puerto Rico, Rio Piedras. He is the author of *What It Means to Be a Man: Reflections on Puerto Rican Masculinity* (1999).

Gordon Rohlehr is Professor of West Indian Literature, University of the West Indies, St Augustine, Trinidad. His research interests include West Indian literature and popular culture, including the calypso. His publications include *Pathfinder: Black Awakening in "The Arrivants" of Edward Kamau Brathwaite* (1981), *Calypso and Society in Pre-Independence Trinidad* (1990), *My Strangled City and Other Essays* (1992), *The Shape of that Hurt and Other Essays* (1992).

David A. Smith is Associate Professor of Sociology, University of California, Irvine, and editor of the journal *Social Problems*. His research interests include transnationalization and international migration. His publications include "Women, Households and Transnational Migration Networks" (with Linda M. Matthei), in *Latin America in the World Economy*, edited by R. Korzeniewicz and W. Smith (1996).